Data Processing for Business

Second Edition

Gerald A. Silver
Los Angeles City College

Joan B. Silver

Harcourt Brace Jovanovich, Inc.
New York   Chicago   San Francisco   Atlanta

COVER: *Evolving Gravity,* computer graphics by Aaron Marcus

Library of Congress Catalog Card Number: 76-52295

ISBN: 0-15-516809-6

Printed in the United States of America

Picture credits and copyright acknowledgments begin on page 586.

PREFACE

Business data processing is an extremely fast changing, dynamic field. New methods, techniques, and devices enter the picture almost daily. Any textbook purporting to teach this discipline must be updated and revised frequently to reflect this phenomenon.

For the second edition of *Data Processing for Business,* we have retained all the features that made the first edition so successful. But we have carefully reviewed and revised textual and illustrative material to reflect current developments. Designed for the first course in data processing, *Data Processing for Business,* Second Edition, presents a contemporary view of computer technology and computer languages. It deals with fundamental concepts, terminology, and theory in logical order, moving from the simple to the complex. Excessive details have been avoided in favor of broad coverage of central topics. The excellent graphics, simple and logical organization, and easy reading style of the first edition have been retained.

Cartoons and anecdotes are used throughout the book to present the ideas, thoughts, and commentary of people who feel strongly about data processing and to remind the student that in data processing, people are as important as machines.

For this edition we have added a chapter on BASIC—one of the major languages now taught to introductory students. We have also added a chapter on the social impact of computers to help the student see the computer in its broader social context. Sections on teleprocessing and information systems have been expanded to reflect their growing importance in the field. All material has been revised, edited, and updated to include discussions of the latest equipment and technology, such as point-of-sale (POS) terminals, electronic funds transfer systems (EFTS), virtual memory systems, and microprocessors.

Data Processing for Business is divided into seven parts followed by four appendixes.

Part One, Introduction, discusses the general subject, defines important terms, and surveys data processing methods and trends.

Part Two, Unit Record Processing/Electrical Accounting Machine Processing, introduces the fundamentals of unit record processing and treats the basic techniques involved in manipulation and reporting.

Part Three, Computer Hardware, considers input, processing, storage and output methods. Numbering and coding systems, conversions, and elementary mathematical operations are included here.

Part Four, Solving a Problem with a Computer, explores computer program planning, algorithms, logic, and flowcharting. Batch, interactive, and supplied programs are discussed and compared.

Part Five, Computer Software, opens with an elementary treatment of operating systems, which lays the groundwork for understanding the design and function of compilers and their relationship to the computer. COBOL, BASIC, and FORTRAN are treated in separate chapters. Another chapter describes such languages as PL/I, RPG, and assembler.

Part Six, Information Systems, explores business systems and their evaluation and covers teleprocessing and information systems, two rapidly growing elements of data processing.

Part Seven, The Computer in Society, discusses the influence the computer is having on the broad spectrum of our everyday lives and the implications for the future.

Appendix A explores the organization of the data processing department and related employment opportunities. Appendix B is a conversion table for the decimal, hexadecimal, and binary number systems. New to this edition, Appendix C teaches the student the terminology of the punched card and how to operate the keypunch machine. Appendix D presents nine case studies, which can be used as springboards for discussion or for a review of the concepts covered in the text.

Each chapter is followed by a list of key terms; a glossary appears at the back of the book. Exercises follow each chapter to aid the student in evaluating his or her progress. Some of the exercises broaden the learning experience by requiring that the student go into the field to interview people or to observe computers and businesses.

A textbook is not the product of one or two individuals. We wish to thank the firms and organizations that graciously provided assistance. We also thank William Cornette of Texas Technological University and Oberita Hager of Eastern Kentucky University for their help in the early stages of the revision and C. C. Calhoon of University of Georgia, James Letterer of Elmhurst College, and Robert Panian of Northern Michigan University for their critical reviews of the final draft.

It is our hope that this book will make learning business data processing an enjoyable and fascinating undertaking.

Gerald A. Silver
Joan B. Silver

CONTENTS

v

PART TWO **UNIT RECORD PROCESSING/ELECTRICAL ACCOUNTING MACHINE PROCESSING   51**

PART THREE **COMPUTER HARDWARE   97**

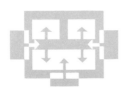

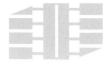

PART SEVEN   THE COMPUTER IN SOCIETY   488

PART ONE

INTRODUCTION

1

DATA PROCESSING

The Machine works on . . . a giant mass of wires and circuits in control of the entire world. It never fails, never tires. It knows all, sees all. It is all. The Machine plans, thinks, and watches. It commands every aspect of our daily lives. It monitors every home, office, classroom, airplane, and ship at sea. All radio and television broadcasts, all telephone conversations are monitored, timed, switched, and processed by the Machine. It is the intellectual center of society. It metes out sentences for law violations, processes our payrolls, writes our plays and books, guides our work and play, educates us, and, of course, it thinks for us. . . .

Huddleston and Bradford, a banking firm in London, England, has issued a list of rules for its office staff:

> Godliness, cleanliness and punctuality are the necessities of a good business. Daily prayers will be held each morning in the main office; the clerical staff will be present. A stove is provided for the benefit of the staff; each member of the clerical staff must bring four pounds of coal each day during cold weather. No member of the staff may leave the room without the permission of Mr. Roberts. No talking is allowed during business hours. The craving of tobacco, wines or spirits is a human weakness, and as such, is forbidden to the clerical staff. Members of the staff will provide their own pens. Clothing will be of a sober nature.*

*"Rules for Clerks," 1854, as quoted in *Creative Computer,* No. V, December 1975, p. 33.

Of course, the two examples above represent extremes. The rapid proliferation of data processing and computers in the last few decades has had a phenomenal impact on our society, but the real world of computer technology lies somewhere in between the land of science fiction and the era of the quill pen.

In 1950 there were only a dozen or so large-scale computers in the United States. By 1970 the number had grown to 80,000. The late 1960s saw the advent of the minicomputer. Minicomputers are hardly larger than an electric typewriter and are at least as fast as their giant ancestors. It is anticipated that by 1983 American business firms will be using over 407,000 of these small-scale computers. (See Figure 1.1.) The early 1970s saw the development of the microprocessor. Microprocessors are computers built on a small silicon chip, a fraction of an inch in size. When incorporated in a complete system, they are capable of performing the data processing tasks of many small and medium-sized business firms at a price such firms can afford. By 1978, more than 700,000 microprocessors alone will be in use. (See Figure 1.2.)

There is no doubt that computers have become an essential and integral part of the American business scene. They are used to control the marketing, manufacture, and financing of a vast amount of goods and services. Computer installations employ thousands of programmers, engineers,

FIGURE 1.1   ESTIMATED NUMBER OF SMALL COMPUTERS INSTALLED (IN THOUSANDS)

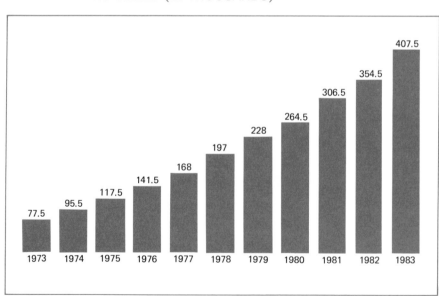

FIGURE 1.2   COMPUTERS IN USE

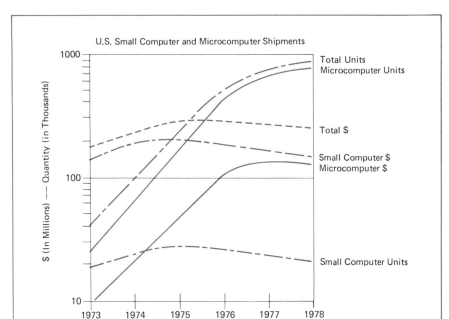

U.S. Small Computer and Microcomputer Shipments

analysts, computer operators, installers, and other people in related and supporting disciplines.

This book will explore the many elements—people, machines, activities, services—involved in the vital, dynamic new industry of electronic data processing.

WHAT ARE COMPUTERS?

Broadly defined, a computer is any device that computes, calculates, or reckons. Thus the abacus, adding machine, and slide rule are all forms of computers.

The definition of a computer has become more limited in contemporary usage. A computer is now defined as an electronic device that processes data, is capable of receiving input and output, and possesses such characteristics as high speed, accuracy, and the ability to store a set of instructions for solving a problem.

What They Are   Computers are electronic devices composed of switches, wires, motors, transistors, and integrated circuits, assembled on frames. The frames form components such as typewriters, line printers, card readers, card punches, magnetic tape drives, and central processing units. These components are wired together into a network called a computing system. The entire system is often called, simply, a computer.

A computing system can read data from hundreds of punched cards in one minute, or type out information at the rate of hundreds of lines per minute. It can store millions of letters or numbers, ready for retrieval.

Computers can perform a variety of mathematical calculations, ranging from simply adding and subtracting to solving complicated math equations that involve thousands of steps. They can repeat a complicated calculation millions of times without error.

Computers can print out whole paragraphs of text matter, write letters, draw pictures, or plot curves and draw graphs. They can sort data, merge lists, search files, and make logical decisions and comparisons.

A computing system may range in size from rather small desk-top devices with limited capability to huge machines occupying several large rooms. It may be constructed as a single, integral device, or as a group of machines, remotely connected but functioning as a unit. The individual parts may be located within the same building or scattered across the country, connected by telephone lines.

A computer program is a series of instructions or statements recorded in a form acceptable to a computer. These instructions direct the computer through a series of steps to solve a problem. Programs are written by individuals, called programmers, who understand the nature of the problem to be solved and who can communicate with the computer.

An important feature of the modern computer is its ability to store a program. Once the instructions in a program are entered into a computer, they remain there until replaced by new instructions. Then the data to be manipulated by the program are entered and the computer carries out the stored instructions step by step. The same program can operate on many sets of data. This arrangement greatly increases the usefulness and general purpose nature of the machine.

Computers can be characterized by their function. Special-purpose computers are built to solve one kind of problem, such as processing airline reservations or controlling a metalworking machine. General-purpose computers can be used for many business, scientific, educational, social, and other applications. These machines are not limited to one type of problem, but lend themselves to the solution of many.

Computers may be generally characterized by the way in which they receive and process data. Some systems process numeric values represented by discrete electronic pulses; others process data of a continuous nature.

Analog computers process data input in a continuous form. Data, such as voltage, resistance, temperature, and pressure, are represented in the computer as a continuous, unbroken flow. In engineering and scientific applications, where quantities to be processed exist as waveforms, or continually rising and falling voltages, pressures, etc., analog computers are very useful. For example, they are used to control processes in the food and petroleum industries. However, they are not suitable for processing business data.

Output from analog computers is usually displayed on cathode ray tubes or plotters. A cathode ray tube converts electric signals into visual forms, much like an ordinary television set. A plotter converts electric signals into lines or a graph on a page.

Digital computers process data in the form of discrete letters or numbers and are therefore more useful in business applications. The output is on line printers, typewriters, punched cards, or paper tape punched in a form convenient for business such as typed reports or paychecks. This book is concerned with business data processing, so "computer" will be understood to mean the digital computer.

The differences between digital and analog computers may be further illustrated by comparing how an increase in temperature is noted by an engineer and an increase in inventory is noted by a businessperson. The increase in temperature, say from 68° to 69°, is not abrupt and may be represented as a continuum. The best way to input this information is by using an increasing electrical voltage, analogous to the rise in temperature. An increase in the number of units of an item in stock, on the other hand, is represented by a discrete number. An inventory total may increase from 105 to 106 units, but not from 105 to $105\frac{1}{2}$ units. Similarly, employees increase in units of one, a paycheck is a discrete amount, and a sales price is quoted as a specific number. This kind of business data is best input to the computer using common numbers.

WHAT ARE DATA AND DATA PROCESSING?

First of all, what are data? Data are useful knowledge, or information of value to an individual or a business. They are factual material used as a basis for discussion, decision, calculation, or measurement. Data are compiled to form reports, letters, facts, figures, records, or documents.

In a narrower sense, data consist of numbers or letters that may be processed or reordered by people or machines to increase their value or utility. The terms data and information are used interchangeably in this book. Some writers prefer to define data as facts, and information as knowledge derived from the manipulation of data.

Data processing, then, is the restructuring or reordering of data, by people or machines, to increase their usefulness and value for some particular

FIGURE 1.3   THE DATA CYCLE

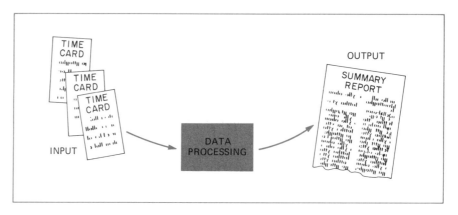

purpose. It includes classifying, sorting, merging, recording, retrieving, calculating, transmitting, summarizing, and reporting.

Data Cycle   Data processing may be done by hand (manually), by simple machines (unit record), or by electronic means (computers). In all three methods, data being processed go through a data cycle, shown in Figure 1.3, that consists of three steps: data input, data processing, and data output.

1. DATA INPUT.   Data input involves converting data from source documents into a form acceptable for processing by computer or other means. Source documents are the original records of a transaction. These records, often written in longhand (such as employee time cards, sales orders, and memos), must be converted and transferred to punched cards for entry into the system. (Other means of entering source documents will be covered later in the book.)

2. DATA PROCESSING.   During data processing, the data are changed in form, order, or structure to increase their value or utility. Sales orders for the week may be totaled. A list of employees may be classified by department. A sales commission may be calculated. Data may be stored for later retrieval and presentation.

3. DATA OUTPUT.   It is not enough that data be input and processed. The results of the processing must be communicated to the user. In the data output phase, the results of the previous steps are made available in a form of maximum use to the business firm. Output may consist of printed forms, statements, or reports; or it may be a table or graph displayed on a cathode ray tube (a visual device that resembles a television set). Data output in one cycle may also be recorded on a storage medium to be used later in further processing, perhaps in a different physical location.

Manual Method
The manual method was the first means employed to process data. Many small business firms still use it. With this method, pencils, adding machines, an abacus, or similar devices are used to process data.

DATA INPUT. Input involves procedures such as writing data on forms or typing in figures.

DATA PROCESSING. Data processing is done mentally, or with paper and pencil, adding machine, or desk calculator. Sorting, merging, and classifying are performed by hand; examples are running up totals to figure gross pay, calculating account balances or credits due a firm, placing employee time cards in sequence by department, and sorting orders by sales personnel.

DATA OUTPUT. Data are output by writing or typing. Examples include writing a receipt or paycheck longhand, or typing a balance sheet, ledger card, or report.

ADVANTAGES. Advantages include simplicity, ease of implementation, and low cost of processing small amounts of data. Since complicated equipment and systems are not involved, changes can be made easily and the method is flexible.

LIMITATIONS. The manual method is slow, inaccurate, and costly when a moderate or large volume of data is involved. It is difficult to standardize procedures and reporting. Manual data processing is also limited by the speed of the human hand and eye. A human may also introduce errors into the system through illness, carelessness, and boredom.

Unit Record Method
The unit record method relies upon human operators and electromechanical devices to process data. It is sometimes called the EAM (electrical accounting machine) process.

In the unit record, or EAM, system, data are stored in coded form or punched cards. Data from each transaction are punched on a separate card, hence the term "unit record." These unit records are manipulated by machines to input, process, and output the data. (See Figure 1.4.) (The unit record system will be studied in detail in Chapters 3 and 4.)

DATA INPUT. Information to be processed by this method is entered into the system from punched cards. The data are punched into the cards by a keypunch machine in the Hollerith code.

DATA PROCESSING. The manipulation of data involves sorting, collating, or merging of decks of punched cards, or the calculation of figures from data input on punched cards. These operations are done by machines that

FIGURE 1.4   UNIT RECORD EQUIPMENT

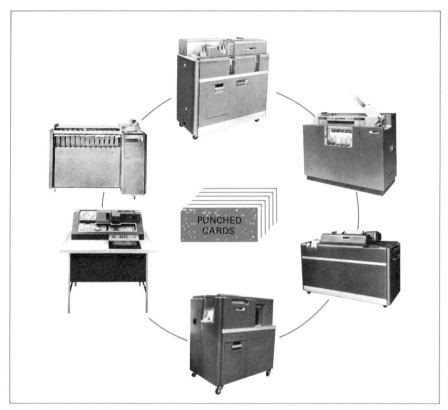

physically move the cards about. Calculations are performed by electromechanical devices that store values in counters.

DATA OUTPUT.   Output is on an accounting machine, which prints out the results of calculations on sheets of paper. These may be reports, forms, or similar documents. Summary data or the results of calculations may also be punched on cards.

ADVANTAGES.   Advantages include simplicity, relatively low cost of equipment, and reliability. The system uses ordinary punched cards for storing and transmitting data. Punched cards are easily filed, mailed, stored, or written upon by hand. Unit record accounting is practical for the small to medium business firm. Its accuracy and speed far exceeds that of the manual method.

LIMITATIONS.   For the large firm, the unit record method has several disadvantages. First, the cost of processing thousands of punched cards precludes their use for high-volume processing. Second, punched cards are bulky to store and are subject to damage and mutilation. In addition, programs for this method are stored externally; wiring boards are usually used, and operators must connect jumper wires to direct the machine.

Electronic
Data Processing—
EDP (Computers)

Computers were a natural and logical outgrowth of the unit record system. (See Figure 1.5.) As companies grew, it became inefficient to move punched cards through machinery to perform the data processing cycle. New methods were clearly needed to input, store, and output data. EDP relies upon the computer and principles of electronics to process data.

DATA INPUT. Data to be processed by this method can be recorded on one of several media for input to the computer. These include punched cards, magnetic tape, and magnetic disks. In some instances, source documents themselves serve as input media for the computer. For example, data printed in magnetic ink are input by Magnetic Ink Character Recognition devices, and handwritten or printed data are read and input by Optical Character Recognition devices. (Data input is explained in more detail in Chapter 6.)

DATA PROCESSING. Once the data are entered in the computer, they are manipulated by electronic means. Data within computers are represented by electric signals, called pulses. These pulses are moved about within the computer in microscopically small circuits, and calculations are performed in billionths of a second.

FIGURE 1.5 ELECTRONIC DATA PROCESSING SYSTEM

DATA OUTPUT.   Various methods of output characterize modern computers. Output can be on high-speed line printers, punched cards, video devices such as cathode ray tube, or by spoken word from an audio response unit. (These devices will be explained in more detail in Chapter 10.)

ADVANTAGES.   The advantages of the computer include high reliability, unsurpassed processing speed, accuracy, and low cost per unit of processing. For large firms, the computer is the most practical of the three means for processing data. The minicomputer and microprocessors bring these advantages to the smaller firm.

LIMITATIONS.   Large computers may cost millions of dollars to purchase, or thousands of dollars per month to lease. Cost may preclude their use for many medium and small firms.

Second, although computers are ideal for solving repetitive problems, they are generally not efficient for nonrecurring problems. It may often be easier for a single problem to be solved by pencil and paper than by computer. It could cost $1,000 to solve a $1 problem.

A third limitation is the nature of the problems that can be solved. Computers can only solve problems stated in quantitative terms. They cannot solve problems that cannot be reduced to precise numbers or values.

WHY STUDY DATA PROCESSING AND COMPUTERS?

A knowledge of the role, capacity, and limitation of data processing is of value to everyone. In fact, it is almost impossible to go through a day without encountering data processing in some form. Government agencies, schools, hospitals, courts and law firms, and businesses of all sizes use data processing in some way. The character and development of modern business is influenced by data processing. Business decisions depend on the quality and accuracy of available data.

Data processing is a growing industry and the source of many jobs. It has been estimated that by 1980 one million people will be employed in electronic data processing.

DEMANDS FOR ELECTRONIC DATA PROCESSING

Electronic data processing was originally developed for scientific and mathematical applications and is still widely used in these disciplines. Because of the specialized nature of early computers, they were impractical for business use. However, the introduction of general-purpose machines and more versatile programming languages greatly increased the computer's utility. Computers are now indispensable tools of business.

Business Needs Electronic data processing is growing because it is capable of meeting a need of modern business firms—the accurate, efficient handling of vast amounts of data. What are the demands faced by business that create this need?

1. NUMBER OF TRANSACTIONS. The growth in size and number of business firms naturally increases the number of business transactions. The computer, with its high capacity and speed, can process thousands of records or business calculations per minute, and with far greater efficiency than any previous method.
2. COST. Competitive pressures have led many firms to adopt computerized methods of data processing. In the past, sales could be written up longhand, orders filled by hand, and the bills and records of the transactions prepared by longhand. However, with a large number of transactions the cost of hand labor precludes this method.

"You're born, you're processed and you die. That's life."

Win Some ...   ... Lose Some

A group of Caltech students with access to a computer won about 20 percent of the prizes in a $50,000 sweepstakes contest staged by the McDonald's Operators' Association of Southern California. Of the students, an 18-year-old freshman won the biggest prize—a new Datsun station wagon and $3,000 worth of groceries.

The students used the computer to print more than a million duplicate entries, which they then submitted to McDonald's. After its lawyers determined that all the entries were valid, the company decided to award additional prizes to other entrants to compensate for the students' winnings.

From now on, however, things will be different: "We're going to change the rules so that entries will have to be handwritten," said the president of the association.

Actually, the computer might have done better. With one-third of the entries, it won only one-fifth of the prizes.

SOURCE: Adapted from "Computer Entries Win 20% of Contest Prizes," *Los Angeles Times*, May 21, 1975.

Engineer Keith Taft hid a homemade computer under his clothes when he took on Lady Luck at the blackjack tables, but she stood up to his challenge.

Taft, 41, spent 1,000 hours studying the mathematics of blackjack. He spent another 1,000 hours developing a winner's computer program. Then he designed and built the $50,000 portable minicomputer he wore beneath his clothing while playing blackjack all over Nevada.

The computer, which had to make as many as 200,000 calculations in less than a second, provided him a readout in the rim of his eyeglasses where color codes flashed to advise him whether to stand pat or take another card. He fed information into the hidden computer through miniature switches connected to his toes.

His toe movements became so feverish— an estimated 10,000 movements per day at the tables—that he broke and replaced connecting wires about every three hours. He never played one casino more than two hours and was always fearful that he had been noticed, because of his swift eye movements and twitching toes.

But trouble came when he went for broke by escalating his betting. He made $1,300 in 90 minutes one weekend, but lost $4,400 in a 30-hour marathon the next. Since he had promised his wife he would risk no more than $4,000 on his venture, he quit.

SOURCE: "Engineer Gambles on Computer, Loses," UPI (dateline Sunnyvale, CA).

3. ACCURACY.   Another pressure on the business firm is the requirement of strict accuracy in many areas. The firm must make decisions, perform calculations, and plan production with precision. A business decision involving millions of dollars may rest on a few pieces of data. Calculations themselves must be performed accurately. An error of only a fraction of a

cent per transaction may not seem too critical, but it is disastrous when one or two million transactions are involved.

With electronic data processing, thousands of calculations can be processed with virtually no errors. The error level in a modern computer is about one error per ten million calculations. No other known device matches this performance.

4. SPEED.   The pace of modern business necessitates the fast flow of data. Decisions must often be made on short notice, or immediately following a transaction. For example, the stock market and the export and import industry rely heavily upon prompt data processing. The computer can process data at speeds unequaled by other means. Data can be moved within a computer in billionths of a second, and complete reports can be printed out in a matter of minutes.

5. SELECTIVITY.   Business people demand selectivity in the ways data are reported. The computer can reorder a collection of data into many different forms. One program can list the sales from the previous day's activities in chronological order. With a few modifications of the program, the computer will categorize the same list by type of merchandise sold, by salesperson, by amount, or by location.

6. INFORMATION.   Good decision making is imperative in business, and good decisions require comprehensive and complete information. This information must often be related to previous experience. Many business managers rely heavily upon ratios, cost comparisons, and time comparisons.

For example, a study of manufacturing costs may require the review of data from hundreds of previous jobs and comparisons between many elements in each job. Unless these comparisons can be made quickly and economically, their value may be lost by the cost of the effort to obtain the data.

One large restaurant chain compares weekly food, linen, labor, and other operating costs for each of their several hundred restaurants. Costs that are out of order are immediately apparent. Such things as theft of linen goods and inefficient or profitless operations are detected before serious losses occur.

7. RECORD KEEPING.   There is a growing need to record transactions at the instant they occur, not hours or days later. Passenger reservations for a 400-seat airliner are valued at thousands of dollars. Because unsold seats are an economic loss to the airline, the airline clerk must know the availability of seats at all times.

Often a sale can be made if current stock, price, or delivery data are available. The lack of data may cost a sale. On the other hand, a sale made on the basis of insufficient credit data may cause a firm to lose thousands of dollars.

The computer can process and record thousands of transactions as they occur. Real-time processing means data are processed and recorded at the moment the physical transaction occurs. Batch processing, on the other hand, means data are collected in groups and processed several hours or days after the physical transaction. With proper equipment, a computer can perform both real-time and batch processing. Such a procedure can mean more sales, better utilization of productive resources, and reduction of credit loss.

8. SERVICE. As businesses grow, it is harder for them to provide individualized service to customers. This problem is alleviated, and sometimes even eliminated, with the aid of high-speed data processing equipment. A department store with 25,000 open accounts must give thorough consideration to each customer each month. Returned merchandise, payments, and charges must be posted promptly and accurately. Without electronic data processing, it would require many more clerks, working full-time, to maintain the accounts.

9. MECHANIZATION. It has been said that "machines should work and people should think." Many business people believe that human resources should be applied to those tasks for which humans are uniquely qualified. Routine transactions, calculations, and processing of data should be done by machines, thus freeing people for more creative activities. Electronic data processing makes possible such a division of labor.

Business Applications

What are some specific uses for computers in business? A representative sampling of current business applications is given below. These and others are considered in greater detail in later chapters.

Sales forecast and control. The computer can prepare an estimate of future sales, called a sales forecast, from sales data. It can be programmed to read historical sales data and calculate trends. With these data, the marketing department can make predictions about coming business cycles—useful information in planning advertising campaigns, stocking retailers, tooling up assembly lines, and contracting with suppliers.

Payroll. The computer can process a firm's payroll. It can be programmed to read payroll records, calculate earnings, deductions, and withholdings, and print out paychecks. Computerized payroll systems can handle hourly or salaried payrolls and commission payments; they can process salaries on a weekly, monthly, or other basis.

Order point calculation. The computer can calculate usage and print out a list of goods and the quantities that must be ordered in advance, based on a review of order times and consumption. It can forecast the number of errors that will probably occur, set safety stock levels, and aid in planning production.

Business management.   The computer can provide reports and data for management. Inventory, sales analysis, credit analysis, and various operating ratios can be calculated.

Accounting.   A comprehensive accounting system can be put on the computer by using electronically stored ledgers in the machine. The computer can print out customer billings, taxes, reports, profit and loss statements, balance sheets, and other financial information required internally and externally.

Personnel management information.   The computer can provide management with data on the compositon of its personnel. It can print out information on job classifications and personnel capabilities, and can list employees by department, by salary schedule, or by both.

Cost accounting.   The computer can print out an analysis of production costs. It can be programmed to perform routine cost accounting tasks with budgeted hourly costs on individual machine rates and overhead figures. It can analyze a production job according to the number of hours required on each machine and in each department, calculate return on investment and profit, and print out a selling price.

Manufacturing information control.   The computer is used in the manufacture and production of goods. It can provide ordering, warehousing, and cost data, based on part numbers or bills of lading.
   The computer can schedule work for an assembly line based upon labor available by shift. It can print out a list of equipment and material needs for the line for a given day and predict output. The same machine can then report the number and units produced and provide follow-up cost data.

Banking and credit.   The computer is used in the finance, credit, and collection industry. It can process deposits, commercial and consumer loans, and revolving charge accounts for banks and department stores. It can prepare credit card statements and maintain trust accounts.

Modeling and planning.   The computer can also be used to simulate business ventures. Actual business conditions can be analyzed and reduced to mathematical terms and the problem fed to the computer. Then different sets of trial data are fed in and the computer prints out results. The firm is spared the time and expense of actually testing the real thing.
   Suppose a manufacturer wants to produce a food product of specific nutritive value. Assume it is not to exceed a given cost, nor a given number of calories per pound. Further assume it must contain certain specified vitamins and a given amount of protein. It is difficult to decide the proper formula if there are many ingredients that can be combined to make the

FIGURE 1.6   LARGE COMPUTER INSTALLATION

food product. The best combination of components to produce the desired result at the lowest cost must be determined. By using a mathematical technique called *linear programming,* the computer can print out a list of ingredients and quantities that most closely meets the manufacturer's requirements.

Size of Installations   Large business firms rely heavily upon electronic data processing. Airlines make ticket reservations, insurance companies handle claims, and large department stores process billing and collections. Manufacturers control assembly lines by computer, railroad companies locate freight cars by computer, and oil and gas companies control the manufacture of their products by computer.

These applications are often complex and require large systems like the one shown in Figure 1.6. Computers such as these, leasing at a cost of from $10,000 to $100,000 per month, are capable of storing millions of pieces of data and can process thousands of instructions per second. Large-scale users may tie computer facilities located at several places across the country into a nationwide network.

Computers are also widely used by firms with from 100 to several thousand employees. Firms of this size, such as loan companies, sales organizations, manufacturers, trucking companies, or insurance companies, use electronic data processing to prepare invoices, handle accounts receivable and payable, review customer credit, and provide management with marketing data, records, and forecasts.

Machines suitable for this level of need are shown in Figure 1.7. They are capable of processing hundreds of instructions per minute, but may be more limited in speed and capability than the large computers. Leasing costs range from $5,000 to $20,000 per month.

FIGURE 1.7   MEDIUM-SIZED COMPUTER INSTALLATION

FIGURE 1.8   SMALL COMPUTER INSTALLATION

FIGURE 1.9   MINICOMPUTER

Improvements in equipment design have brought about lower cost computers, which can be leased for $1,000 to $10,000 per month. (See Figure 1.8.) Another development is the minicomputer, a small desk-top computer costing between $1,000 and $25,000. (See Figure 1.9.)

Terminals, such as the one shown in Figure 1.10, bring the power of the computer to even the smallest firms. These typewriterlike devices are located in business establishments and are connected by ordinary telephone lines to computers at a remote location. Remote computer terminals, discussed in more detail in Chapter 21, lease for as little as $35 per month, plus the charges for computer time and line charges.

In 1970 approximately 50,000 remote terminals were in use in retailing establishments. It is predicted that by 1980 approximately 800,000 of these terminals will be in use. (See Figure 1.11.) Such terminals can be used by food, department, and discount stores to handle credit authorization.

FIGURE 1.10 PORTABLE DATA TERMINAL

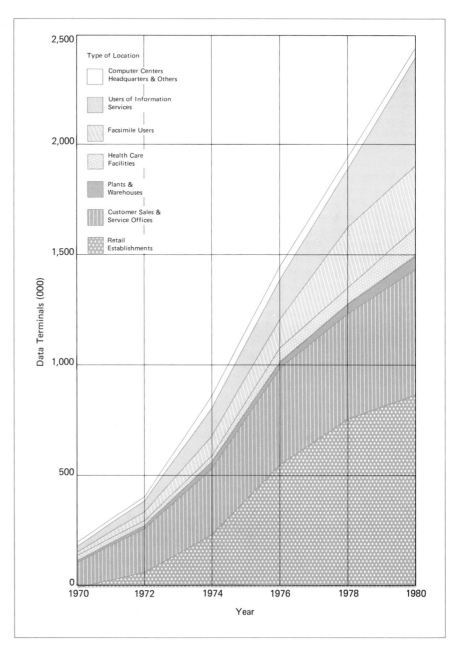

FIGURE 1.11   FORECAST NUMBER OF DATA TERMINALS,
1970–1980

DATA FLOW IN BUSINESS

A business enterprise is dependent upon the efficient flow of data, both internally and externally. Accurate, prompt, and complete data is essential in the decision-making process. Business executives must have adequate data to properly direct the operations of the business enterprise. The manufacturing, marketing, and distribution departments need data for production and shipment of goods.

External data flow in a business enterprise is illustrated in Figure 1.12. The firm is in the center of the diagram, surrounded by the groups with which it interacts. Data flow back and forth between the center—the firm—and the peripheral elements—the vendors, customers, government, and the public. Some examples of external data flow are reports on employee withholding

FIGURE 1.12   EXTERNAL DATA FLOW

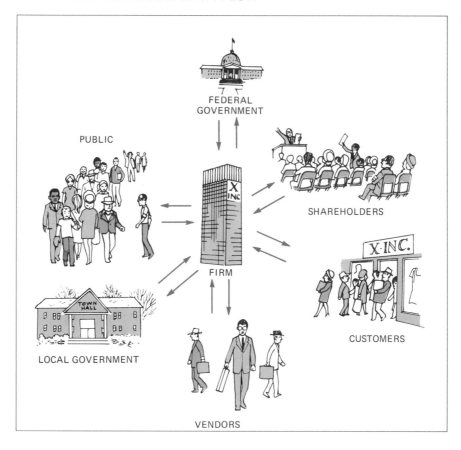

FIGURE 1.13   INTERNAL DATA FLOW

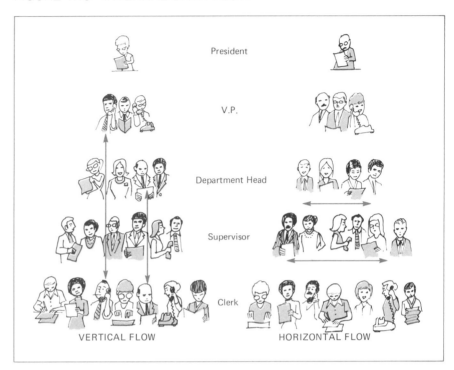

and unemployment tax reports, earnings reports, specifications to vendors, and sales orders.

Internal data flow takes place within an organization both horizontally and vertically. (See Figure 1.13.)

An example of vertical data flow is information passing from a foreman to line employees, or from the president to branch managers. Data may also flow from employees in lower echelons to their supervisors or to the president of the company. Horizontal data flow refers to information passing between personnel on the same level of the organization. For example, the head of manufacturing may supply salary information to the head of the payroll department. Or an employee on the shipping dock may sign for goods and supply data to a clerk in the purchasing department.

Time Factor   To be of optimum value to an organization, certain data must be available at specific points in the business cycle. A system of processing data must take the time element into account. The storage and retrieval of data is an important function of data processing. The accuracy and thoroughness of data processing are of little value to a firm unless the results it produces are presented at the correct times and places. For example, data on the credit standing and reputation of a prospective customer must be in the hands of the sales department prior to a sale. Credit data delivered after the transaction may be little consolation for the sales manager who has extended credit to an account incapable of repayment.

KEY TERMS   Analog computers   Information
              Computer   Input
              Data   Internal data flow
              Data cycle   Microprocessor
              Data processing   Minicomputer
              Digital computers   Output
              EAM   Program
              Electronic data processing   Source documents
              External data flow   Unit record

EXERCISES   1. Give four reasons why a study of data processing is of value.
              2. What is the difference between an analog computer and a digital computer?
              3. Diagram the data cycle of a particular business firm. List source documents, processing requirements, and output.
              4. Define the term "computer." Explain how the use of this term has changed.
              5. What is a computer program? Write a set of approximately ten instructions that tell, step by step, how to perform a task such as balancing a checkbook or determining monthly payments on a loan.
              6. Diagram the vertical data flow in your college. Show kinds of information that flow vertically and the individuals involved.
              7. Diagram the horizontal data flow in a firm or organization with which you are familiar. Show the kinds of information that flow horizontally and the personnel involved.
              8. Why is the time factor important in data processing? Give several examples of the effect of the time factor on the value of data.
              9. The demands on the business enterprise are discussed in this chapter. Select a business firm with which you are familiar and give examples of how these pressures affect it.
             10. Only a few of the many applications of data processing have been studied in this chapter. Visit a business firm that does not have electronic data processing. List at least three applications of electronic data processing that would be of value to that firm.
             11. Name four types of businesses that process data and might be able to use terminals.

12. Select a business firm to study. Interview its owners or employees. Draw a simplified diagram of its external data flow. (See Figure 1.12.) (Show the firm at the center, and list the names of the firms and organizations with which it interacts.)

13. Describe three data processing tasks that are profitable for the small firm to do manually.

14. What are the advantages of electronic data processing over unit record?

2
TRENDS IN
DATA PROCESSING

A study of the history of data processing shows that in the past, years—even centuries—elapsed between the introduction of new inventions. Today, the gap has closed. New machines, new methods, and improved systems enter the industry daily. (See Figure 2.1.) Advancements in data processing technology may be divided into two categories:

1 hardware developments

2 software developments.

In the computing field, hardware is defined as machines, devices, mechanisms, or physical equipment used to process data. Output printers, computer terminals, and the machines illustrated in Chapter 1 are examples of data processing hardware.

Software is defined as programs, computer languages, procedures, and documentation used in data processing. A computer program giving instructions for the steps involved in preparing and printing out employees' checks is an example of software. The language used to communicate with the computer and a diagram of the flow of business information in a firm are also software.

Computers and other data processing equipment could not be used without adequate software. Early software was crude or very limited. Computer languages were difficult to understand and to learn, and no systems were available to efficiently schedule jobs for the computer. Much

FIGURE 2.1   DATA PROCESSING HISTORY

PAST	Finger counting Decimal system Abacus
1300s	Double-entry bookkeeping system
1600s	Napier's bones Slide rule (analog computer) Pascal's numerical wheel calculator Leibnitz calculator
1800s	Jacquard punch card loom Babbages' Analytic Engine and Difference Engine Baldwin calculator Felt's comptometer Key-driven multipliers Hollerith code
1900s	Monroe calculator EAM processing FIRST GENERATION, ENIAC, stored program, assembler language
1950s	SECOND GENERATION, transistor FORTRAN language COBOL language
1960s	THIRD GENERATION, multiprogramming, teleprocessing, optical character recognition, magnetic ink character recognition Magnetic tape and disk, Minicomputers, audio response unit, BASIC language Integrated circuits
1970s	FOURTH GENERATION, monolithic circuits, cryogenics Microprocessors
1980s	?

of the growth and change in data processing in the last decade has been in the area of software.

This chapter will trace important developments and trends in both hardware and software technology.

DEVELOPMENTS IN HARDWARE

Throughout history people have used their creative powers to invent and develop devices and systems to help in their tasks. The manipulation, processing, and recording of data is no exception.

The human fingers were the first devices used to process data. This readily accessible, but limited, means of counting and calculating formed the basis for the decimal numbering system. Later, crude methods such as piling rocks or gathering sticks were used to indicate larger quantities and added another dimension in mathematical computation.

The abacus was one of the first mechanical devices developed to perform mathematical tasks. Although its origin is uncertain, the abacus was used by many civilizations, including the early Chinese and Romans. It is still in use today in many parts of the world.

The oriental abacus consists of a frame and rods, with beads strung along the rods to represent quantities. Addition and subtraction and other arithmetic operations are performed by manipulating the beads. The Romans moved pebbles, called calculi, in slots to perform computations. (See Figure 2.2.) The abacus is the earliest known direct ancestor of the digital computer.

Around 1617, John Napier invented the device, later called Napier's bones, shown in Figure 2.3. Napier's bones are rods with numbers engraved upon them. By rotating the rods, they can be made to perform multiplication, division, and root extraction.

The slide rule was an early example of an analog computer. This device appeared in several forms during the 17th century. Gunter's Scale, shown in Figure 2.4, was one such example. It was approximately two feet long and was used to perform multiplication.

In 1642 Blaise Pascal successfully built an adding machine. This primitive device, shown in Figure 2.5, performed calculations by means of wheels and cogs indexed to represent varying quantities.

In 1671 Gottfried Leibnitz completed a machine that could add, subtract, multiply, and divide. The Leibnitz calculator, shown in Figure 2.6, operates on the principle of the stepped reckoner and pin wheels, features still found in some mechanical desk calculators.

The next major step in the evolution of data processing was the development of a device completely unrelated to early calculators and slide rules. In 1801 in France, Joseph Marie Jacquard perfected an automatic system for weaving patterns into fabric. He used cards with punched holes to guide the warp threads on his loom, shown in Figure 2.7. The holes in the card controlled the pattern that was woven into the fabric. The Jacquard card, illustrated in Figure 2.8, was the forerunner of the cards used in unit record systems today.

About ten years later, in England, a visionary mathematician began work on a calculator that would perform extremely complex arithmetic functions

FIGURE 2.2   ROMAN ABACUS

FIGURE 2.3   NAPIER'S BONES

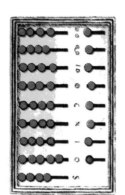

FIGURE 2.4   GUNTER'S SCALE

FIGURE 2.5
PASCAL'S NUMERICAL
WHEEL CALCULATOR

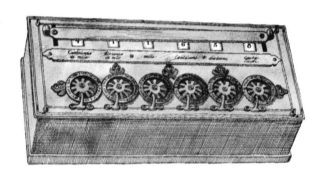

FIGURE 2.6   LEIBNITZ CALCULATOR

and calculations. Charles Babbage spent part of his life and fortune attempting to build his "Difference Engine." Figure 2.9 shows the portion that he completed in 1833. Later, he abandoned this machine in favor of a more complicated one, called the "Analytic Engine," which would perform arithmetic functions on data read in from punched cards. Neither device was ever completed because of the limited technology of the day.

Charles Babbage has earned his place in the history of data processing as the man who attempted to construct the first complex computer. The hundreds of drawings and plans he left have served as inspiration and education to the inventors and mathematicians who came after him.

Although a century would elapse before such a complex computer would finally be built, many small steps were taken during the next few decades. The era of industrialization and mechanization had begun. American inventors were actively pioneering new machines and devices. Many of these are the forerunners of our modern desk-top calculators.

Nineteenth century inventors successfully developed machines that performed some of the operations Babbage envisioned for his Analytic Engine. In 1872 Frank Stephen Baldwin built a calculator that performed all four basic mathematical functions. This marked the beginning of the calculating industry in the United States.

In 1887 Dorr E. Felt patented a "comptometer." This machine, shown in Figure 2.10, opened the way for adding multidigit numbers.

In 1890, Herman Hollerith successfully combined the concepts of Jacquard's cards and data recording and manipulation. He devised a coding system that could be punched into cards to represent data. Figure 2.11 shows the machine he built to read and manipulate data read in from the cards. This system was used to process the 1890 U.S. Census in one-fourth the time it had taken to do the 1880 Census. The Hollerith coding system became the standard data representation method for the unit record system.

Hollerith left the Census Department to manufacture and sell his data processing machine. The company he founded merged eventually with two others to become the International Business Machines Corporation, or IBM—a leader in the production of electronic data processing machines.

The capability of the calculating machine was further expanded in 1892 when W. S. Burroughs developed a 90-key model that could process up to nine decimal digits. And around 1914, the Monroe calculator was designed and built by Jay R. Monroe and F. S. Baldwin.

Birth of the Computer   In 1944 Howard G. Aiken, a physicist at Harvard University, brought Babbage's dream to fruition. Aiken perfected the first general-purpose computer, the Automatic Sequence Control Calculator, Mark I. The Mark I was an electromechanical device composed of numerous telephone relays and rotating mechanical wheels. Punched paper tape and punched cards provided data input.

FIGURE 2.7   JACQUARD LOOM

FIGURE 2.8   JACQUARD CARDS

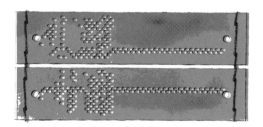

FIGURE 2.9
BABBAGE'S
DIFFERENCE ENGINE

FIGURE 2.10

FELT'S COMPTOMETER

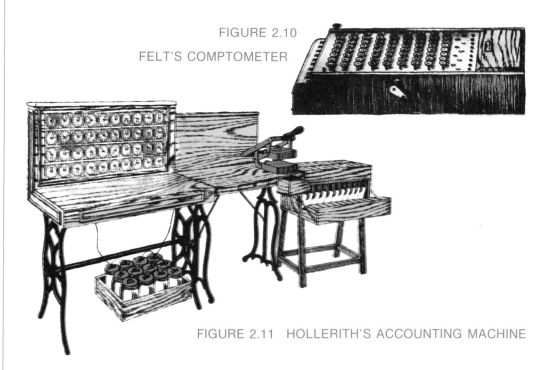

FIGURE 2.11   HOLLERITH'S ACCOUNTING MACHINE

Shortly after the Mark I was introduced, John W. Mauchly and J. Presper Eckert of the University of Pennsylvania developed a prototype computer called the ENIAC, the Electrical Numerical Integrator and Calculator (Figure 2.12). It differed from Aiken's computer in that it used vacuum tubes instead of telephone relays and therefore operated much more rapidly than the Mark I. The ENIAC did not look much like today's computer, but it was fully electronic in nature and had no moving parts.

Next came the development of the internally stored program—a concept basic to modern computers. Princeton mathematician John von Neumann (Figure 2.13) joined Eckert, Mauchly, and others in designing a machine, the Electronic Discrete Variable Automatic Computer (EDVAC), that would accept and store a set of instructions (or program).

Previously, all computers were programmed physically by soldering wires to terminals to direct the circuitry. Some devices used wiring boards— replaceable panels containing circuitry permanently wired to perform a sequence of operations. Early computer capabilities were thus greatly limited because each program or sequence of steps required a particular wiring, and changing programs was a slow, cumbersome, and inconvenient process.

Von Neumann's stored program concept replaced the inconvenient wiring board with instructions read into the machine on punched cards. These instructions directed the machine to carry out a sequence of steps. The internally stored program gives the computer much of its power. The advantages of the internally stored program are

1. The computer can be reprogrammed by entering instructions from another set of cards, instead of rewiring or using wiring panels.

2. The program may be written and tested before the actual data are available.

3. The machine is self-directing; a human operator does not have to guide each step.

Mauchly and Eckert were also involved in designing and building the first commercial computer, the Universal Automatic Computer (UNIVAC). (The company they formed eventually became the UNIVAC division of Sperry Rand Corporation.) The UNIVAC was the first computer to be sold to private business and to be used for commercial purposes. It was also one of the first machines to use magnetic tape as a means of inputting and outputting data. The UNIVAC received national attention in November 1952 when it predicted the victory of Eisenhower over Stevenson in the Presidential election.

In the past several decades, there have been many significant innovations in computers. These include a reduction in size of equipment and an increase in storage capacity and speed of operation. There have been so many innovations that computers have been grouped into categories called generations.

FIGURE 2.12

ENIAC

FIGURE 2.13

JOHN VON NEUMANN

First Generation First-generation computing systems were composed of tubes and relays but had the ability to store a program internally. They received their input data via paper tape or cards. The machines were large and often unreliable because of the many vacuum tubes which frequently overheated and burned out.

First-generation machines date to the late 1940s. They proliferated in use in the mid-1950s.

Second Generation The introduction of the transistor led to smaller, more dependable, and faster machines. Second-generation computing systems were characterized by greater speed and storage capacity than first-generation machines, but were more compact and cost less. Data were input by paper and magnetic tapes, or, most often, by punched cards. The late 1950s and early 1960s saw the introduction and proliferation of these machines.

Third Generation New manufacturing techniques and development of the microtransistor led to improvements in computer design. Third-generation computing systems were characterized by further reduction in size, lower cost, and improved methods of storing data.

The third-generation machines were distributed during the latter 1960s.

Faster, more efficient, and large-capacity means of data input, output, and storage were developed: two of the major ones are magnetic tape and magnetic disk.

MAGNETIC TAPE. (See Figure 2.14.) A $\frac{1}{2}$-inch-wide ribbon of tape, similar to the $\frac{1}{4}$-inch tape used on home tape recorders, is coated with iron oxide and spooled on reels of varying length. Data are placed on tape by magnetizing small areas of the coating. These areas represent bits of data. It is a process similar to recording information on a home tape recorder except that digital data are encoded.

Magnetic tape media allow large amounts of data to be stored in a comparatively small volume. Tape can be fed to a computer much faster than punched cards, is more economical, and can be stored conveniently.

All data are stored on the tape in the same sequence in which they were recorded. To access data, the computer searches the data in sequence for the desired information. Thus, the storage medium is called sequential access storage. (Magnetic tape is discussed in more detail in Chapter 9.)

MAGNETIC DISK. (See Figure 2.15.) Several disks, resembling ordinary phonograph records, are assembled into a conveniently carried disk pack. The top and bottom of each disk in the pack is coated with iron oxide. Data are magnetically recorded on the disks as they revolve at high speed.

A disk pack can store up to several million characters in a system called random access storage. Data can be accessed directly from the moving disk without searching in sequence. A single character, or group of characters,

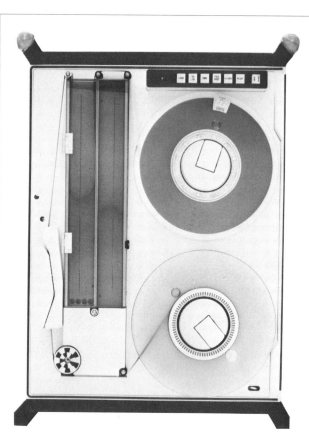

FIGURE 2.14
TAPE STORAGE DEVICE

FIGURE 2.15
MAGNETIC DISK DEVICE

can be retrieved from or recorded on the revolving disk in a fraction of a second. (Magnetic disks are discussed in more detail in Chapter 9.)

Fourth
Generation

Fourth-generation machines appeared in the 1970s, utilizing new technology such as integrated circuitry and monolithic circuits. Physically they are characterized by new types of terminals and miniaturized computers, such as minicomputers and microprocessors.

The integrated circuit is a significant development in computer hardware. Barely larger than the end of a pencil, it contains thousands of separate electronic components. Integrated circuits have made possible a substantial reduction in the size of computers and the amount of power required to run them. Large-scale integrated (LSI) circuits contain thousands of components on a single chip. Each chip may perform the functions of an entire machine such as a computer or calculator.

Figure 2.16 illustrates an integrated circuit, with a dime for size comparison. Figure 2.17 shows how circuitry has diminished in size in the course of the four computer generations.

COMPUTER TERMINALS.   Computer terminals have been an important development during this fourth generation. A computer terminal is a device,

FIGURE 2.16   INTEGRATED CIRCUIT

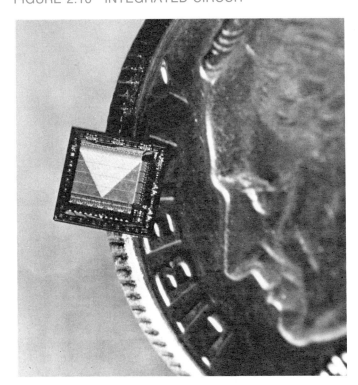

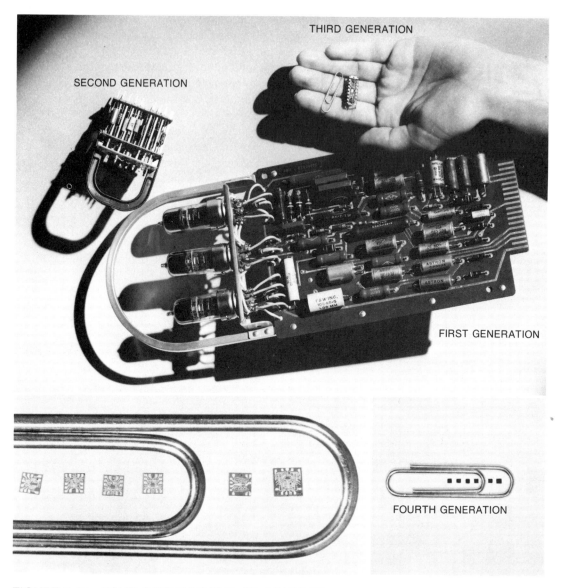

FIGURE 2.17 FOUR GENERATIONS OF COMPUTER CIRCUITRY

often at a location different from that of the central computer, that allows the user to gain access to the computer. Data are transmitted to the computer, and the results of processing may be returned through the terminal. Communication links, such as telephone or telegraph wires, microwave transmission, or leased wires, tie the terminal to the central computer.

Terminals can be used by large and small retailers to handle accounting, bookkeeping, and credit, by insurance companies to process claims, and by hospitals to process patients' records. Remote terminals make practical the processing of data that could not be done profitably or quickly enough at central locations.

The term teleprocessing refers to the terminals, communication links, and programs that facilitate the remote processing of data. Because it has shortened the time gap between the receipt of data and the delivery of results, reports, or solutions to problems, teleprocessing has had a strong influence on computer use.

Many different types of terminals are available to meet differing business needs. Some terminals print out typewriterlike copy, others display images on a video screen (cathode ray tube), some punch out cards or paper tape, and still others record on magnetic tape.

Hard-Copy Terminals. The first terminals, patterned closely after Teletype terminals (see Figure 2.18), are called "hard-copy" terminals, because they generate a printout resembling a page from a typewriter.

FIGURE 2.18   TELETYPE TERMINAL

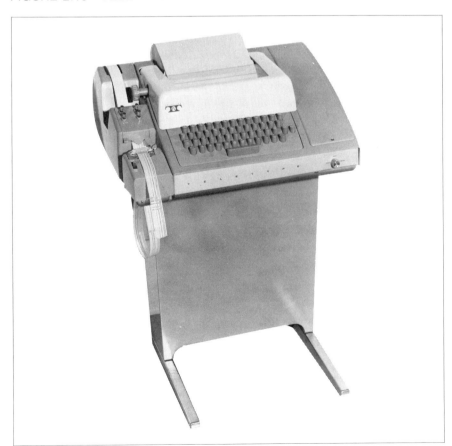

To input data from a hard-copy terminal, the operator strikes a key that sends an electronic pulse over telephone lines to the computer and also types out the character. After the data are entered, they are processed and the results are sent back to the terminal.

Some hard-copy terminals such as the Teletype Keyboard Send and Receive (KSR) can enter data only through the keyboard. The Teletype Automatic Send and Receive (ASR) can also punch and send data via paper tape. When the latter is used, the data on the tape are sent through the terminal to the computer.

Tape and Card Terminals.   A second major group of terminals handle data from punched cards or magnetic tape.

Data returned from the computer to the terminal are punched into cards rather than printed out on a typewriter. Some punch results on paper tape or record them on magnetic tape. Although these forms of output are not as easily read, they are valuable because the data are in a medium that can be used by other machines.

Video Terminals.   The cathode ray tube (CRT), or video terminal, is an example of a soft-copy terminal. It looks like a television with a keyboard. (See Figure 2.19.) Data being transmitted between the terminal and the computer are displayed on a CRT. Results can be displayed in the form of drawings, graphs, or charts. Since no hard copy is generated, the display

FIGURE 2.19   VIDEO TERMINAL

of new data erases the old, unless some provision is made to save the data or copy the screen.

The advantages of video terminals are speed, low cost, and display capacity. Hundreds of characters can be displayed on a screen at one time, as well as lines, graphs, and curves.

Audio Response Terminals.   The audio response terminal is capable of producing a verbal output. Data are entered in the computer by keyboard or other means, and results of the processing are returned over a telephone as words spoken in English. Hard or visual copy is not generated.

Audio response terminals store recorded statements of the human voice, such as sentences, balances, telephone numbers, stock levels, or credit ratings. The computer will select the appropriate phrase or word and construct a verbal message. New messages or different text may be recorded as required.

MINICOMPUTERS.   One of the major developments in the fourth generation was the introduction of minicomputers. They were developed during the late

FIGURE 2.20 MICROPROCESSOR

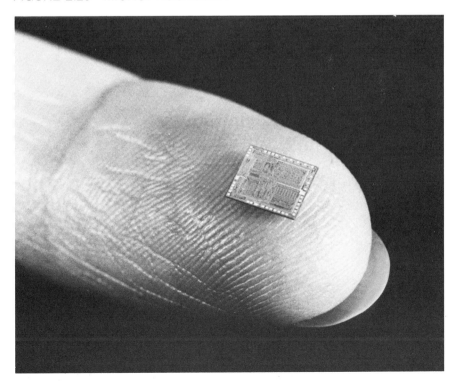

John von Neumann and the All-Purpose Computer

In the 25 years since John von Neumann designed the first fully modern electronic computer, tens of thousands of the controversial machines have dramatically altered the shape of today's society. John von Neumann, a warm outgoing mathematical genius, already stands as one of the giants of twentieth century thought.

Von Neumann was a true mathematical genius. As a six-year old in his native Budapest he could divide two eight-digit numbers in his head. At 24 he had developed "game theory," a mathematical method of studying competitive and cooperative interactions. Three years later he wrote a treatise on quantum mechanics that was to be a cornerstone of this branch of atomic physics. During World War II he was involved in the Manhattan Project, which produced the atomic bomb. In 1955, von Neumann was named to the Atomic Energy Commission. He died in 1957 at the age of 53.

Von Neumann's contribution converted the electronic computer from a special-purpose machine to a flexible, all-purpose device. Previous computers relied on slow mechanical methods [using plugboards] of storing the program, the set of instructions that direct the computer's operations. Von Neumann developed a concept that did away with the plugboard method. He designed a machine in which the program could be written in numbers and stored in the memory exactly as if it were numbers to be manipulated in the computation.

The internally stored program made possible a general-purpose computer that could, almost instantaneously, electronically reorganize its internal circuits to meet special needs simply by feeding in a set of numbers.

This design, which included a new organization of the computer subassemblies —once referred to as the "von Neumann architecture" or the "von Neumann machine"—remains the basic pattern for nearly all digital computers.

SOURCE: Abstracted from "Man and Computer: Uneasy Allies of 25 Years," by Boyce Rensberger, *The New York Times*, July 27, 1972, p. 43.

1960s and proliferated during the early 1970s. Minicomputers are desk-top computers possessing the major features of large-scale machines—at a much lower cost. They store from 4,000 to 64,000 characters in primary memory, weigh from 25 to 100 pounds, and cost from $2,000 to $20,000. They are used largely for small business and office applications, and sometimes as part of a larger computer system.

MICROPROCESSORS.   Developed during the 1970s, the microprocessor is an even smaller version of a computer. It is manufactured on a small chip of silicon, less than $\frac{1}{4}$ inch square (Figure 2.20). Microprocessors have many of the features and capabilities of the larger systems.

The cost of microprocessors has dropped substantially since their introduction and by 1980 is expected to be as low as $5.00. This reduction in cost will bring about a significant increase in the number in use. By 1980 it is estimated that more than 125,000 microprocessors will be used in the field of industrial automation and in medical applications alone. (See Figure 2.21.) The major application for microprocessors lies in the field of industrial automation, where they are used to monitor and control various manufacturing processes. Their low cost and light weight make it feasible to carry them on site or into the field or to package them with other portable equipment as part of a larger system.

"To be frank, Wimberly, we don't *exactly* pension you off.
Ever been stored on a disc before?"

FIGURE 2.21   MICROPROCESSOR SHIPMENTS

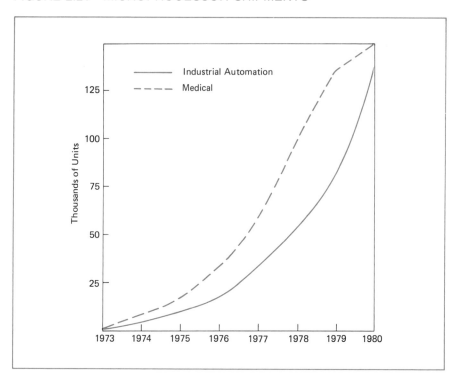

DEVELOPMENTS IN SOFTWARE

Evolution of
Programming
Languages

Software for data processing has passed through many phases of evolution, moving from crude numbering systems, such as Roman numerals, to modern computer languages, such as COBOL and FORTRAN. One of the earliest numbering systems involved Roman numerals. Later, two significant developments improved our ability to manipulate data: the concepts of the zero and the adoption of the Arabic numbering system. Our understanding of the mathematical laws also expanded. Long division, logarithms, square roots, trigonometric functions, and countless other advances have their place in the history of the development of computer software.

These early mathematical discoveries represent milestones in the development of software. However, the real breakthroughs that have facilitated *people–machine communications* occurred during the last several decades, when computer languages were introduced.

WIRING BOARD.   The earliest form of instructing data processing equipment was via the wiring board. This method consists of a wiring panel with terminals and groups of jumper wires. (See Figure 2.22.) To program the system, the operator physically connects the appropriate terminals with the jumper wires to form electrical paths that direct the machine to carry out various functions. Errors in programming are hard to locate with this method, and programs are not easily transferred from one machine to another. Unit record machines are programmed in this manner. The earliest computers were also programmed using wiring boards, a very slow and awkward means of programming.

MACHINE LANGUAGE.   Development of the stored program created a major change in the way computers could be directed to perform tasks. Instructions in a program could now be read into memory locations and stored internally in the machine. At first this was accomplished by a system of relays and switches. Later, magnetic core storage systems were developed.

Internal program storage avoided the necessity for physically wiring the set of instructions in the computer. New programs could be read in quickly to replace the old, without the tedious necessity of rewiring. This greatly increased the machine's general-purpose capabilities.

FIGURE 2.22   WIRING CONTROL PANEL

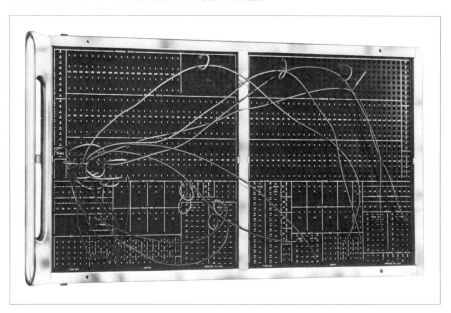

However, early computer programming could be done only in machine language by computer engineers who were familiar with the internal mechanisms of the machine. Machine language is the only language a computer can directly understand. The instructions are coded in the form of 1s and 0s to represent the two-state characteristic of the electronic components involved: on or off, high or low, right or left. Programming in machine language is time consuming and tedious and therefore impractical for modern business applications. Another drawback is that each computer has its own language. Programs written for one machine usually will not run on anther type of machine or that of another manufacturer.

ASSEMBLER LANGUAGE.   Assembler language developed from improvements in computer design and a further study of people–machine communication. In assembler language, instructions are given to the computer in symbols or abbreviations called *mnemonics*. These mnemonics, such as ADD, OR, and PACK, tell the machine to perform certain functions.

Assembler language is much easier for the programmer than machine language because it involves words or wordlike symbols rather than 0s and 1s. However, since the computer operates in machine language, assembler language must be translated by a special program stored in the machine. The assembler program automatically performs the function of translating assembler instructions into machine instructions. In assembler language an instruction must be given for each individual step or operation in the program.

PROBLEM-ORIENTED LANGUAGE (POL).   Since people prefer to communicate in a language that closely resembles their own, new languages were needed. Languages that stressed problem-solving features and eliminated many of the programming details required in machine and assembler languages were designed.

Instructions written in these problem-oriented languages must be translated into machine language before the computer can execute them. This is done by a compiler, a complex program written by a manufacturer or user. A different compiler is used to translate each problem-oriented language into machine language.

One of the important advantages of problem-oriented languages is that each instruction written by the programmer need only give the broad steps, such as read a card or compare values. The compiler will translate each broad step into many minute steps to direct the computer through the action specified.

One of the first of the problem-oriented languages, FORTRAN (for FORmula TRANslating system) was developed during the 1950s. FORTRAN has become one of the major languages in use today. Programs written in FORTRAN can be run on most computers with a FORTRAN compiler with little or no modifications. This language and others are explained more fully in later chapters.

The second major language to appear was COBOL (COmmon Business Oriented Language), which has become widely used for business programming. COBOL is still undergoing improvements and changes.

During the past several years, many new languages have come into use. They have such exotic names as RPG, SNOBOL, BASIC, ALGOL, APL, SIMSCRIPT, PL/I. Each has its advantages and limitations. But without these languages it would be difficult for the programmer to communicate with computers.

Operating Systems

As the volume of work thrust on computers increased, it was essential to develop better methods of scheduling work and assigning input/output devices for each program.

Early computer programs were set up and run one at a time, while the operator stood by to handle errors and problems. If an error appeared, the computer had to be stopped. This procedure was satisfactory as long as only a few programs had to be run.

But as the volume of work increased and the cost of computers rose, the need for a better method became imperative. Special programs, called operating systems, were written to replace the human attendant in scheduling work. These programs are discussed later in the book. Operating systems start programs, stop them when they do not run properly, and deal with error conditions and interruptions efficiently without stopping the computer.

Multiprogramming

Improvements in operating systems further expanded the computer's utility by allowing multiprogramming. Several programs can be processed simultaneously, by sharing the computer's available resources.

A bank can use its computer to service data entered from remote teller terminals while it also prepares the payroll. Both functions can be manipulated at the same time by a system of slicing the computer's time into fractions of a second.

Time Sharing

Time sharing of computers developed to enable many users to share the cost and burden of one large installation. Time sharing brings the benefits of modern EDP to many small users who could not afford to lease or buy the computer alone.

Time sharing has become an important part of business data processing and has led to the development of new software, operating systems, and hardware. Many firms have been established to provide time-sharing services to business establishments. These firms buy a computer and sell time on it. A client gains access to the computer by telephone and enters data and programs through remote terminals. The client receives a monthly bill for the amount of time used.

Time-sharing firms offer their customers many other services, including systems design and programming. They may also have ready-made programs that can handle many common business problems stored on the computer. Such programs may deal with interest, stocks and bonds, capital investments, cost analysis, or other mathematical and statistical procedures. Users dial the computer firm from their personal terminal, call out the required programs, and enter in their data.

Proprietary Programs

One of the newest areas of software expansion is proprietary software. Proprietary software is a program written by a firm for sale or lease. Many companies now provide computer users with package programs at a fixed price or monthly rental. The programs include personnel management, systems, report writers, file maintenance routines, and account billing. This decade should see a growth in the numbers and types of firms offering ready-made programs.

KEY TERMS

Analytic Engine
Assembler language
COBOL
Compiler
Computer generation
ENIAC
FORTRAN
Hard-copy terminals
Hardware
Hollerith code
Jacquard system
Machine language
Magnetic disk
Magnetic tape

Microprocessor
Minicomputer
Multiprogramming
Operating system
Problem-oriented language
Proprietary program
Random access storage
Sequential access storage
Soft copy terminals
Software
Stored program
Teleprocessing
Video terminals

EXERCISES

1. Explain the differences between hardware and software.
2. What were the major developments in data processing techniques before 1900?
3. What is a stored program? What are the advantages of using one?
4. Outline the major developments in the first, second, and third generations of hardware. What generation are we presently in?
5. Explain the differences between sequential access storage and random access storage.
6. How do minicomputers differ from other computers, and what are their advantages?

7. What are microprocessors? Where are they used?
8. What kinds of services do proprietary software firms offer?
9. Define teleprocessing.
10. What advantages do hard-copy terminals have over video terminals?
11. Write a sentence that might be stored in an audio response terminal. Underline the words or numbers in the sentence that the computer will vary, depending on the individual problem it is solving.
12. How does machine language differ from assembler language?
13. What are the advantages of POLs?
14. What is time sharing? List six applications for remote time-sharing users.

PART TWO

UNIT RECORD
PROCESSING/
ELECTRICAL
ACCOUNTING
MACHINE
PROCESSING

3

UNIT RECORD AND DATA CAPTURE PRINCIPLES

Dr. Herman Hollerith, Census Bureau statistician, faced a dilemma. It would soon be time for the 1890 Census, and the United States population had increased greatly in the last decade. How could his office tabulate, summarize, and report the data before it became obsolete? With the existing manual methods, the job would take so long that the results would be meaningless.

Hollerith turned to the principle used by Joseph Marie Jacquard to direct his weaving machine. As mentioned in Chapter 2, cards with holes punched in them were used to control the patterns of the loom. Adapting the punched-card principle to record and process statistical data, Hollerith was able to complete the 1890 Census in $2\frac{1}{2}$ years, a record for the time.

This marked the beginning of the punched-card method of data processing. This mode of processing is called unit record, electrical machine accounting, or just "punched card" processing. (See Figure 3.1.)

To develop and produce unit record equipment, Hollerith originally formed the Tabulating Machine Company, which, after a series of mergers, evolved into the International Business Machines Corporation, or IBM. Today IBM is one of the world's largest manufacturers of unit record and computer data processing equipment.

From 1930 to 1960, the electrical accounting machine (EAM) method was the major method of processing data for large firms. While it is still used today by many companies, it has been largely replaced by computerized systems.

FIGURE 3.1   DATA PROCESSING IN THE EARLY 1900s

The EAM method is discussed here because of its importance and relationship to the development of computer systems and because it provides a convenient and graphic means of explaining many of the concepts involved in data processing principles.

Regardless of the data processing method used—manual, unit record, or electronic—the principles involved in organizing, manipulating, and reporting the data remain very much the same. All data will move through the steps that compose the EAM cycle.

EAM CYCLE

The EAM cycle consists of three phases: input, processing, and output. (See Figure 3.2.) In the first phase, data are input to the system by keypunching on cards. In the processing phase, cards containing data are sorted, collated, duplicated, and manipulated in various ways. The data may be entered into calculations such as determining net wages. Output consists of converting the processed information into a form that is convenient and useful to a business firm. Updated inventories may be listed, paychecks may be printed, and so on.

Data processing systems can be classified by the way in which individual records are handled and processed. Records may be grouped in lists, journals, rosters, and reports where data are all on the same form. The element common to these forms is that many items are grouped on the same document, called a collective list. Some examples of collective lists are

1 a roster of a class, listing names of students and test scores;

2 a typed list of accounts receivable, showing firm names and balances due;

3 a stock list, containing the names, description numbers, and quantities of parts in stock.

Unit Record System   A second method of processing and handling data is by unit records. Here data concerning individual items are kept on separate records. Collective lists, rosters, or journals are not maintained. Machines can more readily locate single cards, remove an item from a group, or update a record that is not physically tied to other records.

In the unit record system, data from source documents are punched on cards. The punched cards are then fed into machines for further processing.

FIGURE 3.2 EAM CYCLE

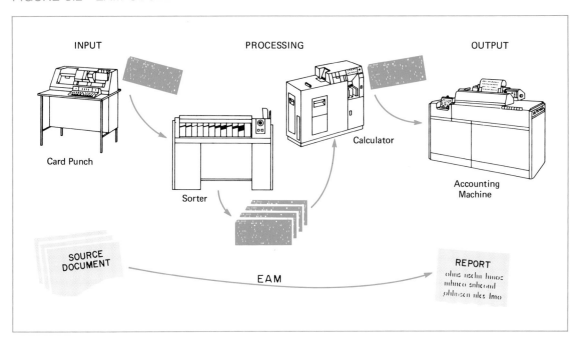

Processing involves the physical movement of cards through the machines to merge groups, sort, perform calculations, etc. The output, or reporting of results, is done by an accounting machine, which prints data on a sheet of paper. Data may also be output on a machine that punches data onto other cards.

The unit record system is based on the principle that each punched card or record contains data or information about only one item. A unit record may contain several pieces of data, but all will refer to the same item. Some examples are

1. a student's name, ID number, and test score;
2. a salesperson's name, employee number, and sales for the month;
3. a part name, description, stock number, and quantity left in stock;
4. a paycheck and stub, issued to one employee, showing employee name, number, deductions, and net salary.

ADVANTAGES. Since only one transaction is recorded on each card, data on one record can easily be changed or updated without disturbing the other records. For example, a test grade for a student can be added, inventory for a part can be adjusted, or, by removing a card, a name can be deleted from a group.

This method of data processing is fast and efficient for small to moderate amounts of data. Punched cards are convenient to handle, as well as easily mailed, written or typed upon, or filed. Equipment costs are moderate, and machine operators can be trained easily.

LIMITATIONS. An ordinary punched card holds a maximum of 80 columns of data. If the data on a transaction require more than 80 columns, two or more cards must be used. The use of more than one card to store data negates the main advantage of a unit record system.

The punched cards can jam in machines, tear, or be mutilated. If holes are not properly punched, or have been tampered with, errors occur. Punched cards cannot be repunched and, at about $1.50 per thousand, are relatively expensive. In addition, storage becomes a problem when thousands of cards are involved.

Since large numbers of cards move relatively slowly through machines, the unit record system is impractical for processing files containing hundreds of thousands of cards. [Time intervals involved in processing data are usually measured in seconds or thousandths of a second (milliseconds) in the unit record system. In electronic data processing, they are measured in millionths of a second (microseconds) or billionths of a second (nanoseconds). (See Table 3.1.)] Furthermore, processing systems that depend on the physical movement of cards are prone to error—cards may be lost, misfiled, or damaged.

TABLE 3.1 RELATIVE SPEEDS

METHOD	APPROXIMATE SPEED
	Measured in
Manual methods	Seconds
Unit record systems	Milliseconds
Early computer systems	Microseconds
Modern computer systems	Nanoseconds

MULTIPLES AND SUBMULTIPLES	PREFIXES	SYMBOLS
$1\ 000\ 000\ 000\ 000 = 10^{12}$	tera (ter'a)	T
$1\ 000\ 000\ 000 = 10^{9}$	giga (ji'ga)	G
$1\ 000\ 000 = 10^{6}$	mega (meg'a)	M
$1\ 000 = 10^{3}$	kilo (kil'o)	k
$100 = 10^{2}$	hecto (hek'to)	h
$10 = 10^{1}$	deka (dek'a)	d
$1 = 10^{0}$		
$0.1 = 10^{-1}$	deci (des'i)	d
$0.01 = 10^{-2}$	centi (sen'ti)	c
$0.001 = 10^{-3}$	milli (mil'i)	m
$0.000\ 001 = 10^{-6}$	micro (mi'kro)	μ
$0.000\ 000\ 001 = 10^{-9}$	nano (nan'o)	n
$0.000\ 000\ 000\ 001 = 10^{-12}$	pico (pe'ko)	p
$0.000\ 000\ 000\ 000\ 001 = 10^{-15}$	femto (fem'to)	f
$0.000\ 000\ 000\ 000\ 000\ 001 = 10^{-18}$	atto (at'to)	a

PUNCHED CARDS

The Hollerith Card

In referring to the punched card, several terms are used synonymously, such as IBM card, punched card, Hollerith card, tab card, unit record, and data card. The standard punched card shown in Figure 3.3 is described below.

FORMAT. Each card is $3\frac{1}{4} \times 7\frac{3}{8}$ inches with corner cut and is available in a variety of colors, printed forms, or with a colored stripe for identification.

The face of each card contains 80 vertical columns. Each column is made up of 12 punch positions and can record one alphabetic or numeric character. Columns are often labeled from 1 to 80, for ease of identification and keypunching. A punch position is the location of one hole punched in a card. Each alphabetic or numeric character has its own combination of punch positions. A punch position is sometimes called a bit (the shortened

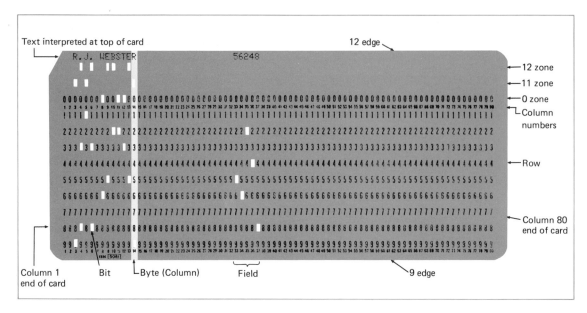

FIGURE 3.3   THE STANDARD PUNCHED CARD

form for binary digit). A group of bits (punch positions) are combined to form each character.

A row is a horizontal group of punch positions across the card. Each row contains 80 possible punches. There are 12 rows, called the 12, 11, 0, 1, 2, 3, 4, 5, 6, 7, 8, and 9 rows, from top to bottom. Only the 0–9 rows are labeled.

A zone is a 12, 11, or 0 row across the top of the punched card. The row at the top of the card is the "12 zone"; the one below it is the "11 zone," sometimes called the "X punch"; the third row is the "0 zone." The 11 and 12 zones are usually not labeled.

A field is one or more columns reserved for related information. Fields can range from 1 to 80 columns in width. For example, a five-digit identification number punched in columns 33 through 37 of a punched card is in a five-column field. A name up to 20 letters long in columns 1 through 20 occupies a "20-column field."

The top edge of the card, nearest the 12 zone, is called the 12 edge. The bottom edge of the card, nearest the 9 row, is called the 9 edge. The left edge of the card, nearest column 1, is called the column 1 end. The right edge of the card, nearest column 80, is called the column 80 end.

Punched Card Codes

Modifications of the Hollerith coding system are used for punching alphabetic and numeric information onto cards. One character—a letter, number, or

symbol—is printed in each column, using a unique combination of holes for
each one. Numbers from 0 to 9 are represented by punching the
corresponding digit in that column. Alphabetic letters require two punches per
column, one in zone 11, 12, or 0, and one in digit rows 1 to 9. Special
characters, such as $*$, $/$, $+$, may require a combination of three holes per
column. This code may vary with the keypunch being used. Figure 3.4
illustrates the code used by the IBM 029 Card Punch. (There is no advantage
in memorizing this code, since the keypunch machine automatically punches
the proper holes when a key is struck.)

SYSTEM/3 PUNCHED CARD CODE.   In 1971 IBM introduced a 96-column
punched card shown in Figure 3.5 for use in their System/3 computers. Up
to 96 columns of data can be punched onto a single System/3 card by using
a coding system in which a combination of six punch positions (bits) encodes
each character. The card is relatively small ($2\frac{5}{8} \times 3\frac{1}{4}$ inches); only 32 columns
of information can be punched across it. Therefore, three layers, or tiers, are
used to encode the 96 characters. Columns 1 through 32 of data are
punched into the first tier, columns 33 through 64 are punched onto the
second tier, and columns 65 through 96 onto the third tier. In the same way,
the printed information is interpreted (printed) across the top of the card
in three rows. The top portion, containing the printed information, is called
the print area, and the lower portion is called the punch area.

FIGURE 3.4   PUNCHED CARD CODE

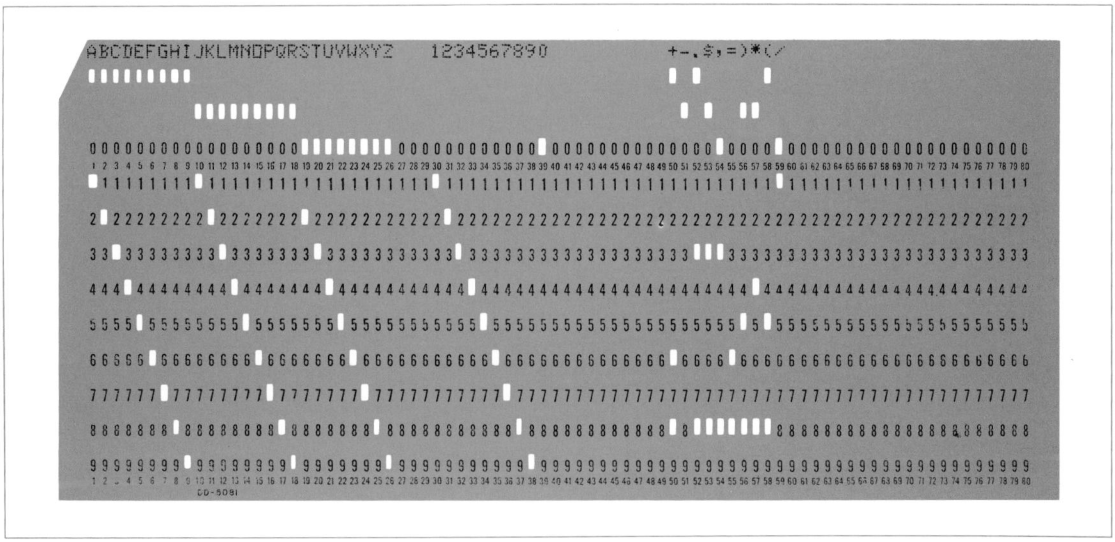

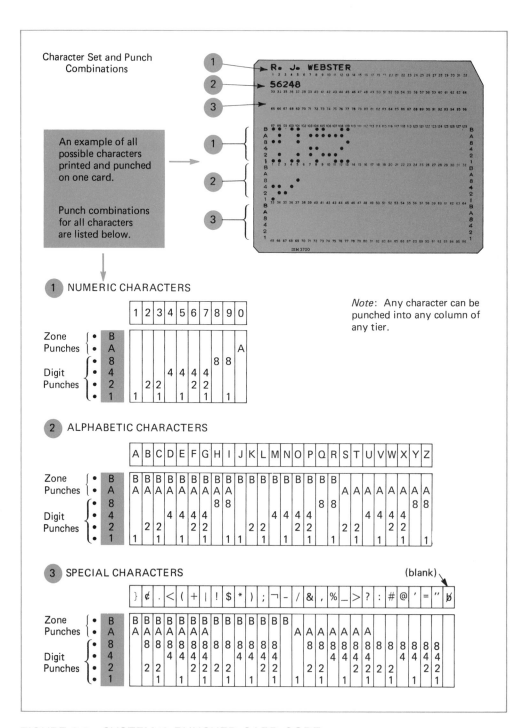

FIGURE 3.5   SYSTEM/3 PUNCHED CARD CODE

FILE ORGANIZATION AND TERMINOLOGY

The principles of file organization and maintenance are basic to all forms of data processing, including computers and unit record. A file is a collection of two or more records in the same category. Figure 3.6 illustrates a file in which each record contains the name of a student and a test score. Files used in business include, for example, personnel lists, lists of accounts receivable and payable, parts lists, inventories, sales for the day, lists of back-ordered items, and lists of goods out to bid.

Files can contain fixed-length records or variable-length records. A fixed-length record contains a predetermined or standard number of columns of data. The length may be set deliberately for consistency or convenience, or determined by the physical limitations of the record. Each fixed-length record requires the same amount of storage space regardless of the number of characters recorded on it. The standard punched card is a fixed-length record, since it allows space for 80 characters. System/3 IBM cards, which accommodate 96 characters, are also fixed-length records.

Variable-length records are limited only by the amount of data that apply to each transaction. Ordinary punched cards are usually too limited to hold variable-length records. Magnetic tape, however, which is discussed in Chapter 9, is an excellent medium for variable-length records.

Variable-length records do not waste space at the end of each record and are therefore more efficient than fixed-length records.

Types
of Records

Records can be classified by content as well as by length. A logical record contains all the data related to a single item. It may be a payroll record for an employee, or a record of all of the charges made by a customer in a department store. Since a logical record has no size limitation, it must often be shortened or condensed if it is to fit on a punched card.

A master record contains information or data of a permanent or semipermanent nature. Master records may contain all available data on an item, even though only a small amount of the data may be used at one time. Selected data may be copied from the master record. An example of a master record is a stock card giving a part's name, size, quantity in stock, supplier, costs, and order point.

A detail record contains selected data copied from the master record or original data that will be added to the master record to bring it up to date. An example of a detail record would be one containing an account name, number, and the amount charged that day. A detail record that contains new information, such as payments to be posted, is sometimes called an activity record.

A summary record contains data that have been summarized, condensed, or reported from other records. For example, a summary card could be

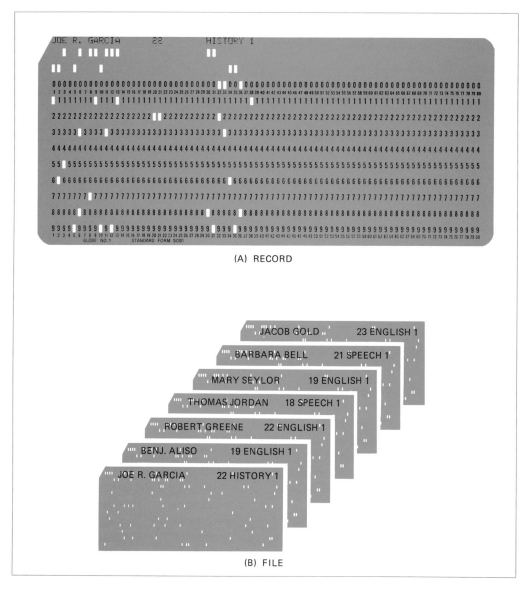

(A) RECORD

(B) FILE

FIGURE 3.6

prepared from a file containing 100 detail cards. Each detail card might contain the title of an account and the balance. The 100 detail cards in the file could then be entered into a machine that would add the individual balances and punch the cumulative total on a card to produce a summary record.

File
Maintenance

Much of the work in data processing consists of keeping files current. To be of value, the information in personnel, cash flow, manufacturing data, and sales and warehousing files must be up to date.

File maintenance includes such tasks as posting debits and credits to accounts, adding new names to personnel lists and removing inactive ones, revising hourly employee records, and changing the number of exemptions on an employee's payroll record.

In unit record processing, file maintenance is usually performed on a machine called a collator. Individual records are pulled from files and updated. Then the new or revised cards are refiled by merging on the collator.

Record Layout

The layout of cards in the unit record system must be carefully planned to hold the maximum amount of data and facilitate processing. Personnel who lay out new records must consider several factors.

Color is frequently used to differentiate files. For example, a red card could be used for accounts payable, a blue card for accounts receivable, a green card for personnel records. Cards with colored stripes printed across their faces can also be bought and used to differentiate files. For example, a yellow-striped card may be used for data from the Los Angeles branch, a green stripe from the Chicago branch, and a purple stripe from the New York branch.

Record layout also involves determining the number, type, and sequence of fields used for recording data. The card designer attempts to use these elements, as well as codes, to place as much data as possible in the 80 columns of a card.

The designer first carefully studies the data to be punched into the card to determine the number and types of fields needed. The order in which the fields appear is important for accuracy and ease of keypunching. Often this sequence will be determined by the design of the source document. It is easier and faster to punch data into a card in the same order in which it appears on the source document. Finally, the designer draws a layout, showing where the fields will be located.

Figure 3.7 illustrates a card layout with eight fields. The fields are labeled and reserved for selected data. In the case illustrated, the first three fields contain alphabetic data and the last five, numerical and coded data. Three fields are left blank. To make it easy to identify data and differentiate fields, forms can be printed directly on the cards in a variety of colors.

Coding Methods

So that maximum information can be recorded on a single record, data are often represented by codes made up of letters, numbers, or a combination of them. For example, a two-digit code system for state names obviously requires a narrower field than if the names were spelled out. The codes used

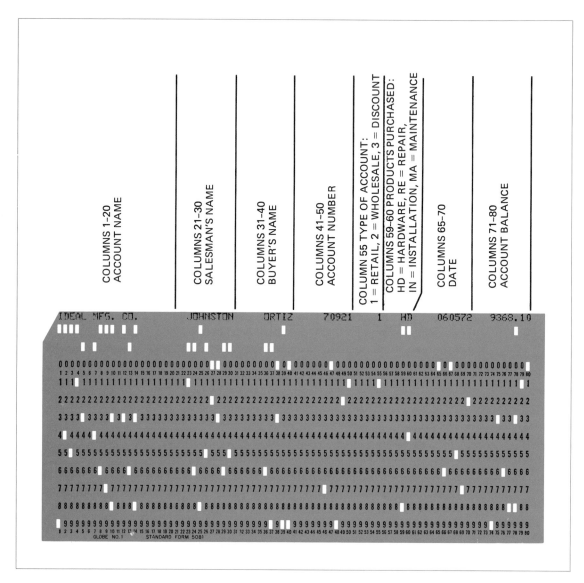

FIGURE 3.7   RECORD LAYOUT

for recording data should not only be convenient to use and easy to interpret, but also expandable so that more items can be added to the list.

The fifth and sixth fields in Figure 3.7 illustrate the use of codes. In the fifth field, column 55, a single digit is keypunched to indicate type of account. In this case, code is used not only to save columns, but also to facilitate later sorting of cards by account type.

In the sixth field, columns 59 and 60, a two-character alphabetic code identifies the product purchased by the account. The two-column code saves many columns for entering other information.

Some commonly used types of codes in unit record systems are the sequence code, the mnemonic code, and the significant digit code.

SEQUENCE CODE.   In a sequence code, each item is assigned a number in sequence, beginning with 1. For example, the departments in a business firm could be coded as follows:

CODE	DEPARTMENT
1	Accounting
2	Advertising
3	Personnel
4	Production
5	Sales
6	Shipping

MNEMONIC CODE.   Mnemonic codes rely upon mnemonic memory devices such as key letters or the sound of words. For example, a mnemonic code for a list of automobile names could be developed as follows:

CODE	AUTOMOBILE
CV	Chevrolet
CA	Cadillac
FO	Ford
OL	Oldsmobile
DA	Datsun

SIGNIFICANT-DIGIT CODE.   Meaning can be assigned to each digit or position in a group of characters to develop a significant-digit code. Strings of letters or numbers can be built into an efficient, compact coding system, allowing more data to be recorded in fewer columns. For example, a code to record dollar volume, salesperson, and type of account could look like this:

CODE	DOLLAR VOLUME	SALESPERSON	TYPE OF ACCOUNT
10 SM W	$10,000	Smith	Wholesale
35 GR R	35,000	Green	Retail
18 CH D	18,000	Chester	Discount

The Man Who Almost Invented the Computer

Charles Babbage had two loves: machines and mathematics. His studies at Cambridge in the early 1800s gave him the opportunity to investigate the principles of mathematics, science, and mechanics. His sizable inheritance gave him the means to pursue his lifelong dream—the development of a calculating machine.

He envisioned a machine that could prepare complex arithmetic tables with a precision and speed far beyond the ability of the human mind. But could he build such a machine? In 1822, The Royal Society persuaded the government to grant him £1,500 to begin his work. He labored eight years without success on the project, and repeatedly requested more money. He himself invested £6,000 trying to perfect the machine he called the "Difference Engine."

Then he dreamed of another device that could perform calculations on data read from punched cards. He abandoned his plans for the Difference Engine in favor of this even more complex device he called the "Analytic Engine."

Building the Analytic Engine proved far more frustrating than the Difference Engine. Babbage returned again and again to the drawing board to change his designs and plans. During the next several years he tried more than 400 different plans and modifications for his Analytic Engine.

When he approached the government for additional funds, he met with such strong opposition that he abandoned the project. After 21 years in engineering and investigating the world's first digital computer, Babbage had to admit defeat. His dreams, far ahead of the ideas and the mechanical technology of his time, were not to come true in his lifetime.

But Babbage's efforts were not all in vain. He wrote several treatises including "The Decline of Science" and "On the Economy of Machinery and Manufactures." His work laid the foundation for the first unit record machines. Three decades after his death, Herman Hollerith relied upon many of his ideas to invent the first successful unit record processing equipment.

Data Input Methods

Originally, all data input to a unit record system were coded onto cards by keypunch machines. Although these machines are still widely used, the past several decades have seen the development of other methods of inputting data such as those illustrated in Figure 3.8. All these methods are suitable for input to electronic data processing systems as well.

KEYBOARD TO PUNCHED CARD.   Keypunch operators punch data directly from keyboards onto cards. Keypunch machines include the standard

80-column ones, such as the IBM 029, the IBM 059 Verifying Machine, the UNIVAC 1810 Verifying Interpreting Punch, the IBM 129, and for System/3 cards the IBM 96-column machines, such as the IBM 5496 Data Recorder.

IBM 029 Card Read/Punch. The IBM 029, illustrated in Figure 3.9, was introduced to punch cards for the IBM/360 Computer. As the operator presses a key, the appropriate code is punched into one column of the card, and the character is printed at the top of the card at the same time.

There are several different keyboard arrangments available on the 029 card punch. The most common layout includes both alphabetic and numeric characters. Another arrangement includes only numeric keys.

Keypunch operators actuate keyboards to punch data directly onto cards. Since a manual activity is involved in converting source data into a form

"Good news, Miss Morgan . . . your keypunch machine will be here tomorrow."

FIGURE 3.8   INPUT METHODS

KEY TO CARD	MARK SENSE	PORTABLE PUNCH	OCR
Source Document	Mark Sense	Portable Punch	Source Document
↓	↓	↓	↓
Keypunch	Punch	Input	Input
↓	↓		
Verify	Input		
↓			
Input			

suitable for input to the system, a certain number of errors will occur. The purpose of verifying is to see that the original data have been accurately punched onto the card. This necessitates keyboarding all data twice, once to keypunch and once to verify. Verification is an essential step to ensure accuracy of data input.

UNIVAC 1801 Verifying Punch.   The UNIVAC keypunch, shown in Figure 3.10, combines automatic printing, punching, and verifying in a single machine. All data to be input are first keyboarded. However, instead of each keystroke punching a code onto a card, the data are entered into a memory device within the machine. After all data have been entered into storage, and verified by a second keyboarding, the machine automatically punches a card. This is done without operator attention, or while data for the next record are being keyboarded.

Primary storage allows the keypunch operator to verify the work in one pass. Data are entered from the keyboard, and the images held in primary storage. Then they are keyboarded again for verification. If the keystrokes match, a card is punched out. If an error is detected, the operator backspaces and enters the correct data.

IBM 5496 Data Recorder.   The IBM 5496 Data Recorder is designed to punch data into the System/3 IBM card. (See Figure 3.11.) The machine is composed of a desk, keyboard, card hopper, and stacker. As keys are pressed on the machine, the data are recorded in an input storage section. Characters can be corrected by backspacing and striking over. After the entire line has been keyboarded, the data are automatically punched into the card.

FIGURE 3.9   IBM 029 CARD READ/PUNCH

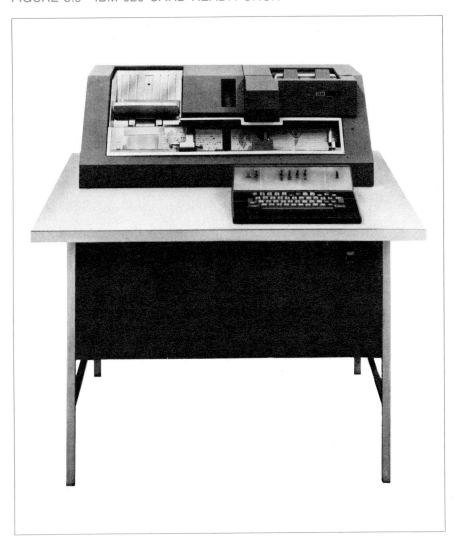

FIGURE 3.10   UNIVAC 1801 VERIFYING PUNCH

FIGURE 3.11

IBM 5496 DATA RECORDER

DIRECT CARD INPUT.   Another data input method involves direct card input. In this process, source data are entered directly on a card ready for entry into the system; no keypunching is required. This increases accuracy and at the same time eliminates the need for verifying.

Portable Punches.   A portable punch can be used to code data onto specially die-cut IBM cards. The card is inserted into a hand-held plastic holder and characters are recorded by punching out appropriate holes in the card with a stylus. Using this method of input, source documents can be prepared in the field with simple equipment. For example, a salesperson can carry a portable punch in a briefcase and enter data directly into cards in the customer's office. Voting systems often use this type of data recording. (See Figure 3.12.)

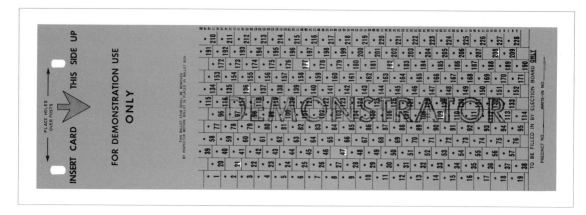

FIGURE 3.12   DIRECT CARD INPUT

Mark-Sense Cards.   Another method of inputting data to unit record systems is with a mark-sense card. (See Figure 3.13.) To record data, the user fills in a bubble (outlined area) with an Electrographic pencil, which leaves a residue of graphite on the surface of the card. Cards that have been mark-sensed are fed through an IBM 519 Reproducing Punch, which reads the marked areas and punches the card accordingly. This method is a convenient, simple way of entering numerical data onto cards without using keypunch equipment. Data such as test scores, prices, order numbers, and stock inventory can be entered directly on cards in the field. Source documents prepared in the field on mark-sense cards reduce the need for verification.

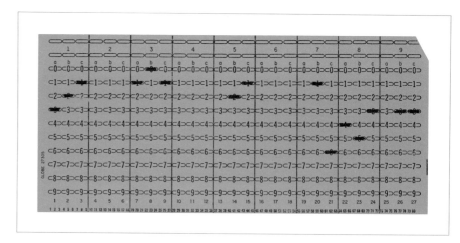

FIGURE 3.13   MARK-SENSE CARD

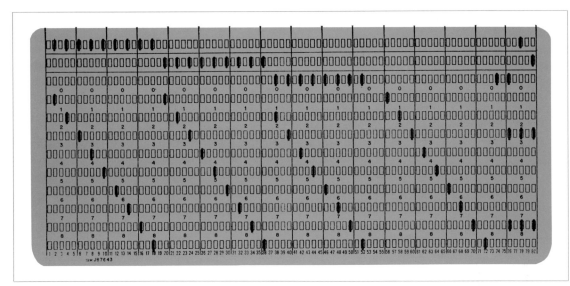

FIGURE 3.14 OPTICAL-SENSE CARD

Optical-Sense Cards. (See Figure 3.14.) In this method, bubbles or outlined areas are filled in with an ordinary pencil or pen. The cards are then fed through a card reader that optically senses the filled-in areas and translates them into electrical pulses, which are sent to the system for processing. No special electronic pencils are required. The card is not punched.

KEY TERMS

Column	Physical record
Detail record	Punched card
EAM	Row
Field	Sequence code
File	Significant-digit code
Fixed-length record	Summary record
Keypunch	System/3 card
Logical record	Unit record
Mark sense	Variable-length record
Master record	Verify
Mnemonic code	Zone

1. Prepare a collective list for use in
   a. your school
   b. a business establishment
2. Mark the following unit record data on three unused punched cards.
   a. The first unit record card should show a student's name, ID number, and test score.
   b. The second unit record should list an automobile by brand, date of manufacture, whether two or four door, and color.
   c. The third unit record should show an account name, number, payment for the month, and a field for returned items.
3. What are the differences between unit records and collective lists? What are the disadvantages of the unit record?
4. Obtain an unused punched card. Draw pencil lines through columns 20, 40, and 60 and through rows 2, 4, and 8. Label the edges of the card to show the 9 edge, 12 edge, column 1 end, and column 80 end.
5. Obtain some used punched cards that have not been interpreted (that is, the English equivalent is not printed at top of each column). To understand how the punched code works, decipher the text on these cards.
6. Obtain six unused punched cards. Assume they are physical records belonging to a file named "Employee Vacation Periods." Mark in appropriate data for each of six employees.
7. Prepare an unused punched card as a master record. Prepare a detail record on another card, using selected data from the master record.
8. Prepare four detail cards, each containing a product and amount in stock. Prepare a summary record from the detail cards.
9. If a machine is available, keypunch a group of cards with your name, address, city, and phone. Put one item on each card in columns 1 to 20.
10. If a machine is available, keypunch your records from Exercises 2, 6, or 8.
11. Obtain some unused mark-sense cards. Using an Electrographic pencil, enter your age, social security number, and school ID number.
12. Develop a single-column sequence code for eight groups of office furnishings and supplies.
13. Develop a two-character mnemonic code for 12 cities located in your state.
14. Develop a significant-digit code giving part name, year of manufacture, and supplier.

4

DATA MANIPULATION AND REPORTING

The process of manipulating and reorganizing data to increase their usefulness includes such operations as classifying and arranging data into groups, selecting a specific record from a file, combining several files into a single file, matching records in files, listing data, and copying records.

In this chapter, we consider the principal concepts involved in data manipulation activities. These include: sorting, grouping, merging, checking, interpreting, reproducing, searching, and reporting. Unit record examples are used to illustrate the basic concepts. In actual practice, files may be processed by computers or other electronic means. In these instances, electrical pulses may be manipulated, and records may be stored on magnetic tape or disk files.

All operations that can be performed by machine can also be done manually, but may take longer and may not be as accurate. A human operator can classify and sequence about 10 cards per minute and sort about 100 cards per minute. Unit record equipment is faster, processing up to 2,000 cards per minute.

Both unit record and manual methods rely upon the physical movement of cards from station to station for processing. Computers use data converted into electrical pulses and move these pulses at speeds measured in nanoseconds. Regardless of the method used, the logic of the basic concepts in the processing activities remains the same.

Sorting   NUMERICAL SORTING. Numerical sorting is the rearrangement of records so that numbers in the same field on each record are put in numerical order.

FIGURE 4.1   NUMERICAL SORTING (ASCENDING SEQUENCE)

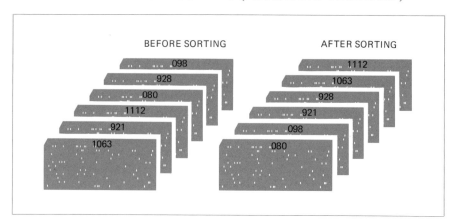

BEFORE SORTING   AFTER SORTING

Before sorting, a file may be in no specific order. A sort may be ascending (lowest number at the beginning and highest at the end) or descending (highest number at the beginning and lowest at the end). Figure 4.1 is an example of a sort in ascending order.

Files are sorted according to a specified field on each record. For example, a file of records may be sorted by account number, date account opened, current balance, or date payment due.

A file can also be sorted into subgroups. For example, a certain file contains student records, giving age, name, and test score. These records are to be placed in order first by age and then by test score within each age group by descending sorts. (The first field to be ordered is called the major sort field. The second field to be ordered is called the minor sort field.) To achieve the required subgroups, the file is first placed in numerical sequence (descending) by sorting the minor sort field, test score. Then it is again sorted by major field, student age. The result will be the record of the oldest student at the top of the file, with the remaining ages in descending order. Within each age group, scores will be sequenced with the highest score on top and the others in descending order.

ALPHABETIC SORTING.   Alphabetic sorting is the processing or rearrangement of files into alphabetical order. Before sorting, a file of records may be in random order. After sorting, the file begins with the letter A and moves through to Z.

A file can be alphabetized by employee name, geographic location, job description, part name, or by any alphabetic data field. Figure 4.2 is an example of a file arranged alphabetically by part name.

Alphabetic sorting is often used in conjunction with other data processing operations on a file. For example, a file of student records containing names and test scores could be grouped by test score and then, within each test score, alphabetized by name. To do this, first the minor (alphabetical) field is sorted and then the major (numerical) field is sorted.

The computer is the most efficient means for performing alphabetic sorts. Sorting by hand is time consuming and tedious. Sorting by unit record machines is also a slow process; a unit record file must pass through the sorter several times before it is correctly alphabetized.

Grouping

Grouping is the procedure of bringing together like records in a file. Before grouping, records in the file are in no specific order. After grouping, records containing similar data are arranged next to each other.

For example, a file of business expenses can be grouped by the name of the department that incurred the expenses. (See Figure 4.3.) Before grouping, records containing the expenditures and department names are in random order. After grouping, all records are arranged in small groups, one composed of manufacturing expenses, another office expenses, another sales expenses, and finally shipping expenses. Files can be grouped by other categories, such as name of individual, month, store where sold, or product line.

Merging

Merging is the operation of combining two files into a single file. Before merging, two separate files exist, each in the same sequence. After merging, all of the cards from the previous two files are contained in one file in sequence. Figure 4.4 is an illustration of merging.

There are many reasons for merging files. A master file containing the account name and balance may be merged with records containing account

FIGURE 4.2 ALPHABETIC SORTING

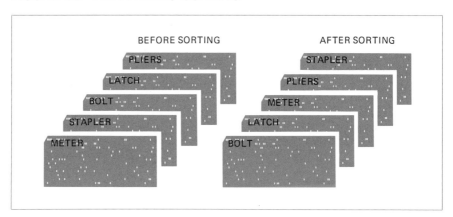

FIGURE 4.3   GROUPING

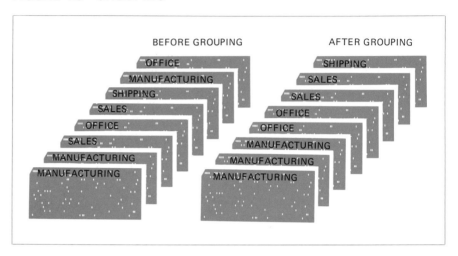

name and monthly payments made. After merging, one file exists with each payment record (activity record) placed behind the master record. An updated file of new master cards can then be prepared from this merged file.

MERGING WITH SELECTION.   The process of merging with selection is similar to merging in that two files are combined. But, in addition, records from one file without corresponding matches in the other file are pulled out, or selected, as the merging operation takes place.

Before merging, there are two files, each in the same alphabetic or numeric sequence. A record in one file may or may not have a match in the other file (matching data in a specified field, i.e., account number, catalog number). After merging with selection, three files are present: the merged file with matched sets of records (one behind the other) and two selected files. Each selected file contains records without a match from one original file. (See Figure 4.5.)

Merging with selection can be used to determine if all parts of a set are ready for distribution or mailing. For example, suppose a credit card and a statement of account card are to be mailed to each customer. In no case is a credit card or a statement of account card to be mailed out alone. The two files, one with credit cards and the other with statement of account cards, are merged with selection. After merging, the paired set of credit cards and statement of account cards are ready for further processing. Any unmatched cards have been put aside into two separate groups.

Checking   MATCHING.   Matching is a checking procedure in which records from two files are compared for matching data but are not merged. Before matching,

FIGURE 4.4   MERGING

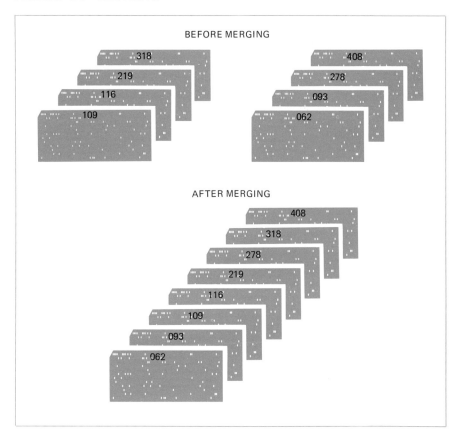

two files are present. Each may contain records without a match in the other file. After matching, the two files remain as separate entities. However, all records without matches are pulled aside. (See Figure 4.6.)

Matching and merging with selection are similar procedures, but differ in the way they rearrange the files. Matching results in four files: two containing records in corresponding order and two with selected records. Merging results in three files: one with matches physically paired and two with selected records.

Matching may be used to determine whether all records that should be in a file are there. This is particularly important when working with master files. For example, suppose the billing department prepares monthly statements for account customers from a master file in the credit department. If a record in the monthly statement file has no match in the master file, it must be put aside for special handling. Conversely, all customers listed in the master file should receive current statements of account. If a monthly statement record

FIGURE 4.5   MERGING WITH SELECTION

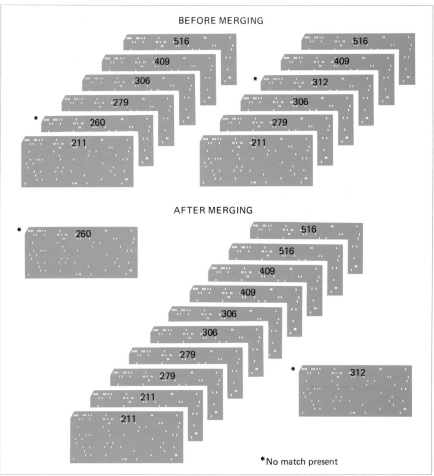

has been lost or has not been prepared, the matching process would detect it by putting aside the master record.

CHECKING SEQUENCE.   The procedure of checking sequence is used to check a file for sequential order. Each record in the file is compared with the one ahead of it. If a record is out of sequence, the machine stops. Files may be checked for either numeric or alphabetic sequence. (See Figure 4.7.)

Files are not physically rearranged; errors are flagged. If sequence checking is being done manually, the operator merely switches records that are out of sequence. If a machine is being used, the device stops to allow the operator to correct the situation. After sequence checking, one file remains with all cards in the proper order.

FIGURE 4.6   MATCHING

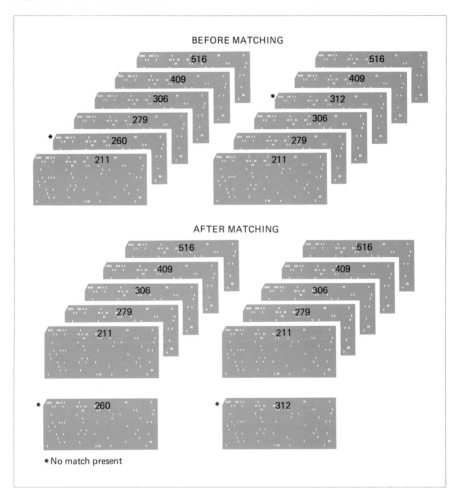

Sequence checking is often done before further processing. Suppose, for example, mailing labels are to be pasted on envelopes containing personally addressed letters. Before labels are pasted on, the operator must be sure that they are in the same order as the envelopes.

Interpreting   Interpreting is the process of decoding holes in a punched card into graphic, readable symbols printed on the face of a card. The hole combinations in a card are read and their symbolic or English language equivalent is printed on the card as shown in Figure 4.8.

Before interpretation, cards in a file are punched with a code. No letters, numbers, or symbols are printed on the face of the card. It is difficult and time consuming for someone to decipher the data on these cards. After

FIGURE 4.7 CHECKING SEQUENCE

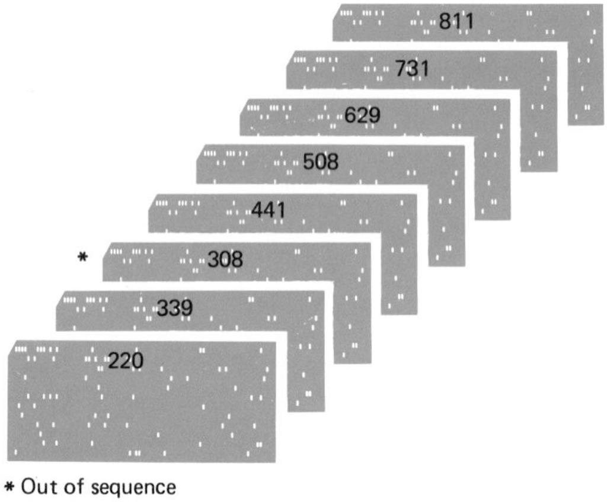

* Out of sequence

interpretation, the graphic equivalent of the punched data is printed on the face of the card. Interpreting may be done in various positions on the face of a card.

Many card punches interpret as they punch.

Reproducing   Reproducing is the process of duplicating records or files. Data may be copied from one medium to another, or a second copy made of the original on the same medium. For example, data on a punched card may be copied onto magnetic tape records or punched into a detail card. All or part of a record may be copied.

80-80 REPRODUCING.   80-80 reproducing is copying all data from one set of records into another set. Data from each original record are punched, or recorded, on a duplicate record in exactly the same order and position. The term "80-80" means that all 80 columns on the original record (a punched card) are copied.

The 80-80 reproducing operation is a convenient way to duplicate card decks as a protection against loss or damage. Also, important computer programs, sets of data, etc. are often copied 80-80 and the duplicate filed. Frequently used punched cards, such as control cards and job order cards, are often reproduced for accuracy and to save time. Rekeypunching may introduce errors. Copies of files or data sets may be sent to different departments in a business.

FIELD-SELECTED REPRODUCING.   Field-selected reproducing is the copying of only selected fields of data, say from a master file, onto new

FIGURE 4.8 INTERPRETING

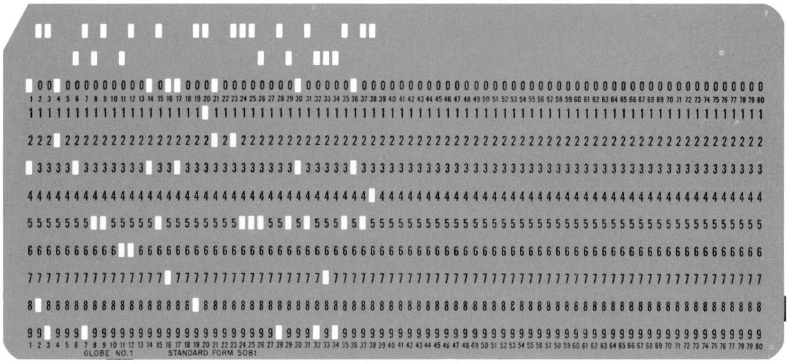

(A) UNINTERPRETED CARD

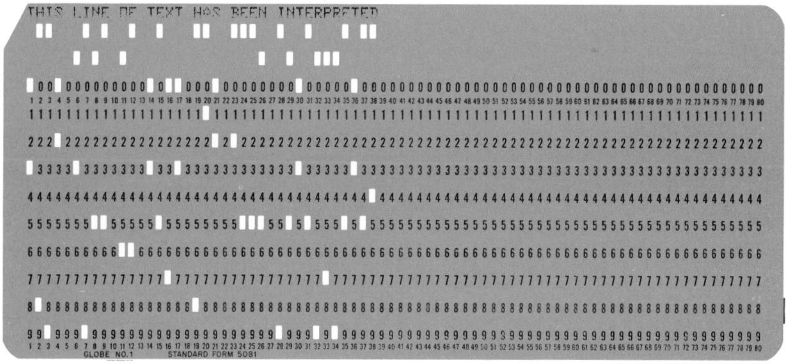

THIS LINE OF TEXT HAS BEEN INTERPRETED

(B) INTERPRETED CARD

records. As many fields as are necessary may be copied from the master to detail records, or from one set of detail records to another.

Field-selected reproducing is useful when confidential business data are included in master records. For example, suppose records in a master file contain a part number, description, confidential wholesale price, and supplier name. Information from this file is needed for warehouse inventory control. The original file is field-selected reproduced to create a detail file listing only the part number and description. This second file can be distributed to the warehouse area without fear of "leaking" confidential company information.

SELECTIVE REPRODUCING. Selective reproducing is the reproduction of only specified records in a file. All or part of the data on a record may be copied, but only from certain cards in the file.

Playing Games
with the Computer

A computer, to most of us, is Big Brother—watching us, admonishing us not to fold, spindle or mutilate. To a growing number of youngsters in the San Francisco area, a computer is another kind of big brother—the kind who never tires of playing games with them and who makes learning fun.

These youngsters can be seen any Friday evening playing games with a computer at the People's Computer Center in the suburban community of Menlo Park. Schools make field trips to the center and hold special classes there. For interested individuals—grownups as well as children—there are afternoon and evening classes, programming workshops and a science-fiction club. Children bring along cakes and hold birthday parties there. People can rent time to play games or try their hand at programming.

Although there are a few other places experimenting with the recreational potential of computers, this is the only one not connected with a university or science museum. The center is run as a nonprofit education corporation on a shoestring budget to keep the price of admission low. (Friday night's two-hour session costs $1.)

Friends help maintain equipment, most of which is on loan, and create new games. They have helped the center to get time on outside computers so visitors can have access to a wider variety of games. High school boys work part-time at the center in exchange for a chance to write games and to program. Other volunteers teach part-time.

"We're a drop-in, neighborhood place," said one of two full-time teachers. "There's nothing else quite like us. We believe in games—computer games that can be played without computers or board games that have been programmed for the computer, especially those with simple rules that can be played at varying levels.

"People think and learn as they play. Games can introduce new ideas. Games encourage imaginative and constructive responses. People playing games develop decision-making capabilities and problem-solving skills."

SOURCE: Adapted from "Big Brother is a Fun Friend," by Harriet Stix, *Los Angeles Times*, June 13, 1975.

OFFSET REPRODUCING. Offset reproducing is the punching of data from selected columns in a master record into different columns on the detail record. Offsetting means that data are copied onto a detail card in a different position from that on the original record.

MARK SENSING. Mark sensing is a data input method in which Electrographic pencil marks on a record are read and data are punched directly into the same record. (See Figure 4.9.)

FIGURE 4.9 MARK-SENSING

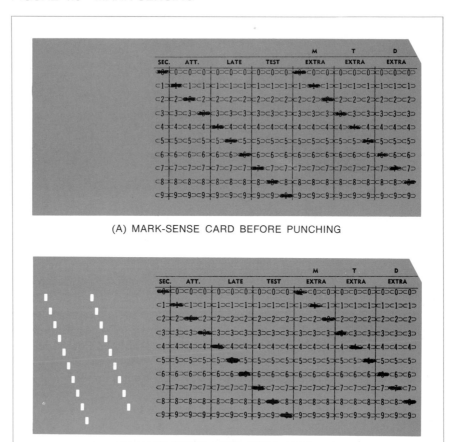

(A) MARK-SENSE CARD BEFORE PUNCHING

(B) MARK-SENSE CARD AFTER PUNCHING

Before mark sensing, a file of cards marked with Electrographic pencil is present. After mark-sense punching, a single file remains, with data punched into the cards. The data can then be read by the machine for further processing.

END PRINTING. End printing is a form of reproducing and interpreting in which selected numbers punched into a card are printed in large display numbers on the edge of the same card, or on a new card. End printing can be done in numbers $\frac{1}{4}$-inch high and in either of two positions on the end of the card. Up to eight numerical characters can be printed on one line. (See Figure 4.10.)

FIGURE 4.10   END PRINTING

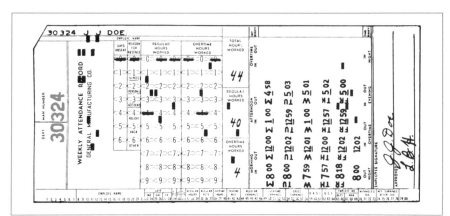

The interpreter reads columns of data punched in a card and prints the information as large numbers on the left-hand side of the card.

Calculating   Calculating is the manipulation of data by arithmetic means. It involves finding sums, figuring balances, paychecks, interest, and so on.

Before calculating, various data from other processes are present. Hours worked, costs of goods, stock levels, and sales figures are all forms of input data. Calculations must be performed on them in order to prepare paychecks, invoices, statements, and other records or documents.

Before the introduction of the computer, calculating was done on EAM machines. Today, most of this processing is done on computers because of their greater capacity, flexibility, speed, and efficiency.

Reporting   Reporting is the process of outputting data in a useful form. The reported data may be the original data fed to the machine or the result of processing. Processing of data usually consists of arithmetic calculations, restructuring, or rearrangement. Data may be reported in the form of tables, statements, invoices, paychecks, and other types of documents.

LISTING (DETAIL PRINTING).   (See Figure 4.11.) Listing is a form of reporting in which data are read from a punched card and printed out on a sheet of paper. All or part of the data on a record may be read and printed on the page. A printout of all 80 columns is referred to as an "80-80 listing."

Listing is used to check the accuracy of files—source documents can be compared with the listing. It is also a convenient way to check sequence of records and to verify that none have been omitted.

PRINTING.   Printing is another form of reporting in which invoices, statements, bills, or other documents are prepared from input data. Printing is usually done on data resulting from some type of restructuring or manipulation.

Printing may be done on continuous pin feed forms, carbon forms, NCR papers, or snap-apart or multipart forms. Pin feed forms are long sheets of paper folded in accordion fashion. Pin holes, small holes similar to sprockets on film, are punched along the edges of the paper to facilitate feeding through the machines and to ensure proper positioning. Carbon and snap-apart forms can be separated after printing and the copies distributed as needed.

Searching

Searching is the process of checking through a file to locate a specific record. Both alphabetic and numeric searches may be made. The data being sought, called the object of the search, must be known in advance.

A file may or may not contain the object of the search. After the search, the file remains intact, and the object of the search has either been found or is known not to be present in the file.

Searches for alphabetic data and multicolumn numeric fields are usually performed by collators or on computers, using search programs.

FIGURE 4.11   LISTING

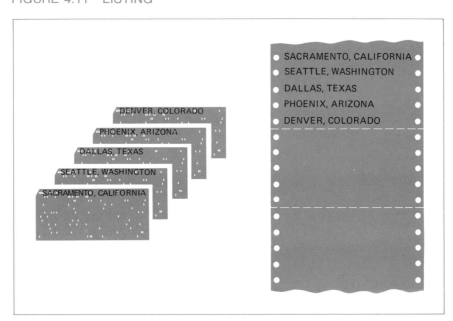

FIGURE 4.12   SEQUENTIAL SEARCH

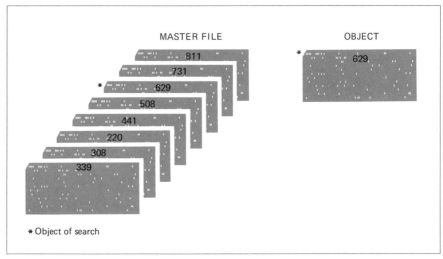

* Object of search

SEQUENTIAL SEARCH.   (See Figure 4.12.) In this procedure, a file is searched starting with the first record and proceeding in sequence through the file until the object of the search is found or until the entire file has been searched.

A search is performed by systematically comparing the search field on each record in the file to the alphabetic or numeric value being sought. Sequential searches are relatively slow when large files are involved, since all records ahead of the one being sought must be searched. The logic, however, is simple and easily programmed, and the records in the file may be in any order.

BINARY SEARCH.   (See Figure 4.13.) A more efficient method of locating an object in a file is with a binary search. In this procedure, the file must first be arranged so that the records are in numerical order by search field. Then the file is split in half and the record at the midpoint is compared with the object of search. If it does not agree, the program determines whether the object of the search is in the upper or lower half of the file. The appropriate half of the file is split and the record at the new midpoint is checked. This procedure continues until the object is found.

STATISTICAL OR PROBABILITY SEARCH.   (See Figure 4.14.) This search procedure relies upon statistical techniques to locate an object of search. The most logical or historical point in the file where the object might be found is determined, and that location is checked first. This is a customized procedure that must be written specifically to fit the characteristics of the file being searched. It is, however, much faster and more efficient to execute than the sequential search.

In this procedure, the file is organized according to the order in which the values are most frequently accessed. The program calculates statistically which point in the file to check first, second, and so on.

FIGURE 4.13   BINARY SEARCH

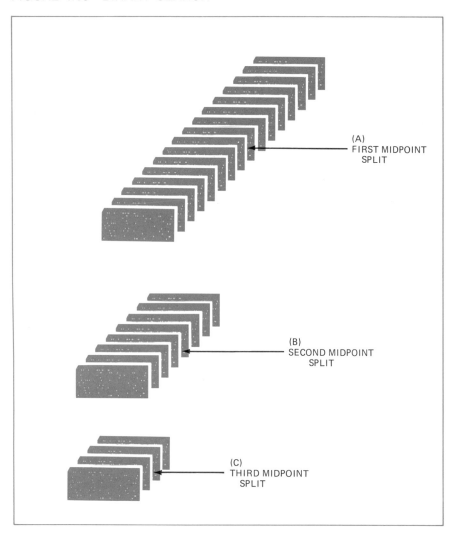

(A)
FIRST MIDPOINT
SPLIT

(B)
SECOND MIDPOINT
SPLIT

(C)
THIRD MIDPOINT
SPLIT

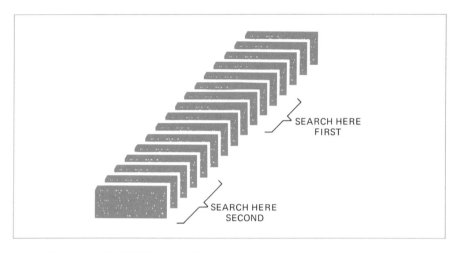

FIGURE 4.14   STATISTICAL SEARCH

UNIT RECORD DATA-MANIPULATING MACHINES

A variety of unit record machines are used to perform the procedures just described. (See Figure 4.15.) However, these machines are practical only when processing small or moderate amounts of data (a few hundred to many thousands of items). When millions of punched cards must be sorted, or huge files merged or searched, it is often more practical to use the power and efficiency of electronic computers. The use of unit record machines continues to decline as more computers come into use.

Sorting Machines Several pieces of equipment sort punched cards. Among them are the IBM 82, 83, and 84 Sorters and the UNIVAC 1720 Sorter, which are all similar in operation. Basically, their function can be described as follows: a card is fed into the sorter, the sorter senses its hole combination and guides the card through a chute into a receiving pocket. These machines will sort numeric or alphabetic data, detect blank columns, or select cards from a file.

Sorters are motor driven and contain a card hopper, column indicator, switches, sort brush (or photocell), and receiving pockets. They sort from 450 to 2,000 cards per minute.

IBM COLLATOR

IBM 557 ALPHABETIC
INTERPRETER

IBM 519 DOCUMENT
ORIGINATING MACHINE

IBM 407 ACCOUNTING MACHINE

FIGURE 4.15
UNIT RECORD
MACHINES

UNIVAC 1720 SORTER

Collating
Machines

Collating machines perform several operations, including merging, merging with selection, matching, and detecting blank columns. They are often used in conjunction with computers and other unit record equipment to prepare files for further processing.

The IBM 85 Collator (Figure 4.15) processes numeric, alphabetic, and special characters. It has two card hoppers for feeding cards from two files simultaneously and four receiving card pockets. Cards can be fed from each hopper at the rate of 240 per minute, or a total of 480 cards per minute from both hoppers.

A wiring control panel is used to direct the machine. This board has many rows of hubs or terminals. The terminals can be wired together in different combinations to cause the machine to perform various collating jobs.

"We've got all the 'Know-How.' We just don't know where it is."

Interpreting
Machines

Interpreting can be done on a keypunch, on the IBM 557 Interpreter, or on a similar machine. (Figure 4.15.) The IBM 557 is motor driven and automatically moves cards from the card hopper past two sets of brushes: the read brushes and the proof brushes.

Type wheels contain alphabetical, numerical, and special characters. As the card passes the type wheels, it is struck from behind by a set of hammers, which force it against the type wheels. A fabric ribbon placed between the card and the print wheel provides inking.

The Interpreter is a flexible machine. The wiring panel can be adjusted so that the machine will repeat print. In this operation, a master card with punched data is fed into the machine. All succeeding cards run through will contain the same data (interpreted, but not punched) as that on the master card. This is a convenient way to prepare information cards, notices, memos, and similar documents, where repetitive copy is desired. The IBM 557 Interpreter can also be used to prepare many business documents such as ledger cards, loan cards, deposit slips, and postcards.

Reproducing
Machines

The IBM 514 and 519 Document Originating Machines (Figure 4.15) dominated the market for reproducing functions until computers became available. These machines, often called reproducing punches, repro punches, or simply punches, are still widely used and are found in many computer installations for short-run work.

A reproducing machine has two feed hoppers, two card pockets (called stackers), and an automatic card feeder. The IBM 519 can process up to 100 cards per minute and will punch, gang punch (punch a number of identical cards), end print, compare, and mark-sense punch. The machine is motor driven and contains a removable wiring control panel. Short jumper wires are connected to hubs on the panel in various combinations to program the different reproducing and checking functions.

Calculating
and Reporting
Machines

Although largely replaced by computer systems such as the IBM 360/20 and UNIVAC 90/30 (Figure 4.16), some unit record machines are still used for calculating and reporting tasks. The IBM 402 and 407 Accounting Machines, IBM 604 and 609 Calculators, and the UNIVAC 1004 Electronic Card Processing machine are examples.

The IBM 407 Accounting Machine, illustrated in Figure 4.15, is designed to do listing and printing on forms and reports. It has a card hopper, card stacker, and printing assembly. It can print 18,000 characters per minute and process 150 cards per minute.

The accounting machine has a paper-feeding mechanism for handling pin feed continuous forms. Paper-tape carriage control mechanisms control vertical spacing and positioning of the print line on the forms.

A limited amount of calculating, mainly addition and subtraction, can be done on the machine.

FIGURE 4.16   UNIVAC 90/30 COMPUTER

KEY TERMS

Binary search
Calculating
Checking sequence
End printing
Grouping
Interpreting
Listing
Mark sensing

Matching
Merging
Reporting
Reproducing
Sequential search
Sort field
Sorting
Statistical search

EXERCISES

1. List the different types of operations in data manipulation.
2. List three instances in which it is more advantageous to input data by mark sensing rather than by keypunching.
3. Lay out and keypunch a master card that contains confidential price data and part descriptions. Then keypunch a detail card for warehouse use, omitting the confidential information.
4. List the major steps in a binary search.
5. What are the advantages and limitations of a sequential search?
6. Label a deck of 25 punched cards with the numbers from 10 to 34. Shuffle the cards and then sequence them in descending numerical order.
7. Prepare 25 punched cards as follows: label five cards PENS, five PENCILS, five ERASERS, five PAPER, and the last five CLIPS. Number the cards in each group with the numbers 1 through 5. After shuffling all the cards, perform a minor sort and a major sort, using the alphabetic data as the minor field and the numeric data as the major field.
8. Develop a sample inventory updating system on unit record cards. Keypunch master and detail cards for this system.
9. Perform a sequence checking routine using the deck from Exercise 6.
10. If you have access to a data center in your school or community, prepare a list of unit record equipment available in the center.
11. Shuffle the same deck as in Exercise 7 and resort it, using the numeric data as the minor field and the alphabetical data as the major field.

PART THREE

COMPUTER
HARDWARE

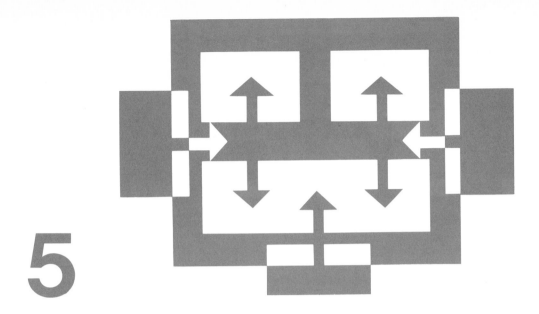

5

FUNDAMENTAL
COMPUTER CONCEPTS

A system is an assembly of methods, procedures, or techniques that interact in a regulated manner to form an organized whole. It is an organized collection of elements necessary to accomplish specific functions. Systems are composed of smaller parts known as subsystems. These smaller units have individual functions but act in accord with the goals of the larger system. A change in one element in a system usually affects one or all of the other elements.

The human organism is one of nature's most perfect systems. The senses, memory, logic, mobility, and other attributes are elements of the total system. Working as a unit, they create an active, integrated, functioning person who is capable of sensing the environment, grasping a problem, structuring a solution, and, finally, affecting the environment. The components of this system could be called input, processing, output, and memory. (See Figure 5.1.) Input is through the five senses. Processing and memory occur in the brain. Humans can remember hundreds of events, places, people, and facts. But memory is not an unlimited, total dependable resource; some things are harder to remember than others, or are easily confused. Therefore, people take notes, make up lists, look up facts in tables or charts, and keep records. These are called external memory aids.

People are capable of goal setting and self-direction. They can select a goal and coordinate their entire capacity to move toward it. Activities and actions are planned and performed, behavior patterns are tested and

FIGURE 5.1   THE HUMAN SYSTEM

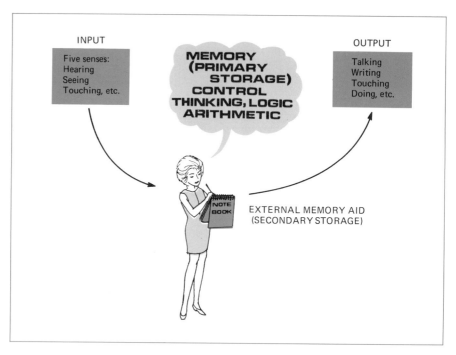

adjusted, until the goal is reached. The human organism is capable of feeding its own output back into the system for reprocessing. As a result, behavior can be changed, corrected, and adjusted to more accurately direct actions toward the goal.

THE COMPUTER SYSTEM

Computers are also systems and are similar in many ways to the human organism. Input, processing, output, and storage are also elements of the computer system. The system is capable of logical deductions and, to a limited extent, self-direction. Figure 5.2 is a block diagram illustrating these functions.

There are, of course, major differences between the two systems. Computers are incapable of long-range planning, generalizing from seemingly unrelated data, "intellectualizing," or "deep philosophical" thinking. However, the ability of the computer to function in business data processing compares favorably with people's. In fact, in some areas the computer far surpasses its creator. For example, computers can perform arithmetic computations much faster than the human mind.

The computer inputs data via a card reader, tape reader, or other input device. It processes information in its central processing unit (CPU), where it performs mathematical calculations and makes logical decisions. The computer is self-directing to the extent that it can follow a set of instructions, process data, and output or store results without human intervention. When it exceeds its internal storage capacity, it may call in external storage devices. Figure 5.3 illustrates the relationships of the parts of a typical system.

COMPUTER SUBSYSTEMS

Each part of the computer is a subsystem that functions as part of the larger system. The major subsystems that can make up a computer are

- Input
- CPU
- Secondary storage
- Output
- Telecommunications

FIGURE 5.2   THE COMPUTER SYSTEM

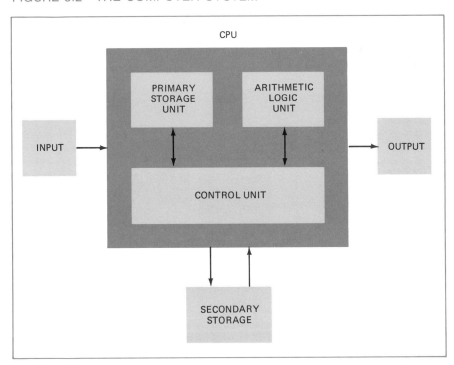

FIGURE 5.3   PARTS OF A COMPUTER SYSTEM

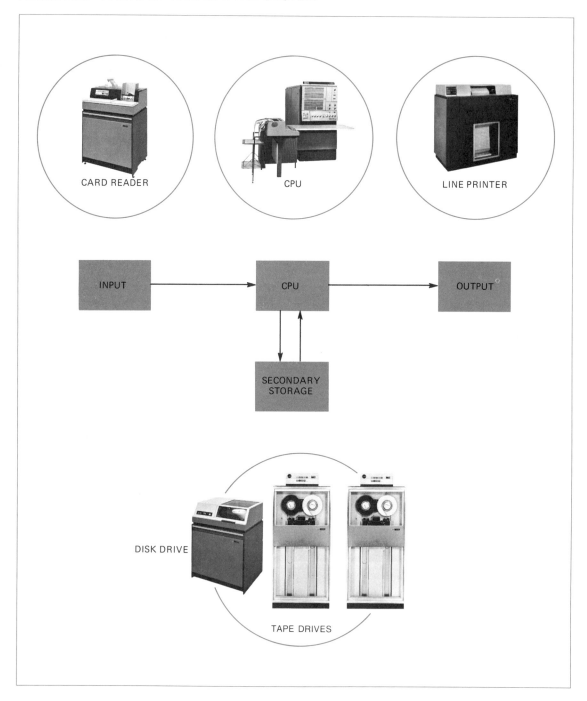

Input System

In sending telegraph messages by Morse code, the telegraph operator converts words into a string of dots and dashes, which are sent over the line. Similarly, the input system of a computer reads data in the form of printed characters on a page, holes on punched cards or paper tape, or magnetized areas on magnetic tapes or disks and converts them into electronic pulses. It then transmits these pulses through wires to the CPU for processing. In a computer, each pulse is called a bit and represents one piece of data. Groups of bits (pulses) are used to represent numbers, letters, or words. (Bit combinations or codes used are discussed in Chapter 7.)

A computer input system may have only one device for reading punched cards or it may have several devices, each handling a different input medium. Large installations often have several card and tape units. The most common modes of computer input are

1. CARD READER.   Holes in a punched card are read and translated into electronic pulses.
2. MAGNETIC TAPE READER.   Magnetized bits on magnetic tape are read and translated into electronic pulses.
3. MAGNETIC DISK DRIVE.   Magnetized bits on a magnetic disk are read and translated into electronic pulses.
4. PAPER TAPE READER.   Holes punched into paper tape are read and translated into electronic pulses.
5. OPTICAL CHARACTER AND MARK-SENSE READER.   Handwritten, typewritten, or printed character forms, or pencilled-in bubbles on a page are read and translated into electronic pulses.
6. MAGNETIC INK CHARACTER READER.   Magnetically coded characters on a page are read and translated into electrical pulses.
7. CONSOLE TYPEWRITER.   Keystrokes on a typewriter cause electronic pulses to be sent to the CPU.

Central Processing Unit

The most complex and powerful part of the computer is the central processing unit (CPU), or processor. The major functions of the CPU are

❶ to control the overall operation of the computer and coordinate its parts;

❷ to perform arithmetic calculations and make logical decisions;

❸ to store the programs and data being processed (primary storage).

The relationship of the CPU to the input and output devices is shown in Figure 5.3. Card readers, magnetic tape devices, line printers, and other system components are wired to the CPU. Data may flow between the input and output machines and register and primary memory units. The control unit performs a switching activity directing the flow of data from primary

FIGURE 5.4   IBM 370 COMPUTER CONSOLE

memory and registers to the input/output units. (Primary memory storage and registers are devices that store strings of electronic pulses during processing; they are discussed in detail later.)

PHYSICAL APPEARANCE.   As shown in Figure 5.4, the CPU resembles the other components of the computer system in size and appearance. Often a desk and typewriter unit, called the console typewriter, is attached. On the control panel, or console, at the front of the CPU are sense lights, buttons, and switches. The sense lights show the status of the machine at all times and indicate the contents of some of the storage locations.

The CPU is sometimes called the mainframe. The related input and output devices that provide the CPU with outside communications are called peripheral devices. Peripherals are any input or output devices associated with a computer but do not include the CPU. The abbreviation I/O is often used to refer collectively to input and output devices.

Internally, the CPU is usually a solid-state device composed of transistors, wires, and integrated and monolithic circuits mounted on circuit boards. (See Figure 5.5.) (A monolithic circuit consists of many microscopic electronic components manufactured on a small piece of glass or crystal. See Figure 5.6.) The CPU also contains several thousand minute magnetic storage devices that hold the program and the data for processing. The circuitry is designed to move, store, and manipulate data electronically and has no moving parts—only the electronic impulses move about inside the CPU. Its major parts are diagrammed in Figure 5.7, and their functions are discussed below.

Functions of the CPU

CONTROL.   Part of the CPU circuitry, the control unit is designed to monitor and supervise the operation of the entire computer. It calls upon the card reader, line printer, tape drives, etc. The control unit provides a system for storing and remembering the instructions in programs and opens and closes circuits that feed data to and from storage.

The control unit is similar in function to the central switchboard at the telephone company or in a large business establishment. Control is effected through the wires that connect all parts of the system to the central control board.

Another aspect of the control function of the CPU is governed by the source program. The source program is written to solve a specific, local problem. This program is entered into the computer, usually with the related data, and instructs the machine to perform mathematical calculations, read data cards, write information on the line printer, store data, etc. The source program is often called the problem program, and the collection of data to be processed is called the data set.

ARITHMETIC AND LOGIC.   Another section of the CPU is designed to perform mathematical calculations, compare numeric and non-numeric values, and make decisions. (These jobs are done with sophisticated electronic circuitry, called gates and registers.) Both arithmetic and logical decisions can be made. For example, the computer can branch to one of three circuits, or paths, depending on whether the value being tested is greater than, equal to, or less than another value.

When arithmetic is to be performed, numbers are read into temporary holding stations called registers. Numbers from several registers may be added, subtracted, or operated upon in some other way. After calculations are completed, data are either returned to computer storage or output.

PRIMARY STORAGE.   Primary storage, often called core storage, is another function of the CPU. This section of the CPU may be composed of millions of

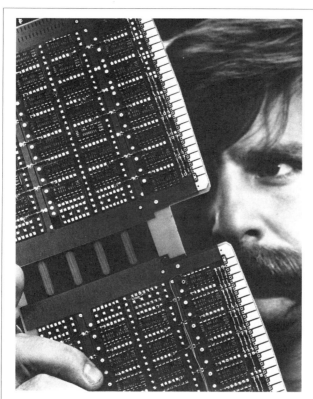

FIGURE 5.5

COMPUTER CIRCUIT BOARD

FIGURE 5.6

MONOLITHIC CIRCUITS

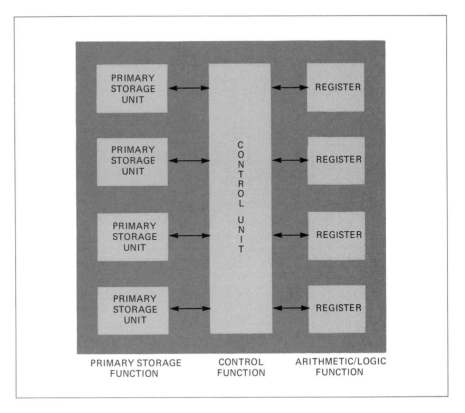

FIGURE 5.7   CPU

magnetic storage devices—magnetic cores, flux rings, or cores printed on thin film.

Primary storage is a reusable, fast storage medium, directly accessible by the control unit. Primary storage capacity varies from one computer to another, ranging from as few as 4,000 bytes to over several million bytes. A byte is a group of bits (pulses) that form a character—a number, letter, or symbol. Usually, one alphabetic character or two numeric characters are stored in a byte. Primary storage is sometimes divided into parts, or sections, as shown in Figure 5.7. Thus the control unit can allocate parts of its storage capacity to different tasks, and each part can function without interfering with the others.

Primary storage is most often used for storing data that must be called in frequently, such as the program under execution and the data being operated upon.

Secondary Storage System   Because the primary storage capacity of most computers is limited, the CPU calls upon its secondary storage system to handle and store large amounts of data. This supplementary storage capacity is usually provided by tape and

The Versatile Computer

The many talents of the computer are popping up in a lot of unexpected places these days—some related to the pleasanter side of life and some to the not so pleasant side.

For example, an electronic ballpoint pen wired to a computer can help to apprehend forgers. Developed by the Stanford Research Institute, the pen records the pressure and motion of the writer as well as the lines in the written characters. A forgery is easily distinguished from writing held on file.

This electronic detective would be extremely valuable in any situations that require signature verification—credit card purchases, the use of traveler's checks or money orders, stock exchange transactions, receipt of registered mail, voting, and access to security areas, for example.

TV shows notwithstanding, fingerprint searches are rarely done because they are very time consuming and costly. But a latent fingerprint system used by the California Department of Justice may change all that. The system, manufactured by the Autonetics Group of Rockwell International, can identify single or partial prints left at the scene of a crime.

Here's how it works. An operator inserts the print into the computer console. It is automatically displayed on an enlarging screen. The operator then marks the print minutiae (points where fingerprint ridges end or fork) with an electronic cursor. The system automatically searches the file for a match. Key to the system's success is its simplicity and speed.

On the other hand, computers are useful in other aspects of life, too . . . one is designed to hold 200 bottles of 46 different brands of liquors, wines, and liqueurs, plus 14 mixers, including fruit juices, water, soft drinks, and soda.

Programmed to mix thousands of different drinks in two seconds or less, it can also calculate drink prices, totals, and taxes.

SOURCE: Van Nuys Green Sheet, June 20, 1975; EDN, June 20, 1976; Van Nuys Green Sheet, September 18, 1975.

---

disk drive systems. Secondary storage allows billions of characters or pieces of data to be stored until needed.

Most computer systems use a combination of primary and secondary storage media. Data can be fed to and from primary storage in only a few billionths of a second. In secondary storage, on the other hand, it takes several thousandths of a second to retrieve a piece of data. Secondary storage is used for large files of data that need not be accessed continually, such as accounts receivable, accounts payable, inventory, and payroll records.

Output System
The output system is designed to report the results of calculations and processing from the CPU. Reporting and outputting may be done on a line printer, card punch, cathode ray tube, or audio unit. The objective of the

output system is to convert electronic pulses from the CPU into documents, cards, or a visual display, giving the results of the processed data in a usable form. The form of the output is chosen for suitability for input into other machines, or for easy readability and comprehension by people. The most common modes of computer output are

1. LINE PRINTER. Electronic pulses from the CPU are converted into readable characters on a printed page.
2. CARD PUNCH. Electronic pulses are translated into a punch code on a punched card.

Sidney Harris

3. MAGNETIC TAPE DRIVE.   Electronic pulses are recorded as magnetized areas on magnetic tape. This tape may be stored or used to input data into other machines.
4. MAGNETIC DISK DRIVE.   Electronic pulses are stored as magnetized areas on a magnetic disk. The disk can be stored or placed on another computer.
5. PAPER TAPE PUNCH.   Electronic pulses are converted into holes punched in a roll of paper tape.
6. AUDIO RESPONSE DEVICE.   Electronic pulses are converted into spoken words or audio responses. These responses are stored on tape. The unit is equipped with a tape or drum head, amplifier, and loudspeaker.
7. CATHODE RAY TUBE (CRT).   Electronic pulses are converted into a graphic display on a cathode ray tube. Drawings, illustrations, graphs, and tables can be displayed.
8. CONSOLE TYPEWRITER.   Electronic pulses from the CPU are converted into typewritten characters by the typewriter attached to the console.
9. PLOTTER.   Electronic pulses are converted into graphic designs, plots, or line drawings on a sheet of paper.

Output is an essential step in the data processing cycle. Unless output is provided to the user in some way, the cycle has little value.

Telecommunications System

Another subsystem of the computer can be a telecommunications network, shown in Figure 5.8. Telecommunications networks vary in complexity and purpose from one computer to another. They are not always tangible devices, such as a card punch, but are often a network of wires, codes, and messages.

Telecommunications systems have two uses: First, they may enable two or more computers to be tied together into a unit, increasing the available CPU power and capacity. This is called a multiprocessing system (see Chapter 21). Second, they facilitate communication between the machine and its users. They allow remote users to access the system, both to transmit data to the CPU and to receive data from it. Telecommunications systems transmit data by means of telephone and telegraph lines and microwave transmission systems.

MODERN COMPUTER SYSTEMS

The systems described below are typical of general classes of systems in industry. Since improvements and changes in design are frequently made in computer systems, these examples should be considered only as illustrations representative of general classes.

FIGURE 5.8 TELECOMMUNICATIONS NETWORK

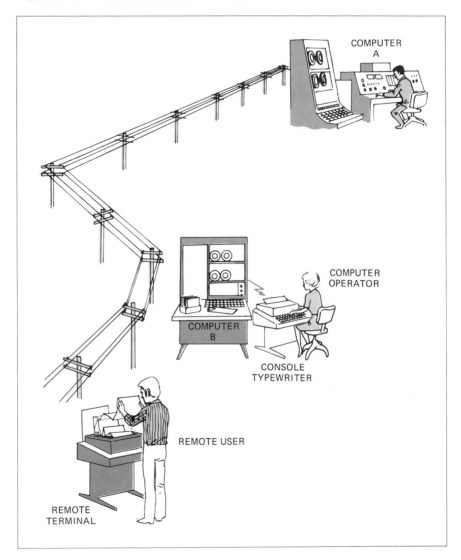

The term K is often used in describing computer storage capacity. It is derived from the decimal prefix kilo, which means 1,000, but in computer terminology it is usually used to represent 2^{10}, or 1,024, units. Thus, for example, 4K bytes means $4 \times 1,024 = 4,096$ bytes.

Digital Equipment Corporation PDP-11

The computer shown in Figure 5.9 is a general-purpose minicomputer. It is a desk-top or rack mounted device, approximately 19 inches wide. The minimum system configuration usually includes a single input/output

FIGURE 5.9

PDP-11 COMPUTER

FIGURE 5.10   NCR CENTURY 50 COMPUTER

FIGURE 5.11   HEWLETT-PACKARD 3000 COMPUTER

device, such as an ASR 33 Teletype terminal. The system may be expanded with additional devices, such as a line printer, card reader, or secondary storage device. Minimum primary storage capacity is 4K bytes. The complete system, including one Teletype terminal, costs approximately $10,000.

NCR 50   Figure 5.10 illustrates a small, general-purpose batch-processing computer system. The system includes a 125 line-a-minute printer, 16K-byte memory capacity, card reader, and dual-disk memory unit. The entire system costs approximately $47,000. Monthly rental is approximately $1,200. The system is designed primarily for small business firms, manufacturing companies, schools, financial institutions, and small government agencies. It is principally a batch-processing, card-oriented system, and can be programmed in COBOL, FORTRAN, and assembler languages.

Hewlett-Packard   The system shown in Figure 5.11 is a small, general-purpose computer
3000   system, designed for multilanguage, concurrent processing. The system will handle local batch jobs and interactive terminals at the same time. The minimum system configuration consists of a CPU and console, one magnetic tape drive, and one magnetic disk drive. Additional input/output devices may be added, including tape and disk drives, line printers, and terminals. The basic memory size is 64K bytes, but it may be expanded to 128K bytes. The

FIGURE 5.12   IBM 370/135 COMPUTER

system can be programmed in BASIC, FORTRAN, or COBOL, and includes editing and sorting programs and a scientific library. Purchase price for the CPU is approximately $100,000. Additional peripheral equipment may add between $25,000 and $200,000 to the total cost of the system.

IBM 370/135   The computer system shown in Figure 5.12 is typical of a medium-sized, general-purpose computer. It consists of a CPU with console, line printer, card reader, punch, and disk storage drives. Main memory may range from 98K bytes to 245K bytes. Additional disk storage devices, magnetic tape drives, printers, card readers, and CRT displays may be connected. The

FIGURE 5.13   HONEYWELL 66/80 COMPUTER

system may be programmed in COBOL, FORTRAN, RPG, assembler, PL/I, and other languages. The system leases for under $20,000 per month.

Honeywell 66/80   This is an example of a large-scale system (Figure 5.13). It has a memory range of 1 million to 4 million bytes. Monthly rental cost is $94,000. The large-scale system includes line printers, magnetic tape drives, magnetic disk drives, card readers, and a CPU.

Burroughs 6700   (See Figure 5.14.) This is a large-scale computer with the capacity of three central processors and three I/O processors combined into a single system. Three levels of memory are available on the system; its total capacity is in excess of 6 million bytes. The system includes line printers, card readers, and numerous tape and disk storage devices. It will support a variety of terminals, including hard copy and CRT displays. The system can be programmed in the major computer languages. The monthly rental for the system is in the $100,000 range, depending on the number and type of peripheral devices on the system.

FIGURE 5.14
BURROUGHS
6700 COMPUTER

FIGURE 5.15
UNIVAC 1110
COMPUTER

UNIVAC 1110,
Sperry Rand
Corporation

The UNIVAC 1110 (Figure 5.15) is one of the largest, most flexible systems in operation. It has a basic primary storage capacity of 65,000K bytes, expandable to many millions. The system includes a central processor that can support numerous I/O devices, including card readers, punches, video display terminals, and even complete remote job entry systems. From these remote processing terminals, jobs may be entered as cards and the results received back on high-speed line printers. The system supports time sharing and multiprogramming. Programming may be done in many languages, including COBOL and FORTRAN V.

KEY TERMS

Central processing
  unit (CPU)
Console
Data set
Input
I/O
Mainframe
Memory
Multiprocessing system

Output
Peripheral devices
Primary storage
Processing
Secondary storage
Source program
Subsystem
System
Telecommunications

EXERCISES

1. Draw a schematic diagram showing the related parts of the computer. Show input and output.
2. List five common external memory aids used by humans.
3. Define "system" and list several examples.
4. What do all computer input systems have in common?
5. What do all computer output systems have in common?
6. Draw a schematic diagram showing the relationship of the parts of the CPU.
7. How does primary storage differ from secondary storage?
8. What is the function of a telecommunications system?
9. What advantages and differences are there between the human system and the computer system?
10. Define *peripheral device* and *CPU* and explain how they differ in function.
11. What kind of data are usually stored by a CPU in its primary storage?

6

DATA INPUT

The function of the computer's input system is to convert data into a form that can be processed by the central processing unit. Data input machines translate the holes in paper tape or cards, the magnetic areas on tape, or the optical images on forms into direct-current pulses. The electronic pulses leave the input devices one at a time, forming a pulse train. These pulses are routed to the CPU through a system of buffers, control units, and channels. (See Figure 6.1.)

Data may be routed directly to the CPU for immediate processing, or they may be recorded and stored for later input and processing. Online data input means that data from the record enter the CPU directly from the input device (Figure 6.2). In offline input, the data are recorded onto a storage medium such as magnetic tape or disk, or punched into cards, and are later input to the system for processing. The advantage of online input is that the data can be processed immediately, without delay. However, offline input may better utilize the computer's resources.

DATA INPUT MACHINES

Online
Input Devices

Modern computers receive data from a variety of input devices, such as card readers, paper and magnetic tape readers, optical character readers, and console typewriters. All are wired directly to the CPU and transmit electronic images, or pulses, of the data from a record.

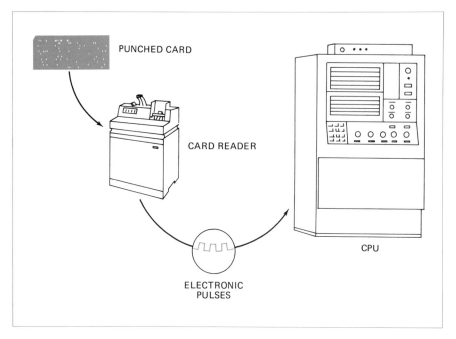

FIGURE 6.1   DATA CONVERTED TO ELECTRONIC PULSES

FIGURE 6.2   ONLINE AND OFFLINE DATA INPUT

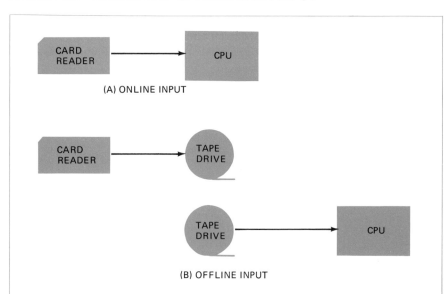

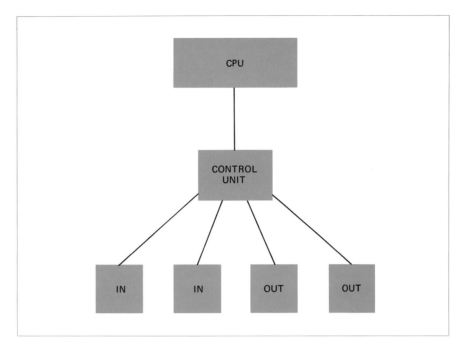

FIGURE 6.3   CONTROL UNIT

Timing is important in data entry. Data must be made available to the CPU at the proper points in the processing cycle. Control units regulate the timing of the input and output machines. Their standard wiring arrangement permits different I/O devices to be coupled to the CPU, or more than one input device to be connected. (See Figure 6.3.)

Control units either stand alone as a separate unit or are part of the CPU. They are signaled by the input device when the data are ready for input. Upon receiving another signal from the CPU, they feed in the data in phase, at the proper speed.

Below are examples of typical online input devices.

CARD READER.   This machine, shown in Figure 6.4, converts data from punched cards to electronic pulses. It is equipped with a card hopper, read station, phototransistors, a light source, and a card stacker. The machine will read 1,000 cards per minute. The card hopper holds 1,200 cards and feeds one card at a time from the bottom of the stack. It is linked to the CPU by a control unit.

A signal from the control unit initiates the reading cycle. An electric motor drives the card-feeding mechanism. First, a card is moved from the hopper and positioned in a preread station. (See Figure 6.5.) The card then moves to

FIGURE 6.4   CARD READER

the read station, where one column at a time is read. A light source focuses
a beam on the column at the read station. The light beam passes through
any holes present in that column and activates one or more of the 12
phototransistors (corresponding in position to the rows and zones of the
column) beneath it. As each phototransistor is activated, it creates an
electronic pulse. If no hole is present in the column, no light passes
through, and no phototransistors are activated.

The columns are read serially, character by character, until all colunns
across the card have been read. The machine is equipped with an
error-detection check. It will determine if cards are properly punched,
if columns contain too many punches, or if punches do not agree with
a valid card code.

The machine shown in Figure 6.4 is representative of the phototransistor
type of card reader. Other card readers use sensing brushes to generate

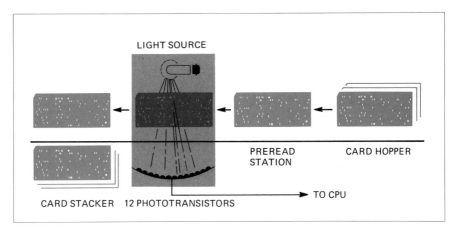

LIGHT SOURCE

PREREAD
STATION

CARD HOPPER

TO CPU

CARD STACKER 12 PHOTOTRANSISTORS

FIGURE 6.5 CARD PATH

pulses. The sensing brushes make electronic contact with a roller below the card, through the holes punched in the column.

PAPER TAPE READER. This device, shown in Figure 6.6, is designed to translate holes in paper tape to electronic pulses, and to relay these to the CPU. The machine reads data from paper tape at up to 300 characters per second.

The reader feeds the tape past a photoelectric device that senses the holes in the tape and translates them into electronic pulses. Several different codes are used for punching data into paper tape. (Details of data representation and other codes are discussed in Chapter 7.)

OPTICAL CHARACTER READER (OCR). The optical input device illustrated in Figure 6.7 is representative of optical character reader machines. It reads data optically and converts them to electronic pulses. Optical character readers are designed to read handwritten or printed numbers and special characters from checks, orders, cash register tapes, adding machine tapes, utility bills, telephone bills, tickets, etc. They read data from a page that can vary in size from $2\frac{1}{4} \times 3$ inches to $5\frac{9}{10} \times 9$ inches. About 550 documents, size $2\frac{1}{4} \times 3$ inches, can be read in one minute. They can also read cash register and adding machine tapes up to 200 feet long at the rate of 3,300 lines per minute.

Documents to be scanned move from the document hopper, past a separator mechanism to the aligner, and then to the read station. (See Figure 6.8.) After a document has been read, it is sent to one of several stackers.

The aligner positions the document for entry into the reading station. The document moves into the read station, where it is again positioned and scanned with a beam of light from a cathode ray tube. As the beam moves

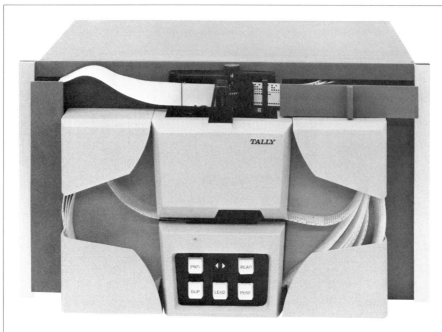

FIGURE 6.6   PAPER TAPE READER

FIGURE 6.7   OPTICAL CHARACTER READER

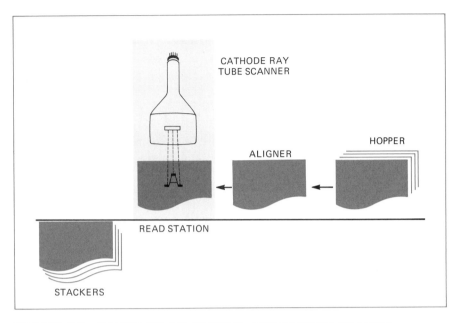

FIGURE 6.8 PARTS OF AN OPTICAL CHARACTER READER

back and forth across the page, images on the document reflect different amounts of light. Light from an image is reflected back to a sensing mechanism that detects minute differences. These differences are converted into electronic pulses to be input to the CPU.

Devices that read cash register and adding machine tapes have input and take-up spindles to hold the rolls of tape. The tape is threaded from the input spindle, through the reading chamber, and onto the take-up spindle. The machine scans 6 inches of tape at a time.

Figure 6.9 illustrates handwritten numeric characters that can be read optically. This is a convenient means of recording data in the field without keypunching. The salesclerk, secretary, or stock clerk can write each character in a separate block on specially printed forms, observing a few simple rules for letter shaping.

In addition to handwriting, OCR devices can read typewriter faces and several printed optical character type fonts. (See Figure 6.10.) They can be programmed to read selected areas on a bill or order form. They can read a price column, skip down to the total, read a printed form number, and read handprinted messages.

MAGNETIC INK CHARACTER READER (MICR). Figure 6.11 illustrates a device designed to read data printed in magnetic ink. It can read magnetically inscribed checks, deposit slips, bills, etc. The machine is equipped with a document hopper, read station, and 13 document-stacking pockets.

FIGURE 6.9   HANDWRITTEN CHARACTERS READ BY OCR

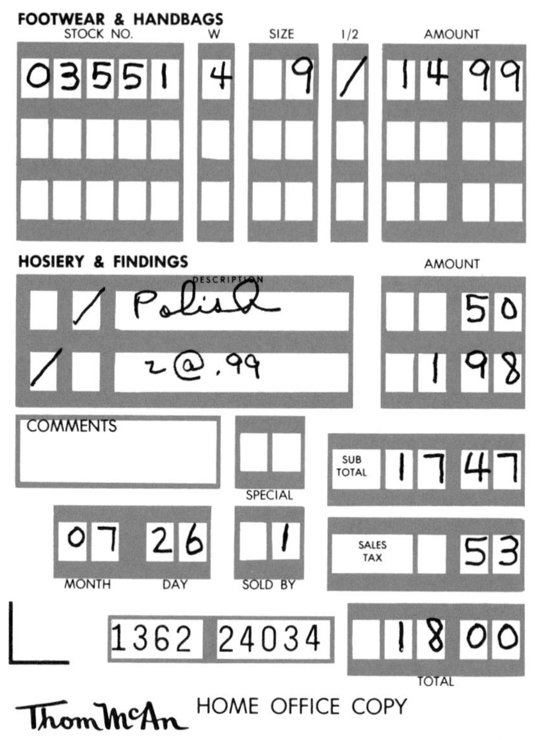

Up to 1,600 documents can be read per minute and sorted into the receiving pockets. The machine will read documents of different sizes and thicknesses, such as a collection of checks from many different banks.

Documents to be input must be printed using special magnetic ink and specially shaped letters, (See Figure 6.12.) Figure 6.13 shows the layout of the check form approved by the American Banking Association.

As the documents containing data to be inputted move through the MICR device, they are scanned for the special ink images. The magnetic images on the page affect a magnetic field in the machine and are recorded as electronic impulses ready for input.

PRINTER-KEYBOARD.   Another common group of computer input devices are the printer-keyboards, or console typewriters. The device shown in Figure 6.14 is representative of keyboard-to-electronic-pulse input devices.

The console typewriter is the operator's means of communicating with the computer. The operator uses it to direct the function of the CPU and

FIGURE 6.10 OPTICAL CHARACTERS

OCR-A

IS AVAILABLE IN UPPER CASE AND WITH COMPATIBLE LOWER CASE AND SHOULD BE USED IN APPLICATIONS THAT ARE PRIMARILY HUMAN FACTORS INSENSITIVE.

The compatible lower case extends the available character set.

OCR-B

With lower case provides good human com-patibility with some compromise for ease of machine reading. It is recommended for applications that are human factors sensitive.

ELITE

When maximum interchange with humans is a requirement, an elite face can be utilized with utmost efficiency, for the total people/machine system.

FIGURE 6.11 MAGNETIC INK CHARACTER READER

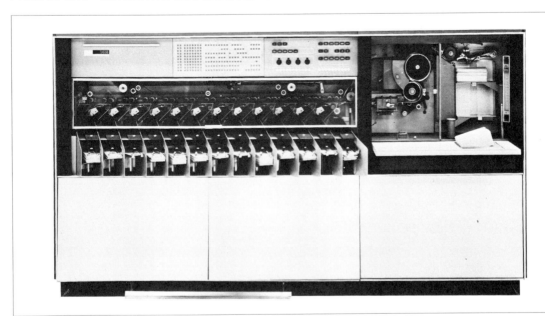

⑆O260⑈O6791⑆　⑉6　O12345⑈

FIGURE 6.12　MAGNETIC INK CHARACTERS

to receive messages from it. It is a means of outputting as well as inputting data. This permits communication between the CPU and the operator concerning a program, computer status, data input for a program, or instructions on how to handle an error condition.

Console typewriters are usually located on the console table and attached directly to the CPU. The keyboard is similar to that of an ordinary typewriter and has rows of numbers, letters, and special characters. The device includes a pin feed platen that feeds paper up to $13\frac{1}{8}$ inches wide. It prints at about 15.5 characters per second.

A group of status lights on the computer inform the operator of its readiness to receive input data. As keys are struck, the machine sends electrical pulses to the CPU and simultaneously types the message. The console, however, is a very slow means of data input and is usually reserved for small amounts of data.

For example, in updating a file, a record can be found and typed out on the console typewriter by the CPU. Then the operator can type a corrected line and instruct the machine to insert it in the file in place of the outdated line.

FIGURE 6.13　APPROVED CHECK FORM WITH MICR CHARACTERS

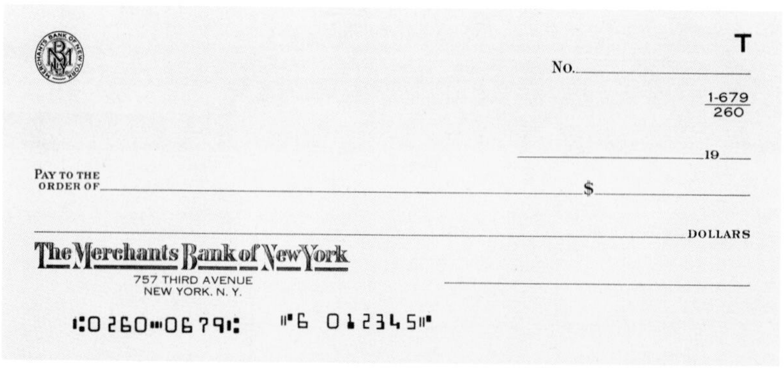

No.___

T

1-679
260

___19___

PAY TO THE
ORDER OF___

$___

___DOLLARS

The Merchants Bank of New York

757 THIRD AVENUE
NEW YORK, N. Y.

⑆O260⑈O6791⑆　⑉6　O12345⑈

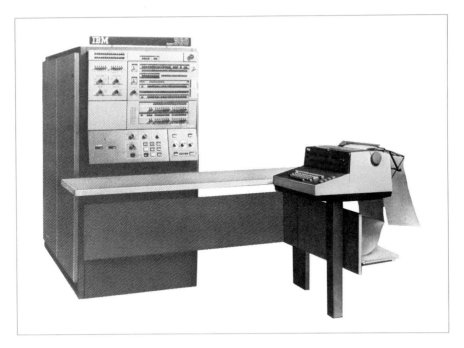

FIGURE 6.14 PRINTER KEYBOARD

POINT-OF-SALE TERMINALS. The terminal illustrated in Figure 6.15 converts data entered from a checker's keyboard into electronic pulses that are sent to a computer for immediate processing. Point-of-sale terminals are located in retail stores and provide a convenient means of preparing invoices and receipts, updating inventory files, and checking credit at the time a sale is made.

Each terminal is provided with keys for entering information such as a product code or price. The computer locates the product code in an information file, often stored on magnetic disk or tape, and processes the sale. It may adjust the inventory to reflect the purchase, post the sale to the customer's account or record the payment, and print out a receipt at the terminal showing the items purchased, price, and sales tax.

Several varieties of point-of-sale terminals are in use. The direct-reading model uses a hand-held wand or laser beam built into the checkout table. Items labeled with the uniform product code (UPC) are moved across the laser beam or are scanned by the hand-held wand to input data to the computer. (See Figure 6.16.) In the keyboard entry model, the clerk must input data, such as the product code or price, via a keyboard for processing. Other models record the information offline on magnetic tape cartridges for later input to the computer.

FIGURE 6.15   POINT-OF-SALE (POS) TERMINAL

FIGURE 6.16   HAND-HELD WAND

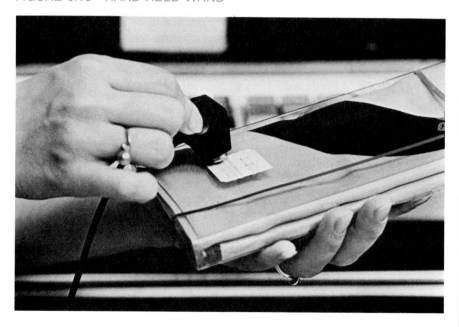

Offline
Input Devices

In offline data input, the data are first recorded on an intermediate medium such as magnetic tape or disk, for temporary storage. This process is performed on devices that are not connected to the computer, usually via a keyboard. Later, the tape reels or disk packs holding the data are placed on an online device for input to the computer. Some media, such as punched cards, and some point-of-sale terminals can be used in either an online or offline mode.

Some examples of typical devices used in offline data input are

KEY-TO-TAPE SYSTEM.   Data are recorded on magnetic tape from a machine similar in appearance to a keypunch. However, this machine records on a cartridge of magnetic tape instead of on punched cards. A plastic cartridge encloses and protects the tape, and provides for easy handling. Cartridges can be easily stored and are reusable. A key-to-tape system is shown in Figure 6.17.

As keys are depressed, 20 characters per inch are recorded on magnetic tape. As each character is typed, it is displayed on a screen before the operator. An end-of-record mark separates variable-length records, which

FIGURE 6.17   KEY-TO-TAPE SYSTEM

Round Versus Rectangular

"Mr. Hollerith, you've got to do something! The Census results will be outdated before they're ready . . . ."

Herman Hollerith of the U.S. Census Bureau knew that something did indeed have to be done. The 1890 Census was about to begin, and the U.S. population had passed the 60-million mark. It would take so many years to do the job with the present manual tabulating and calculating methods that the results would be meaningless before they were obtained.

Hollerith investigated many ideas and inventions. Finally, he discovered a system Joseph Jacquard had developed to weave patterns into fabric. Jacquard used cards containing codes in the form of punched holes to control a machine. Hollerith realized that if the holes in a card represented data, a machine could tabulate the information by sensing the hole combinations.

Since holes came in different sizes and shapes, Hollerith made several decisions of historic import without being aware of it. He designed his system to punch rectangular holes across the face of a card in a single tier, or row. This, it seemed to him, was the most efficient and practical means of recording data.

What finally emerged from his efforts was a punched card, a coding system, and a punched card machine. Each time the operator pressed a key, the machine punched a combination of rectangular holes into the card, in serial order.

Hollerith's system worked, and the 1890 and 1900 Census were processed in record time. But Hollerith wasn't satisfied. He envisioned his fantastic data coding system being used by businesses throughout the country. In 1896, he formed the Tabulating Machine Company to manufacture and sell his invention. In 1924 his company merged with two others to form IBM Corporation.

In the meantime, James Powers replaced Hollerith in the Census Department. This brash young man had his own ideas and believed that the system needed several important improvements. First, the rectangular holes had to go. So Powers built his own punch card machine, which punched 90 round holes in several tiers in cards. It also had a mechanism to store the keystrokes. After the operator keyed all the characters, the machine punched them into the card simultaneously.

Power's machine was very successful and before long he founded the Powers Accounting Machine Company (later known as UNIVAC Division of Sperry Rand).

The battle was on! Hollerith stressed the advantages of rectangular holes; Powers the virtues of round holes. Throughout the 1920s and 1930s, the giants, IBM and UNIVAC, were locked in a marketing struggle. By the late 1950s, the marketing strategy of IBM proved superior. The rectangles pulled ahead and emerged victorious. Cards with 80 rectangular holes punched in a single tier became the industry standard.

In 1970 UNIVAC introduced a new series of keypunch machines to punch rectangular holes in a standard 80-column card. Powers had been repudiated. It seemed that Hollerith had been right.

But the conflict wasn't over yet. IBM was planning a new series of electronic equipment, envisioned as the most up-to-date, modern punched card computer system on the market. Their new system would need the most efficient, practical, and advanced punch coding system that could be created. IBM engineers searched, investigated, and experimented.

Almost the day that UNIVAC announced their decision to go rectangular, IBM introduced their new System/3 Computer. It accepts only cards with 96 round holes, arranged in three tiers and punched simultaneously.

Was James Powers right after all?

may be as long as 720 characters. A record counter keeps track of the number of records entered on each tape.

To verify data, the tape is rewound to the beginning and the source document keyboarded a second time. An error is corrected by backspacing and rekeying.

TAPE POOLER. Data recorded on magnetic tape cartridges at 20 characters per inch must be condensed to 800 to 1,600 characters per inch for input to a computer. A tape pooler (Figure 6.18) is a specialized machine that converts widely spaced characters on a magnetic tape cartridge to tightly spaced characters on magnetic tape. The tape pooler can handle variable-length records up to 720 characters per record.

KEY-TO-DISK SYSTEM. The system shown in Figure 6.19 is a keyboard-to-magnetic disk system. Data are keyed into magnetic disk packs from a cathode ray tube terminal. The disk pack is then placed on an online disk drive for input to the CPU.

FIGURE 6.18 TAPE POOLER

FIGURE 6.19   KEY-TO-DISK SYSTEM

Keying source documents directly onto a disk eliminates the need for a pooler to condense the characters for computer input. The Inforex System 3300 includes a microprocessor, which facilitates text editing and data entry. The system tutors the operator by displaying formatted data on the screen. Data entered by the operator are then stored on disk. The system includes a verifier. If errors are detected, it will interrupt the operator and wait for correct information to be inserted.

THE PROBLEM OF SINGLE ACCESS

Early computers had only one input and one output device. A pair of electrical wires connected to the CPU served as the route for both the input

and output pulses. (See Figure 6.20.) To feed in data, the input device
(usually a tape reader) was connected by a switch to these wires. When the
time came to print out data, the switch disconnected the input device and
connected the output unit. This set of wires was called an I/O channel.

With only one input and one output device to serve, a single I/O channel
was sufficient. But the amount of data that could be processed was limited by
the speed of the I/O devices. As computers became more complex, the CPU
became capable of processing data much more rapidly than the data could
be transmitted. Because the CPU was idle while data were being read
into storage, much of the increased processing capacity was wasted.

This input bottleneck can be illustrated as follows. A business office
served by only one elevator is located on the tenth floor of a large
metropolitan office building. Regardless of the number of employees and
the speed at which they work, only those customers that gain access to
the tenth floor by the single elevator can be serviced. If more elevators are
installed, more customers can enter and leave, increasing the throughput.
An even greater volume of transactions can be processed if individuals are
employed to regulate elevator traffic.

"It heard one of the machines is going in for repairs,
and it's taking up a collection for it."

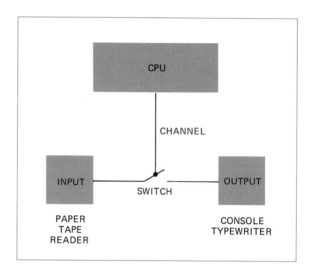

FIGURE 6.20   SINGLE I/O CHANNEL

Multiple Channels
To increase input/output capability, computer designers developed a multichannel I/O system. At first, several devices, such as tape or card readers, were wired to the CPU through a single channel. Each device was switched in and out of the system manually, by a selector switch. (See Figure 6.21.) The number and variety of devices connected to the system increased the computer's flexibility but did not improve throughput. The total number of jobs read in or out was still limited by the single channel.

Computer engineers then added more input and output channels between the CPU and the I/O devices. Figure 6.22 shows a CPU with four channels. Two card readers are permanently connected to channels 0 and 1. Two line printers are permanently connected to channels 2 and 3.

All channels can operate simultaneously, allowing the computer to receive the data from more than one job at a time. The input channels can be feeding in data from different jobs while the output channels are printing out the results of previous jobs. The CPU keeps the data from one job from being intermixed with that from another. This system greatly increases the throughput.

The next step was to have each channel serve more than one I/O device for increased flexibility. This way, two tape readers (or a card reader and a tape reader) could input data at one time. And a line printer and a tape drive (or two line printers) could output simultaneously.

Channel Address
As the number of input and output devices on a system increased, a problem of identifying each unit arose. The mechanical selector switch was replaced by an electronic switching arrangement and an addressing system. Each I/O

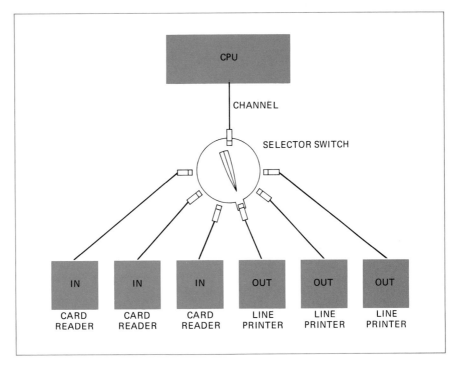

FIGURE 6.21   MULTIPLE INPUT-OUTPUT WITH SELECTOR SWITCH

FIGURE 6.22   MULTIPLE CHANNELS

(SIMULTANEOUS OPERATION)

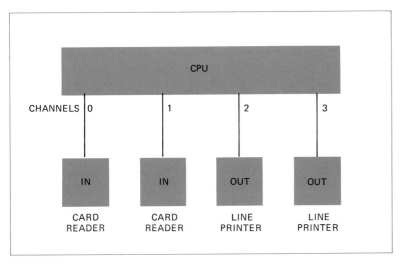

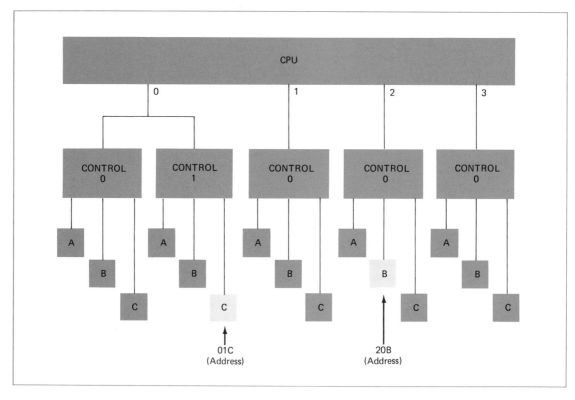

FIGURE 6.23   CHANNEL ADDRESSING

unit on the system is given a unique number, called a channel address, composed of channel number, control unit number, and device number.

The CPU in Figure 6.23 has 15 input/output devices, located on four separate channels. Each channel contains a control unit between the CPU and the I/O device. The function of the control unit is described later. Each channel has a number (0 to 3), each control unit has a number (0 to 1), and each I/O unit is referred to by an alphabetic character (A, B, or C) or a number (such as 181).

The specific address for a given unit is composed of its channel number, control unit number, and device number. Figure 6.23 identifies several devices on the system by these addresses. For example,

CHANNEL	CONTROL UNIT	DEVICE NUMBER
0	1	C
2	0	B

This system of addressing allows a programmer to identify which of several hundred devices connected to a CPU is to be used. The programmer can also reassign devices to meet the needs of the program.

Channel
Scheduler

The channel scheduler is a system used by a computer to keep track of which input/output devices are busy and what jobs are waiting to use them. It also starts the input and output operations. When the end of the file is reached or an error is detected, it will stop the input/output operations. If the channel scheduler detects an error, it will try to correct it, print out an error message on the console, or terminate the job without processing it. Then it will start the next job waiting in line.

Queuing

A system can become overloaded if its I/O or storage devices have more jobs assigned to them than they can handle. When the entire system is in use, the channel scheduler places waiting jobs in a line until a device is available. This waiting line is called a queue. It has provisions for keeping track of jobs and processes them on a first-come, first-served basis.

Sometimes several jobs being processed at the same time will specify the same I/O device, while others wait unused. This slows down throughput. The channel scheduler may override the programmer's device specification and adjust I/O assignments to suit the load. It electronically connects input and output devices to the channels to allow maximum utility of the channels and the CPU.

In these instances, the channel scheduler is performing the same function as an elevator scheduler in a busy office building who routes passengers to different elevators. The scheduler sees that some cars are going up, some down, that none are idle while people wait, and that none leave only partly full during peak hours. He or she also adjusts the load for morning and evening conditions.

Figure 6.24 shows ten jobs to be input and output. Five jobs are waiting to be input to channel 0, three to channel 1. Two jobs are waiting to be output on channel 2, while channel 3 is idle. The channel scheduler can override the I/O address specified by the programmers and assign the loads to gain maximum throughput. In this case, it could assign one of the input jobs from channel 0 to channel 1, and one of the output jobs from channel 2 to channel 3. (See Figure 6.25.) The output and input channels now have balanced loads.

THE PROBLEM OF DIFFERENT SPEEDS

Because of their physical nature, input devices convert data to electronic pulses at different speeds.

Since electromechanical devices, such as line printers, card punches,

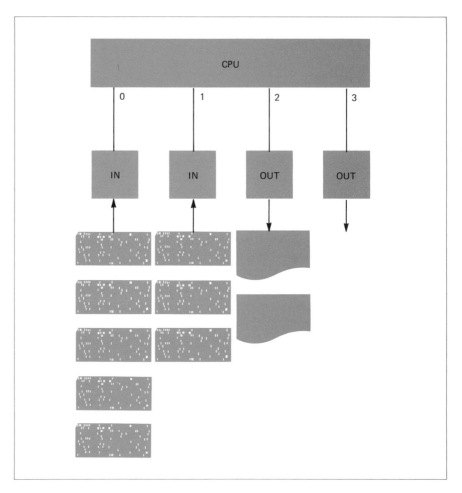

FIGURE 6.24   CHANNEL SCHEDULING (BEFORE)

card readers, and console typewriters, physically move cards or activate mechanical printing mechanisms, they transmit or receive only a few hundred characters per second. This speed is too slow for direct transmission to the CPU.

Devices that read, write, and record characters electronically are high-speed units. They transmit or receive several hundred thousand characters per second, and therefore can transmit data directly to the CPU. These devices include magnetic tape drives, magnetic disk drives, and drum storage devices.

The differences in speeds of input/output devices present several input problems. A CPU manipulates data at a high rate of speed. Data coming from all input devices must enter the CPU at the same speed. Buffering and

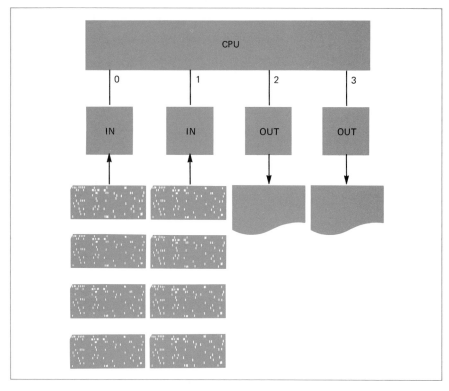

FIGURE 6.25   CHANNEL SCHEDULING (AFTER)

multiplexing are two techniques that have been used to resolve these problems.

Buffering   One method of reconciling the differences in speed between input units is to use a buffer between the input device and the CPU. The buffer is a storage unit that saves up a group of characters (bytes) coming from a slow input device. When sufficient data are accumulated, they are fed from the buffer to the CPU in a burst at high speed. Burst input speed (hundreds of thousands of bytes per second) equals the speed at which most CPUs are designed to manipulate data.

Buffers are usually composed of core storage systems, which hold data electronically. They may be physically located within the input device, the CPU, or elsewhere (Figure 6.26).

Buffering increases computer efficiency. Suppose four card readers are feeding data to a computer with four channels. Each could be connected directly to a separate channel. But this would tie up all channels, and only a relatively small amount of data would enter the CPU because of the slow speed of the card readers.

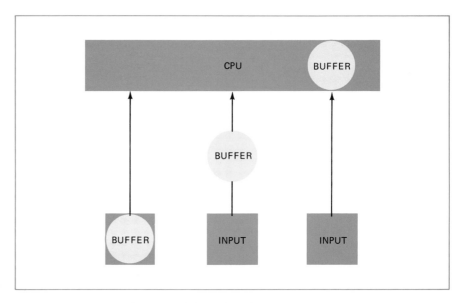

FIGURE 6.26   PHYSICAL LOCATION OF BUFFERS

A better arrangement would be to provide buffering for each card reader and tie all four to one input channel. When a buffer has received all the data from one record, it is switched online and transmits the data to the CPU. As a result, all four card readers can operate simultaneously, with buffers holding data until the line is open. (See Figure 6.27.) This leaves the other three channels open for other input/output tasks.

Multiplexing   Another method of compensating for differences in speed between input devices is to multiplex, or interleave data. Bytes of data coming from several input devices are interleaved, one after the other. In buffering, one or more records are held in storage and fed to the CPU in a burst. In multiplexing (Figure 6.28) data are picked up one byte at a time from several input devices, in turn. Both buffering and multiplexing allow a maximum amount of data to be fed over a single channel, increasing throughput.

Suppose data from four slow devices are to be fed to a CPU designed to receive data at high speed. The data can be buffered and sent in bursts from each card reader, or they can be multiplexed. In either case, only one channel is required. If the data are to be multiplexed, one character at a time is transmitted from each of the card readers. Once in the CPU, the multiplexer separates each byte, and the original records are reconstructed in separate storage areas.

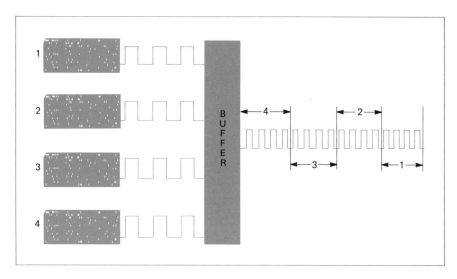

FIGURE 6.27   BUFFERING FOUR CARD READERS

FIGURE 6.28   MULTIPLEXING FOUR CARD READERS

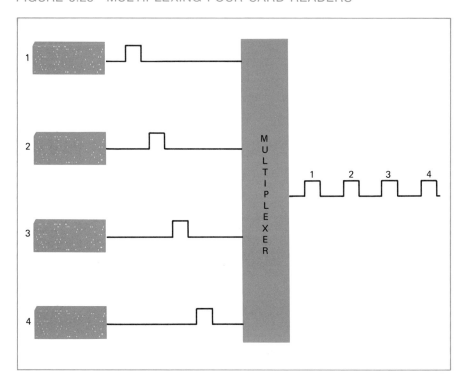

KEY TERMS   Buffer   Multiplex
                 Channel address   Offline input
                 Channel scheduler   Online input
                 Control units   Point-of-sale terminal
                 Interleave   Pulse train
                 I/O channel   Queue

EXERCISES   1. Explain the system used for detecting holes in a punched card and
                 converting them to electrical pulses.
              2. How are characters converted from the printed page to electrical pulses
                 by the Optical Character Reader?
              3. What is the disadvantage of using the printer-keyboard to feed data in
                 and out of the computer?
              4. Draw a sketch of a simple computer, showing one access channel.
              5. What are I/O channels? What function do they serve?
              6. What is the difference between online and offline data input?
              7. What is channel scheduling, and how does it improve computer
                 throughput?
              8. Why are slow input devices a problem for the CPU? List four slow devices
                 and four fast devices.
              9. Define the term buffering. How is it used in the computer system?
             10. Define multiplexing. How does it differ from buffering?
             11. Visit your data center on campus and list all input and output devices
                 on the system. Categorize each according to whether it is fast or slow.
             12. Visit a market or department store using point-of-sale terminals. Briefly,
                 describe what information is input, how it is input, and what information
                 is output by the terminal.

7

DATA REPRESENTATION AND COMPUTER ARITHMETIC

In written communication, it is necessary to use symbols in place of actual objects or events. The use of symbols makes it easier to process data. One way to represent data is with numbers (0, 1, 2, 3, 4, 5, 6, 7, 8, 9), each number being the symbol of a certain quantity. The alphabet is another way of representing data. Each combination of symbols has a specific meaning. For example, by convention the symbols *Jane Smith* form a name that represents a person.

In electronic data processing, data are represented by coding systems that can be converted to electronic pulses for manipulation by a computer.

EARLY DATA REPRESENTATION

The first attempt to represent data probably consisted of using fingers, rocks, or sticks. To add two and two, a person might, for example, have raised two fingers on one hand, and then two on the other. Four raised fingers then represented the sum of the objects being counted.

Each rock, stick, or finger represented one object or thing. Since there were few objects or things to count, this simple system was adequate. The skins of 100 animals could conveniently be represented by 100 sticks.

	OBJECTS	ROMAN NUMERAL SYSTEM	DECIMAL SYSTEM
	○	I	1
	○ ○	II	2
	○ ○ ○	III	3
	○○○○○ ○○○○○	X	10

FIGURE 7.1   USE OF SYMBOLS TO REPRESENT OBJECTS

This early numbering system was based on two principles: First, each unit represented only one object (1). For example, two units had to be used to represent two objects (11); ten to represent ten objects (1111111111). Second, only two states could be represented: an object existed or it did not.

As people's needs changed, this crude system of data representation became inadequate. A shorthand method of representing larger numbers was needed.

Numbering systems developed that used different symbols to represent quantities of more than one. For example, consider the Roman system, shown in Figure 7.1, which uses letters as symbols. In Roman numerals, I represents one unit, and III represents 3. But a V represents 5 units; an X, 10 units; and a C, 100 units.

But since people could conveniently remember and use only a limited number of symbols, the next step was to devise a system where the position of the symbol gave it a different value. This led to the development of number systems that used bases and place values.

The base of a numbering system is the number of states it recognizes. For example, a system with ten states (0, 1, 2, 3, 4, 5, 6, 7, 8, 9) is called base 10. A system with four states (0, 1, 2, 3) is called base 4.

Place value is that value assigned to a symbol according to its position or place in the number. (See Figure 7.2.) It is an important concept; it greatly increases the flexibility and capacity of a numbering system. Place value is a power of the base of a numbering system. In base 10, the rightmost position, or the symbol before the decimal (or reference) point, is equal to the symbol times 10^0 or 1. [Any number to the zero power (N^0) equals 1.] The position to its left is equal to the symbol times 10^1 or 10; the next, the symbol times 10^2 or 100 (10 × 10); the next position, the symbol times 10^3 or 1,000 (10 × 10 × 10), and so on.

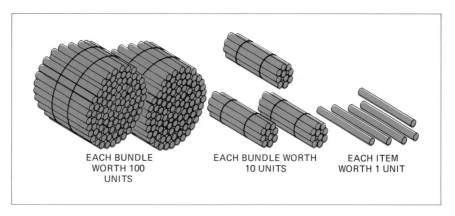

EACH BUNDLE
WORTH 100
UNITS

EACH BUNDLE WORTH
10 UNITS

EACH ITEM
WORTH 1 UNIT

FIGURE 7.2   PLACE VALUE

BASE 10 SYSTEM

Our common numbering system is the base 10 or decimal system. **Ten different symbols represent the states: 0, 1, 2, 3, 4, 5, 6, 7, 8, and 9.**

The decimal system also uses place value. In the following example, each digit in the number 345 has a different place value.

Power	10^2	10^1	10^0	
Place value	100	10	1	
Digit	3	4	5	$= 300 + 40 + 5$

The value of each digit depends upon its position with respect to the other digits. The number in the right-hand column (5) represents five units because it is in the units, or ones, column. The number 4 is in the tens column and represents 10 $\times$ 4, or 40 units. The number in the left column (3) is in the hundreds column and represents not 3 units, but 3 $\times$ 100 or 300 units. It is the place value that determines the actual quantity a numeral represents.

Looking at it another way, we see that the number 345 is the same as

3 $\times$ 100	100
	100
	100
4 $\times$ 10	10
	10
	10
	10

$$
\begin{array}{cc}
5 \times 1 & 1 \\
& 1 \\
& 1 \\
& 1 \\
& \underline{1} \\
& 345
\end{array}
$$

The decimal system needs only three digits to represent the quantity instead of a string of 345 ones—a definite improvement over the system used by early people.

In the decimal system of representation, the following place values and symbols are used:

Place values

10^5	10^4	10^3	10^2	10^1	10^0
Hundred thousands	Ten thousands	Thousands	Hundreds	Tens	Ones
100,000	10,000	1,000	100	10	1

Symbols used

0, 1, 2, 3, 4, 5, 6, 7, 8, 9

"I can use base ten, and you can't."

It is interesting to speculate about what would have happened had people been born with only eight or as many as twelve fingers. In all likelihood, our numbering system would be quite different. With only eight fingers, our numbering system might be base 8 and look like this:

Place values

Power of 8	8^4	8^3	8^2	8^1	8^0
Decimal equivalent	4,096	512	64	8	1

Symbols used

0, 1, 2, 3, 4, 5, 6, 7

Had we been born with 12 fingers, our system might be base 12. A base 12 system would need 12 symbols.

Although the decimal, or base 10, system can be used, the base 2 (binary) and base 16 (hexadecimal) systems have been found to be more efficient in data processing. The remainder of the chapter is devoted to these important number systems.

BINARY REPRESENTATION

Early computer engineers designed machines that used the decimal system. But since these computers had to be able to represent and store ten states, they proved to be complicated and inaccurate. There was a need to represent data in a form compatible with computer hardware capabilities. Computers, in fact most electronic devices, are inherently "two-state" machines. Switches, relays, lamps, diodes, memory cores, etc. are either off or on, charged or not charged, conducting or not conducting. Therefore, a number system with only two states is the most efficient for the machine. Binary representation is ideal because it is based on only two conditions: on or off. And two symbols represent these states: 1 and 0.

These two states are represented electronically as a pulse train. (See Figure 7.3.) An electrical voltage of zero lasting a given length of time represents a binary zero. A positive electrical voltage lasting a given length of time represents a binary one.

Each storage unit of the computer is capable of representing only one of two possible states, "1" or "0." But to have any value, a numbering system must represent more than two numbers. By connecting storage units in series, positions for place value are created, and larger numbers can be represented. Thus, any number that can be represented as a decimal can be represented as a binary number, and all mathematical operations, such as addition, subtraction, and multiplication, can be performed upon it.

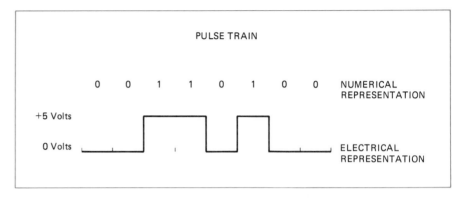

FIGURE 7.3   PULSE TRAIN

Place Values   The binary numbering system uses place values to represent numbers larger than its base, just as the decimal system does. Each place value is a power of 2 (the base) and increases in magnitude as it moves to the left. The first eight binary place values (given here in familiar decimal system terms) are

Place value	2^7	2^6	2^5	2^4	2^3	2^2	2^1	2^0
Decimal equivalent	128	64	32	16	8	4	2	1

The following table gives some examples of binary numbers and their decimal equivalents.

BINARY NUMBER								DECIMAL EQUIVALENT		
128	64	32	16	8	4	2	1	100	10	1
0	0	0	0	0	0	0	1			1
0	0	0	0	0	0	1	1			3
0	0	0	0	0	1	0	1			5
0	1	0	0	0	0	0	1		6	5
1	0	0	0	0	1	1	0	1	3	4
1	1	1	1	1	1	1	1	2	5	5

With eight place-value positions (each capable of only two conditions), any number from 0 to 255 can be represented. Larger numbers can be represented by adding more place values. The number of numerals that can be represented is doubled each time a place value is added.

To a human, the binary system appears inconvenient and awkward. It requires many more place-value positions to represent a number than does the decimal system. But an electronic device can manipulate long strings of binary bits both efficiently and rapidly.

Binary
Mathematics

Any mathematical operation can be performed on numbers stored in the computer in binary representation. The principles involved are very similar to those used in manipulating decimal numbers. Although it is unnecessary for you to become proficient in binary mathematics, you should have some understanding of the process. Here are some fundamental rules for binary mathematical operations.

BINARY ADDITION.   Addition of binary numbers is performed in a manner similar to adding decimal numbers. Follow these rules:

1. Zero plus zero equals zero (0 + 0 = 0)
2. Zero plus one equals one (0 + 1 = 1)
3. One plus zero equals one (1 + 0 = 1)
4. One plus one equals zero with one to carry (1 + 1 = 10)

The following is an example of binary addition. The result is given below with the decimal equivalent to the right.

$$
\begin{array}{rr}
0\,1\,1\,1 & 7 \\
+0\,0\,1\,1 & 3 \\
\hline
1\,0\,1\,0 = 10 &
\end{array}
$$

Begin at the right-hand side and add each column of digits. Place the sum below the line, just as in decimal addition. Remember, if the sum of any two digits in a given column exceeds 1, a carry must be made.

Step 1. Add 1 + 1. The sum is greater than 1 and the answer is 0 with 1
        to carry.
Step 2. Add 1 + 1 + 1. This results in 1 with 1 to carry.
Step 3. Add 1 + 1. Again, 0 is below the line and 1 is carried.
Step 4. Add 1 + 0. The answer is 1.

The resulting binary number, 1010, is the sum. This is how it looks expressed by place value and converted to its decimal equivalent:

$$
\frac{8\;4\;2\;1}{1\;0\;1\;0}
$$

This shows that binary 1010 is the same as

$$
\begin{array}{rr}
\text{one group of 8 units} = & 8 \\
\text{one group of 2 units} = & +2 \\
\hline
& 10 \text{ decimal units}
\end{array}
$$

George Boole, Mathematical Wizard

What a disappointment George Boole turned out to be. He had been such a promising mathematician as a youth. At 16, he became an assistant master in a private school and founded a very successful school by the time he was 20. A brilliant teacher, he was later made Professor of Mathematics at Queen's College, Cork, Ireland, a post he held for the rest of his life.

He began his investigation in experimental mathematics while at Queens College. A fantastic new scheme came to him—a system of mathematics and algebra that was a perfect plan of logic using only ones and zeros. He envisioned sets and subsets, unions, intersections, universals, and complements. It all fit together nicely.

In 1847 he wrote a statement describing his new system and in 1854 he published his monumental work on Boolean algebra, but it brought him only frustration and disappointment. No one cared or even pretended to be interested. One colleague asked him why he wasted his time developing a new system when a perfectly good decimal system already existed. And besides, who would want a primitive system using only ones and zeros?

Librarians had such trouble cataloging his writings that even they wished he hadn't strayed from the beaten track. (Where would you put "An Investigation of the Laws of Thought, on Which Are Founded the Mathematical Theories of Logic and Probabilities"? under philosophy? mathematics? logic?) In December of 1864, George Boole died, leaving a mathematical system no one wanted.

For almost a century Boole's work lay unused. Then in the late 1940s, scientists and engineers created a device capable of processing decimal numbers. But it kept adding two and two and getting five. What was needed was a system of mathematics based on ones and zeros—a system suitable to the on-off states inherent in computer hardware. Then an engineer came upon a rare work—Boole's treatises. It was the perfect match, a mathematical system apparently custom-made for the modern computer.

Today, almost every digital computer in the world performs its mathematical computations in circuitry based on Boole's scheme. From kindergarten to college, students are studying new math. And, for the modern twentieth-century computer technologist, the most important mathematical scheme that exists is the Boolean system of algebra.

Here are several other examples of binary addition:

8 4 2 1		16 8 4 2 1		8 4 2 1	
0 1 0 1	5	0 1 0 1	5	0 1 1 0	6
+1 0 1 0	10	+1 1 1 1	15	+0 1 1 1	7
1 1 1 1 = 15		1 0 1 0 0 = 20		1 1 0 1 = 13	

BINARY SUBTRACTION.   The computer performs subtraction by using a method called subtraction by the twos complement.

In a computer, a series of transistors or other devices can easily be changed from one state to another (from conducting to nonconducting, for example). Thus, it is an easy matter to convert a string of ones and zeros to their opposite, or complement, string. For example,

Binary number:	0 1 1 0	0 1 0 1
Twos complement:	1 0 0 1	1 0 1 0

This feature makes it convenient to perform subtraction using the twos complementary addition method. By this method, the subtrahend is converted to its complement and added to the minuend. Then a binary 1 or 0 (called and end-around carry) is added to the units position to give the answer.

For example, here is how the computer would subtract 7 from 9 using the twos complement method:

Step 1. Binary 0111 (the subtrahend) is converted to its complement, 1000.
Step 2. The number 1000 is added to the minuend 1001, giving 10001.
Step 3. The digit in the highest place value, "1," is carried around and added to the units position, giving the answer 0010, a decimal 2.

$$
\begin{array}{ccc}
1001 & 1001 & 9 \\
+1000 & +1000 & -7 \\
\hline
10001 & \textcircled{1}0001 & \\
& \searrow\ 1 & \\
\hline
& 0010 & 2
\end{array}
$$

In the above example, the end-around carry is 1, indicating that the answer is a positive number. When the end-around carry is 0, the answer will be negative; it must be complemented again and a negative sign attached.

For example:

$$
\begin{array}{ccc}
7 & 0111 & 0111 \\
-9 & -1001 & +0110 \\
\hline
-2 & & \textcircled{0}1101 \\
& & \searrow\ 0 \\
& & 1101 \rightarrow -0010
\end{array}
$$

In an example using numbers as small as 9 and 7, this method may appear to be overly complicated and not worth the effort. But in dealing with numbers involving long strings of binary bits, it makes more efficient use of the computer.

BINARY MULTIPLICATION AND DIVISION. Multiplication is actually a shorthand way of doing a series of addition problems. 3×7 is the same as adding three sevens, or $7 + 7 + 7 = 21$. And $50 \times 3,891$ is the same as adding fifty 3,891s. Both equal 194,550.

Division, of both decimal and binary numbers, is a shorthand method of doing a series of subtractions. $30 \div 10 = 3$ means that one can subtract 10 from 30 three times. And $135 \div 25 = 5$ with a remainder of 10, whether it is done by the traditional method or as a series of subtraction problems.

The computer performs multiplication as a series of addition problems and division as a series of subtraction problems. This is more efficient for the machine and it can use the same circuitry set up for addition and subtraction. The mechanics of these processes are performed internally by the computer without operator intervention or instruction. The programmer has only to supply the values to be operated upon.

Converting Binary and Decimal Numbers

The CPU performs arithmetic calculations on binary data. Usually, however, data are entered into the computer in decimal form. The CPU will automatically convert numbers from decimal to binary for processing, and reconvert the results to be output into decimal form.

Occasionally, however, a programmer must know how to make this conversion. Many tables and charts are available that give the equivalent binary and decimal values. Or, since the principles involved are fairly simple, the programmer can make the necessary calculations easily.

DECIMAL TO BINARY CONVERSION. There are two common methods of converting decimals to binary numbers. One is a system of division and the other involves regrouping the units under the new place values.

Division by Two. One way to perform decimal-to-binary conversion is by dividing the decimal number by 2 (the base) repeatedly, writing down the remainder each time. For example, here is how the binary equivalent of 71 would be found:

$$
\begin{array}{rcl}
71 \div 2 &=& 35 + 1 \\
35 \div 2 &=& 17 + 1 \\
17 \div 2 &=& 8 + 1 \\
8 \div 2 &=& 4 + 0 \\
4 \div 2 &=& 2 + 0 \\
2 \div 2 &=& 1 + 0 \\
1 \div 2 &=& 0 + 1 \\
\end{array}
$$

$$1\ \ 0\ \ 0\ \ 0\ \ 1\ \ 1\ \ 1$$

In this system, the remainders from the series of divisions form the binary equivalent of the decimal number.

Regrouping Units. A second way to convert a number from one base system to another is to regroup the number of units according to the new place values. As an example, we will convert decimal 48 to its binary equivalent. We will need enough binary places to represent 48 units (the first six place values). To determine the number of places we start at the right and add place values until the total reaches or exceeds 48. The total for the first five places is $1 + 2 + 4 + 8 + 16 = 31$. Going one more place to the left we reach a total of 63. So we list the six places:

$$32 \quad 16 \quad 8 \quad 4 \quad 2 \quad 1$$

Then we regroup 32 of the 48 units by placing a ''1'' under the place-value position that represents 32 units.

This still leaves 16 units to be regrouped. There is a binary place value representing 16 units, so we write a ''1'' under it, and fill in the place values to the right with zeros:

$$
\begin{array}{rl}
48 & \text{units} \\
-32 & = 1 \text{ group of 32 units} \\
\hline
16 & \text{units} \\
-16 & = 1 \text{ group of 16 units} \\
\hline
0 &
\end{array}
$$

32	16	8	4	2	1
1	1	0	0	0	0

The binary representation of 48 units is 110000.

Other examples:

Decimal 73 is expressed as binary 1001001.

$$
\begin{array}{rl}
73 & \text{units} \\
-64 & = 1 \text{ group of 64 units} \\
\hline
9 & \text{units} \\
-\;8 & = 1 \text{ group of 8 units} \\
\hline
1 & \text{unit} \\
-\;1 & = 1 \text{ unit} \\
\hline
0 &
\end{array}
$$

64	32	16	8	4	2	1
1	0	0	1	0	0	1

Decimal 101 is expressed as binary 1100101.

```
101    units
─  64 = 1 group of 64 units
 37    units
─  32 = 1 group of 32 units
  5    units
─   4 = 1 group of 4 units
  1    unit
─   1 = 1 unit
  0
```

64	32	16	8	4	2	1
1	1	0	0	1	0	1

BINARY TO DECIMAL CONVERSION. To convert from binary to decimal numbers, add the number of units represented by each binary place value.

As an example, let's convert binary 1110101 to its decimal equivalent. First determine the place value of each digit in the binary number. Then sum the number of units they represent.

64	32	16	8	4	2	1
1	1	1	0	1	0	1

```
There is one group of   64 units
     + one group of   32 units
     + one group of   16 units
     + one group of    4 units
     + one group of    1 units
                   = 117 decimal units
```

Binary 1110101 is equivalent to decimal 117.

BCD
Numeric Code

Although binary representation of numbers is efficient for use by the computer, it is awkward and inconvenient for us to use. It is easier for us to read and understand numbers that more closely resemble the decimal place-value system.

A modified form of the binary numeric system is called the Binary Coded Decimal (BCD) Numeric Code. In this system, only the binary codes for the numbers 0 to 9 are used. Four binary digits are required to express these values.

DECIMAL		BINARY (BCD)	DECIMAL		BINARY (BCD)
0	=	0000	5	=	0101
1	=	0001	6	=	0110
2	=	0010	7	=	0111
3	=	0011	8	=	1000
4	=	0100	9	=	1001

A decimal number is expressed by translating each digit in the number to its binary code. For example, decimal 213 would be expressed as

Decimal	2	1	3
BCD	0010	0001	0011

(The pure binary representation of decimal 213 is 11010101.)
Decimal 5,168 would be expressed in BCD as

Decimal	5	1	6	8
BCD	0101	0001	0110	1000

Decimal 1,009 would be expressed in BCD as

Decimal	1	0	0	9
BCD	0001	0000	0000	1001

HEXADECIMAL REPRESENTATION

Although the BCD system increases the flexibility and ease of programming numeric data, it does require more computer space to record each number. Four binary digits are necessary to express the ten values of the BCD system, but in this system there are six unused combinations of four digits. These unused combinations represent empty storage space in the computer.

The hexadecimal (hex) system, using base 16, incorporates the convenience of the BCD system with the full storage capability allowed by using all code combinations of pure binary. Strings of binary bits, representing a number, are divided into groups of fours. A group of four zeros and ones has 16 possible combinations: the 16 states of the hex numbering system. The first ten states have the same values and symbols as the decimal system. The last six are represented by the first six letters of the alphabet.

Table 7.1 lists the symbols required to represent the first 16 numbers in the decimal, hexadecimal, binary, and BCD systems.

TABLE 7.1 VARIOUS NUMBERING SYSTEMS

DECIMAL	HEX	BINARY	BCD	
0	0	0000	0000	0000
1	1	0001	0000	0001
2	2	0010	0000	0010
3	3	0011	0000	0011
4	4	0100	0000	0100
5	5	0101	0000	0101
6	6	0110	0000	0110
7	7	0111	0000	0111
8	8	1000	0000	1000
9	9	1001	0000	1001
10	A	1010	0001	0000
11	B	1011	0001	0001
12	C	1100	0001	0010
13	D	1101	0001	0011
14	E	1110	0001	0100
15	F	1111	0001	0101

Each hex place value is expressed in binary by one group of four digits. Therefore, a hex number with two place values requires eight binary digits and one with three place values, 12 binary digits. For example,

HEX	BINARY	DECIMAL
A5	1010 0101	165
2E7	0010 1110 0111	743
F00	1111 0000 0000	3,840

With only 16 combinations to remember, programmers can easily refer to large binary numbers by their hexadecimal names, such as

$$0010 \quad 1111 \quad 0001 \quad 1110 \quad 1100 = 2F1EC = 193{,}004$$
$$2 \qquad F \qquad 1 \qquad E \qquad C$$

and

$$1110 \quad 0010 \quad 1110 \quad 0000 \quad 1101 \quad 1010 \quad 1011 = E2E0DAB = 237{,}899{,}179$$
$$E \qquad 2 \qquad E \qquad 0 \qquad D \qquad A \qquad B$$

Conversion of large binary numbers to the decimal system is simplified. First the hex name for the binary number is determined. Then the hex number is converted to the decimal number. Conversion from decimal to binary is also simplified by first converting the number to hex and then to binary. The computer, of course, makes this conversion automatically.

TABLE 7.2 HEXADECIMAL TO DECIMAL CONVERSION

HEX	DEC	HEX	DEC	HEX	DEC	HEX	DEC	HEX	DEC	HEX	DEC	HEX	DEC	HEX	DEC
0	0	0	0	0	0	0	0	0	0	0	0	0	0	0	0
1	268,435,456	1	16,777,216	1	1,048,576	1	65,536	1	4,096	1	256	1	16	1	1
2	536,870,912	2	33,554,432	2	2,097,152	2	131,072	2	8,192	2	512	2	32	2	2
3	805,306,368	3	50,331,648	3	3,145,728	3	196,608	3	12,288	3	768	3	48	3	3
4	1,073,741,824	4	67,108,864	4	4,194,304	4	262,144	4	16,384	4	1,024	4	64	4	4
5	1,342,177,280	5	83,886,080	5	5,242,880	5	327,680	5	20,480	5	1,280	5	80	5	5
6	1,610,612,736	6	100,663,296	6	6,291,456	6	393,216	6	24,576	6	1,536	6	96	6	6
7	1,879,048,192	7	117,440,512	7	7,340,032	7	458,752	7	28,672	7	1,792	7	112	7	7
8	2,147,483,648	8	134,217,728	8	8,388,608	8	524,288	8	32,768	8	2,048	8	128	8	8
9	2,415,919,104	9	150,994,944	9	9,437,184	9	589,824	9	36,864	9	2,304	9	144	9	9
A	2,684,354,560	A	167,772,160	A	10,485,760	A	655,360	A	40,960	A	2,560	A	160	A	10
B	2,952,790,016	B	184,549,376	B	11,534,336	B	720,896	B	45,056	B	2,816	B	176	B	11
C	3,221,225,472	C	201,326,592	C	12,582,912	C	786,432	C	49,152	C	3,072	C	192	C	12
D	3,489,660,928	D	218,103,808	D	13,631,488	D	851,968	D	53,248	D	3,328	D	208	D	13
E	3,758,096,384	E	234,881,024	E	14,680,064	E	917,504	E	57,344	E	3,584	E	224	E	14
F	4,026,531,840	F	251,658,240	F	15,728,640	F	983,040	F	61,440	F	3,840	F	240	F	15
8		7		6		5		4		3		2		1	

The listings of information that computers print out about a program after it has unexpectedly stopped are usually in hex. To understand them requires a knowledge of hex and the ability to convert data between the decimal and the hex systems. A knowledge of hexadecimal conversion is also necessary for writing programs in assembler.

Appendix B illustrates the relationship of hexadecimal, decimal, and binary numbers. A close look at the three systems will indicate the efficiency of the hex numbering system.

HEXADECIMAL TO DECIMAL CONVERSION.   Conversion between the two systems is most easily accomplished by using a table such as Table 7.2. This table will convert hex numbers up to eight place values or positions. The place values are numbered from 1 to 8, right to left, along the bottom of the table. Each place value is a power of 16, the base, and represents these units:

8	7	6	5	4	3	2	1
268,435,456	16,777,216	1,048,576	65,536	4,096	256	16	1

A hex 1 in position 3 means there is one group of 256 units in a number. An A in that position means there are ten groups of 256 units in the number, or 2,560 decimal units. A hex B position 2 means there are 11 groups of 16 units or 176 (11 $\times$ 16) decimal units, etc.

The table provides a convenient method of simplifying the conversion of hex and decimal numbers. The decimal value of each hex position is found and added to give the equivalent decimal number.

Here are several examples of hex to decimal conversion, using the place values listed above.

1. HEX 1CB3 = DECIMAL 7,347

    hex 3 in position 1 = 3 × 1   =   3 in decimal
    hex B in position 2 = 11 × 16   =   176 in decimal
    hex C in position 3 = 12 × 256 = 3,072 in decimal
    hex 1 in position 4 = 1 × 4,096 = 4,096 in decimal
                                       7,347

2. HEX 1010 = DECIMAL 4,112

    hex 0 in position 1 = 0 × 1   =   0
    hex 1 in position 2 = 1 × 16   =   16
    hex 0 in position 3 = 0 × 256 =   0
    hex 1 in position 4 = 1 × 4,096 = 4,096
                                       4,112

3. HEX 14BBB = DECIMAL 84,923

    hex B in position 1 = 11 × 1   =   11
    hex B in position 2 = 11 × 16   =   176
    hex B in position 3 = 11 × 256   = 2,816
    hex 4 in position 4 = 4 × 4,096 = 16,384
    hex 1 in position 5 = 1 × 65,536 = 65,536
                                       84,923

DECIMAL TO HEXADECIMAL CONVERSION. A reverse procedure will convert decimal numbers to hexadecimal values, also by using Table 7.2. It is basically the process of rearranging the units represented by a number into new groups corresponding to the place values of the hex system.

For example, look at the steps involved in converting the decimal value 32,184 to its hex equivalent:

1. Find the decimal number on the table equal to or almost as large as the number being converted. In this case, it is 28,672 in position 4. The hex equivalent is 7___. The number will contain four place values, and the leftmost digit is a hex 7. This means the decimal number contains 7 groups of 4,096 units (7 × 4,096 = 28,672).

2. Now subtract 28,672 from 32,184 since these units have been regrouped. This leaves 3,512 units.

                       32,184
                    −28,672   7___
                       3,512

3. The closest decimal value to 3,512 is 3,328 in position 3. Its hex equivalent is D__. 3,512 contains 13 groups of 256 units, with 184 units still left to be regrouped. The hex number now looks like this:

$$
\begin{array}{r}
3,512 \\
-3,328 \\
\hline
184
\end{array}
\qquad 7D \_\_
$$

4. Decimal 176 is the closest value to 184 and its hex equivalent is B_, with 8 units left. The number is now

$$
\begin{array}{r}
184 \\
-176 \\
\hline
8
\end{array}
\qquad 7DB\_
$$

5. Eight decimal units are equal to 8 hex units, and these are added to give the final answer. The decimal number 32,184 is equal to hex 7DB8.

Here are two more

DECIMAL   12,431 = HEX 308F

$$
\begin{array}{rl}
12,431 & \\
-12,288 = & 3\_\_\_ \\
\hline
143 & \\
-128 = & 08\_ \\
\hline
15 & \\
-15 = & \underline{\qquad F} \\
\hline
0 & 308F
\end{array}
$$

DECIMAL   10,396,652 = HEX 9EA3EC

$$
\begin{array}{rl}
10,396,652 = & \\
-\ 9,437,184 = & 9\_\_\_\_\_ \\
\hline
959,468 & \\
-917,504 = & E\_\_\_\_ \\
\hline
41,964 & \\
-40,960 = & A\_\_\_ \\
\hline
1,004 & \\
-\ \ \ 768 = & 3\_\_ \\
\hline
236 & \\
-224 = & E\_ \\
\hline
12 & \\
-12 = & \underline{\qquad C} \\
\hline
0 & 9EA3EC
\end{array}
$$

ALPHABETIC CODING SYSTEMS

The coding systems discussed up to this point represent only numeric data, since any system using four bits can represent only 16 different characters. (Hex represents 16 numbers; BCD represents ten numbers and has six unused combinations.) But a coding system using five bits is able to represent 32 characters; one with six bits, 64 characters; and so forth. Such systems allow for coding of alphabetic data and special characters, such as $, +, and (.

Several codes have been developed, many based on the BCD coding system, to convert alphabetic and special characters to binary bits that can be processed by the computer. Each coding system is designed to meet certain needs. For example, some are for transmitting data over telephone lines, others for storage of data within the CPU. Modern coding systems are able to represent as many as 256 different characters.

Terminology has been developed to describe specific aspects of coding systems. Intelligence bits are those bits that are part of the code for a character. Some codes include extra bits, used for accuracy control. The BCD code, for example, has four intelligence bits. A six-bit code might have five intelligence bits and one bit for checking accuracy.

In the early years of telegraph transmission, paper tape was used to feed data. The code combination for each character was punched across the width of the paper tape. The row of holes formed by each punch position along the length of the tape was called a channel. There were as many channels as there were bits in a code.

Tape codes commonly have from five to eight channels. A channel may contain intelligence or accuracy bits, but never both. Those with intelligence bits are called intelligence channels. Provisions for maintaining accuracy, called parity checks, have also been developed and included in some of the codes. These are provided in parity channels. See Figure 7.6.

Tracks are similar to channels, except they are related to magnetic rather than paper tape. Magnetic tape may have from seven to nine tracks depending on the code used.

Parity Check Early in the development of data transmission and coding systems, a serious problem arose. It was not uncommon for a bit to be lost in transmission because of a mechanical or electronic failure. (See Figure 7.4.) If the loss went undetected, the character received on the other end of the line was incorrect. By the same token, if an extra bit found its way onto a tape or into the transmitted signal, incorrect data resulted.

To prevent this from happening, the parity system was developed to detect errors in coding. Each character, or byte, is composed of a different combination of bits. Some characters have an odd number of bits and

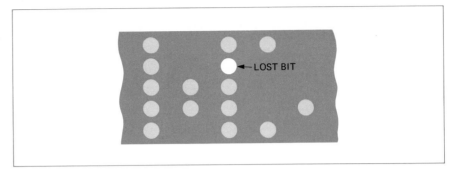

FIGURE 7.4 LOST BITS (NO CHECK PRESENT)

some an even number. For example, these code combinations have an odd number of bits turned on:

$$1 = 0001$$
$$7 = 0111$$
$$8 = 1000$$

These have an even number:

$$6 = 0110$$
$$5 = 0101$$
$$3 = 0011$$

To use the parity system, an extra bit, called a check bit, is added either to all the combinations with an odd number of bits, or to all the combinations with an even number.

EVEN PARITY. Even-parity codes place a check bit with each uneven byte. [See Figure 7.5(A).] Since it is transmitted only with characters composed of an uneven number of bits, all characters transmitted will have an even number of bits. The check bit is transmitted to and from the computer along with the character code. If a bit is lost (or added) in transmission, the system will detect its loss. An uneven number of bits received in a code string composed of even bits will signal an error.

ODD PARITY. Odd-parity codes punch an extra check bit with code combinations that have an even number of bits. [See Figure 7.5(B).] Thus, all characters transmitted will have an odd number of bits. Odd and even parity are similar in nature. They are both designed to signal an error in the event data are lost or added.

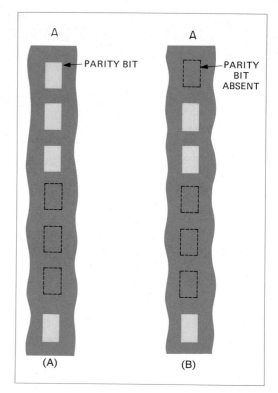

FIGURE 7.5   (A) EVEN PARITY (LETTER A, SEVEN-BIT CODE)
(B) ODD PARITY (LETTER A, SEVEN-BIT CODE)

LONGITUDINAL PARITY.   Longitudinal parity is used for checking accuracy when recording and transmitting on magnetic tape. In this form, all characters in a track are tallied along the length of the tape. At the end of each track a check bit is added to maintain even or odd parity. (See Figure 7.6.) Longitudinal parity can be even or odd and can be used in addition to the parity system used to check each byte.

Data Transmission Codes

The following codes are used to transmit data between the CPU and input and output devices, and between CPUs of different computers. Some codes are limited in the number of characters they can transmit; some do not contain parity checks.

BAUDOT PAPER TAPE CODE.   This code, shown in Figure 7.7, was developed by a French engineer, Jean Baudot, for use in telegraph communication. It has five intelligence channels. Two sets of 32 characters allow a total of 64 characters to be transmitted. A special combination of

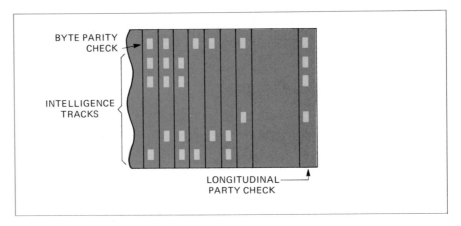

FIGURE 7.6 LONGITUDINAL PARITY

characters, called shift codes, identifies each set. The Baudot code has no parity check. A row of small sprocket holes in the tape does not contain data, but is used to drive the tape through a tape feeder.

TWX PAPER TAPE CODE.   This code, shown in Figure 7.8, is an extension of the Baudot five-channel code. It consists of eight channels. Six are intelligence channels, the seventh is for the parity check, and the eighth is an end-of-line control bit. This code is used extensively by telegraph and Teletype users. With the proper decoding device, these tapes may be used for computer input.

AMERICAN STANDARD CODE FOR INFORMATION INTERCHANGE (ASCII). This code, shown in Figure 7.9, consists of seven intelligence channels and an eighth check-bit channel. The channels are numbered 1, 2, 3, 4, 5, 6, 7, 8. It resembles the TWX code but makes more efficient use of the channels. Since it uses seven channels for intelligence, it can represent 128 charaters. (This code was formerly referred to as USASCII, United States of America Standard Code for Information Interchange.) One of the two most widely used codes for transmitting data to computers, ASCII is also used for data transmission between many terminals and CPUs.

EXTENDED BINARY CODED DECIMAL INTERCHANGE CODE (EBCDIC). This code, shown in Figure 7.10, is an extension of the ASCII code. It has nine tracks: eight for intelligence and one for parity check. It is capable of representing 256 characters. It allows both upper- and lower-case characters, many special symbols, and control characters to be transmitted. EBCDIC coding system was originally used by IBM in its 360 series computers. It is one of the two codes most widely used for data transmission.

FIGURE 7.7 BAUDOT PAPER TAPE CODE

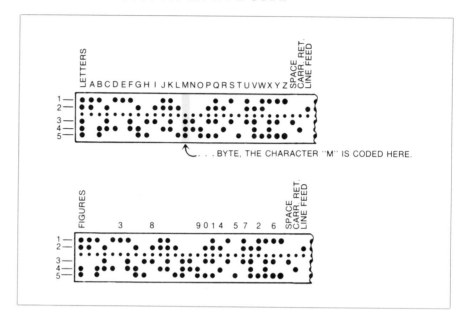

EBCDIC possesses one major advantage over other codes. It allows two numbers to be packed into one byte, thereby increasing efficiency and storage capabilities. Since eight intelligence tracks are available, two BCD numbers (each using only four tracks) can be stored in one byte. The ninth track holds the check bit to maintain accuracy. This system is very efficient for transmitting and storing large amounts of numerical data.

FIGURE 7.8 TWX PAPER TAPE CODE (SIX-BIT, EIGHT-CHANNEL CODE)

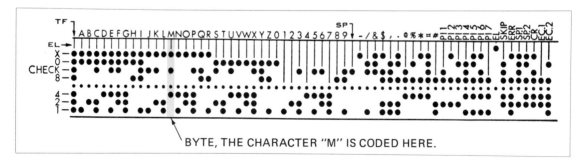

BYTE, THE CHARACTER "M" IS CODED HERE.

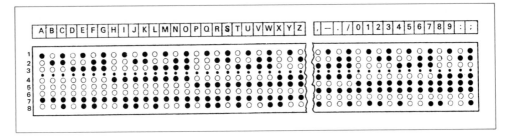

FIGURE 7.9   AMERICAN STANDARD CODE FOR
             INFORMATION INTERCHANGE (ASCII) (SEVEN-BIT,
             EIGHT-CHANNEL CODE)

FIGURE 7.10   EXTENDED BINARY CODED DECIMAL INTERCHANGE
              CODE (EBCDIC) (EIGHT-BIT, NINE-TRACK CODE)

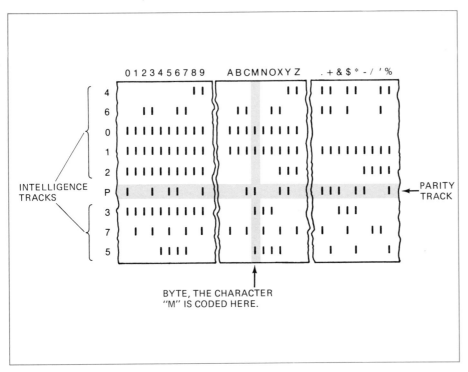

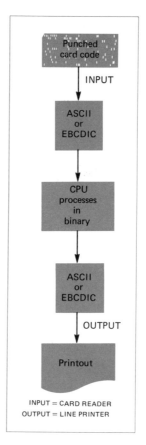

FIGURE 7.11   DATA CONVERSION WITHIN THE COMPUTER

Data Conversion Data are converted into different codes during the cycle of input, manipulation by the CPU, output, and storage. The computer will automatically handle the conversion. Human operators need only feed data to computers as punched cards or coded on paper or magnetic tape. (See Figure 7.11.)

Input devices accept source data recorded in one of several representation codes. Card readers, for example, accept data punched in the 12-bit Hollerith code or System/3 code. They convert these hole combinations to electronic pulses for input to the CPU. Data recorded on magnetic tape in ASCII or EBCDIC are converted to electronic pulses and entered directly to the CPU.

The CPU automatically converts input data into binary for manipulation. When processing is completed, the CPU automatically reconverts the data into ASCII or EBCDIC for outputting. The output device will convert it back to the proper form. For storing on tape, the electronic pulses will be converted to magnetic bits in ASCII or EBCDIC. Data are output by a line printer in a form understandable to humans.

KEY TERMS   ASCII   EBCDIC
             Base   Hexadecimal notation
             Baudot code   Intelligence
             BCD   Parity check
             Binary notation   Place value
             Channel   Track
             Check bit   TWX paper tape code
             Decimal notation

EXERCISES   1. What is meant by the term "base 10 system"?
             2. List three advantages and several disadvantages of binary representation.
             3. Give the decimal equivalents of the following binary numbers:

                      1101   0010   0110   0111

             4. Write the binary equivalent for each of the following decimal numbers:

                      16   8   3   32

             5. Add the following binary numbers. Perform the work in binary.

                      0010   1111   1010
                     +0110   +0010   +1110

             6. In what ways are the rules of binary addition similar to those for decimal addition?
             7. Convert the following hexadecimal values to decimal numbers:

                      7BC0   ABC1   111C4

             8. Convert the following decimal numbers to hexadecimal values:

                      1,356   17,000   299

             9. What is the function of the parity check? How does the parity system detect the loss of a bit?
             10. How do even and odd parity differ?
             11. What is the function of longitudinal parity?
             12. Refer to Figure 7.9. Write your name in ASCII code.
             13. Obtain a piece of punched paper tape from your instructor or data center. Compare it with the illustrations in this chapter. Label and translate 20 characters punched into it.
             14. Using the same tape as above, determine whether even or odd parity is used. Redraw the code, changing the parity.

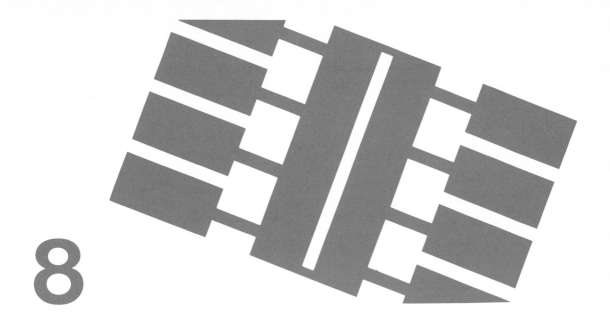

8

THE CENTRAL PROCESSING UNIT: FUNCTIONS AND COMPONENTS

The central processing unit (CPU) is the heart of the processing system. It is that portion of the computer that contains the control, main storage, and logic units. It is designed to make arithmetic calculations and logical decisions. The CPU is capable of storing a program and executing it, line-by-line, on data. It controls and schedules the overall operation of the computing system.

The CPU is linked to the I/O devices through I/O channels (discussed in Chapters 6 and 10). Data from tape readers, magnetic storage devices, card read punches, etc., flow to the CPU through these channels. Data are processed in the CPU and results are fed back through the channels for output on the I/O devices.

The CPU uses registers, primary storage areas, and secondary storage areas to provide storage and working space for all data during the processing of a program.

This chapter is concerned with the three principal functions of the CPU: primary storage, arithmetic and logic, and control. Secondary storage is explained in the next chapter. This chapter also includes a brief discussion of how the CPU executes programming instructions.

PRIMARY STORAGE

Primary storage is the basic means of storing data within the CPU itself. It holds a special program called the operating system (discussed in Chapter 14), which controls the computer. Primary storage acts as the main memory and holds source programs, data files, and frequently used routines; it also provides a temporary work area for data produced by intermediate calculations and manipulation. Data ready for output are held in primary storage in the format required by the source program.

Primary storage (sometimes called core storage) is a reusable storage area. It is like a huge scratch pad, instantaneously available to the computer for saving directions, answers, and data, but easily erased by reading new data into the same area, on top of the old.

Advantages and Limitations

Data can be retrieved from primary storage in millionths of a second. Access is random (direct), and each item is located by its address.

Primary storage is limited by the physical composition of the CPU. This storage area must be shared by the control program of the CPU, the programming instructions, and the data for processing.

Small computers may provide only 4K bytes of core storage. That is, only 4,096 characters can be held in primary storage at one time. Larger computers may have from 64K to more than a million bytes of primary storage.

A large primary storage capacity is expensive because data are stored in physical hardware. Each byte of data in primary storage must be held in a device, such as a ferrite core, flux ring, plate wire, or semiconductor.

Since data are held in fixed locations within the CPU, they cannot be physically removed, filed, or carried from the computer. Data can be transmitted to other computers, but information in primary storage remains tied to the physical hardware.

A large primary storage capacity allows many instructions and a large amount of data to be held for instantaneous use. This means that complex programs can be processed faster. Smaller machines require a complex program to be broken into sections or modules, which are executed one at a time.

Virtual Storage Memory

Some computer systems overcome the physical space limitations of primary memory by using an arrangement called virtual storage memory. (See Figure 8.1.) This system is composed of the computer's physical primary storage (real memory) and a disk storage device (referred to as its virtual memory or apparent memory). In operation, the full disk storage capacity can be drawn upon as if it were part of the computer's primary memory.

When a job is run, all instructions and data in the program are assigned to a storage space on the disk memory device. Then small parts of the

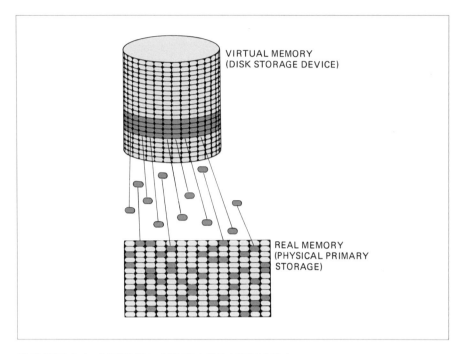

FIGURE 8.1 VIRTUAL STORAGE MEMORY

program are transferred to primary memory and executed, one by one, until the entire program has been processed. Each of these parts is called a page.

The process of swapping pages of information between the virtual storage device (disk) and the real memory is handled automatically by the computer's operating system.

This system allows extremely large programs to be processed in a relatively small machine. A computer with only 256K bytes of primary memory can appear to have 16 million bytes.

Types of Media
A variety of primary memory media have been employed in computers. These include ferrite core storage, magnetic film, semiconductor, magnetic bubble, and charge-coupled devices. (See Figure 8.2.) The most common primary memory system in use is the ferrite core, which is magnetized to represent data. The semiconductor memory system, which uses transistors to store data, is increasing in utility. Other media, such as bubble memory, plated wire, and charge-coupled devices, are under development. They promise greater memory capacity and faster data transfer, at a lower cost and in less physical space.

RAM and ROM Memory
Memory systems may be divided into two distinct categories: Random Access Memory (RAM) and Read Only Memory (ROM). In RAM, data can be written

FIGURE 8.2 PRIMARY STORAGE MEDIA

(A) MAGNETIC CORE MEMORY

(B) MONOLITHIC MEMORY

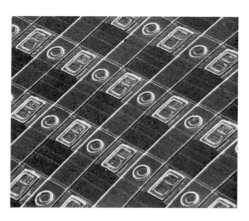

(C) THIN FILM MEMORY

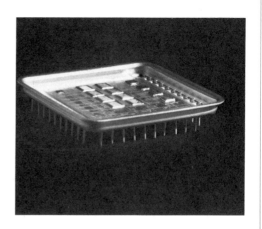

(D) LSI MEMORY

into memory (recorded) and later read out (played back). It is much like recording and playing back on a home tape recorder. The RAM system is used in the computer's primary memory to hold data that will change, source programs, data sets, and so on.

The ROM type of memory system provides only readout (playback) capacity. (See Figure 8.3.) Important instructions or programs are permanently written into the memory device during manufacture. They can be read out as often as desired, but new data or programs cannot be recorded over the old. This is similar in concept to a domestic phonograph recording, which can be played many times but not changed.

Read Only Memory is generally used to hold a set of instructions that are frequently needed. For example, a control program, a language compiler, mathematical routines, or conversion routines may be implemented in ROM memory.

Ferrite Core Storage

ORGANIZATION.   Ferrite core storage is composed of thousands of cores, strung on wires to form a network. The cores are tiny doughnut-shaped objects pressed from iron ferrite. [See Figure 8.4(A).] Each core may be magnetized in either the clockwise or counterclockwise direction. Cores magnetized in the clockwise direction may represent the "zero" state; in the

FIGURE 8.3 READ ONLY MEMORY (ROM)

FIGURE 8.4   (A) FERRITE CORE; (B) CORE PLANES

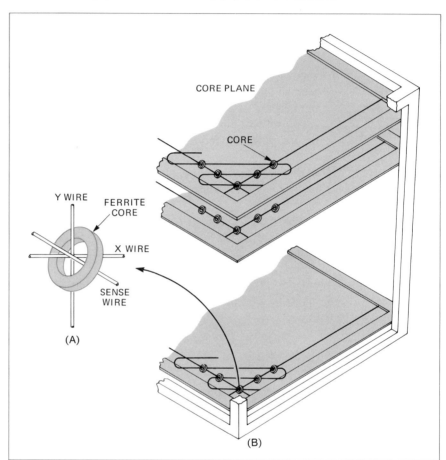

counterclockwise direction, the "one" state. Once charged, the cores hold their direction of magnetism, or flux, until new data are read in.

Each core is capable of holding one bit of data. The core networks are called planes. A flat surface with a core arrangement on it is a core plane. [See Figure 8.4(B).] The core planes are stacked in groups of eight or nine, depending upon the particular computer. If data are stored in the EBCDIC code (mentioned in Chapter 7), nine planes are necessary to allow eight bits of intelligence and one parity to be stored. A column of bits representing one character is a byte.

The ASCII code system requires eight planes to allow for seven intelligence bits and one parity bit.

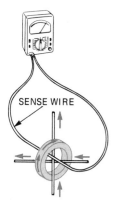

SENSE WIRE

READING DATA IN. Each core is strung on a group of wires, called the X wire, Y wire, and sense wire, as shown in Figure 8.4. To read in a bit of data, a specific core is magnetized by passing a small current of electricity through the X and Y wires. (See Figure 8.5.) Half the current is sent through the X wire; half through the Y wire. Only the core at the intersection of the two wires receives the full current and will be magnetized or selected.

READING DATA OUT. Data can be read out of core and copied into another area by sensing which cores have been magnetized. Basically, this is done by passing a voltage through the X and Y wires of each core, in succession, and monitoring the output on the sense wire. A charged core, receiving a full current through the X and Y wires, emits a weak electrical pulse, and the sense wire relays the pulses out of the core plane. Only one wire is required to sense all the cores on one plane. (See figure at left.) The data in the core do not change when they are read out. They will remain the same until the direction of magnetic flux is changed by another pulse.

Data flow from the cores in serial fashion, forming a pulse train. Each pulse represents one bit of data. A group of pulses represents a byte or

FIGURE 8.5   SELECTING A CORE

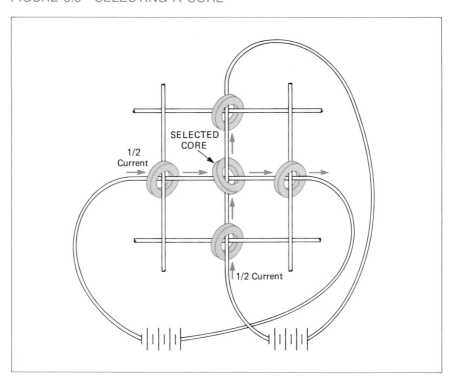

Computerized Job Finding

Within a few years, you will be able to walk into a U.S. Employment Service office and feed an application into a computer. Zap—it will tell you where in the United States there is a job for you.

The Labor Department is involved in an effort to develop and install a nationwide computer system to match job seekers with job openings. The computer will also be used to speed the processing of unemployment insurance claims.

The job-matching system has already been tried in a few cities on an experimental basis. In Portland, Oregon, for example, employers can place a job order with the local government employment office and have its computer search the file for compatible applicants. On the other hand, individuals looking for a job can walk in, give a clerk information about their work experience, education, and skills, and receive a printout of appropriate job openings.

When the system is completely in operation, it will provide instant or overnight service in job referrals on a local and state-wide basis. When all states are tied in, a job seeker in Boston will be able to learn about a job opening in San Francisco.

The job-matching system is scheduled to be completed nation-wide in 1981. However, by 1979 the computers will be able to process unemployment insurance claims, providing local offices immediately with determinations of applicants' eligibility. The total cost is estimated at more than $100 million.

SOURCE: "Computerized Job Finding Slated Within Five Years" (Associated Press), *Los Angeles Times,* May 14, 1976. Reprinted by permission of The Associated Press.

character. These pulses are read into another work or storage area or sent to an output device.

A ferrite core retains its magnetic charge even when the electrical power is lost or turned off. Therefore, the data that are in storage when a machine is turned off will still be there when it is turned on again.

Semiconductor Storage   CONSTRUCTION. Several types of semiconductor memory systems are employed in computers. These include Metal Oxide Silicon (MOS) transistors and bipolar transistors. These systems use the two-state characteristics of transistors as switching devices to store data in binary form. Thousands of

FIGURE 8.6   METAL OXIDE SEMICONDUCTOR (MOS) MEMORY

semiconductors are manufactured in groups or arrays on a single, small chip. (See Figure 8.6.)

READING DATA IN.   Data in the form of electrical pulses are fed to the semiconductor memory devices to place them in either the 1 or 0 state. They will remain in that state until changed by another pulse.

READING DATA OUT.   Data are read out of these devices by sensing their electrical characteristic or the state of each semiconductor in the array. One of the limitations of semiconductor memory is its volatility. If the electrical power is removed from the semiconductors, they will lose the data in storage. Thus, standby electrical power must be provided at all times with semiconductor memory. Even a short power failure or interruption will cause loss of data.

Storage   The primary storage areas of the CPU are divided into smaller sections, called
Addresses   storage modules. These modules, in turn, are broken down into small units

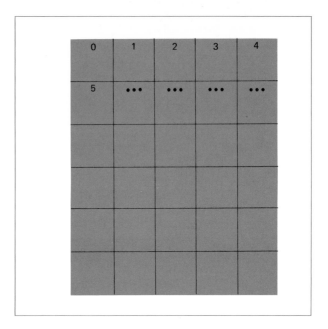

FIGURE 8.7 STORAGE ADDRESSES

composed of groups of storage locations, each of which has its own address. (See Figure 8.7.) Usually the first position or location in storage is assigned the address 0. The next one is 1, the next 2, and so on.

The number of bits in a storage location varies from one computer to another. All the bits stored in one location are treated as a unit and form a computer word. In some machines, each word has its own address. These machines are word addressable. Other machines are byte addressable. In these, a word is addressed by the location of the first byte of the word.

A computer is built to store fixed- or variable-length words. Some computers can handle both. In a computer with fixed-length words, all words have the same number of bytes. In a machine using variable-length words, the words will vary in the number of bytes they contain. (See Figure 8.8.)

We address primary storage in a manner similar to the way we address apartment buildings. The storage module can be compared to an apartment building where one street address refers to the whole building and all the apartments in it. Each apartment in the building is the same as a storage location (or word) with an individual number or letter, A, B, C, and so on. In a fixed-length building, each apartment would have the same number of rooms. In a variable-length building, apartments would have different numbers of rooms.

In a computer with fixed-length words, every address refers to the same number of bytes. For example, assume a machine has a fixed word length of

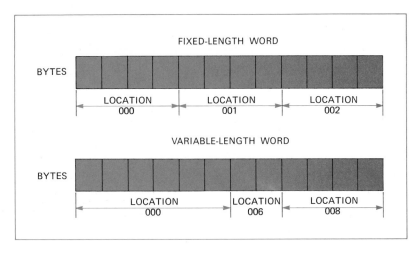

FIGURE 8.8 WORD LENGTH

six bytes and uses an eight-bit code. Data from location 120 are needed. The CPU will go to that address and read out the data from the next 48 locations (6 bytes $\times$ 8 bits = 48). The information stored in that location may be a two-digit number and fill only two of the available six bytes. The remaining four bytes will be unused storage space and may contain leading zeros.

In a computer with variable word length, each byte has its own address. It would be very time consuming and tedious to address each letter in a name, or each digit in a number individually. It is much more convenient to tell the computer that ten bytes in locations 205 to 214 belong together and form a word. To do this, it is necessary to signal the computer when the end of the word has been reached. One method is to use a word mark or control bit in the data representation code. It is turned on only in the last byte of each word.

A second method is to indicate in the programming instructions the number of bytes in each word. Some systems allow variable-length words to include as many as 256 bytes. Thus, one or two sentences, containing up to 256 characters, punctuation marks, and spaces, can be considered one word and can be easily referred to by one address and manipulated by one instruction.

Some computers can operate with both fixed-length and variable-length words, depending on the language used or the programmer's instructions.

DATA IN STORAGE. A clear distinction exists between the data stored in a given location and the address itself. Let us return to the apartment building analogy. An apartment has an address and an occupant. They are not the same thing. The address refers to the location and does not change, but the occupant may change from time to time. Although an occupant can be located by his or her address, the address refers to an apartment and not to a person.

In the same way, a computer address does not refer to data stored in a location, but to the location itself. (See Figure 8.9.) The data it holds will change, but the address will not. Each storage location is, in effect, a reusable container. Different data may be read in and out of one location several times during a program. To call data from storage, the programmer need not know the actual contents of the data, only the address at which they are stored. The circuitry will locate the value stored in the location and relay it for processing.

The ability to locate data from their address gives the CPU much of its power. The programmer can instruct the computer to perform a series of operations on the contents of an address. In this way, a series of operations can be repeated many times during a job, each time on a new piece of data read into a particular storage location. The programmer has only to instruct the computer to store the data in the proper location.

To illustrate, suppose a programmer directs the computer to read two numbers into locations 013 and 214. The numbers are to be added, and the answer is to be sent to location 041 and then printed out on the line printer.

FIGURE 8.9   DATA IN STORAGE LOCATIONS

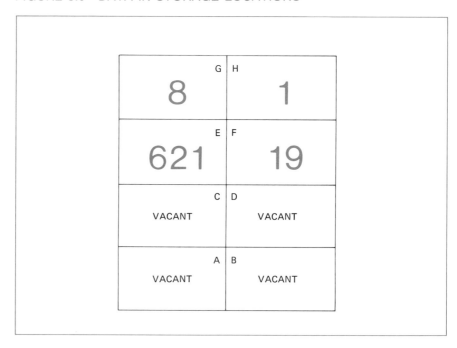

Then the computer is to return to the beginning of the program and repeat the cycle on two more numbers.

When executing the program, the CPU will first read the two numbers, (say 109 and 216) into storage locations 013 and 214. Later the CPU will call them and feed them to the arithmetic unit for processing. Here they will be added and the result fed to location 041. Instructions then direct the computer to print out the contents of location 041 on the line printer. The number 325 will be printed out. Then the CPU will begin the next cycle, bring in two new numbers (say 382 and 418), and read them into locations 013 and 214. It will add, send the result (800) to location 041, and print it out. The cycle will be repeated until all numbers have been added.

ARITHMETIC AND LOGIC UNIT

The arithmetic and logic unit (ALU) section of the CPU performs the arithmetic and logic functions of the system. The ALU is equipped with a series of registers and gates. These devices perform various logical comparisons and mathematical operations in binary.

Registers   The CPU contains a group of storage areas called registers, which are similar in concept to core storage but hold only a few bytes of data, or a limited number of words. (See Figure 8.10.) Registers serve different purposes. Some are used by the control function of the CPU, some by the arithmetic and logic unit, and others serve as temporary storage devices. Data can be read in and out of these registers in millionths of a second.

Registers are electrical circuits composed of semiconductor transistors or magnetic cores. Being electronic devices, transistors are either on or off, in either an emitting or a nonemitting state. An emitting transistor represents the value "1" stored in that position. A nonemitting transistor represents the value "0." Similarly, magnetic cores can represent "1"s or "0"s.

FIGURE 8.10 CORE REGISTER

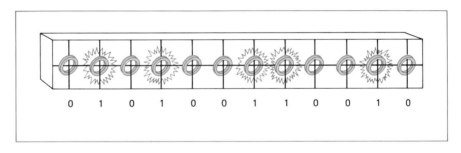

General- and
Special-Purpose
Registers

The system of registers is an indispensable part of the CPU and gives it its ability to "process" data. The electrical changes that take place in the transistors or cores of the registers allow the computer to count, store data, compare electrical pulses, and perform mathematics. There are two kinds of registers: general purpose and special purpose.

A general-purpose register can be used for many functions in addition to those operations performed by the special-purpose registers. For example, general-purpose registers will index (act as a counter), act as an accumulator, and hold addresses or data for processing. In most systems, general-purpose registers are available to the programmer.

Special-purpose registers are reserved by the CPU for specific jobs. They include the address register, instruction register, storage register, and accumulator register.

INSTRUCTION REGISTER.   One instruction at a time is pulled from primary storage by the CPU and placed in registers for execution. The instruction register holds the part of an instruction that indicates what process is to be performed.

ADDRESS REGISTER.   The address register holds the part of an instruction that indicates where the data to be used are stored.

STORAGE REGISTER.   A storage register acts as a temporary storage area for data awaiting processing. (Actual processing does not take place in storage registers—they are more like waiting rooms where data needed for the next step in an operation are kept ready.) While part of the CPU is operating on one piece of data, another part can retrieve the next piece from memory and have it ready in a readily accessible storage register.

ACCUMULATOR REGISTER.   The accumulator register holds results of calculations. Accumulator registers hold binary bits of data, such as numbers, sums, quotients, and products. Each time a new value is added to a running total, for example, it is added to the accumulator register, updating the total. When the calculations have been completed, the results in the accumulator register can be read into storage or another register for further processing.

Mathematical
and Logical
Circuitry

The mechanics of addition, subtraction, and logical decisions are performed by a group of specialized circuits within the ALU. These circuits use gates. Gates are transistors and diodes wired in special arrangements that open different pathways, depending on the pulses they receive.

Many kinds of gates wired in different arrangements and combinations are used in a CPU. Gates are capable of adding and subtracting binary numbers; comparing values to determine whether a value is equal to, or greater than, another; etc. Gates are the heart of the computer's mathematical

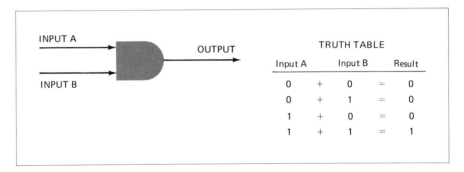

FIGURE 8.11 AND GATE

and logical ability. Some common CPU gates are the AND gate, OR gate, and NOR gate.

The use of gates can be illustrated with a brief description of the AND gate, which is used in performing addition. This gate is a special transistor circuit with two input wires and one output wire. If pulses are sent to both input wires, the transistor conducts a signal to the output wire. If a pulse is received by only one of its input wires, it will not conduct a signal. An AND gate will trigger its output wire *only* if pulses are sent to both input wires simultaneously. (See Figure 8.11.)

Some gates emit a pulse only when one input wire receives a pulse. Other gates continue to emit pulses until they are stopped by a pulse to an input wire.

To perform a mathematical operation, the numbers to be processed will be called out from storage and fed into registers. Electrical pathways are set up that feed the pulses representing these numbers to the proper gates. The output from the gates passes through other circuitry and into accumulator registers. From there, the pulses may go back to storage, be used for other processing, or perhaps sent to an output device.

Logical decisions are made in gates similar to the mathematical gates described above. Logical gates test the voltage from one value against another. They can indicate whether a given value is equal to, greater than, or less than the other value. This result can then be used by the CPU to branch control to one of several paths specified in a program.

CONTROL UNIT

The last major element of the CPU is the control unit. This part of the CPU includes a cycle clock, counters, decoding circuits, and other components necessary to control the overall operation of the CPU. The control unit schedules the movement of data within the CPU and directs the movement of data between primary memory, registers, and the ALU. It also governs the instruction and execution cycles described later in this chapter.

Cycle Clock   A major component of the CPU is the cycle clock, which sends out pulses at the rate of billions of cycles per second. These electrical pulses are sent to parts of the CPU to control its operations and timing. The pulse causes electrical circuits to open or close. Completed circuits create new paths for the pulse to follow and, in turn, these open other paths. All operations of the CPU are actually only a matter of different paths that the circuitry opens. Each change in the electrical condition within the CPU is in time with, and in response to, the pulses from this clock. Each step the computer takes to solve a problem is governed by this internal clock.

Counters   CPUs contain modules called counters, which have only one function: to count and remember the number of pulses sent to them. They are not mechanical devices, but groups of transistors and diodes arranged in a "flip-flop" circuit. (See Figure 8.12.) Flip-flop circuits increase the count by one each time they receive an electrical pulse.

A transistor in a flip-flop circuit reverses its electrical state when a pulse is received. If it is already conducting and is fed another pulse, it passes the current on to the next transistor and changes to a nonconducting state.

At the beginning of the counting cycle, all transistors are set to zero and are nonconducting. The first pulse turns on the first transistor (creating a binary 1). The second pulse causes it to flip flop, turn on the next transistor, and turn off (creating a binary 2). The next pulse turns on the first transistor again (creating binary 3), and so on.

Counters can work in a positive or negative direction. They are controlled by the CPU and used for specific functions during the processing of a job. For example, counters are used to keep track of the number of times a given series of steps is carried out. If the computer is to repeat a cycle, say 100 times, the counter will add one each time a cycle is completed. When the counter reaches 100, the computer will go on to the next instruction. Or if a number is to be multiplied by itself (raised to a power)—for example, increase from 10^0 to 10^6, a counter will increase each time the number is multiplied, until the limit 6 has been reached.

Counters also keep track of instructions. Instructions are assigned consecutive storage spaces in primary storage. The instruction counter will be indexed to the address of the first instruction. This counter will increase each time the CPU processes an instruction, indicating the address of the next instruction to be processed.

Suppose a series of 30 instructions is held in primary storage in positions 000 to 029, as shown in Figure 8.13. A counter is set to 000, the address of the first instruction. The CPU will call the contents of storage space 000 and

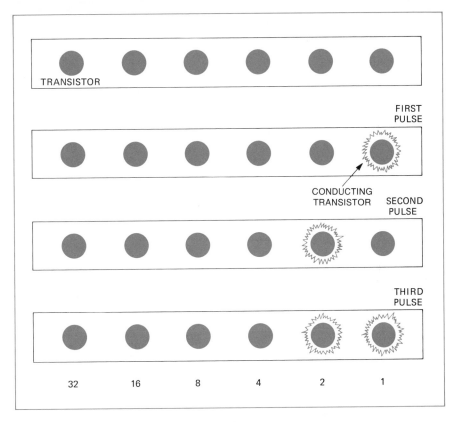

FIGURE 8.12   FLIP-FLOP COUNTER

perform the operations directed by the instruction. Meanwhile, the counter will increase and equal 001. When the CPU is ready, it checks the counter to learn the location of the next instruction. Then this instruction is called and executed, and the counter again increases by 1. This procedure will continue until all 30 instructions have been processed.

Decoder   A decoder is an electronic device in the CPU that sets up an electrical pathway in response to a specific code.

Operation decoders convert an instruction into the electrical paths or circuits that will perform the proper operation. For example, suppose the computer is directed to perform addition. Say that in the computer language being used, the word ADD is the code for addition. In binary, ADD might be expressed as 0101 and 1010. This string of binary bits is sent to a decoder. The decoder senses the bit pattern and prepares the circuitry that performs addition. It will allocate storage registers to hold the numbers to be added and the sum.

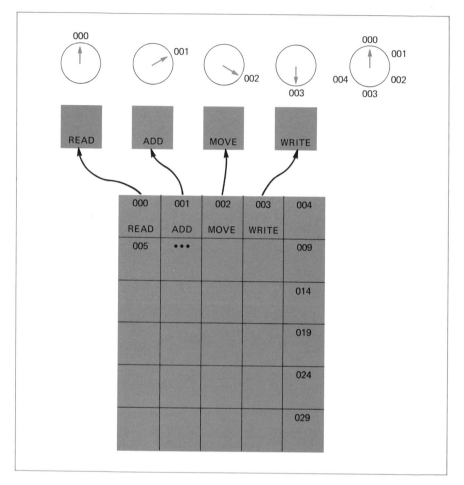

FIGURE 8.13   ADDRESS COUNTER FOR INSTRUCTIONS

Command decoders prepare the proper pathways for program instructions that have been input from the console. Other decoders convert expressions from a code to a more easily understood form. For example, decoders convert binary strings to their decimal equivalents.

Encoders are similar devices that convert an expression into a coded form. For example, they will change a decimal number into its binary value for use by the CPU.

INSTRUCTION AND EXECUTION CYCLES

The previous sections of this chapter discussed the individual parts of the CPU and their functions. All components are electrical devices that operate only when they receive a signal from another electrical component or from the program. The end result of all this activity is to process the job. The CPU takes the series of pulses representing data from a payroll or sales orders, for example, moves them around, changes their order, and restructures the data into another form.

The computer cannot perform any of these activities on its own. It must be fed a list of the operations to be performed. These directions trigger the circuitry needed to process the job. Some of these instructions are from the control program stored in the CPU.

Other instructions are prepared by the programmer to fit the needs of the particular job. These programming instructions are entered into storage units of the CPU and stored in consecutive storage locations.

Programming Instructions Computer instructions have two basic parts: the operation code and the operand.

INSTRUCTION:

OPERATION CODE   OPERAND

The operation code (op code) tells the control unit what function is to be performed and the computer prepares the circuitry that performs that function. ADD, SUBTRACT, MOVE DATA, and COMPARE are typical operations.

Sidney Harris

The operand indicates the location of the data to be operated on.
Most instructions will use two operands called OPA and OPB. The data
represented by OPA and OPB may be manipulated in different ways. OPB will
be subtracted from OPA. OPA will be added to OPB. OPB will be stored in
the location indicated by OPA, etc. How an instruction with two operands
will look is shown below.

INSTRUCTION:

OP CODE	OPA	OPB
SUB	BAL	PAY

In this case, SUB is the code for the operation that is to be performed.
BAL is the location of the first piece of data; and PAY, the location of the
second piece of data. When the computer executes the above instruction, it
will perform the activity directed by OP CODE on the data indicated as OPA
and OPB.

Machine Cycles The procedure for executing programming instructions involves two cycles,
which are synchronized with the pulses coming from the cycle clock. These
cycles are the instruction (I) cycle, which sets up circuitry to perform a
required operation, and the execution (E) cycle, during which the operation
is actually carried out.

Computers alternate between the two cycles millions of times per second,
in time with the pulses from the cycle clock. The first cycle is always the
instruction cycle, and it is followed by the execution cycle. The time spent
on the instruction cycle is called I time; that spent on the execution cycle,
E time.

During the instruction cycle, the computer locates the instruction in
storage and places it in a storage register. The operation code is sent to the
instruction register and the operand to the address register. The operation
decoder converts the op code into the specific circuitry necessary to perform
the job. During I time, the address counter increments, informing the
computer of the location of the next instruction.

The function of the execution cycle is to manipulate the data as specified
in the op code of the instruction. The data specified by the operand is pulled
from storage and sent to the proper devices by the circuitry initiated by the
op code. During the execution cycle, the computer may move data
electronically from primary storage to register, and vice versa. It adds
numbers, moves data, subtracts values, etc. The results of these or other
functions are placed in appropriate registers or storage. After execution is
completed, the cycles are repeated for the next instruction. This continues
until the last instruction in the program has been executed.

KEY TERMS   Computer word   Operand
             Core plane   Page
             Core storage   Primary storage
             Counter   RAM
             Cycle clock   Register
             Decoder   ROM
             Execution cycle   Semiconductor transistor
             Fixed-length word   Storage address
             Gate   Variable-length word
             Instruction cycle   Virtual storage
             Op code   Word mark

EXERCISES   1. Draw a ferrite core and label each of the wires it is strung on.
             2. What are the differences between ferrite core and semiconductor
                storage?
             3. What are the differences between fixed-length and variable-length words?
             4. What functions does primary storage perform?
             5. In what ways does register storage differ from core storage?
             6. Briefly define the functions of the following:
                a. Address register
                b. Instruction register
                c. Storage register
                d. Accumulator register
             7. What is the function of the cycle clock?
             8. What are gates and what is their function?
             9. How is counting performed in the CPU?
            10. Arrange a group of dominos or other objects into a flip-flop counter.
                Increase this counter by manipulating the dominos.
            11. What are the differences between the instruction and execution cycles?
            12. What are RAM and ROM memory systems?
            13. What is the purpose of having two operands in an instruction?
            14. Draw core storage capable of holding 20 bytes of data. Label storage
                positions and assign addresses.
            15. What are the advantages of virtual storage systems?

9

SECONDARY STORAGE SYSTEMS

As discussed in Chapter 8, primary storage is located within the CPU and is directly accessible to it. Data can be read in and out of primary memory in only a few millionths of a second. Secondary storage is located in devices connected to the CPU. These devices are not fully electronic and are therefore slower in operation. However, they provide the CPU with additional, virtually unlimited storage facilities. Data that the CPU will need only occasionally (files, for example) are kept in secondary storage.

Three principal means of secondary storage have been developed and are widely used in data processing: magnetic tape, magnetic disk, and magnetic drum.

ACCESS TIME

The average time required to locate and retrieve a given piece of data from storage is known as the average access time. To illustrate, estimate how long it would take you to look up information in your class notes. Obviously, if your notes are with you in class and consist of only a few pages, it would not take as long as it would if they filled several notebooks and were at home.

The time necessary to locate the required information could be called your access time. Thus, access time is a function of

❶ The location of the data

❷ The amount of data to be searched

❸ The speed of the hardware

Because primary storage is located within the CPU, it naturally has a shorter access time than secondary storage. Primary storage, too, is limited in capacity and thus contains fewer data. These factors combine to make primary storage more readily accessible than secondary storage.

ACCESS METHODS

Two methods are used to access data in secondary storage: sequential access and random access.

Sequential access means that to locate a given piece of data each item in a file must be searched in sequence. Magnetic tape is the most commonly used form of sequential access storage. Data are stored on magnetic tape in the order in which they were recorded. To find a piece of data, the computer rewinds the reel of tape to the beginning and checks each item on the tape until it finds the specified data.

Random access storage devices can retrieve data directly from storage without searching in sequence. To do this, the storage medium is divided into storage locations, and addresses are assigned to each location. Each data record being read into storage is assigned to one of these locations. Given the address, the computer can locate a specific piece of data without searching through every item in the file. Because the computer can go directly to the item in storage, random access is often referred to as direct access. Data stored on random access devices can, of course, be accessed sequentially as well. Magnetic disks and drums are common random access devices.

Understandably, random access devices are faster than sequential access devices.

MAGNETIC TAPE STORAGE

Magnetic tape is a sequential access storage medium. One or more tape units may be placed online with the CPU to give the computer access to data stored on more than one reel of magnetic tape at a time.

FIGURE 9.1   (A) MAGNETIC TAPE
             (B) REEL WITH FILE PROTECTION RING

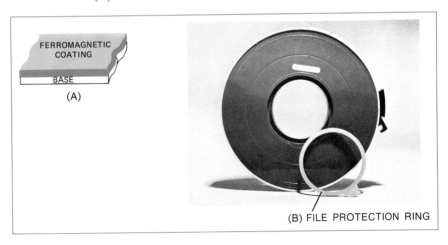

FERROMAGNETIC
COATING

BASE

(A)

(B) FILE PROTECTION RING

The Medium   Magnetic tape is ½-inch-wide plastic ribbon that has been coated with a thin layer of ferromagnetic material and wound on reels (See Figure 9.1.) The two most common reel sizes are 10½ inches in diameter, holding 2,400 feet of tape, and 8½ inches in diameter, holding 1,200 feet.

Data are recorded on the tape in the form of magnetized areas. From 200 to 1,600 bytes can be recorded in one inch of tape, depending on the model.

The tape reel is equipped with a special plastic ring, called the file protection ring. (See Figure 9.1.) When the ring is in place on the reel, new data can be recorded or old data erased from the tape. When the ring is removed, no new data can be recorded over the existing bits of information. The removal of this ring serves as a protection against accidental destruction of important data, since it requires a deliberate act by the computer operator to replace the ring.

Recording   Data are recorded by magnetizing areas of the coating as the tape passes
Data   under a write head. The head converts electronic pulses (representing alphabetic and numeric characters) to magnetized spots on the moving tape. Data are read from the tape by a reverse procedure. The read head senses the magnetized spots on the tape, induces a current in a pickup coil, and converts the magnetic fields to electronic pulses. These pulses, representing coded data, are sent to the CPU for processing. The same head may be used for both writing and reading and is often referred to as read/write head. (See Figure 9.2.)

CODE SYSTEM.   The two code systems commonly used to record data on magnetic tape are the seven-channel BCD alphameric code and the

FIGURE 9.2   RECORDING ON MAGNETIC TAPE

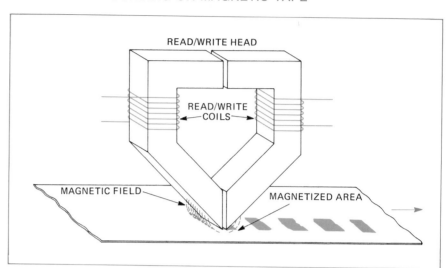

nine-channel EBCDIC code. The BCD alphameric code requires seven tracks of data: six for intelligence and one for a parity check. In the EBCDIC code, nine tracks are used to record data: eight for intelligence bits and the ninth for a parity check bit.

Since magnetic tape is a sequential access medium, the access time, or time required to locate a given record on the tape, is a function of the speed of the drive, the stopping and starting rates, number of records on the tape, and location of the particular record. The average access time for magnetic tape is 5 seconds.

Each reel of magnetic tape contains two indicator marks, which note the beginning of usable recording tape and the end of the reel. These marks are called

load-point mark: beginning of usable tape

end-of-reel mark: end of usable area on tape

The indicators are small pieces of reflective foil bonded to the edge of the tape that are sensed by photocells in the drive mechanism. (See Figure 9.5.)

File Organization

TAPE RECORD.   A tape record is a group of bytes relating to a single transaction. Tape records can be either fixed or variable in length. A record can be only one byte or as many as several thousand. Each record on the tape is separated by a 0.6-inch-wide space, called the inter-record gap (IRG), shown in Figure 9.3. When a computer reads a file, the tape drive comes to a stop after each record, starts again, moves to the next record, stops again, etc. Approximately 0.6 inch of tape will be reeled during the time required for the drive to go from a stopped position to the proper speed for reading or writing.

FIGURE 9.3 INTER-RECORD GAP (IRG)

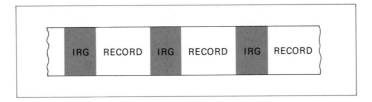

Inter-record gaps occupy space on the tape, however, and fewer bytes of data can be stored on a reel. One method of avoiding this loss is to block or combine several records without IRGs, as shown in Figure 9.4. Each block is separated by an IRG, sometimes called an interblock gap (each record is separated by a group mark inserted during programming).

Tape Files   A reel of tape may contain all or part of the records for one file, or for more than one file.

In any file maintenance procedure, care must be taken to see that the correct files are being processed. Updating the wrong inventory file, or posting charges to the wrong list of customers, would cause many problems. A file identification system is especially important in secondary storage systems, where data are stored in a magnetic code that the human operator cannot read to verify identification.

LABELING.   Data processing techniques have been developed to accurately identify files and prevent errors. These techniques are based upon volume and file labels. The labels are similar to a book's table of contents. They contain information on the files stored on a reel of tape or a disk, and where they are located. Volume and file labels are not physical labels applied to the cell, disk, or reel of tape, but are magnetized bits of information recorded on the media. Physical labels (readable by humans) may also, of course, be applied to the media.

FIGURE 9.4 BLOCKING RECORDS

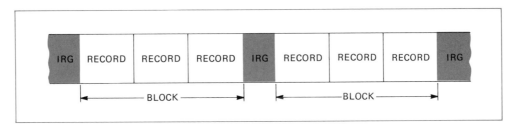

FIGURE 9.5   TAPE FILE ORGANIZATION   (MULTIFILE VOLUME)

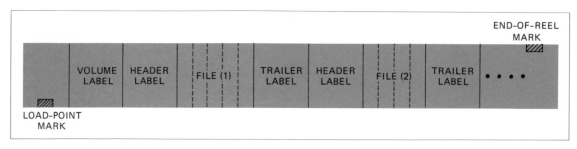

In order to assure that the correct reel of tape is loaded for processing, a system of external and internal labels is used. The external label, readable by the operator, is on the outside of the reel. Internal labels are records on the tape that are readable by the computer and contain identifying information. (See Figure 9.5.) Each reel of tape has a volume label just after the load-point mark to indicate the number of that volume or reel. Next to it, and before each file on the reel, is a header label that identifies the file and gives information such as the file name and the date after which it can be destroyed. (See Figure 9.6.)

The trailer label appears at the end of each file and gives the same information as the header label, along with a count of the blocks of records that are in the file. This is used during processing to assure that all records are processed.

Files that require more than one reel of tape are called *multivolume files.* In these instances, each reel or volume has a volume label and header label that identifies that particular volume and a trailer label that is called an end-of-volume label. The trailer label in the last volume of the file is called an end-of-file label.

When more than one file is recorded on a reel of tape, it is called a *multifile volume.* Each reel has a volume label. Each file on the reel has its own header and trailer labels.

Processing
Tape Files

Magnetic tape can be used for both input and output during processing. Very often, detail files, recorded on magnetic tape or punched cards, will be merged with a master file recorded on magnetic tape, and a new, updated master file will be output on another magnetic tape. A tape device is required for each tape file involved. (See Figure 9.7.)

Figure 9.8 illustrates the updating of a master file where both the master and detail files are on magnetic tape. The input master file contains the master records, each of which includes an account number, account name and address, and old balance. The account numbers are in sequential order. The other input file contains the detail records, which show any transactions that have occurred during the month. Each record shows the account

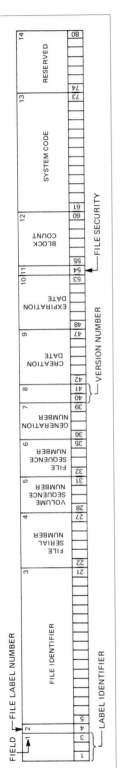

FIGURE 9.6
HEADER LABEL

FIGURE 9.7   MAGNETIC TAPE STORAGE DEVICE

FIGURE 9.8   TAPE FILE PROCESSING

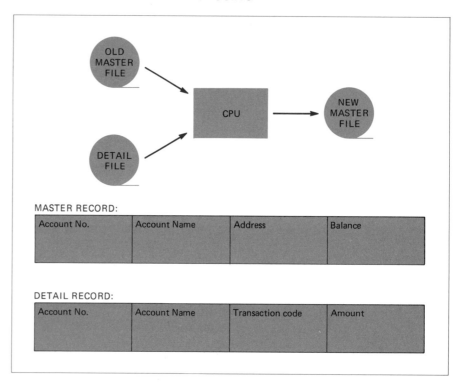

MASTER RECORD:

Account No.	Account Name	Address	Balance

DETAIL RECORD:

Account No.	Account Name	Transaction code	Amount

number and name, the kind of transaction, and the amount. Some accounts may have more than one transaction to be posted; others may have none. The records in the detail file are also in sequential order by account number (having been previously sorted and merged in another operation), with records for the same account grouped together.

The program will merge the two input files and produce an updated master file. Documents such as reports or statements could also be produced at this time. Since tape is a sequential access medium, each record must be read or scanned in turn before the next one in line can be read.

The program will first read a record from the old master file and one from the detail file into primary memory and check to see if the account numbers match. If they do, the transaction is posted. The next detail record is read and the account numbers checked. After all transactions for that account have been posted, the new updated master record is written onto the output tape file. If the account numbers do not match, it is assumed no transactions have occurred that month and the old master record is copied onto the new master file. In either case, the next master record is read in and the process continues until all records have been posted and written.

Many error-checking routines are executed during a program run by either the operating system or the source program. Some routines check the identity

Horror Story

Not too long ago, researchers at Stanford Medical Center in California were horrified to discover that several years of data that were stored on magnetic tape had disappeared. The tapes hadn't disappeared—just the data. The discovery was made when they attempted to retrieve some of the data for analysis but found only "garbage" recorded on the tapes. Even more disturbing was the fact that these tapes were supposed to be ultra reliable. They had been especially developed for storage of important research data and used a fully redundant recording technique for improved reliability. (The data recorded on one side of the tape are duplicated on the other side.)

First, the researchers thought (prayed) that their tape decks were malfunctioning. Not so. Diagnostic checks were made and the tape equipment was working properly. Next, the tapes were examined. Nothing was wrong with them, physically, and in fact, new data could be recorded on them and retrieved without difficulty. They asked others around the Medical Center if they had encountered similar problems (there

are about 50 computers at the Stanford Medical Center). None had.

Then they looked for environmental causes, but there appeared to be none. The temperature and humidity recorders, common to biomedical research facilities, indicated no significant fluctuations. There had been no fires, no chemical accidents, and there was no X-ray or high power electronics gear in use nearby. The tapes had been in their individual boxes, just like the tapes of the other computer facilities in the Medical Center, and these boxes had been neatly stored on the bottom shelves of a cabinet, well out of the way of possible harm. It was a most frustrating puzzle.

Finally, however, the mystery was solved. It seems that the janitor had made his biannual floor polishing rounds, using a heavy duty rotary floor polisher. The magnetic radiation from its massive motor, in proximity to the low shelved tapes, had raised havoc with the bit patterns that had been recorded on the tapes.

The researchers now store their tapes on the top shelves.

SOURCE: Abstracted from "Horror Story," by Jim C. Warren, Jr., *Byte Magazine*, January, 1976.

of the input and output files to assure that the proper tapes have been loaded for reading and writing. Other routines perform blocking and deblocking operations, detect errors in the data set, monitor the reading and writing operations, check sequence of account numbers, and so on.

RIGID DISK SYSTEMS

The Medium   A magnetic disk is a round metal plate coated with a thin layer of ferromagnetic material. Each disk is approximately 14 inches in diameter and has from 200 to 500 concentric tracks per surface. Data are recorded

FIGURE 9.9   DISK PACK

one byte at a time along each track. Depending on the system used, from 3,625 to 7,294 bytes of data can be recorded on each track. Each track holds the same amount of data.

A disk pack is a collection of two or more disks (usually six) mounted on a common shaft. (See Figure 9.9.) The vertical alignment formed by tracks in the same position on all disks in the pack is called a cylinder. (See Figure 9.10.) A disk drive rotates the pack at 2,400 revolutions per minute. Each disk pack weighs about ten pounds and can be removed from the drive mechanism and stored in a filing cabinet.

The disk storage device shown in Figure 9.11 has a group of read/write heads that move in unison. It has a spindle for mounting disk packs, a switch panel, and related circuitry. Disk packs can store from $7\frac{1}{4}$ million to 100 million bytes of data, depending upon the particular system. Average access time ranges from 5 milliseconds to 75 milliseconds. The data-transfer rate from the disk to the CPU ranges from 156,000 bytes per second to over 806,000 bytes per second.

Recording and Accessing Data   Data are recorded on both the top and bottom surfaces of each disk (except for the top and bottom surfaces of the pack). A disk pack with six disks will

FIGURE 9.10   DISK CYLINDER

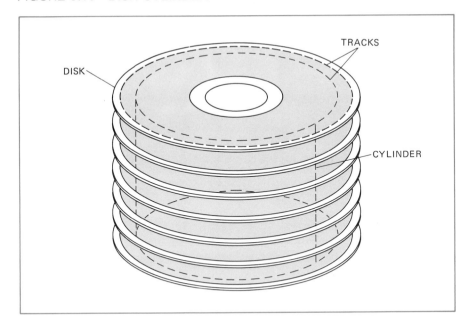

FIGURE 9.11   RIGID DISK STORAGE DEVICE

FIGURE 9.12   DISK ACCESS MECHANISM

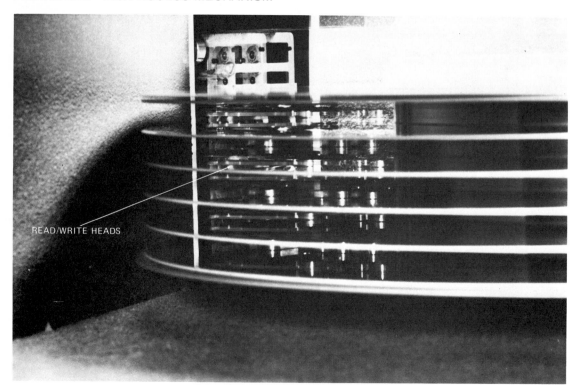

READ/WRITE HEADS

have ten recording surfaces. A group of read/write heads attached to movable arms record and read data on the disk pack. (See Figure 9.12.) The arms move back and forth across the surfaces of the disks. Two read/write heads attached to one arm service the bottom of one disk and the top of another. On some models, the heads may move in unison, with each accessing a track of the same cylinder. On other models, the arms work independently. Disk storage is a random access medium. To locate a given piece of data, the arms advance across the disks to the appropriate cylinder. A read head senses the magnetized areas on the revolving disk and converts them into electronic pulses.

Average access time to locate a given record is approximately 30–60 milliseconds.

Other disks have a fixed read/write head positioned over each track. Data are recorded or read as the track rotates beneath the stationary head. Average access time in this arrangement is 5 milliseconds.

File Organization   DISK RECORD.   Records stored on a disk can be either fixed or variable in length and are separated by gaps. Storage locations on a disk pack are

FIGURE 9.13 COUNT-DATA FORMAT

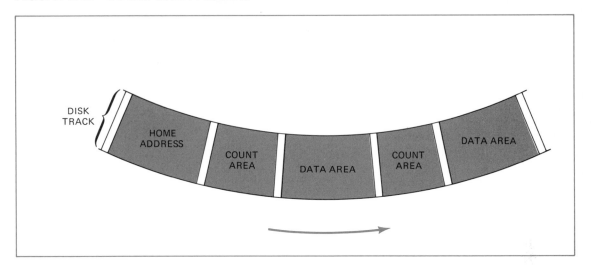

identified by disk surface number, track number, and the physical address of the location on the track.

DISK FILE. There are two formats that can be used to organize records in a disk file: the count-data format and the count-key-data format. In the count-data format, each record is referenced by its physical address—its actual location on the disk track. Each track has one home address area followed by count and data areas for each record (See Figure 9.13.) The home address area identifies the surface and track number. The count area specifies the disk address of the following data area, and the data area holds the information in the record. An end-of-file record appears as the last record. This type of arrangement is used to store records that are accessed either sequentially or directly by their physical location.

The count-key-data format is similar to the count-data method, except that a key area is located between each count and data area. (See Figure 9.14.) The key area contains information that identifies the record that follows it, such as an account number, part number, or employee number. This type of arrangement is used to store records that will be accessed by identification number rather than by address. Since the key areas consume some space on the track, fewer records can be stored than in the count-data format.

File Processing   Records in a disk file can be processed sequentially or randomly, depending on the needs of the program. If the records are being processed sequentially, they are usually blocked to save space and time.

Figure 9.15 illustrates file updating when the master file is recorded on

FIGURE 9.14   COUNT-KEY-DATA FORMAT

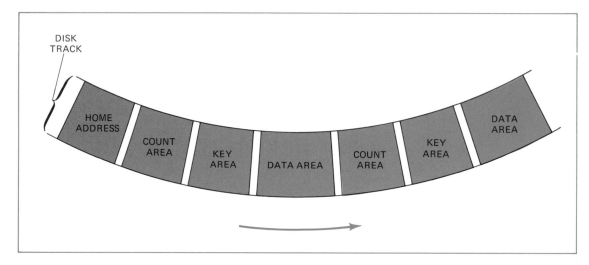

disk and the transaction file is on magnetic tape. The records in the master file are recorded in the count-key-data format with the account number in the key area. Since this is a random access medium, the program reads in each transaction record in turn, goes directly to the master record with the same account number, copies it into primary storage, performs the posting, and writes the new master record over the old. This method is considerably faster than the sequential method necessary in processing tape files.

To prevent loss of information if disks are stolen or damaged, and to have the old record available for reference, a copy of the new master file is sometimes made on magnetic tape and stored in a separate location.

FIGURE 9.15   DISK FILE PROCESSING

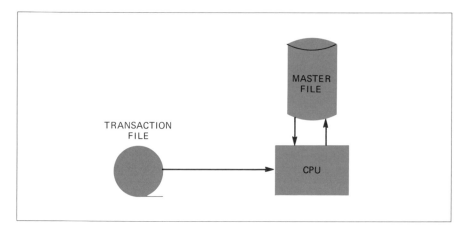

FLEXIBLE (FLOPPY) DISK SYSTEMS

The Medium
The floppy disk is a thin, flexible plastic disk coated with a layer of ferromagnetic material. It is approximately 10 inches in diameter and is housed in a square plastic envelope with an aperture that allows a read/write head to access the disk with the envelope in place.

Floppy disks are similar to phonograph records. They can be removed from the disk drive, filed, mailed, or otherwise easily handled. Their low cost makes them competitive with other storage media. Concentric tracks on one side of a floppy disk can store approximately 400,000 bytes of data.

The flexible disk drive shown in Figure 9.16 has provisions for mounting the flexible disk while it remains in its envelope. The drive rotates the disk under a read/write head. Typically, data may be transferred at the rate of 250,000 bytes per second. The average access time is approximately 6 milliseconds. Flexible disk (floppy) drives are generally smaller and more economical to manufacture than rigid disk systems.

Recording Data
To record data, the disk, still in its envelope, is inserted in a drive. The disk rotates within the envelope at several hundred revolutions per minute, and data are recorded by a read/write head through the aperture in the envelope.

FIGURE 9.16   FLEXIBLE (FLOPPY) DISK DEVICE

Records and files are organized and processed in the same way as with rigid disk systems.

MAGNETIC DRUM STORAGE

Magnetic drum is a random access device similar in principle to the magnetic disk. The magnetic drum usually has a smaller storage capacity than either magnetic tape or disk, but a much faster access time. It is used like a scratch pad to record data that will be used repeatedly during a job, such as programs, operating systems, or mathematical functions.

Physical Description

A metal cylinder coated with a thin layer of ferromagnetic material is mounted on a drum storage drive. There are 200 tracks around the circumference of the drum, numbered 0 to 199. Each of these tracks, in turn, is made up of four subtracks, making a total of 800 tracks. Each of the main tracks will store up to 20,483 bytes of data. Over four million bytes can be stored on a single drum. Access time is 8.6 milliseconds.

Sidney Harris

FIGURE 9.17   DRUM STORAGE DEVICE

The unit shown in Figure 9.17 has a drum drive system, which rotates the drum at 3,500 revolutions per minute. A group of fixed-position read/write heads are located across each track. Data is transferred from the drum to the CPU at the rate of 303,800 bytes per second.

Recording Data

As the drum rotates, data are recorded on its surface by a read/write head (See Figure 9.18.) To retrieve data from the drum, a read head senses the magnetized areas on the rotating drum and converts them to electronic pulses, which are fed to the CPU for processing.

CODE SYSTEM.   Encoded data are recorded on the drum in addressable tracks. The EBCDIC code is used to record data.

DRUM RECORDS.   Storage locations are addressed by track numbers. Drum records may be fixed or variable in length. Records can be from 1 to 65,535 bytes in length.

FIGURE 9.18   DRUM STORAGE PRINCIPLE

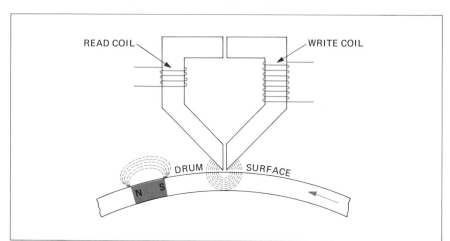

ADVANTAGES AND LIMITATIONS OF SECONDARY STORAGE

Secondary storage is an efficient, compact means of storing large amounts of data in a limited amount of physical space. The cost per byte of storage is much less than for primary storage.

Secondary storage devices, such as magnetic tape, disk packs, or flexible disks are easily carried or filed. Disk packs, for example, can be carried from one computer to another. Magnetic tape reels and flexible disks can be filed in racks, carried about, or sent through the mails. Tape reels can be given to computer centers not directly connected to the CPU. Files are often delivered to other departments for additional processing, or made available to other firms or governmental agencies.

SELECTION OF STORAGE MEDIA

The selection of storage devices largely depends on the needs of the business firm. Firms that have millions of records to be filed will need large secondary storage systems. A firm must also consider whether files are in sequential or random order, the cost of storage systems, data access speeds, and primary storage capabilities. Most computer installations use a combination of media to provide high-speed access for certain files and high-capacity storage for others.

A reel of magnetic tape, which weighs about four pounds, will hold an

TABLE 9.1   COMPARISON OF ACCESS DEVICES

MEDIA	AVERAGE ACCESS TIME	CAPACITY	METHOD
Magnetic tape	5 seconds	40 megabytes	Sequential
Movable head magnetic disk	30 milliseconds	100 megabytes	Random
Magnetic drum	8.6 milliseconds	4 megabytes	Random
Fixed head magnetic disk	5 milliseconds	11.2 megabytes	Random

amount of data equivalent to what could be stored on 200,000 punched cards. Magnetic disk storage is even more efficient. A ribbon of magnetic tape, about 2,400 feet long, costs less than $20. The punched cards needed to store the same amount of data would cost approximately $200.

It also requires less time to load a reel of magnetic tape than to load the equivalent number of punched cards into a computer. There is far less chance of individual records being lost or damaged, and magnetic tape can be erased and reused.

Magnetic tape is, however, subject to breakage, limited to sequential access methods, and has a much slower access time than a magnetic disk.

Magnetic disks can be accessed sequentially or randomly, are less apt to be broken or damaged, and have a fast access time. However, it costs more to store data on magnetic disk than on tape or punched cards, and for this reason magnetic tape is usually used as a backup medium.

Average access times differ among secondary storage devices, but all are slower than primary storage. Capacity also depends on the medium and the particular model being used. Table 9.1 compares average access time, storage capacity, and access methods of several common media.

KEY TERMS

Access time
Blocking
Count-data format
Count-key-data format
Disk pack
End-of-reel mark
Flexible (floppy) disk
Header label
IRG

Load-point mark
Magnetic disk
Magnetic drum
Magnetic tape
Random access
Read/write head
Sequential access
Tracks
Volume label

EXERCISES
1. Define primary and secondary storage.
2. Give three uses for primary storage and three for secondary storage.
3. What features do magnetic disk, tape, and drum storage devices have in common?
4. Explain storage capacity and why it is important in secondary storage systems.
5. Define average access time. What factors affect it?
6. Ask a friend to look up five words in the dictionary at random. Using a stop watch, record his minimum and maximum access times. Calculate the average.
7. What are the advantages of random access storage and sequential access storage?
8. What is the purpose of labeling files?
9. Draw a disk track and indicate several records stored in the count-key-data format.
10. What kinds and types of secondary storage are available on the system in use at your data center?
11. Select one storage device used in your data center. Determine how it is used, what its average access time is, and how it is called in and out by the programmer.

10

DATA OUTPUT

Data output devices convert the electronic pulses emitted by the CPU into a form that can be understood by people or stored for further processing by machines. Output may be printed matter, graphs, video images, sounds, punches on tape or cards, or magnetized areas on tapes or disks. Earlier chapters have discussed many of the principles involved in such output. In this chapter we shall first discuss a number of output devices. Then we shall see how various problems of output are dealt with.

Data output devices may be classified as hard copy or soft copy machines. Hard copy output devices generate a permanent physical copy or printout of the data that may be filed, duplicated, mailed, etc. Examples include punched cards and printed reports and forms. Soft copy output devices provide only a temporary copy of the output data. Examples are spoken words or an image on the face of a cathode ray tube.

Generally, hard copy output devices operate more slowly than soft copy devices, and since they require paper and other supplies, costs are higher. Advantages are that they generate a permanent copy that can be filed, copied, or otherwise manually processed or mailed. Soft copy output is more economical; large volumes of data can be displayed at a low cost.

However, since the output is not permanent, its usefulness for many applications is limited. Computer systems often include a combination of hard and soft copy output devices that can be switched in and out as the program requires.

HARD COPY DEVICES

A variety of hard copy devices provide output in the form of typewritten characters, punched holes, photographic images, and graphs.

Character Printing Sequence
Characters are printed in two ways: serial and parallel. In serial printing, letters are struck one at a time. For example, a line of 100 characters would be printed letter by letter, usually from left to right. The ordinary typewriter, type bar, and type element printers use this principle. Generally, serial printing is not used for high-volume computer output. It is, however, economical from a machine design standpoint and hence used for low-cost or low-volume output systems.

In parallel printing, all characters on a line are struck at the same instant. The type wheel printer uses this principle. To produce a line 100 characters wide, the output device will index 100 type wheels across the page to the proper images. At a signal, 100 hammers will strike the page, forcing it against all the type images at the same instant. Naturally, parallel printing is much faster than serial printing. The following sections discuss some examples of typical hard copy output devices.

Serial Impact Printers
Most typewriters use the type bar principle. Type hammers form the images by striking a ribbon against a sheet of paper. (On each hammer is a character in relief.) Type-bar output is slow and is therefore not suitable for high-volume data processing.

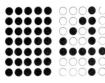

ABCDEFGH
IJKLMNOP
QRSTUVWX
YZ012345
6789-.;8
/◇$+#%@=
(+)

Another method used to print characters is a type element or type ball. (See Figure 10.1.) A set of numbers and characters (called a font) is molded on each type element. To print a character, the element is indexed to the proper position and struck against the ribbon onto the sheet. Type element output is used on some console typewriters and small computers. The type element prints at a speed of up to 30 characters per second—too slow for high-volume computer output. However, the advantage of type element printers is that type sizes and styles can easily be changed by substituting elements.

The device shown in Figure 10.2 uses the type element principle.

Printed characters can also be generated with a wire matrix. (See the figure in the left margin.) A group of 35 wires or rods is arranged in a 5 × 7 matrix pattern. Numbers and characters are formed by selectively striking the ends of the rods or wires. To print the digit "4," for example, the rods that

FIGURE 10.1 TYPE ELEMENT

form the image of the number are struck from behind and forced against the paper and the image is transferred. (A ribbon inserted between the rods and the page provides inking.) Keypunch machines and some computer printers use this principle. (See Figure 10.3.)

A comparatively new method of generating characters uses heat and heat-sensitive paper. Letter forms are generated by heating selected rods in a matrix. When the ends of the selected rods touch the heat-sensitive paper, the image is transferred. Though thermal imaging is relatively slow, it is practical for low-volume output.

The type wheel printer, shown in Figure 10.4, is a fourth method of generating characters. Each type wheel contains a full font of characters. To print a character, the wheel is rotated until the appropriate character is in position. An image is made by a hammer striking the sheet from behind or moving the type wheel forward against the page. One type wheel is used in each print position. Some systems use one wheel, which travels across the page.

FIGURE 10.2

TYPE ELEMENT PRINTER

FIGURE 10.3   WIRE MATRIX PRINTER

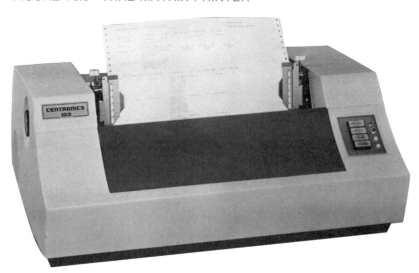

FIGURE 10.4   TYPE WHEEL PRINTER

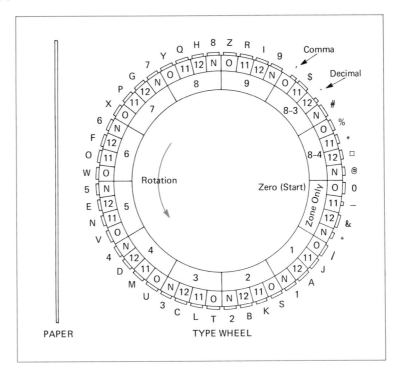

Type wheel printers are faster than type element or type bar machines (they can print 200 to 300 lines per minute). However, they are also too slow for high-speed data output.

High-speed output is possible with a chain printer, illustrated in Figure 10.5. Type slugs are mounted on a moving train, or type chain. Gears move each slug into printing position. A ribbon is placed between the page and the train. To print a character, a hammer behind the paper forces the sheet up against the moving type chain. When the sheet is brought into contact with the moving train, a letter image is transferred to the paper. Chain printers can produce up to 2,200 lines per minute. One or more full fonts of characters are available on each train. Figure 10.6 illustrates a chain-printing machine.

Photographic Printers Photographic techniques can also be used to create output images. (See Figure 10.7.) A beam of light is focused through a rotating disk containing a full font of characters. The image of a character is projected onto a piece of film or photographic paper. The print or negative is developed and fixed, similar to ordinary photographs. This form of output prints out high-quality, letter-perfect images and is often used in bookmaking.

PHOTOTYPESETTER.   The machine shown in Figure 10.8 outputs data as typeset characters on photographic film or paper. It is similar in purpose to

FIGURE 10.5   CHAIN PRINTER MECHANISM

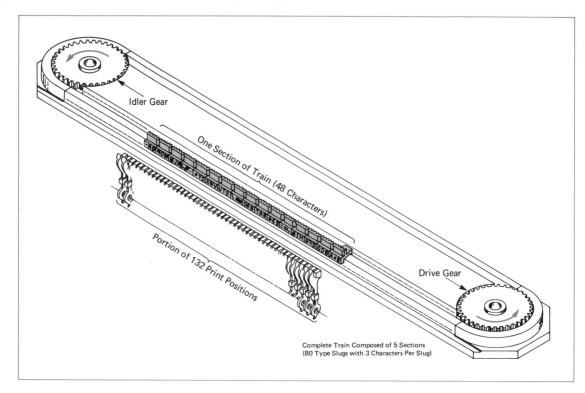

Idler Gear

One Section of Train (48 Characters)

Portion of 132 Print Positions

Drive Gear

Complete Train Composed of 5 Sections
(80 Type Slugs with 3 Characters Per Slug)

the line printer but produces a high quality, letter-perfect image, suitable for reproduction.

The machine is equipped with a paper tape feeder, a photographic exposure system, changeable type matrix, and film-transport mechanism. It is used to set type from computer-generated tape for newspapers, books, etc. The length of the printing line can be varied as needed and can be set justified (even right- and left-hand margins) at speeds up to 30 lines per minute.

Images are formed by passing a beam of light through letter forms on a revolving type disk. The projected image is focused onto sensitized photographic paper or film. The exposed film is processed in a separate unit, and the output can be reproduced by the printing process.

ELECTROSTATIC IMAGING.   Images or letter forms on the face of a cathode ray tube can be made permanent by copying them on a device similar to an ordinary photocopy machine. In the terminal shown in Figure 10.9, pulses from the CPU are sent to both the cathode ray tube and the hard copy machine at the same time.

FIGURE 10.6   CHAIN PRINTER

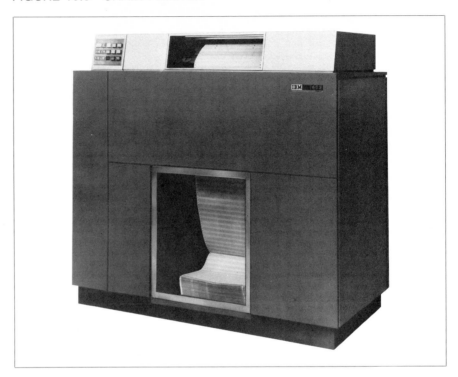

FIGURE 10.7   PHOTOGRAPHIC IMAGING

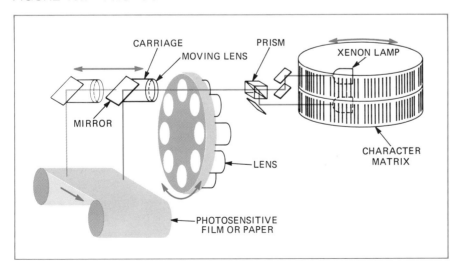

FIGURE 10.8　PHOTOTYPESETTING MACHINE

FIGURE 10.9　CRT TERMINAL WITH HARD COPY OUTPUT

The Computer Goes to Congress

Thanks to a computer, a congressman working in an office can now push a couple of buttons on a television-type device and read a summary of the debate he or she is missing on the House floor.

At the push of a few buttons on the device's keyboard, the screen will display a summary of the day's debate on the House floor. The summary is updated every few minutes, with a lag of no more than 10 minutes from the time the debate takes place.

A gadget attached to the screen can print the summary on a roll of paper. A printer unit has been installed in the House Press Gallery, where newspaper reporters work.

The debate summary is being prepared by a seven-member team, including writers, editors, and two secretaries. It is written on the House floor. The writers paraphrase the debate in short paragraphs every few minutes and send the summary to an editor stationed in a room near the chamber. The editor reviews the summary before it is placed in the computer.

Representative Don Fuqua (Democrat-Florida), chairman of the task force directing the project, spoke about the computer system in glowing terms. "When I'm busy in my office, I can find out what is going on on the floor," he said. "You can cover an hour's debate in two minutes of reading. It gives you a better utilization of your time."

If the machines, which each cost $180 a month, are put into wide use around the Capitol, they may be wired into various government information networks. It then could be possible, for example for a member of Congress or a staff assistant to view on the machine's special television-type screen the Library of Congress card file, the Department of Justice's computerized record of the entire U.S. legal code and Supreme Court decisions, or a digest of every bill pending before the House and Senate.

SOURCE: "Capitol Computer Keeps Congress Plugged In" (Associated Press), *Los Angeles Times*, May 2, 1976.

Computer Output Microfilm (COM) The computer can be used to generate output in the form of microfilm or microfiche. Computer Output Microfilm (COM) units transfer output data from the computer onto standard 4 × 6 inch microfiche cards. A magnifying display viewer is used to read the film images. COM has several advantages over paper output. Microfilm requires substantially less space to store records, cards can be easily mailed, and data can be retrieved easily. COM output machines can print out the equivalent of 14,000 lines of data per minute. A one-inch stack of microfiche records contains the same amount of data as 25,000 pages of computer printout. (See Figure 10.10.) It costs approximately one-tenth as much as line printer output and is generated approximately 10 times as fast.

FIGURE 10.10
MICROFICHE OUTPUT
VS. PAPER PRINTOUTS

FIGURE 10.11   CARD READ PUNCH

Card Read Punch The device shown in Figure 10.11 converts electronic pulses to holes in a punched card. The machine is equipped with a card-feed hopper capable of holding several hundred cards, and a transport mechanism that moves the cards past a read station and a punch station to either of two card stackers.

To punch cards, data received from the CPU in the EBCDIC or ASCII code are checked for parity and then stored in a punch buffer. The buffer holds each byte of data until a full record is received. When the device is ready, the data are moved to the punch station where a group of punch dies convert the code into punched holes at a rate of 500 cards per minute.

Paper Tape Punches Paper tape is sometimes used as computer output, particularly in small computer systems. Devices such as the one shown in Figure 10.12 convert electronic pulses from the CPU into holes in paper tape. These devices output data at a rate of up to 300 characters per second, using the ASCII or other codes. Paper tape output is convenient for outputting small amounts of data and can be sent through the mail or stored.

FIGURE 10.12   PAPER TAPE PUNCH

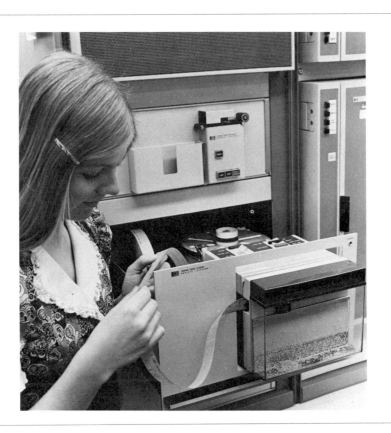

FIGURE 10.13 PLOTTER WITH SAMPLE OUTPUT

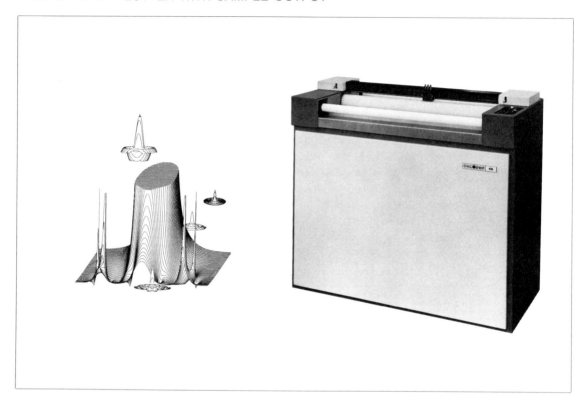

Online Plotters These machines convert data emitted from the CPU into graphic shapes, such as lines, curves, or figures. (See Figure 10.13.) The plotter is equipped with a pen, movable carriage, drum, and chart paper holder. The pen moves across the page along the *y* or horizontal axis, and the drum drives the paper along the *x* or vertical axis.

Digital information received from the CPU causes either the drum to rotate or the pen to move across the carriage. This creates a visual line representing the output data. Line drawings, curves, analogs, and similar *x-y* axis output are prepared on the plotter.

Some plotters will produce lines up to $29\frac{1}{2}$ inches wide at speeds up to 7 inches per second. Very precise charts, lines, and figures can be prepared because the pen can be positioned in any one of 45,000 points in each square inch.

The plotter can be used to plot many different kinds of business and scientific data, such as stock market curves, utility price curves, trend lines, and supply and demand curves, and to construct figures, symbols, and bar graphs.

SOFT COPY DEVICES

A variety of devices are used to provide output in the form of images displayed on a cathode ray tube, or as spoken words.

Below are examples of typical soft-copy output devices.

Cathode Ray Tube (CRT) Devices The cathode ray tube (CRT) is frequently used to output a "soft copy" of data. The principles involved are similar to those in forming images on an ordinary TV screen.

An electron beam is scanned back and forth across the face of a phosphor-coated tube at high speeds. The beam of electrons is modulated

Sidney Harris

"It can print information at the rate of 5,600 words per minute. Run a help wanted ad for someone who can read 5,600 words per minute."

FIGURE 10.14   VIDEO DISPLAY TERMINAL

(turned on and off) as it swings back and forth. When the beam is on, it activates the phosphor coating on the inside of the tube and causes it to glow. The glowing spots on the tube create patterns visible from the outside. Messages, tables, curves, lines, and other figures can be generated in this manner.

VIDEO DISPLAY TERMINAL.   The machine shown in Figure 10.14 resembles an ordinary television set with an attached keyboard. It converts electronic pulses into visual images and displays them on a cathode ray tube. Such devices may display up to 1,920 characters at any one time.

Instructions, input data, and corrections can be typed on the keyboard and inputted to the CPU. The corrected information will be displayed instantly on the screen.

The device is connected to the CPU by a control unit, which converts the pulses from the CPU into characters for display. Characters displayed on the

FIGURE 10.15 . LIGHT PEN DISPLAY CONSOLE

face of the tube look like images on a television screen. Each character remains on the screen until replaced by new data from the CPU, or until the unit is turned off. No hard copy is generated.

LIGHT PEN DISPLAY CONSOLE.   The light pen display console resembles the video display terminal and performs a similar function. However, in addition to numbers and characters, it can also display lines, graphs, curves, and drawings. A unique feature called a *light pen* is used to change or replace data displayed on the screen. When touched to the screen, a light beam from the pen will modify the data as desired. (See Figure 10.15.)

The device is coupled to the CPU by a controller. A small, self-contained computer, the controller generates characters from code received by its CPU and relays them to the cathode ray tube for display. The machine has a display screen approximately 12 $\times$ 12 inches. A point on a graph or chart can be placed at any of the intersections on the grid. A full screen of data can be displayed in 32 microseconds. Data remain on display until replaced by new output from the CPU, or until the unit is turned off. No hard copy is generated.

FIGURE 10.16   AUDIO RESPONSE UNIT

Audio Response Unit   The audio response unit, shown in Figure 10.16, converts data outputted by the CPU into an audible signal that sounds like a human voice. It outputs data as sentences, numbers, words, or phrases. The unit is physically located near the CPU. Users query the CPU and receive answers via ordinary telephone lines.

A caller dials the computer and enters a query by means of a touch-tone phone, push-button phone, or other instrument that allows numbers to be fed in by depressing buttons. The query can be a request for price information, inventory, credit rating, etc. The CPU will process the inquiry and retrieve data from a record or file as needed. Then the CPU directs the unit to assemble a verbal reply to be outputted over the telephone. The audio response unit assembles an audible message from a prerecorded vocabulary stored on a direct access storage device and then plays it into the telephone.

In a brokerage house, a master file of over-the-counter stock prices can be put online and queried by buyers and sellers. In a bank, a master file of accounts, balances, and credit ratings can be queried by bank tellers. And in the hotel-motel industry, a master file of available rooms, facilities, and rates can be queried by travel or sales agents. Messages of varying length and vocabulary to suit a particular need can be stored on the device.

PROBLEMS IN DATA OUTPUT

Like input, data output is limited by the difference between the operating speed of output devices and that of the CPU. For example, the CPU can perform thousands of calculations in the time it takes a line printer to type out one line. When the CPU has completed processing a block of data, it must have some place to put it. If the only output medium is a slow line printer tied up with the previous job, trouble arises. The CPU must wait until the line printer is ready before it can output its data and begin processing the next job.

A system is said to be I/O bound when the input or output devices on the system prevent the CPU from processing the maximum number of jobs during a given time period. Several methods are used to ease this bottleneck.

Multiple Outputs Several input devices can be connected online simultaneously to increase computer throughput. Additional output devices can be coupled in the same way. Selector and multiplexer channels can also be used to feed data to a number of line printers, card punches, etc. at the same time.

Channel addresses are assigned to each output unit on the system, just as they are to input devices. Using these addresses, the programmer can call specific units in and out of service during the program run. Card punches, line printers, tape punches, etc. may be indicated by referring to the assigned channel, control unit, and device number. (See page 36.)

Buffering Buffering has special importance in data output. Buffering involves holding bytes of data or records in temporary storage until either the designated unit or the CPU is ready to process it.

If the output device has a buffer, the CPU can transfer processed data into the buffer and proceed with the next job. The output device can operate at its own speed and print out the data from the next job in line.

Spooling and offline I/O operations are other ways to take better advantage of the CPU's speed.

Spooling Spooling, illustrated in Figure 10.17, allows the CPU to process data at maximum speeds without waiting for slow output devices. In spooling, the CPU records the output on an intermediate storage device, such as a magnetic drum. The jobs are transferred to the output devices when these units are ready.

FIGURE 10.17   SPOOLING

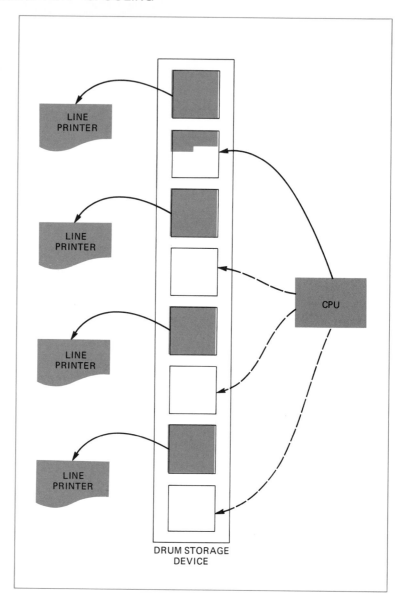

Assume, for example, that four line printers and a drum unit are used in a spooling operation on a computer system. A control program coordinates assignment of jobs to the output devices.

Data are fed at maximum speed from the CPU, stored on the drum, and sent to slower devices for output as the devices become available. As a result, the CPU can output at maximum speed, while several relatively slow output units operate simultaneously to process it. Spooling can also be used to buffer a job.

ONLINE/OFFLINE OUTPUT

In recent years there has been a proliferation of output media. The selection of a particular medium depends upon the needs of the user, facilities available in the computer center, cost, and quality factors. Online output machines receive pulses directly from the CPU. Transmitted data are recorded on output records without being held in intermediate storage. Offline machines receive data recorded on paper tape, magnetic tape, or other storage media and are not connected directly to the CPU. The tape is placed on the offline machine to produce charts, graphs, pages for reproduction by the printing process, etc.

FIGURE 10.18   OFFLINE I/O OPERATION

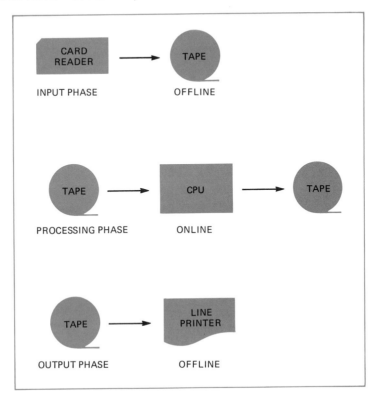

A means of breaking the I/O bottleneck is to provide offline data input and output facilities. (See Figure 10.18.) Some computer installations do not feed data directly to the CPU from card readers, paper tape readers, etc., nor do they connect the line printers directly to the CPU. Instead, all data are inputted and outputted via high-speed tape units.

For example, input data from punched cards are first recorded on offline magnetic tape units. These reels of tape are then placed on the computer for processing. Similarly, output data are recorded on magnetic tape by the CPU. Later these tape reels are placed on an offline line printer to generate the final output.

Tapes used as an intermediate offline step markedly increase throughput. A system of offline I/O allows data to be sent to the CPU without delays due to mechanical problems. It is not uncommon for a CPU to remain idle while the operator removes a torn card from the card reader or loads paper into the line printer. In the time taken to remove a card from the card reader, the CPU could process another 1,000 records or more. Tapes also give the data processing department increased flexibility. Card-to-tape and tape-to-printer units allow a job to be processed in discrete steps at different times.

KEY TERMS

Cathode ray tube	Plotter
Chain printer	Serial printing
Electrostatic imaging	Spooling
Font	Thermal imaging
Offline output	Type bar
Online output	Type element
Parallel printing	Type wheel
Phototypesetter	Wire matrix

EXERCISES

1. List three applications suitable for video display terminals. List three applications for which they are not suited.
2. What are plotters and what kinds of information do they display?
3. How does the audio response unit respond to queries from a user?
4. Why is buffering critical for output devices?
5. What is the difference between an I/O-bound system and a CPU-bound system?
6. What is spooling? Why is it useful?
7. How does offline I/O differ from online I/O? What problems does it solve?

8. Compare the advantages and disadvantages of type bar, type wheel, and type element printers.
9. How does serial printing differ from parallel printing?
10. Visit your data center and determine if the bulk of the computer's I/O is online or offline. Does the center take full advantage of the capability of its CPU?

PART FOUR

SOLVING
A PROBLEM
WITH
A COMPUTER

11

PROGRAM PLANNING

The human organism and the computer differ in the methods they use to solve a problem. Generally, humans attempt to solve problems in an "all-at-once" fashion. They don't spell out all the procedures before actually beginning to execute them and often carry out the first steps before structuring the last. There are advantages to this procedure. The plan for solving a problem becomes intermixed with and responsive to the results. This kind of activity allows humans to solve problems rapidly with creativity and insight.

COMPUTER PROBLEM SOLVING

The resources of the computer can be applied to a problem only when the method for solving the problem has been reduced to a series of discrete, logical instructions coded in a language the computer understands. It must be told where to find the required information, what logic to use, what calculations to perform, and in what form to output the answer.

Planning   A computer programmer studies the problem or procedure the machine is to process and prepares a plan of action. He or she decides which steps the machine must take to reach the results and specifies the form of input and output. Then this plan of action is converted into a set of steps in a programming language.

These instructions are prepared for input to the computer by keypunching into cards or paper tape or by recording on magnetic tape. The set of instructions, ready for input, is called a source program, a problem program, a program deck, or simply program. It is entered into the computer via an input device that converts it to electronic impulses.

Computers can only process data in machine language (1s and 0s). Instructions coded in any other language must be translated into machine language for processing. This is done with a program called a compiler or assembler.

Execution After the program has been converted to machine language, it is ready to be executed and run. In this phase, the steps in the program are carried out on the data set and the output is generated.

Stored Program It is the computer's ability to follow the instructions of the stored problem program without further human intervention or direction that gives it a degree of self-direction. But it is limited to following the steps in the program. It cannot examine its own output, decide something is wrong, and change the procedure it is following.

This ability has advantages and disadvantages. If the programmer has made an error in procedural logic, the results outputted by the machine may be incorrect, sometimes without the programmer realizing it. On the other hand, once a program is known to be logically sound and accurate in coding, the programmer is assured that the procedural steps and level of accuracy will not vary from one run to another.

The stored program has other major advantages. A program can be written and tested before the data to be processed are available. The programmer uses symbolic names to refer to the quantities manipulated in the program. For example, instructions could tell the computer that the values punched in columns 30–35 of the records in the card reader are the amount an employee has earned and are referred to as EARN in the program; and that the employee's deductions, called DEDUC, would be found in the third field of each record on a magnetic tape. The computer can then be instructed to subtract DEDUC from EARN and print out PAY on the check form in the line printer. The use of symbolic names gives the computer a great deal of power and flexibility.

PREPARING A COMPUTER PROGRAM

Figure 11.1 illustrates the steps carried out in implementing a computer program. Generally, the evolution from problem to program includes:

❶ Problem analysis
❷ Algorithm and flowcharting

FIGURE 11.1 IMPLEMENTING THE PROGRAM

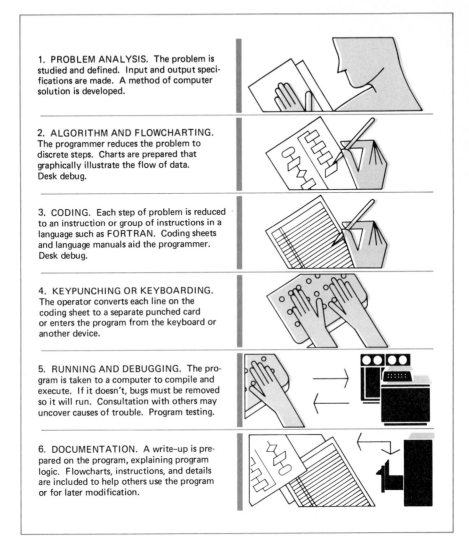

1. PROBLEM ANALYSIS. The problem is studied and defined. Input and output specifications are made. A method of computer solution is developed.

2. ALGORITHM AND FLOWCHARTING. The programmer reduces the problem to discrete steps. Charts are prepared that graphically illustrate the flow of data. Desk debug.

3. CODING. Each step of problem is reduced to an instruction or group of instructions in a language such as FORTRAN. Coding sheets and language manuals aid the programmer. Desk debug.

4. KEYPUNCHING OR KEYBOARDING. The operator converts each line on the coding sheet to a separate punched card or enters the program from the keyboard or another device.

5. RUNNING AND DEBUGGING. The program is taken to a computer to compile and execute. If it doesn't, bugs must be removed so it will run. Consultation with others may uncover causes of trouble. Program testing.

6. DOCUMENTATION. A write-up is prepared on the program, explaining program logic. Flowcharts, instructions, and details are included to help others use the program or for later modification.

③ Coding
④ Keyboarding or keypunching
⑤ Running and debugging
⑥ Documentation

These phases may vary from one computer installation to another and with the needs of a given firm. Some installations require keypunching, whereas others allow the program to be entered via a terminal. Some firms require extensive documentation, others may not. In any case, all steps must be considered.

Problem Analysis

The problem to be solved by the computer must first be carefully analyzed and defined in terms of end results. The programmer must determine what data are to be processed, what form they are in, what information is to be output, and how the data must be manipulated to produce this output.

One of the elements often considered in problem analysis is the feasibility of solving the problem on the computer. Such things as costs, error rate, and time factor must be considered. If it appears that the computer solution is practical, then the programmer will proceed with the next phase.

In problem analysis, the programmer generally follows four steps:

1. *Problem Definition.* In this step, the elements in the problem are determined. All input and output conditions are specified.
2. *Description of Variables in Quantitative Terms.* Next, the programmer converts all elements to be processed into quantitative terms—all variables must be converted into measurable quantities. For example, qualitative terms such as "poor credit," "Christmas bonus," "good employee," and "best accounts," must be converted into terms such as "delinquent more than 45 days," "$50," "absent less than five times," "purchases over $10,000." The expected outcomes are expressed in terms of these quantitative variables.
3. *Reduction to Specifics.* In this phase, the programmer determines which operations and manipulations must take place to restructure the data to produce the desired output. These operations are expressed as specific discrete steps. Next, the programmer must determine the order in which the steps are to be taken. For example, in preparing a payroll, the number of hours worked by each employee, pay rate, and number of exemptions must be input before income tax calculations can be made.
4. *Establishment of Relationships.* The purpose of this phase is to establish relationships between all the elements and factors involved. The programmer must determine what actions are to take place if certain conditions exist. For example, if the employee has a credit payment due, the program must branch to the appropriate routine to subtract the payment.

DECISION TABLES. If many possible alternatives and relationships are present in a problem, the programmer may illustrate them with a decision table. Decision tables are graphic means of showing the alternatives and branches in a program. They visually document all possible conditions and the actions to be taken in each case. The details of preparing complex decision tables are often the responsibility of the system analyst or advanced programmer. The programmer often uses the decision table when coding for assurance that all possible conditions and actions have been accounted for.

Decision tables for computer programs are also based on the IF/THEN relationship. IF the customer orders more than 1,000 units of an item, THEN a "low inventory" message must be sent to the stockroom. IF the employee worked more than 40 hours, THEN overtime must be added to the paycheck. Each entry is then translated into coded instructions in the program.

Programmers often prepare decision tables on a form similar to the one shown in Figure 11.2. A decision table is divided into four portions. (See Figure 11.3(A).) The *condition stub* (upper left portion) lists all possible conditions that may be encountered. The *condition entry* portion (upper right portion) includes various combinations of conditions that may be present. The *action stub* (lower left portion) lists all possible actions to be carried out in the program. The lower right portion, called the *action entry,* indicates the actions to be taken for a given set of conditions.

Condition entries are usually a Y (yes) to indicate a positive condition, or an N for the negative condition. Other symbols, such as =, >, <, could be used to indicate relationships. The action entries are usually indicated with an X and describe the action to be taken for each set of conditions. Each vertical column (containing Ys, Ns, and Xs) is called a *rule* or alternative. Each rule represents a given set of conditions and the actions that must be taken for that particular set.

To use a decision table, the programmer locates the rule that meets a given set of conditions and programs the computer to carry out the action entries checked within that rule.

FIGURE 11.2 DECISION TABLE FORM

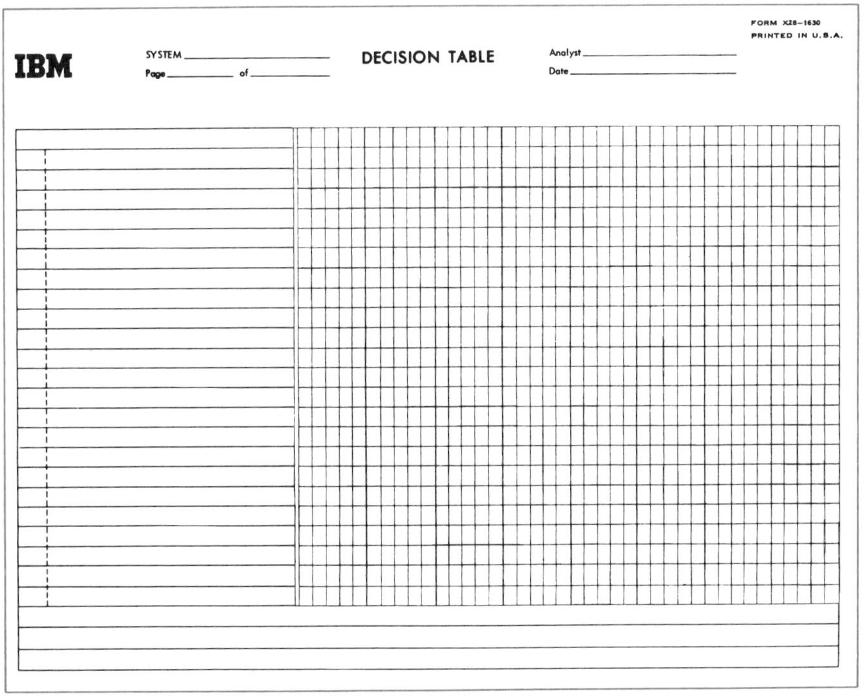
FORM X28-1630
PRINTED IN U.S.A.

IBM

SYSTEM ______
Page ______ of ______

DECISION TABLE

Analyst ______
Date ______

FIGURE 11.3   (A) PORTIONS OF DECISION TABLES
            (B) DECISION TABLE—HOLIDAY BONUS PROGRAM

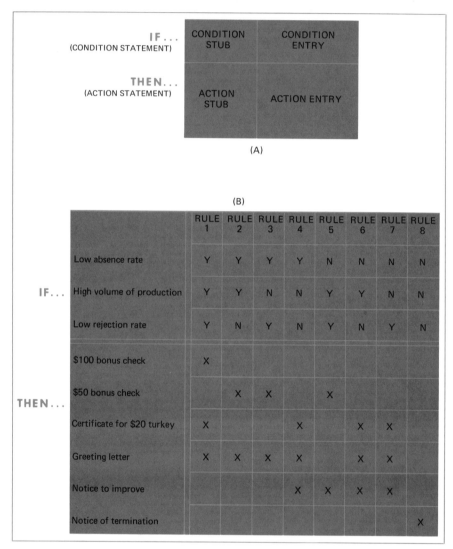

		RULE 1	RULE 2	RULE 3	RULE 4	RULE 5	RULE 6	RULE 7	RULE 8
IF...	Low absence rate	Y	Y	Y	Y	N	N	N	N
	High volume of production	Y	Y	N	N	Y	Y	N	N
	Low rejection rate	Y	N	Y	N	Y	N	Y	N
THEN...	$100 bonus check	X							
	$50 bonus check		X	X		X			
	Certificate for $20 turkey	X			X		X	X	
	Greeting letter	X	X	X	X		X	X	
	Notice to improve				X	X	X	X	
	Notice of termination								X

Figure 11.3(B) is a decision table for a program that will prepare a holiday
bonus mailing to employees. Bonus checks, holiday greetings, certificates
for turkeys, and letters from management or from the personnel department
are to be mailed to each employee, depending upon certain conditions.
These conditions are employee absenteeism, level of production, and
rejection rate.

A decision table defines the intent and objectives of the program and
ensures that all conditions and actions have been accounted for.

Algorithm and Flowcharting

After all elements and relationships in the problem have been analyzed and defined in quantitative, specific terms, they must be expressed as steps that the computer can perform. This sequence of steps, a strategy for solving the problem, is called an algorithm. The programmer will design and consider several alternative algorithms and select the most suitable one for the particular problem and system.

One way the programmer can illustrate the sequence of steps in an algorithm is with a flowchart. This is a graphic device in which symbols are used to represent the various operations a computer can perform.

Flowcharting allows the programmer to detect errors in an algorithm and facilitates coding, which is the next step to be performed. Problem logic and flowcharting techniques are discussed in more detail in Chapter 12.

Coding

After a problem has been flowcharted, it must be converted into a set of instructions understandable to the computer. Coding is the process of converting the steps in the algorithm to a set of instructions written in a programming language.

The computer cannot be instructed by simply writing a set of commands such as

PLEASE FIGURE OUT WAGES PAID AND CASH RECEIVED FROM LAST MONTH'S BOOKS. ADD THEM TOGETHER AND GIVE THEM TO THE CONTROLLER.

"All we can figure is that they broke in and programmed the computer to transfer all our assets to a numbered account in Switzerland."

In the future a compiler may accept instructions given in a free conversation form, but at present, programming instructions must follow a precise format and set of conventions for each language. The instructions must direct the computer through each step in the algorithm and define each calculation in detail. They must give the computer such information as the size and type of numbers to be read in and out, their location on the records, and the exact form and layout of the output desired.

Programming instructions given to the computer must conform to the rules of spelling, structure, order, etc. for a particular language. Below are examples of excerpts from programs coded in COBOL and FORTRAN.

COBOL:

```
1070 READ-DATA.
1080     READ WAGE-FILE INTO WAGE AT END GO TO END-OF-JOB.
1090     READ CASH-FILE INTO CASH AT END GO TO END-OF-JOB.
1100      ADD WAGE, CASH, GIVING TOTAL.
1110 WRITE-DATA.
1120     MOVE TOTAL TO OUTPUT-AREA.
1130     WRITE OUTPUT-AREA AFTER ADVANCING 2 LINES.
```

FORTRAN:

```
READ (5,10) WAGE, CASH
TOTAL = WAGE + CASH
WRITE (6,20) TOTAL
```

The codes in these examples are very efficient and compact. Some interactive computer languages (discussed in Chapter 18) permit more freedom than the above examples. However, even in these languages the programmer must adhere to specific conventions.

CODING FORMS.   Programming statements are coded on a standard form ruled off in columns and lines. Each column on the coding sheet corresponds to a character or column on a punched card, and each line to an individual record. Each coding form is designed to conform to the conventions of one of the programming languages. Figure 11.4 illustrates several of the forms in use. All the forms have the same function: they provide uniform pages on which to write computer instructions.

Keypunching or Keyboarding   In this step, the coded instructions in the program are converted to a machine-readable form for input to the computer. This is done either online or offline, depending on the type of language used and the design of the system.

BATCH PROCESSING.   In batch processing, the instructions are prepared offline for later entry and processing by the computer. Instructions are keypunched into punched cards, or keyed into paper tape or magnetic tape or disk. Each line in the program is converted into one punched card or a

FIGURE 11.4 DIFFERENT CODING FORMS

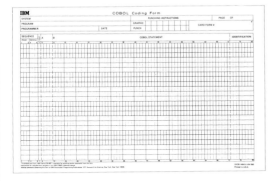

COBOL

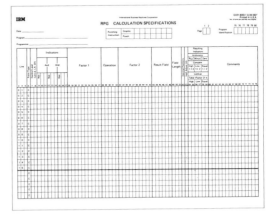

RPG

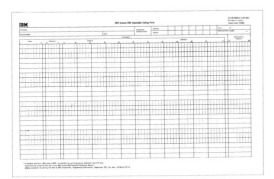

ASSEMBLER

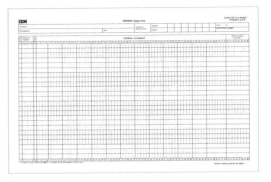

FORTRAN

FIGURE 11.5 JOB STREAM

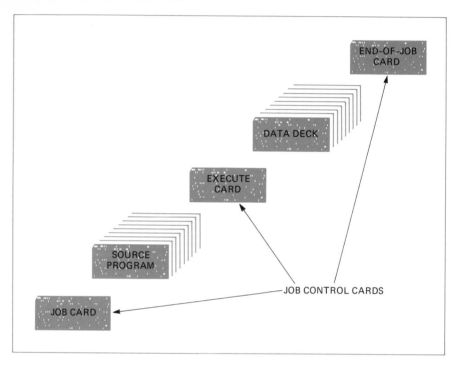

record on magnetic tape or magnetic disk. The set of punched cards or records that is generated is called the program.

The data on which the program is to operate may also be prepared at this time on punched cards or magnetic tape or disk. The program and data set may be recorded on the same or different media, depending on the design and needs of the programs.

If the program has been keypunched, the cards are assembled with job control language cards into a job stream ready for input to the computer. (See Figure 11.5.) Job control instructions tell the computer such things as a new job is being presented or a job is ending, the language in which it is coded, and the user's name and location.

INTERACTIVE PROCESSING.   In interactive processing, programs are input, line by line, directly to the computer for immediate processing. As each instruction is keyboarded on a terminal, it is converted to a machine-readable form and sent directly to the computer. In some systems, the computer will immediately indicate if an error is present in the line and wait for the programmer to make corrections.

After all lines have been entered, they may be listed on the terminal and checked for accuracy by the operator. Additions or changes may be made at this time using various editing techniques.

The data to be manipulated by the program may be entered from the terminal at the time of execution, or recorded on a storage medium such as paper or magnetic tape and called in by the program at the appropriate time.

Running and
Debugging

COMPILATION. After the instructions in a program have been converted into machine-readable form and input to the computer, they must be translated into machine language before they can be executed. This is done by an assembler, compiler, or other translating program.

An assembler program is used to translate assembler language into machine language. Each type of computer has its own assembler language and therefore its own assembler program. Assemblers usually are capable of generating only one line of machine language for each line of code. This, of course, requires the programmer to spell out many more processing details in writing a program.

Compilers, interpreters, and other translating programs translate instructions coded in languages such as FORTRAN, BASIC, and COBOL into machine language.

A compiler is capable of generating many lines of detailed instructions in machine language from each coded statement. A separate compiler is required for each language and each variation of a language.

The CPU calls a compiler for a particular language from secondary storage and loads it into primary storage. The compiler checks each coded instruction to see that it follows the rules for that language, uses proper punctuation, spelling, etc. All acceptable instructions are translated into machine language and stored. This process is called compilation.

DIAGNOSTIC MESSAGES. When a compiler discovers errors in a program, it will communicate this information to the programmer in one of several ways depending on whether processing is batch or interactive in mode. In batch programming, diagnostic messages will be listed by the computer after it has attempted to compile the program. These messages will appear on the line printer or other designated device, along with a listing of the program instructions. In interactive programming, the diagnostic messages will be listed on the terminal, either as each line is entered or at the end of the listing.

Figure 11.6 illustrates some typical error messages. The errors have been flagged by the compiler as the program was listed. As an instruction is read, the compiler checks to see that it conforms to the language rules, syntax, etc. Those that do not conform have been flagged or marked in different ways. Some computers place a dollar sign ($) below the point of error; others use a caret or similar symbol. Execution errors are printed out at the end of the listing.

If no coding errors (or only minor ones) are present and all instructions in the program have been corrected, translated, and stored, the source program is said to have compiled and is now ready for execution.

FIGURE 11.6 DIAGNOSTIC MESSAGES

```
            C      CALCULATES AVERAGE
    0001         10 DC 50 I=1,5
    0002         20 READ(5,30)POPULATICN1,PCPULATICN2
                           $            $
*************01)  IEY003I NAME LENGTH*************02)   IEY003I NAME LENGTH********************
    0003         30 FORMAT(F5.0,F5.0
                                                                       $
*************01)  IEY013I SYNTAX***********************************************************
    0004         40 MEAN=(PCPULATICN1+PCPULATICN2)/2
                   $
*************01)  IEY013I SYNTAX***********************************************************
    0005            CONTINUE
    0006         30 WRITE(6,70)MEAN
                   $ $
*************01)  IEY005I ILLEGAL LABEL***********02)   IEY006I DUPLICATELABEL****************
    0007            FORMT(1H0,I5)
                    $
*************01)  IEY013I SYNTAX***********************************************************
    0008         90 STCP
    0009         100 END
                    $
*************01)  IEY036I ILLEGAL LABEL WRN.***********************************************


                        IEY021I UNCL CC LCCP-COMP TER
    50


                        IEY022I     UNDEFINED LABEL
    50              70                    100
```

Execution is the final step in processing the problem. It is the phase
in which the CPU follows the step-by-step instructions in the program. As
directed, it will read in data from the card reader or tape or disk drive, print
out headings on the line printer, perform mathematical calculations, make
logical decisions, rearrange data, control movement of data between
secondary and primary storage, and output results.

Most problem programs manipulate a collection of data. For example,
a program that prepares a company's payroll operates on the file of
employees' payroll records. This file is the data set. When running the job,
the data set is entered in the computer after the source program has been
compiled and loaded. The combination of a source program and one or
more data sets is called a job.

One source program can execute on many data sets consecutively. This
is an important advantage of the computer. Once written, the program can be
saved and used as many times as required. For each run, the program is
entered into the computer followed by a data set.

If, as often happens, the initial run of the program is unsuccessful, it is
said to blow up (that is, fail to compile or execute as planned). Few programs
with more than a dozen instructions compile and execute the first time
through a computer. The fault lies not with the computer but with bugs in
the program. Bugs are logical or clerical errors that prevent the computer
from properly compiling or executing the program. The programmer must

The Newest Hobby

Computers—for a long time highly sophisticated and vastly expensive machines requiring platoons of technicians, programmers, mathematicians, and engineers to run—are now being sold and used by amateurs. It's happening just the way ham radios and high-fidelity sets passed into the hands of hobbyists of earlier generations.

The nation's first electronic computer, developed at the University of Pennsylvania's Moore School in the 1940's, took several years to build and cost close to $20 million. But technological developments have made it possible to build an equivalent computer for as little as $500.

The advance that made hobby computers possible is the microprocessor. Inexpensive and versatile, these fingernail-sized computers can be used for many things, from playing games to solving very technical problems.

They can be connected to the television to play video games like Ping-Pong or connected to a speaker to play music. Teachers can use them to grade students' tests. One hobbyist uses a microprocessor to play backgammon and chess, to control security devices in his house, and to save paperwork by storing tax information.

Until recently, inexpensive computer equipment was not readily available to the general public. But by mid-1976 about a dozen computer hobby shops had sprung up across the nation. Their customers, who range in age from 10 to 65 and over, can buy all kinds of computer parts, including processing units, memory units, and connections to hook computers to items already in the home. An entire system runs from $700 to $1,200. When completed it looks like a small box and can fit on a table.

Said an MIT professor, "Now that there are low-cost computers, the pressure is mounting to develop programs to do domestic tasks. They have become cheap enough so that we can expect them to have a serious impact on household management within the next decade."

Computer societies and magazines catering to the computer hobbyists are appearing all over the country.

According to the owner of a computer hobby shop in Burlington, Massachusetts, "With the low cost and availability of these computers, they are going to be as much a part of everyday life as the toaster. The younger people are going to be in the computer age whether they like it or not."

SOURCE: " 'Ham' Computers Latest Hobby Craze," (Associated Press), *Los Angeles Times*, June 9, 1976.

change the program to correct errors in logic, coding, etc. This process is called debugging.

TYPES OF BUGS. There are two major types of bugs in a program: compilation errors and execution errors. If either are present, the program will not run properly or will give inaccurate results.

Compilation Errors.   Compilation errors are discovered by the compiler and include

- Spelling errors
- Syntax errors
- Improperly sequenced statements
- Improperly labeled statements

- Conflict in names
- Illegal names or statements
- Invalid statements
- Missing punctuation

Execution Errors.   Execution errors are discovered by the computer's operating system during the process of execution and include

- Numbers too large for storage area
- Incorrectly written input statements
- Mispunched characters in the data set

DEBUGGING PROCEDURES.   The debugging phase of the programming effort requires patience and insight and can be the most frustrating part of programming. One small clerical or logical error may result in many trips to the computer center to run the program, check the results, make keypunch changes, and then resubmit the job.

A programmer looks for and corrects compilation errors in keypunching, coding, syntax, etc. If all these errors are corrected and the job compiles but still does not run, the programmer considers execution and logical errors. For example, the columns of the record being read by a computer must contain data, or the results may be erroneous. Because of a wrong input description a computer may read in 359 as 59 or 3,590. Errors in logic may prevent a job from running properly. A loop may begin the cycle at the wrong statement, or an error in branching may cause the computer to skip an important step.

A programmer attempts to find and eliminate these bugs by carefully checking a printout of the set of computer instructions and by reexamining the logic. He or she will trace a piece of test data through the program manually, checking at each step to see the results of the computer run. The program may be modified to have the computer print out the intermediate results after performing each operation.

When all errors are removed and the job compiles and executes properly, it is considered a running program ready for documenting.

One disadvantage of batch processing is that errors and incorrect statements are not detected until the entire program has been keyboarded and submitted to the computer for running. This is avoided in interactive processing.

Documentation   Completing documentation is the last step in the implementation of a program. Final documentation is explanatory material, flowcharts, instructions to the computer operator, sample test data, and other information relating to the details of a program, written and filed as a permanent record.

PURPOSES.   Documentation explains the program algorithm to others. It is a tangible record of logic, details, and input and output specifications—all easily forgotten items. Programmers find documentation useful when writing new programs. Well-documented programs are a source of notes, routines, algorithms, and other pertinent information.

Documentation is essential if programs are to be modified or revised. It is much easier to retrace logic and follow through calculations with the help of documentation. Also, there is less chance of creating a logical error if the logic is clearly outlined on paper.

Documentation is important in production runs. The computer operator needs specifications to set up the machine properly, load the correct I/O units, and handle errors and problem situations.

Documentation varies according to the needs of individual firms and the purpose of the program. Sometimes a program listing is sufficient. At other times, a complete case history of the program is necessary.

CONTENTS OF THE DOCUMENTATION FILE.   There are no rules about what must be placed in a documentation file. It should be complete enough to enable changes and modifications to be made without difficulty. The following items are often placed in the file:

Abstract.   A one- or two-paragraph summary of the purpose of a program and its major features and options. It may include a bird's-eye view of the algorithm and general procedures followed.

The sample abstract in Figure 11.7 includes sufficient information to explain the basic program, yet avoids unnecessary detail.

Descriptive Narrative.   A written description of the program. It defines the problem and explains the algorithm, methodology, and logic followed in the program. All mathematical calculations and formulas should be shown. Any options are listed, with an explanation of how they are called out or used. A good narrative should be clearly written and avoid undefined terms.

Graphic Narration.   Adequate graphic and visual devices to illustrate a program and its relationship to the system. Program flowcharts, system flowcharts, block diagrams, and coding sheets are used.

Program Listing.   An accurate program listing. The listing serves as the master record against which copies and revisions of the program are checked.

Layout of Input and Output Records.   A complete set of specimen input and output records. Input records should be pasted down on a sheet of paper

FIGURE 11.7 ABSTRACT

Program Name: Medical Record Screening Program

Program Author: Susan Tyler

Inquiries Handled By: Susan Tyler, Med. Rec. Div.,

Eastern Hospital, X 233

DESCRIPTION:

This program performs a data screening and
sort routine on medical records. The program
screens data for selected characteristics.
Common data input to the program includes
patient's name, medical record number,
descriptive physical information, number of
days lost, type of injury, and class of
coverage.

Program outputs a group of reports
categorized by type of injury, number of
days lost, and occupational class. A summary
report is also prepared, giving descriptive
data on the selected population, by age,
height, weight, and other parameters.

SOFTWARE SYSTEM:

This program operates under a disk
operating system, with interactive terminal
support.

MINIMUM HARDWARE CONFIGURATION:

UNIVAC 90/30, with 32K of core, including
two disk drives, card reader, line printer,
and CRT.

LANGUAGE:

ANSI FORTRAN IV.

FIGURE 11.8 INPUT/OUTPUT RECORD DOCUMENTATION

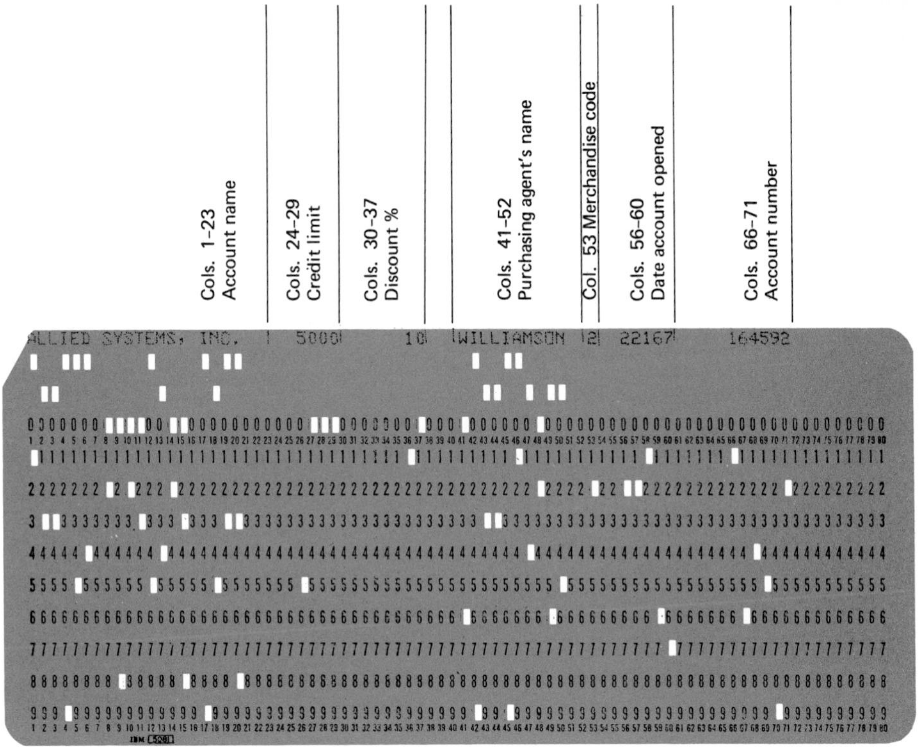

Card Style   5081   Vendor   IBM Corp.

Color   Manila   Back Ptg.   None

Corner cut   Top, left   Stub   None

Stripe   None   Score, Perf, Tint   None

PROGRAM: Credit Authorization

and each field labeled. (See Figure 11.8.) If an alphabetic or numeric code is used to group data, it should be indicated and explained in the documentation.

If several data records, such as master and detail records, are used, they should all be shown and described in detail. A visual job stream will be helpful here to show the sequence of the input. (See Figure 11.9.)

Specifications for output records should be shown and described. The fields for each piece of data on the records should be indicated. If output is

FIGURE 11.9   VISUAL JOB STREAM

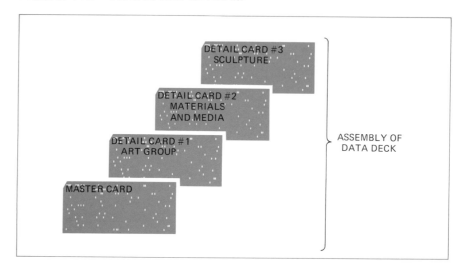

to be printed, a sample should be included, and the size of the form and type of paper it is printed on noted.

Test Data for Checking.   Test data sets are valuable testing and debugging aids. They should include data that forces the computer to execute all branches and possibilities in the program. Carefully checked printouts should be included as known standards for checking future runs.

Lapse Time.   Summary of the time required for compilation and execution of a program. This statement helps the operator later discover any malfunctions in the run.

Run Manual.   Documents necessary to actually run the job on the computer. This includes information such as job stream setup, sequence of data cards, and layout of input and output records.

A run log or continuing record, showing changes or modifications made in the program during the run, is sometimes kept.

KEY TERMS   Algorithm   Diagnostic messages
            Assembler   Documentation
            Coding   Execution
            Compilation   Execution errors
            Compilation errors   Flowchart
            Compiler   Problem analysis
            Debugging   Symbolic name
            Decision table

EXERCISES

1. List and describe the six major steps in implementing a computer program.
2. Define coding. What is its purpose and how is it done?
3. List three instructions that are too general to be coded. List three commands that are specific enough to be coded.
4. Select a simple business problem, such as calculate interest, or figure a bank balance. Break the problem down into a series of discrete steps.
5. List some items normally found in the documentation file.
6. Compare several coding forms for different languages. How do they differ?
7. What is the relationship between the lines on a coding form and the punched program deck?
8. What is the purpose of running and debugging a program?
9. List three types of compilation errors.
10. How do compilation errors differ from execution errors?
11. What are diagnostic messages, and how are they indicated by various compilers?
12. How do programmers debug a program?
13. What is the function of documentation?

12

PROGRAM LOGIC
AND FLOWCHARTING

Once the program planning and definition is completed, the programmer must design and flowchart the algorithm. Flowcharts should always be prepared *before* a program is coded, not after. This reduces the chances of error.

FLOWCHARTS

Definition A flowchart is a diagram, prepared by the programmer, of the sequence of steps involved in solving a problem. It provides either a detailed view or an overview of the program and indicates the direction of program flow. A flowchart is like a blueprint in that it shows the general plan, architecture, and essential details of the proposed structure.

A flowchart illustrates the strategy and thread of logic followed in the program. It allows the programmer to compare different approaches and alternatives on paper and often shows interrelationships that are not immediately apparent. Figure 12.1 is a flowchart of a washing machine's cycles. In a similar way, a sequence of data processing steps may be diagrammed.

FIGURE 12.1   WASHING MACHINE CYCLES

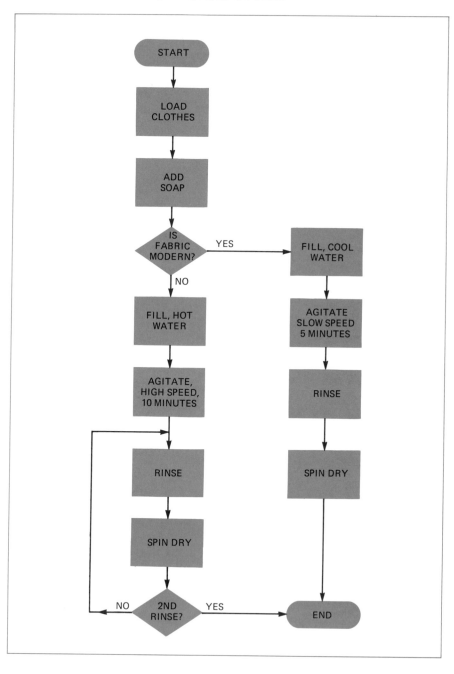

The flowchart is an essential tool for the programmer. By forcing him or her to state the logic in clear terms and to state the essential details, a flowchart helps the programmer avoid fuzzy thinking and accidental omissions of intermediate steps. The flowchart is also a communication tool used to link the programmer, the user of the program, the systems analyst, and the computer operator.

Types and Functions
A flowchart may be drawn informally in longhand, lettered in pen and ink, or typed by machine on a sheet of paper. It can be written either horizontally or vertically and may take from one to as many as several dozen pages.

A flowchart serves as a map or guide for the programmer in the course of writing a program. Each programmer uses the flowchart in a way that best suits the problem-solving activity he or she faces.

Flowcharts are divided into two basic types: the *system flowchart* and the

FIGURE 12.2   SIMPLE SYSTEM FLOWCHART

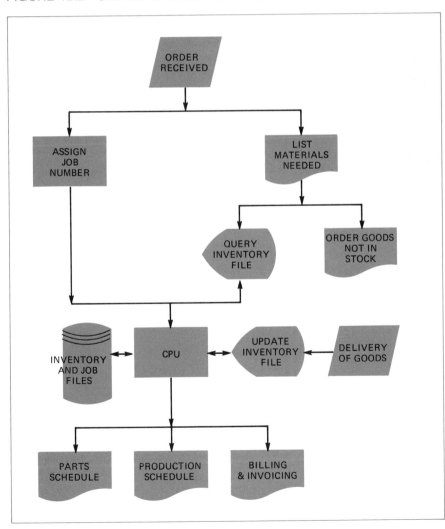

program flowchart. The program flowchart is further divided into modular and detailed program flowcharts.

SYSTEM FLOWCHART.

The system flowchart is designed to present an overview, or bird's-eye view, of the data flow through all parts of a data processing system. The system flowchart stresses people, activities, documents, and media. It shows the data-flow relationships of the various departments and work stations to the whole. It describes data sources, their form, and the stages through which they will be processed.

Figure 12.2 illustrates the channels of data flow and processing in a merchandising system. It includes activities such as generating source documents, keypunching, and computerized sorting and processing.

MODULAR PROGRAM FLOWCHART.

The modular program flowchart is sometimes called a block diagram or macro flowchart. Each block in the flowchart represents a major step in the program logic.

The modular flowchart shows only the gross phases of the solution and does not obscure essentials with details. It provides the programmer with a broad-brush picture of the strategy and flow of data in a particular situation.

More refined and detailed flowcharts can be prepared from this flowchart for use in the actual writing of the program. Each block in the modular flowchart may be expanded and exploded into many programming steps. The module "CALCULATE BASIC SALARY" in Figure 12.3, for example, may contain dozens of steps and calculations.

DETAIL PROGRAM FLOWCHART.

A detail program flowchart is sometimes called a micro or detail flowchart. It outlines each step, calculation, test, and comparison involved in the solution of the problem. It provides a microscopic view of each element in the system.

The detail program flowchart expands the blocks of the modular flowchart into programmable steps, used as a guide for writing the program. This flowchart helps the programmer make sure that all steps are included, that branches refer to the correct points in the program, etc.

In Figure 12.4, the programmer has drawn in each decision point, branch, and calculation.

Common Flowchart Symbols

Each type of operation the computer is to perform can be indicated by the use of a different shape, called a flowchart symbol. About two dozen widely used symbols cover the most common programming situations. A template, Form X-20-8020-1, available from IBM, is a convenient aid in drawing flowcharts. Templates in various sizes are also manufactured by Rapid Design, Inc. to conform to the ANSI X3.5 standard. (See Figure 12.5.) Most programmers prepare working and development flowcharts with a template, pencil, and scratch paper. Permanent flowcharts are usually drawn in ink, although a computer can be used to print them. The most common flowchart symbols are as follows.

FIGURE 12.3 MODULAR PROGRAM FLOWCHART

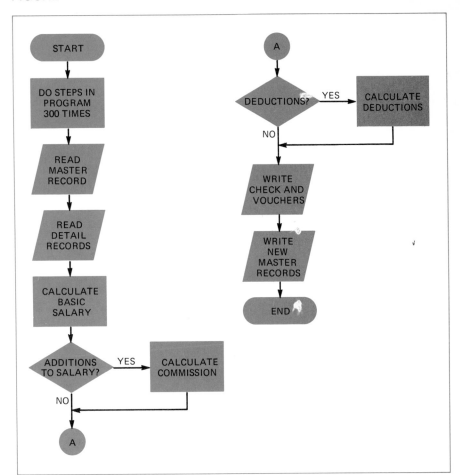

TERMINAL. The terminal symbol is an oval and the words START, STOP, or HALT are usually written in the center. START, the first symbol of the flowchart, marks the beginning of the logic train. STOP or HALT, the last symbol of the flowchart, marks the end of the logic train. This symbol is also used at other points in a program to show where different branches terminate or where the program is to stop due to an error condition. Used in this manner, the oval means a programming step, not a remote or display terminal.

INPUT/OUTPUT (GENERAL). A parallelogram indicates where data are to be input or output during a program. It is a general form and is used for all input/output media, such as read or punch a card, write on a printer, or display on a video tube. A few words in the center of the symbol describe the input or output action and the data involved.

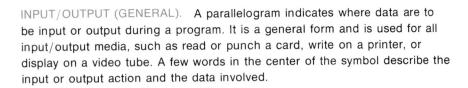

FIGURE 12.4 DETAIL PROGRAM FLOWCHART

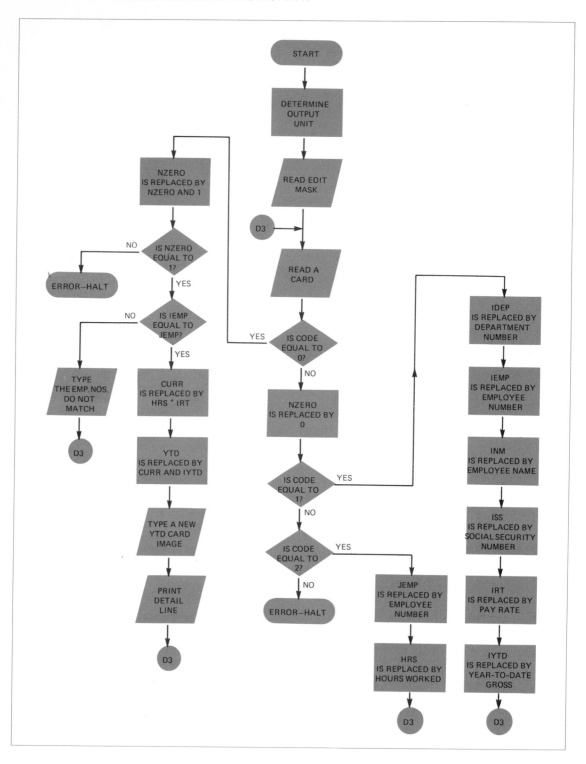

PROCESS. The process symbol, a rectangle, indicates an operation that is to be performed by the computer. It may be a mathematical calculation such as add, subtract, compute, or find square root. The specific action should be identified in the center of the box.

CONNECTOR. The connector symbol, a small circle, is used to tie parts of a flowchart together. It allows the programmer to draw portions of a chart elsewhere on the page. Keys such as GO TO 19 or GO TO READ CARD help the reader follow the continuity of the program. The symbol is useful when charts have many branches or run onto many pages.

DECISION. A diamond-shaped symbol indicates that a branch or decision point, has been reached in the program. A few words within the symbol briefly describe the decision that must be made. Labeled arrows leading from the decision symbol indicate the action the computer should take for each possible answer. For example, FIELD = 999? may appear within the symbol, and labels such as YES or NO, GO TO A, GO TO B, or GO TO C may identify possible paths.

PUNCHED CARD. A symbol shaped like a card indicates that data are to be read or punched on a card. It differs from the general input/output symbol in that it represents only punched cards.

DOCUMENT. The document symbol, which looks like part of a sheet of paper, shows that a hard-copy document is being read or generated. The term hard-copy document refers to a paper or sheet of printout. It should not be confused with microfiche or microfilm "documents." The document symbol is a specialized form of the general input/output symbol and is used where data are to be read from, or output on, a document, such as an invoice, check, or order form.

MAGNETIC TAPE. A circle with a horizontal line at the bottom is another specialized input/output symbol. It is used to represent data being read from or written on magnetic tape.

DIRECT-ACCESS STORAGE DEVICE. A portion of a round drum cylinder is a specialized input/output symbol. It is used to represent data stored on random access media such as disk or drum.

COMMUNICATION LINK. This jagged symbol, which looks like a bolt of lightning, indicates that data are being transmitted from one location to another via communication lines.

The symbols on a flowchart are connected by straight lines. Arrows along the straight lines show the direction of program flow. Figure 12.6 illustrates some symbols with a statement in each to facilitate following the logic.

FIGURE 12.5   FLOWCHARTING TEMPLATE

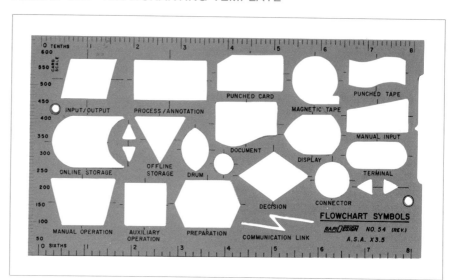

PROGRAM LOGIC

Algorithms   A strategy for solving a problem must be established before the actual programming efforts are begun. This strategy is the *algorithm.* An algorithm is a list of steps, or a set of rules, leading to the solution of a problem.

A problem can often be solved by more than one strategy or algorithm. For example, monthly statements can be prepared in several different ways. One way would be to process the whole group of statements in separate steps. First, debits and credits would be posted to all the accounts. Next, the entire group of statements would be typed. Then the envelopes would be prepared, and, finally, the statements would be folded and inserted into the envelopes.

Another way to achieve the same result would be to prepare each statement separately. The debits and credits are posted to an account and the statement and envelope typed. The statement is then folded and inserted, ready for mailing. Then the statement for the next account is prepared.

The end results would be the same, but the strategies used are different. The choice of algorithm is affected by factors such as personnel, available equipment, time considerations, and office layout. The algorithm that best suits all conditions will be selected.

As another example, consider the ways in which a credit and collection letter could be processed. Assume each account must pay $20 per month. Customers who pay less receive an appropriate collection letter, those who pay $20 receive an acknowledgement, and those who overpay receive a letter indicating a credit has been posted toward next month's payment.

FIGURE 12.6   COMMON SYMBOLS

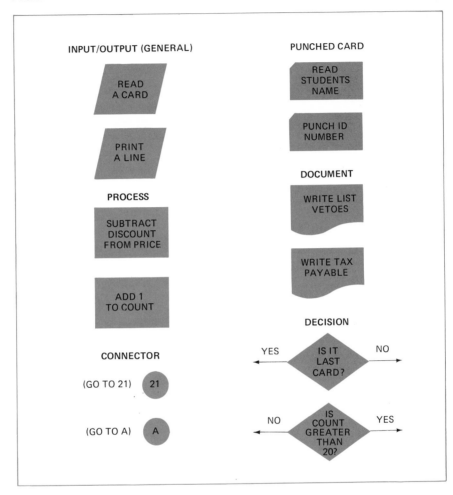

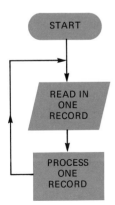

One algorithm for solving the problem would involve sorting the accounts into three categories: those who paid less than $20, those who paid $20, and those who paid more than $20. Then each group of letters could be prepared as a batch. The top left figure flowcharts this algorithm.

An alternative strategy would be to check one customer payment at a time and prepare the appropriate letter. The bottom left figure illustrates this approach.

To use the computer to best advantage, factors that bear on the problem, such as computer storage capability, number of steps in the instructions, and access time, must be examined. The algorithm that best meets all the needs is selected. Once the algorithm is chosen, the actual programming details can be worked out.

Murphy the Time Sharer

Ages ago an eminent scientist by the name of Murphy set forth an irrefutable law comprised of three hypotheses. Briefly stated, Murphy's Law says:

1. If anything can go wrong it will.
2. Nothing is as simple as it seems.
3. Everything takes longer than it should.

Scientists throughout the ages have proven these laws again and again; in fact, many times nonscientific persons have experienced their veracity. While Murphy lived before the age of computer time sharing, it is obvious that the old gentleman foresaw this age when he formulated his hypotheses.

Consider a few proofs of Murphy's Law when computer timesharing.

Hypothesis 1: If anything can go wrong it will.

You have just completed typing a large quantity of data to the computer. You are about to save it when:

a. You kick the terminal power plug with your foot.
b. The terminal becomes hopelessly jammed.
c. The phone company unplugs you.
d. The computer center has a power failure.
e. A friend slaps you on the back and you bump the "off" switch.
f. Lightning strikes your terminal.
g. A bulldozer knocks over a telephone pole.
h. A violent electrical storm disrupts all communications.
i. In swatting at a mosquito you hit the "off" switch.
j. You discover that you really weren't "online" after all!

Hypothesis 2: Nothing is as simple as it seems.

You wish to make a minor modification to an existing program (which is used regularly by 300 people). Taking full advantage of the ease in modifying a program with computer time sharing, you:

a. Replace the wrong statement.
b. Add a line of "garbage" to the program, rendering it inoperable.
c. Use a previously used statement number.
d. Cause the program to loop endlessly. (This takes 15 minutes to discover.)
e. No longer can duplicate the test problem results. (Further checking shows that the original program has never given correct results.)
f. Destroy the old program and forget to save the revised program.
g. After result (f) you discover that you don't have a listing of the program.

Hypothesis 3: Everything takes longer than it should.

It is five minutes before a very important conference (which includes the company president). You need some additional calculated results, and a program is available on the time-sharing service. Taking full advantage of the "instant results" provided by time sharing, you rush to the terminal and discover that:

a. There is no paper at the terminal.
b. A 6-foot, 5-inch, 250-pound bully is already using the terminal.
c. The telephone has been disconnected.
d. You can't remember your "ID".
e. The last user became frustrated and buried an ax in the terminal.
f. The computer has just been taken "off-line" for a 10-minute test.
g. Management has removed all the terminals as part of an austerity program!

While these are just a few isolated examples, which prove that Murphy may have been a time-sharing user, more evidence is collected each day to substantiate this possibility. Therefore, the user of time sharing will do well to remember that Murphy's Law does control him when he is at the terminal. Hopefully, a forewarned user can minimize the wrath of this law.

SOURCE: "Murphy, The Time-Sharer," G. L. Kaes, *Modern Data*, June, 1970. Reprinted by permission of *Modern Data*.

Programmers use several basic procedures in planning and writing programs. The choice of procedures depends on the complexity of the program. Some programs are simple and have only a few steps. Others are complex and branch into one of several tracks, test against known values, and loop through a set of calculations, comparisons, or operations many times.

Some of the most common procedures used by programmers are discussed below.

SINGLE-PASS EXECUTION.   The most elementary program moves through a set of statements in sequence, from beginning to end. Figure 12.7 illustrates a program that computes shipping charges. The program involves only one pass through the calculations.

First, a shipping rate schedule is read in and stored by the computer. Next, it reads the weight of the shipment and computes the shipping charges. Finally, it writes out the answer. The computer will move through the sequence from START to END only once. The program has no branches or loops and is executed the same way each time it is run. If a new set of

FIGURE 12.7   SINGLE PASS

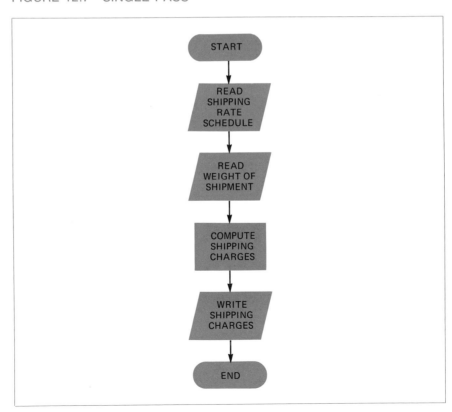

values is to be read and computed, the program must be fed into the computer with the new set of data.

BRANCHING TO PARALLEL TRACKS.   The computer can also read a value and select one of several courses depending on the value read. In Figure 12.8, the computer reads a part name and category number. Depending on the category, it will select one of four paths to follow. Each path directs the computer to write out the part name and description of the category in which it belongs.

Basically, this is a single-pass execution—the program will read only one record, perform the classification only once, and then direct the computer to terminate execution. The computer, however, has a choice of paths to follow. The selection of the particular path depends upon the category code read.

FIGURE 12.8   BRANCHING TO PARALLEL TRACKS

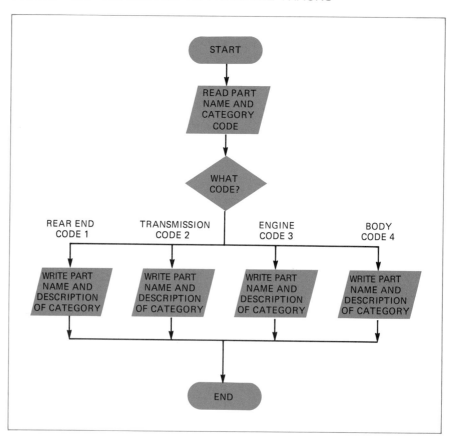

FIGURE 12.9 SIMPLE LOOP

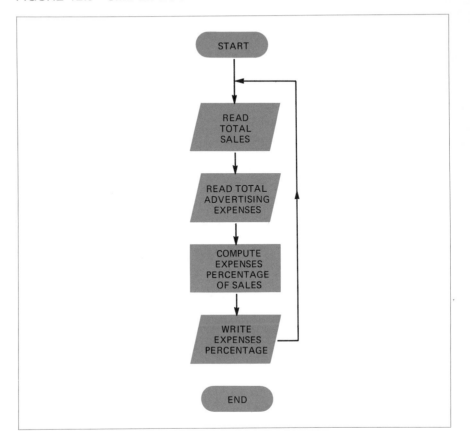

SIMPLE LOOP.   Figure 12.9 is an example of a program that directs the
computer to perform calculations several times. It computes the percentage
of sales represented by advertising expenses for each office of a large
company.

Upon completing the first pass through to the WRITE statement, the
program will loop back to the beginning and read another record. It again
computes the expenses percentage, writes the answer, and loops back. As
the program is now written, the machine will continue to perform the looping
operation and calculations until it runs out of data records. In practice, a
method of indicating that the end of the file has been reached would be
written into the program.

A loop enables the programmer to instruct the computer to perform an
operation many times without having to write new instructions for each pass.
The computer will automatically repeat a cycle until directed to stop. The
weakness of the simple or unconditional loop is that the programmer has no
control over, or knowledge of, the number of times it is executed.

FIGURE 12.10 LAST-RECORD LOOP

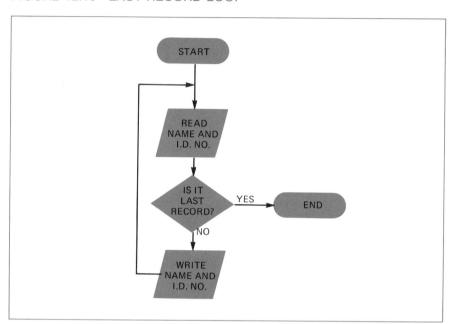

LAST-RECORD LOOP.   Figure 12.10 shows another type of looping. The machine is to read and write a list of identification numbers from a file until it encounters the last record in the file. In this example, a signal punched card (differentiated by a code in a specific field) is inserted as the last record in the data set. This card is sometimes called a trailer record/ or end-of-file record.

As the program is written the computer will read a record and test whether it is the last record. If not, it will write the name and I.D. number and go back to read another record. When it finally encounters the last record, the computer will direct control to END.

The trailer record is an accepted method of indicating to the computer that it has reached the end of the file. The programmer, however, has no way of knowing how many times the loop has been executed and can limit it only by the number of records in the file.

LAST RECORD LOOP WITH BRANCH.   On reaching the last record, the computer does not have to stop. It can branch to another leg of the program and perform other calculations and steps. This concept is illustrated in Figure 12.11. The computer is instructed to read in salaries from a record, add the salary to a subtotal, and then write out a paycheck. When the last record is encountered, the computer does not immediately stop; it first writes out a value for the total salaries processed.

FIGURE 12.11 LAST-RECORD LOOP WITH BRANCH

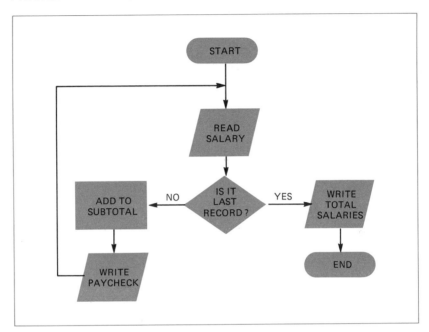

LOOP WITH COUNTER.   A programmer may find it necessary to limit the number of times a loop is to be executed. One way to do this is to write a counter into the program. The counter is incremented each time the computer passes that instruction. The program directs the computer to branch out of the loop when the counter reaches a predetermined value.

In Figure 12.12, the programmer uses a counter to print out a roster. The computer is instructed to read the name of a student, add the name to a roster, and add one to the counter. The counter is tested to see if it equals 50. When it equals 50, the computer is instructed to write out the list of 50 students assigned to the class.

The programmer sets the initial value of the counter. Normally counters start at zero, but they can be initialized at any number. Counters may be set to increase by 1 during each loop, or by 5, or by 7, or by any number. Counters can also be initialized to a value calculated within the program. Counters may run in a positive direction, that is, adding one each time, or in a negative direction, that is, subtracting one each pass.

Counters can simplify the work of the programmer and reduce programming effort. A great variety of algorithms can be developed with counters. For example, they can be used to keep track of the number of data records read in. This count can be printed out later, or used in mathematical

FIGURE 12.12   LOOP WITH COUNTER

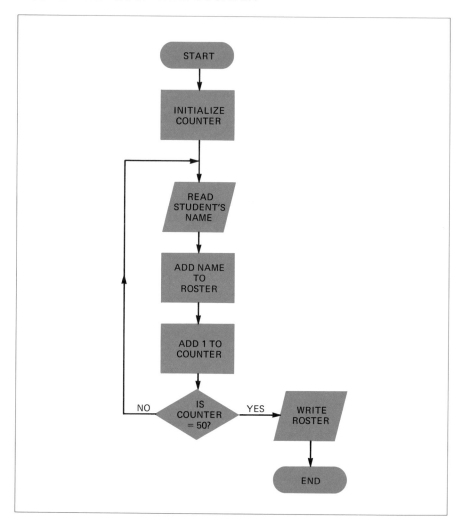

calculations, such as finding averages. And since counters may be set up anywhere in a program, they can be used as indices to keep track of calculations, to count, or to limit the number of times a step is executed.

LOOP WITH COUNTER AND TEST FOR LAST RECORD.   Another common algorithm is a loop with a counter and a test for last record. This loop is limited by the test for last record (end of file). The counter is incremented each time the loop is executed and indicates the number of cycles performed. That is, if a loop reads in records from a file, the value of the counter will tell the number of records read.

In Figure 12.13, the computer reads in a value called quality control and tests for last record. If it is not the last record, it adds one to a counter and performs some calculations. Upon reaching the last record, the computer writes out the count of records and prints out a report on the calculations.

LIMITED LOOP. A programmer often does not know the number of times a loop must be executed, but needs to set the maximum. There may be a limited amount of computer storage space available or the programmer may want to group data for statistical procedures.

One way to limit a loop is with a two-part test. One part sets the maximum times the loop may be repeated, and the other tests for last record. In this way, the computer will break out of the loop either when the last

FIGURE 12.13 LOOP WITH COUNTER AND TEST FOR LAST RECORD

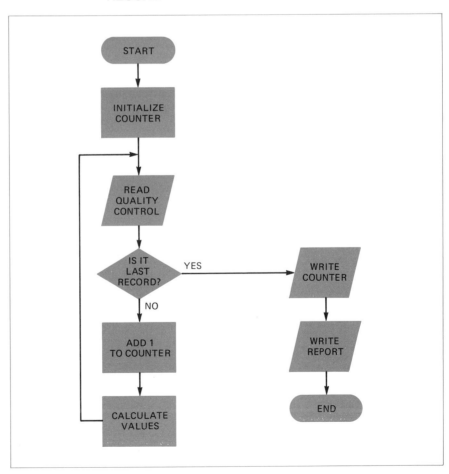

FIGURE 12.14   LIMITED LOOP

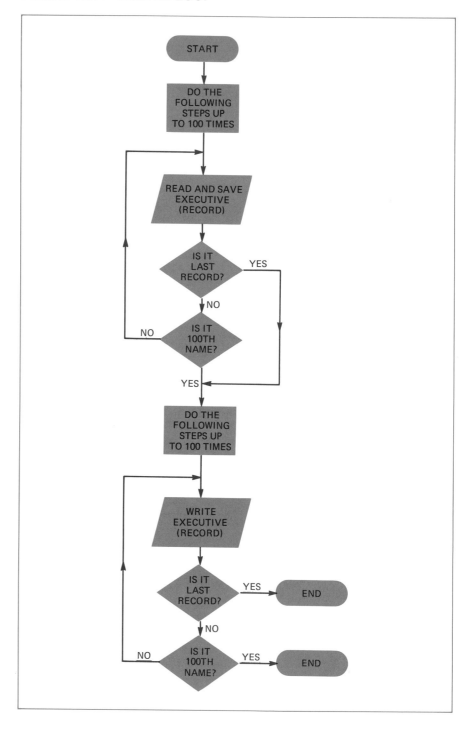

record has been encountered or when the loop has been executed the predetermined number of times.

In Figure 12.14, the computer is to read the names of a group of executives and print out a list. The computer will read and list up to 100 names. If the computer encounters a trailer or end-of-file record before reading the hundredth name, it will break out of the loop and go to the next procedure in the program. If, on the other hand, there are more than 100 records in the file, it will read the first 100 names, break out of the loop, and go on to the next procedure, ignoring the rest of the names. If the programmer needs to know how many times the loop was executed (names read and printed out), a counter could be included.

Grin and Bear It by George Lichty,
courtesy of Field Newspaper Syndicate

"Who's the wise guy who programmed nostalgia
into the design computer?"

SOME ELEMENTARY FLOWCHARTS

The programmer frequently combines the elementary programming logic steps illustrated in the previous section into larger working units. Some typical business data processing problems and their flowcharts will be described in the remainder of this chapter.

    To better illustrate the examples, detailed and modular flowcharting concepts are used on the same chart. For example, a module such as "WRITE REPORT" would actually be composed of a dozen or more programming steps such as "WRITE HEADING," "WRITE TITLES," and "WRITE TEXT MESSAGE." "IS IT LAST RECORD," on the other hand, might represent only one programming step.

Franchise Report   Figure 12.15 illustrates the use of a loop to print out a series of operating reports for a group of franchisees and a report for the franchisor.

FIGURE 12.15   FRANCHISE REPORT

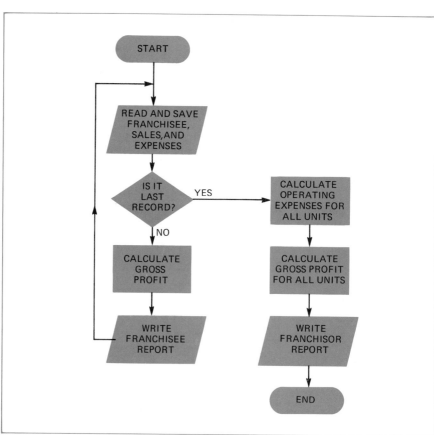

FIGURE 12.16   BILLING AND COLLECTION PROGRAM

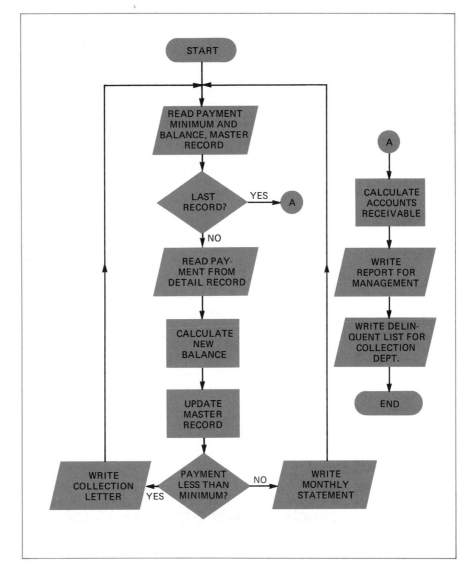

The computer reads a record containing gross expenses, receipts, and other cost data from a franchisee. The computer calculates the operating expenses and gross profit and prepares a report summarizing these data for that franchisee. This completes one loop. The computer then cycles back to read a record from another franchisee, perform the calculations, and prepare another report. The computer continues to cycle through the loop until the last record in the file has been reached, at which point the computer branches to a management routine. The management routine is designed to prepare summary data for the franchisor. In this routine, operating expenses and gross profits for all units are calculated. Then a management report is printed out.

This problem illustrates a typical programming situation in which individual records are processed, and a summary report is prepared on reaching the last record in the file.

Billing and Collection Program

In Figure 12.16 an accounts receivable file is maintained, and two reports, in addition to collection letters and monthly statements, are prepared.

The computer reads a record from a master file, which contains the current balance and minimum payment due for each account. Then it reads a record from the detail file, which contains monthly payments made. The program calculates the new balance for each account and updates the master file. It then decides whether the monthly payment received is less than the minimum amount due for that account. If it is, it prints out a collection letter to inform the account of the overlooked payment. The computer then loops back to read another account record. If the payment received is greater than or equal to the minimum amount due, the computer prepares a monthly statement for the account and loops back to read another account record.

After each master record is read, an end-of-file test is made. When the last record has been processed, the computer branches to a management report routine. This routine calculates total accounts receivable and prints out a report of the status of all accounts. Then the computer prepares for the collection department a special report containing the names, addresses, and phone numbers of all overdue accounts.

KEY TERMS

Algorithm
Branching
Counter
Detail program flowchart
End-of-file record
Flowchart
Flowchart symbols

Last record loop
Loop
Modular program flowchart
Single-pass execution
System flowchart
Trailer record

EXERCISES

1. Why do programmers flowchart a problem?
2. What is the difference between a system flowchart and a program flowchart?
3. What is an algorithm? Select a problem and give several solutions to it.
4. Using the algorithms and solutions developed in Exercise 3, prepare flowcharts for each.

5. What is the difference between a single-pass execution and a simple loop?
6. List three problems that might be solved by using an algorithm that involves branching to parallel tracks.
7. What are loops? List four situations in which loops may be used.
8. Define a last-record loop. What is its function? Describe how it is used in a program.
9. Extend the flowchart in Figure 12.7 to change it from a single-pass execution to a limited loop.
10. Use another method to limit the loop in Exercise 9.
11. Flowchart programs to perform the following functions:
    a. Single-pass execution, which reads in balance, deposits, and withdrawals from a punched card, and computes and prints out the new balance.
    b. Read a part name and code from a record and branch to one of five parallel tracks.
12. Flowchart programs to perform the following functions:
    a. Perform a simple loop that reads in a list of names from a record and writes the list on the line printer.
    b. Read a record containing the number in stock and cost per unit. Multiply to find total cost and print it out. Then loop back to read another record. Include a "test for last record."
13. Flowchart programs to perform the following functions:
    a. Compute simple interest due on each account in a file.
    b. Read in the number of parts left in stock. If under 100, write a "short supply" message. If 100–500, write "adequate supply" message. If more than 500, write an "oversupply" message.

13

BATCH, INTERACTIVE, AND SUPPLIED PROGRAMS

The previous chapters discussed how to analyze, plan, flowchart, and code a computer program. This chapter discusses the common modes of program execution—the batch (stand alone) and interactive methods—and gives an example of each.

It is not always necessary to develop an original program to solve a specific problem. Programs for solving general problems are often already available—either in the computer's system library (on tapes or disk), or from manufacturers, proprietary software firms, or time-sharing companies. This chapter concludes with a discussion of these kinds of programs, which are called *library* or *supplied programs*.

THE BATCH PROGRAMMING MODE

The distinguishing element of the batch program is that it is written as an independent, self-sufficient package. All instructions, data, and details for solving the problem are submitted to the computer as a unit. The program is processed under the control of the CPU without any intervention by the programmer.

The programmer designs and writes a set of instructions to solve a specific problem. It may be a generalized program or one suited to immediate, limited needs. Usually, the cost of writing the program is borne by the firm that will use it to solve an internal data-processing problem, but batch programs can also be written by computer manufacturers for distribution.

Advantages   The batch program is best suited for repetitive problem-solving activities, although it is often very valuable for solving a one-time, complex problem that involves repetitive steps. Once the program has been written and tested, it may be used over and over to process different sets of data.

Because the program is written to solve a particular problem, the form of the input and output data and the method used to solve the problem can be designed for a specific user's needs. Such programs are written to do a specific firm's accounts receivable, billing, collection letters, inventory, etc.

Disadvantages   A major disadvantage of the batch program is that since the problem is specific, a unique set of instructions must be written to solve it, requiring considerable programming time and effort. Another disadvantage is that results are not usually available immediately. Since most data centers run batch programs as a group, scheduling arrangements in the data center will also have an effect.

SAMPLE BATCH PROBLEM

We now follow a simple example of a batch data processing problem through implementation.

Problem Analysis   A business firm wants a program that will indicate when there are fewer than 1,000 units of a given part in stock. Some units are kept in the sales department, and some are stored in the warehouse. The number of units available in each department is recorded on a separate card by that department. The two files are in matching sequence by part number. The computer must calculate the total number of units in stock for each part. If less than 1,000 it must print a message telling the order department to order more.

Algorithm and   The programmer studies the problem and defines the steps the computer
Flowcharting   must take to solve it. He or she decides that the best algorithm would be for the computer to read in the card from the sales department file and then the one from the warehouse for each type of part, and then add the two quantities to get the current inventory. Then test the inventory. If it is less than 1,000, write a message indicating that more parts must be ordered. If the inventory is 1,000 or greater, print a notice that sufficient parts are on hand.

FIGURE 13.1 FLOWCHARTING THE PROBLEM

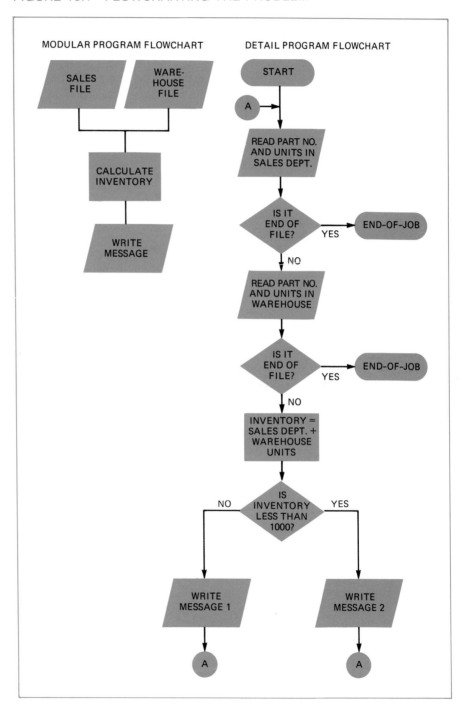

Figure 13.1 illustrates a modular program and a detail program flowchart for this example. They show how the programmer has converted the logic in the program into modular steps. These, in turn, are expanded to detailed steps the computer can follow to solve the problem.

Coding the Problem

The program must be coded in a language the computer can understand, such as COBOL. Assume the data are available on the data records in the following format.

Records from the Sales Department:

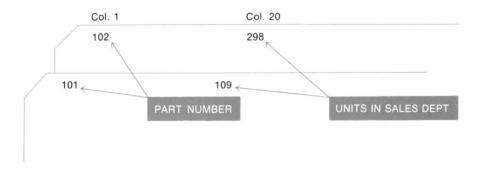

Records from the Warehouse Department:

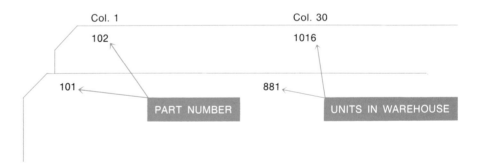

The first step is to break the problem down into workable smaller units. Some programmers develop a list from the flowchart:

- Start program
- Read a data card from the Sales Department file
- Test for end-of-file
- Read a data card from the Warehouse file

- Test for end-of-file
- Add UNITS-IN-SALES-DEPT to UNITS-IN-WAREHOUSE
- Compare INVENTORY to 1,000
- If INVENTORY is less than 1,000, write out the message "REPLENISH STOCK OF PART-NUMBER xxx ORDER MORE UNITS IMMEDIATELY."
- Go back and read another data card from the Sales Department file
- If INVENTORY is equal to or greater than 1,000, write out the message "THERE IS AN ADEQUATE SUPPLY OF PART-NUMBER xxx."
- Go back and read another data card from the Sales Department file
- END-OF-JOB close program

The next step is to actually write the instructions. Figure 13.2 shows some of the coded statements on the COBOL coding form. Figure 13.3 is a listing of the instructions the programmer has given the computer.

FIGURE 13.2 SAMPLE COBOL CODING

```
IBM                                    COBOL Coding Form

SYSTEM                                          PUNCHING INSTRUCTIONS          PAGE   OF
PROGRAM   COBOL CODING EXAMPLE                  GRAPHIC                CARD FORM #
PROGRAMMER                         DATE         PUNCH

SEQUENCE                           COBOL STATEMENT                     IDENTIFICATION

5020  START-PROGRAM.
5030     OPEN INPUT SALES-FILE, WAREHOUSE-FILE, OUTPUT PRINT-FILE.
5040  READ-DATA.
5050     READ SALES-FILE INTO HOLD-INPUT, AT END GO TO END-OF-JOB.
5060     MOVE UNITS-IN-SALES-DEPT TO WORKAREA-1.
5070     READ WAREHOUSE-FILE INTO HOLD-INPUT, AT END GO TO END-OF-JOB.
5080     MOVE UNITS-IN-WAREHOUSE TO WORKAREA-2.
5090  CALCULATIONS.
5100     ADD WORKAREA-1, WORKAREA-2, GIVING INVENTORY.
5110     IF INVENTORY IS EQUAL TO 1000, GO TO WRITE-MESSAGE-1.
5120     IF INVENTORY IS GREATER THAN 1000, GO TO WRITE-MESSAGE-1.
5130     IF INVENTORY IS LESS THAN 1000, GO TO WRITE-MESSAGE-2.
5140  WRITE-MESSAGE-1.
5150     MOVE PART-NUMBER TO MESSG1.
5160     MOVE MESSAGE-1 TO PRINT-LINE.
5170     WRITE PRINT-LINE AFTER ADVANCING 2 LINES.
5180     GO TO READ-DATA.
5190  WRITE-MESSAGE-2.
5200     MOVE PART-NUMBER TO MESSG2.
5210     MOVE MESSAGE-2 TO PRINT-LINE.
5220     WRITE PRINT-LINE AFTER ADVANCING 2 LINES.
5230     GO TO READ-DATA.
5240  END-OF-JOB.
5250     CLOSE SALES-FILE, WAREHOUSE-FILE, PRINT-FILE.
```

*A standard card form, IBM Electro C61897, is available for punching source statements from this form.
Instructions for using this form are given in any IBM COBOL reference manual.
Address comments concerning this form to IBM Corporation, Programming Publications, 1271 Avenue of the Americas, New York, New York 10020.

GX28-1464-5 U/M 050
Printed in U.S.A.

FIGURE 13.3 COBOL PROGRAM LISTING

```
LINE NO. SEQ. NO.          SOURCE STATEMENT
     1     5020 START-PROGRAM.
     2     5030     OPEN INPUT SALES-FILE, WAREHOUSE-FILE, OUTPUT PRINT-FILE.
     3     5040 READ-DATA.
     4     5050     READ SALES-FILE INTO HOLD-INPUT, AT END GO TO END-OF-JOB.
     5     5060     MOVE UNITS-IN-SALES-DEPT TO WORKAREA-1.
     6     5070     READ WAREHOUSE-FILE INTO HOLD-INPUT, AT END GO TO END-OF-JOB.
     7     5080     MOVE UNITS-IN-WAREHOUSE TO WORKAREA-2.
     8     5090 CALCULATIONS.
     9     5100     ADD WORKAREA-1, WORKAREA-2, GIVING INVENTORY.
    10     5110     IF INVENTORY IS EQUAL TO 1000, GO TO WRITE-MESSAGE-1.
    11     5120     IF INVENTORY IS GREATER THAN 1000, GO TO WRITE-MESSAGE-1.
    12     5130     IF INVENTORY IS LESS THAN 1000, GO TO WRITE-MESSAGE-2.
    13     5140 WRITE-MESSAGE-1.
    14     5150     MOVE PART-NUMBER TO MESSG1.
    15     5160     MOVE MESSAGE-1 TO PRINT-LINE.
    16     5170     WRITE PRINT-LINE AFTER ADVANCING 2 LINES.
    17     5180     GO TO READ-DATA.
    18     5190 WRITE-MESSAGE-2.
    19     5200     MOVE PART-NUMBER TO MESSG2.
    20     5210     MOVE MESSAGE-2 TO PRINT-LINE.
    21     5220     WRITE PRINT-LINE AFTER ADVANCING 2 LINES.
    22     5230     GO TO READ-DATA.
    23     5240 END-OF-JOB.
    24     5250     CLOSE SALES-FILE, WAREHOUSE-FILE, PRINT-FILE.
    25     5260     STOP RUN.
```

The first two statements direct the computer to prepare the input and output devices that will be needed.

```
START-PROGRAM.
    OPEN INPUT SALES-FILE, WAREHOUSE-FILE, OUTPUT
    PRINT-FILE.
```

Next the programmer instructs the computer to read a card from the SALES-FILE with this code:

```
READ-DATA.
    READ SALES-FILE INTO HOLD-INPUT, AT END GO TO
    END-OF-JOB.
```

The computer will move all 80 columns of the input record into a temporary storage area called HOLD-INPUT. It will check the card to see if it is a specially coded end-of-file card. If it is, the computer will branch down to the routine called END-OF-JOB. If it is not, the computer goes on to the next instruction.

Since the program logic calls for only two values, UNITS-IN-SALES-DEPT and UNITS-IN-WAREHOUSE, to be added, the programmer will direct the computer to separate these quantities from the rest of the data on the record and move them into temporary working areas for manipulation.

MOVE UNITS-IN-SALES-DEPT TO WORKAREA-1.

This instruction tells the computer to move the quantity named UNITS-IN-SALES-DEPT to the temporary storage area named WORKAREA-1.

READ WAREHOUSE-FILE INTO HOLD-INPUT, AT END GO TO
  END-OF-JOB.

This statement tells the computer to read a record from the WAREHOUSE-FILE and move all 80 columns into HOLD-INPUT. This new data will replace the information read in and stored there from the last card. The card is tested to see if it is the last card in the file. If it is, the computer will branch down to the END-OF-JOB routine. If it is not, the computer goes on to the next instruction.

MOVE UNITS-IN-WAREHOUSE TO WORKAREA-2.

The computer is instructed to separate the quantity needed for manipulation from the rest of the data on the record. It will be moved into temporary storage area named WORKAREA-2.

Now the programmer is ready to calculate the total current INVENTORY. The computer is instructed to add the quantities stored in WORKAREA-1 and WORKAREA-2 and place the answer in the storage area named INVENTORY.

CALCULATIONS.
  ADD WORKAREA-1, WORKAREA-2, GIVING INVENTORY.

To test INVENTORY to see whether it is greater or less than 1,000 the programmer uses this code:

IF INVENTORY IS EQUAL TO 1000, GO TO WRITE-MESSAGE-1.
IF INVENTORY IS GREATER THAN 1000, GO TO WRITE-MESSAGE-1.
IF INVENTORY IS LESS THAN 1000, GO TO WRITE-MESSAGE-2.

The computer will perform the test as directed and branch to the appropriate paragraph.

The instructions that write the messages are

WRITE-MESSAGE-1.
  MOVE PART-NUMBER TO MESSG1.
  MOVE MESSAGE-1 TO PRINT-LINE.

The computer will move the PART-NUMBER stored in HOLD-INPUT into the reserved field in the MESSAGE-1 area. Then it will move MESSAGE-1 to the PRINT-LINE area.

> WRITE PRINT-LINE AFTER ADVANCING 2 LINES.

This tells the computer to double-space and print the data stored in the PRINT-LINE area on the line printer.

> GO TO READ-DATA.

With this statement, the programmer directs the computer to begin another loop and read in the next record from the SALES-FILE.

If INVENTORY is less than 1,000, the computer will branch to the second message.

> WRITE-MESSAGE-2.
>   MOVE PART-NUMBER TO MESSG2.
>   MOVE MESSAGE-2 TO PRINT-LINE.
>   WRITE PRINT-LINE AFTER ADVANCING 2 LINES.
>   GO TO READ-DATA.

It will move the PART-NUMBER from the HOLD-INPUT area to the field reserved for it in the MESSAGE-2 area. Then it will move the entire group to the line printer for output. Again the machine is instructed to double-space before printing MESSAGE-2 on the line printer. Then the computer will loop back to read another record from the SALES-FILE.

When the computer reads in the end-of-file card from the SALES-FILE, or WAREHOUSE-FILE, it will branch to the END-OF-JOB routine.

> END-OF-JOB.
>   CLOSE SALES-FILE, WAREHOUSE-FILE, PRINT-FILE.
>   STOP RUN.

Here the programmer tells the computer that there will be no more records to write or read. STOP RUN informs it that it has reached the last statement in the program.

At this point, the computer compiles the COBOL statements and executes the instructions on the data files. Figure 13.4 is an example of the output that would be generated by this program.

This example was a simplified program used for illustration. It was assumed that each file contained matching cards in the same sequence. In practice, several more steps would probably be included, to verify matching of part numbers, to reinitialize numerical areas before each loop, and even to have the computer print out the reorder forms. The coding shown is only part of the entire program. Chapter 15 gives a more detailed discussion of the structure of the COBOL language.

Keypunching   After the programmer has written the set of coded instructions, each line on the coding sheet is converted into a separate punched card. Data for the Warehouse and Sales files and the required job control information are

FIGURE 13.4 OUTPUT FROM COBOL PROGRAMMING EXAMPLE

REPLENISH STOCK OF PART-NUMBER 101 ORDER MORE UNITS IMMEDIATELY

THERE IS AN ADEQUATE SUPPLY OF PART-NUMBER 102

punched into cards. Finally, all cards are gathered together and assembled into a single deck called a job.

Running and Debugging Depending upon the type of installation, the job is either run by the programmer or submitted for run. One or more passes through the computer may be required to check the program for accuracy and to eliminate bugs or errors. Most programmers compare computer-generated results against known results calculated manually.

Documentation Documentation is the last step in program preparation. The programmer gathers together in a file the program listing, a copy of the sample data set, a narrative description of the program, and the flowchart.

THE INTERACTIVE PROGRAM

An interactive program is a program written either by a user or by a manufacturer that permits the user to enter data, branch, receive results, or change the course of the program flow during execution. It differs from the batch program in that it is designed to stop and wait for the programmer's directions. Many firms have interactive programs available on their computer systems. Time-sharing companies also provide interactive programs.

A user interacts with the program via a remote terminal keyboard connected to the CPU by telephone lines. Figure 13.5 shows a remote terminal. A remote terminal allows the user to interact with the program in a conversational way, to enter commands and data during processing, and to receive data as an immediate response.

Interactive programs have many branches and options. The branches are determined at key points during the processing, as the user selects options and feeds in parameters and variables. Interactive programs allow a user the flexibility of selecting procedures based on the results of a previous step.

FIGURE 13.5   REMOTE TERMINAL

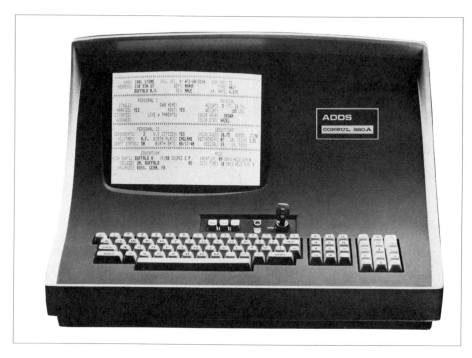

Advantages   A major advantage of the interactive program is its real-time feature. Data are processed instantaneously and results are made available immediately. Since the remote terminal can be placed wherever a telephone is located, it brings the power of the computer to the points in the business enterprise where and when it is most needed. The programmer or user does not have to go to the computer site to process data.

Interactive programming is practical for one-time-only problems as well as production work. If a program is available for a procedure, no time need be lost writing a program for a single problem or solving it manually.

Disadvantages   Costs may be higher for the interactive program than for the batch program. CPU time must be made available for all users on the system in a time-sharing arrangement. Communication lines, which must be either rented or purchased outright, must be provided to each online terminal.

The limitations of some terminals preclude their use for production runs. Since most terminals are designed to accept keyboard or paper tape input, large data files cannot be easily or economically entered. Some firms do store data files at the data center. An operator then loads them online when they are queried from a remote terminal—a procedure that requires time and negates some of the advantages of the interactive program.

Transmission line failure can cause troubles with online systems. The interruption of telephone service or electric power at a terminal will lock out that terminal. Data cannot be processed until the service is restored.

Problem Analysis   Interactive programs may be written by the user for a one-time-only execution and then erased, stored on a secondary storage medium for repeated execution, or called in from a library of programs available on the computer.

How these programs are implemented depends on which type they are.

ONE-TIME-ONLY-EXECUTION.   Programs to be executed only once might solve a particular mathematical problem in much the same way as an adding machine is used. The user examines the data and decides which operations are necessary to perform the desired manipulation. He or she then structures a simple program to carry these out and goes online to the computer. The computer is instructed to load the appropriate interactive compiler into primary storage. Then the user keyboards the lines in the program and directs the computer to execute them. The data can be written into the program or entered during execution from the keyboard. If any mistakes are present, they can be corrected immediately or other changes can be made, and the program is then rerun. When the problem is solved, the user signs off from the computer, making no attempt to save the keyboarded instructions.

LIBRARY PROGRAMS.   Programs called in from the computer's library may be written by the user or manufacturer to solve frequently run problems where the results are desired immediately. Examples are programs for calculating interest or loan payments.

The user must have a clear idea of the input data and the procedures that will have to be performed. The problem must be stated in quantitative terms suitable for solution by the computer. (In this respect, implementation is the same as in the batch program.)

After reviewing the programs available on the interactive terminal, the user selects a program and studies its documentation to determine its suitability for the problem at hand. Will it print out the results in the form and style required? Is the logic and algorithm followed in the program acceptable? What are the input and output specifications? What options are available?

The user goes online and directs the computer to call out the particular program from storage and make it available for execution. The program takes over, usually responding by giving a list of the options or routines it includes.

The user must determine the options needed to process the problem and then enter their names. The computer will ask questions and give instructions. At appropriate points in the execution, the computer will indicate that data should be entered and then will continue to process the information. Errors made when entering data are corrected immediately by retyping the new data. Results of the processing will be printed by the keyboard of the terminal.

REPEATED EXECUTION. Programs that solve frequently run problems can also be written by the user and stored on a secondary storage device ready for repeated execution. They are planned and coded in the same manner as batch programs. They can be designed to allow data to be entered from the keyboard during execution, read in from a secondary storage medium, or written into the program. These programs may include options that can be selected during execution, allowing the user the flexibility of solving specific problems.

This type of programming might be used to prepare reports based on keyboarded data, calculate carpeting needed for a given house size, calculate the price of a commodity, and so on.

To implement these programs, the user plans, flowcharts, codes, and debugs the program instructions and then directs the computer to store them on a secondary storage medium such as magnetic tape or disk. Each time the program is run, the user goes online and directs the computer to load the appropriate program into computer storage ready for execution. Depending on the design of the program, the user may enter data when requested by the program or indicate where it is stored, and selects options as desired. After execution is completed and the results are obtained, the user signs off from the computer.

BATCH PROGRAMS. Programs written in the batch mode can also be executed on an interactive terminal. The user goes online, instructs the computer to load the program from a secondary storage medium, indicates where the data will be found, and directs the computer to execute the program. The computer will then proceed without any further intervention from the user.

Documentation　An interactive programming session is self-documenting. The printout generated contains a record of the dialog between the computer and the user. It shows the computer's questions, the user's responses, the options used, and the data entered. Results of the processing are displayed on the printout and are thus available for further checking.

Most firms or data centers offering interactive programs usually provide comprehensive user manuals, which include not only documentation of the program, algorithm, and input/output specifications, but also directions for calling out and executing the program and a summary of available options. The interactive mode is often used to solve one-time-only problems, and hence less documentation is required than on the repetitive production runs usually handled by the batch program.

SAMPLE INTERACTIVE PROBLEM

The following example illustrates interactive programming. To illustrate one form of interactive programming, let us suppose a loan consultant has a customer applying for a $25,900 home loan at 7% interest. The customer asks the difference in monthly payments between a 20- and 30-year mortgage and the amount of equity that would have accumulated at the end of 10 years for each mortgage alternative.

The consultant has reviewed several interactive programs and selected a program that will perform the analysis needed. He or she is seated before an interactive terminal connected via telephone lines to a computer. Let

"Yes, it computed the answer in a billionth of a second and printed it instantly, but until I find my glasses . . ."

us follow the activity.[1] (The remarks typed by the computer are flush with the left margin, and the programmer's comments are printed in color. A brief discussion of each message is in the column at the right.)

OLD   NAME—MORTGE***   First, we call up the program.
READY.
          RUN   Then we type RUN, carriage
                                                         return. We request the
MORTGE   12:25   MON.   08-18-77   program to compute the
                                                         payment amount.
RATE = 1; LIFE = 2; AMOUNT BORROWED = 3; PAYMENT
AMOUNT = 4

ENTER THE NUMBER YOU WANT TO FIND [1,2,3, OR 4]?
     4

NUMBER OF PAYMENTS PER YEAR?   You can designate any
     12   number of payments in a
                                                         year. Since we want monthly
                                                         payments, we type 12.

NOMINAL ANNUAL RATE USING DECIMAL NOTATION?   This is the nominal annual
     .07   rate in decimal form.

LIFE OF THE MORTGAGE: YEARS, MONTHS   The life of the mortgage in
     20,0   this case is 20 years,
                                                         0 months.

AMOUNT TO BE BORROWED?   The total amount to be
     25900   borrowed is $25,900.

FOR HOW MANY CALENDAR YEARS DO YOU WANT THE   We want to show the equity
MORTGAGE TABLE PRINTED OUT?   for 10 years, so we
     10   type 10.

MONTH [JAN = 1; ETC.] AND YEAR IN WHICH THE MORTGAGE   Since the mortgage becomes
LOAN WILL BE MADE?   effective in September, 1977,
     9,77   we enter 9,77. The program
                                                         assumes that the first
                                                         payment is made after the
                                                         mortgage becomes effective.

---

[1]The illustration is from Call-A-Computer, General Library, "Interest, Mortgage, and Annuity Programs," pp. 5–6.

TYPE A ONE [1] IF YOU WANT ONLY AN ANNUAL SUMMARY OF THE MORTGAGE TABLE; TYPE A ZERO [0] FOR A MONTHLY TABLE?

1

The annual summary will suffice since we want to know the amount of equity, so we type 1. By typing 0, we would get a monthly (periodic) listing by year of interest, principal repayment, and outstanding principal.

*** MORTGAGE TERMS ***

NOMINAL ANNUAL RATE = 7 PERCENT
LIFE OF MORTGAGE = 20 YEARS, 0 MONTHS
AMOUNT BORROWED = $25900.00
PAYMENT AMOUNT = $200.80

This gives us a chance to check our data. It also indicates the payment amount.

*** MORTGAGE TABLE ***

YEAR	INTEREST	PRINCIPAL REPAYMENT	ENDING PRINCIPAL OUTSTANDING
77	452.378	150.029	25749.971
78	1782.635	626.994	25122.976
79	1737.310	672.320	24450.656
80	1688.708	720.922	23729.734
81	1636.592	773.037	22956.697
82	1580.709	828.920	22127.776
83	1520.787	888.843	21238.933
84	1456.532	953.098	20285.835
85	1387.633	1021.997	19263.838
86	1313.752	1095.877	18167.961
87	1234.531	1175.098	16992.862

Equity is the difference between loan amount and principal outstanding.

The consultant will then call up the same program and repeat the process, inserting data for a 30-year mortgage. The two printouts can then be compared and the customer can choose the mortgage alternative best suited to his or her needs.

Batch programs can also be processed over remote terminals, but not in the interactive mode. The batch program and data sets are entered via paper tape or keyboard and the computer takes over. It processes the job and prints the results on the remote terminal. There is no interaction between the program and the user, and the course of the program cannot be changed during execution.

The Interactive
Terminal

An interactive terminal is an online, real-time terminal designed to input and output data from a keyboard. As you recall, online means the terminal is directly connected to the computer. This connection allows the user to change the course of execution of the program, to add in data, or to handle queries from the CPU at the time and place that are most convenient. Real time means that the CPU processes the data or queries at the instant the keyboarding takes place.

The interactive terminal is remotely connected to the CPU over telephone lines and need not be in the same building or even the same city as the computer. It can be located where it has the greatest value to most users; many firms have more than one terminal available in different offices or departments.

Some Available
Interactive
Programs

The following list of programs, available from the General Electric Time Sharing Services, illustrates the varieties of programs available in this mode.[2]

Auditing: Appraises the results of an audit and calculates confidence limits with different ratios. Calculates the size of an audit sample necessary to satisfy certain cost questions.

Accounting: Handles journals and chart of accounts, maintains general ledgers, prepares departmental income statements, balance sheets, and schedules for selected accounts.

Business modeling: Sets up a working model of any system. Provides statistical measures of system operation.

Bond analysis: Calculates potential gains on presently held securities and compares potential return on investment for each bond to determine average of trade. Calculates price that should be paid for bonds to realize a specified yield.

Cash flow analysis: Calculates the discounted rate of return and the present worth of cash flow over life of investment.

Inventory control: Simulates an inventory system, forecasts customer demand and time needed to build and maintain inventory. Calculates optimum inventory level.

Loans and interest: Calculates payment or withdrawal annuity variables and prints out annuity tables. Calculates nominal and effective annual interest rates for installment loans.

Management decisions: Makes yearly projections from average percentage change. Evaluates and compares alternative methods of plant and production expansion by the Monte Carlo simulation method.

Marketing and economic forecasting: Correlates as many as ten time series of data. Finds best-fit curve.

---

[2]General Electric Information Systems, Program Library Index #800000 4-70, p. 3.

Computer Assists in Childbirth

Doctors and nurses in the obstetrics ward at Oak Knoll Naval Hospital in Oakland, California, are receiving help from a new kind of midwife: a computer.

"It's a lot different from the days when about all we had to work with was a stethoscope," said one of the doctors. The stethoscope was a limited tool during labor because it could not be used during contractions when the mother was moving around.

Now the computer monitors critical functions during labor—and it, in turn, is monitored by another device.

About 10 years ago the monitoring system became available to hospitals, but Oak Knoll is the first to have the scanner that checks all information in the computer.

The system keeps track of the fetal heartbeat patterns. It is capable of analyzing heart rates and discerns the contraction pattern of the uterus during labor. This information is fed into a "read-out station" at the nurses' desk. When the alert system detects a problem, a light flashes on and a beeper sounds.

Despite the presence of all this hardware there is still plenty of personal attention by nurses and doctors.

The system brings to the attention of the physician problems he or she couldn't even recognize before. The monitoring is expected to greatly reduce mental retardation and other brain damage that occurs because of lack of oxygen to the fetus.

SOURCE: "Computer Plays Role of 'Midwife' at Hospital," UPI (dateline Oakland, CA).

Production analysis: Projects work effort based on average work unit. Calculates output based on average learning curve theory.

THE SUPPLIED PROGRAM

A supplied program is a program written by someone other than the user. It may be provided by a computer manufacturer, a private or public institution, or by a firm that specializes in writing programs for sale (proprietary software house). Such programs may be made available at no charge, at a flat fee, or on a monthly lease or rental arrangement.

Supplied programs are available to process many different business, scientific, and statistical problems. These programs may be delivered as a set of punched cards ready to be run on the user's computer, as a program recorded on magnetic or paper tape, or on a disk pack. Some supplied programs are available only as a program listing, and the user must keypunch a program deck or record it on tape or disk.

Some business firms find it cheaper to buy or lease a program from a proprietary firm than to pay for the programming effort and debugging time required to develop the program. In addition, off-the-shelf programs provided at no charge by computer manufacturers are attractive to users.

Since the supplied program is already written and tested, the user has only to check it out and prepare the modifications. Sometimes supplied programs include extra services that a firm finds useful but would not pay to develop specifically. And, in some cases, the supplier provides maintenance, revisions, and modification serivces as part of the rental agreement. For example, modifications resulting from changes in the tax rate or calculations or new laws affecting the program might be supplied as part of the maintenance agreement.

Since sophisticated, documented programs are available, a user with little or no programming experience or mathematical skills can perform mathematical and financial analysis procedures. The program asks the questions and provides the algorithms and logic; the user supplies the data and decides which algorithm to use.

A disadvantage of the supplied program is that it may be too generalized for a given firm's needs. The conversion costs or reprogramming effort required to bring it in line with needs may be as great as those for writing an original program. If the demand for a supplied program falls below a certain point the manufacturer may withdraw it from circulation and the user will lose supporting services, such as revisions, updating, and maintenance, that were formerly available.

MANUFACTURER-SUPPLIED PROGRAMS.   A primary source of supplied programs is the computer manufacturer. Firms such as Burroughs, General Electric, and IBM provide customers with ready-made programs. Available programs are listed in a catalog, which is supplied without charge to users and includes descriptive information and an abstract for each program. For a partial listing of supplied programs, see Table 13.1.

The manufacturer provides documentation, more details, and a copy of a specific program upon request. The documentation file may contain a copy of the program flowchart, program listing, descriptive material on the algorithm, and application notes. These programs are sometimes called "off the shelf," because they are readily available.

Manufacturer-supplied programs are generalized in nature and designed for common business applications. The following IBM-supplied programs are typical of the range available:

· Finance: Investing, borrowing, stocks, bonds, taxes and auditing

TABLE 13.1 SOME PROGRAMS SUPPLIED FOR MARK II[a]

ACCOUNTING

BIGGL$***   Expanded version of PLBAL$ that handles up to 550 chart-of-accounts records.

JEDIT$***   Edits journal entry files prior to their input to PBAL$ ro BIGGL$ for detecting invalid account codes or out-of-balance conditions. Also prints total income or loss resulting from journal entries for income tax determination.

PLBAL$***   Maintains the general ledger for a business and produces specified trial balances, detailed general ledger listings, total and departmental income statements, balance sheets, and schedules for selected accounts.

AUDITING

APSAM$***   Appraises the results of an audit by calculating the confidence limits on the cost questioned, using difference and ratio methods.

RANUM$***   Generates random numbers within specified range.

RASEQ$***   Generates sets of random numbers.

SAMSI$***   Calculates the size of an audit sample necessary to satisfy specified confidence limits on cost questioned.

BUSINESS MODELING

GENPS$***   Performs operating simulation of any system—mechanical or human. Provides a variety of statistical measures of system operation.

FINANCIAL ANALYSIS

ANNUIT***   Calculates payment or withdrawal annuity variables and prints annuity tables.

DEPREC   Calculates depreciation schedules.

FINAN$***   Prepares seven types of financial analyses and can handle ten historical and ten projected years.

LESEE$***   Determines net advantage of leasing with respect to borrowing funds and to buying the asset, with annual cash flows and sensitivity analysis.

LESIM$***   Calculates the risk of investing in an asset and then leasing.

LESØR$***   Calculates rate of return from investing in an asset and then leasing the asset to another party, with annual cash flows and sensitivity analysis.

[a]General Electric Company, Information Service Department, 7735 Old Georgetown Road, Bethesda, Md. 20014. *Program Library Index,* "Mark II Applications Programs," p. 3.

- Cost accounting: Labor, work in progress
- Payroll and benefits: Payroll, employee benefits, profit sharing, retirement, credit union
- Personnel: Recruiting, hiring, training, wages, salary
- Manufacturing: Scheduling, loading, job reporting, bill of materials
- Inventory: Stocking, inventory, equipment and tool inventory
- Purchasing: Preparation of purchase orders, accounts payable, purchase analysis
- Marketing: Sales forecasting, bid analysis, territory analysis

User-Supplied Programs

Another group of supplied programs is provided by computer users themselves. These programs are made available by users, without charge, to the manufacturer, who in turn passes them along at no charge.

Users may supply programs similar to those provided by the manufacturer. However, user-supplied programs are often more limited in application, since they are written by private firms to meet specific local needs.

Schools and universities often make their programs available to other institutions. Although these programs may have required thousands of hours of programming time and many dollars in preparation, they are usually offered at little or no charge. The Biomedical Programs researched and developed by UCLA include dozens of routines for the health sciences. Many of these are statistical and analytical programs that can also be used to solve business problems. The entire group of programs is available on magnetic tape with a printed manual that outlines and documents the programs.

Proprietary Programs

Many programs have been written by private firms, consultants, and banks and insurance companies and are available to other users at a charge. Proprietary software firms specialize in developing, writing, and marketing programs for profit. These firms offer general programs for a flat fee or a monthly lease or rental arrangement.

The number and types of firms providing this service have grown in the past decade. Businesses often find that programs supplied by software firms are better written and cost less than programs written by users themselves, because software firms employ specialized, highly qualified programmers.

The following proprietary programs will give some idea of the scope and type available:

- File maintenance: Maintains large files such as payroll, personnel inventory, and sales. Routines include searches, merges, file updating, and removing inactive names or records.

- Payroll and taxes: Handles tax preparation for a range of business personnel. Calculates withholding taxes and prepares government and internal reports. Also calculates earnings, deductions, and tax liability, and prints paychecks.
- Accounts receivable: Handles a firm's accounts receivable and order processing, customer payments, aged balances, and current inventory stock level and generates up-to-date reports, invoices, and statements.

TABLE 13.2   PROGRAMMING MODE COMPARISON

	BATCH PROGRAM	INTERACTIVE PROGRAM	SUPPLIED PROGRAM
ALGORITHM	Selection of algorithm by user or vendor	Selection of algorithm by user or vendor	Algorithm supplied by vendor; reviewed by user
CODING	By programmer on coding sheets	By programmer on coding sheets	By vendor
KEYPUNCHING/ KEYBOARDING	Program keyboarded by user or vendor; data keyboarded by user or stored on secondary storage media	Program, responses and data entered directly from terminal	Program keyboarded by vendor; data keyboarded by user or punched by user
RUN AND DEBUG	Careful check after run of data and program by user	Careful check after run of data and program by user	Done by vendor; revised by user; modifications prepared and tested by user
DOCUMENTATION	Complete file written by user or vendor	Complete file written by user or vendor	Supplied by vendor; modifications written by user
PROGRAMMING COST	Borne by user or vendor	Borne by user or vendor	Borne by vendor; modifications at user's expense
APPLICATION	To solve specific, one-time-only, or frequently run problems	To solve specific, one-time-only, or frequently run problems	Generalized routines for application by many users

· Finance company accounting: Processes all data, calculations, and operations. Calculates collections, fees, loans, and balances, records payments, prepares ledger and summary statements, and prints mailing labels.

· Data plotting: Plots a variety of business, educational, and scientific data. Data may be computed or read in from cards and printed on the line printer as a plot.

· Commercial banking: Handles a variety of commercial banking and savings and loan tasks. Processes mortgage payments and certificates of deposits, provides management reports, and prepares the general ledger.

Implementing the Supplied Program

The potential user of a supplied program first obtains an abstract. If the program appears to solve the problem at hand, additional documentation, such as flowcharts and sample input and output records, is ordered. Some factors considered are: Will the program run on the available computer? What modifications will be necessary? Would it be more economical to write an entirely new program?

If it is suitable, the program is recorded on cards, tape, or disk. The program is obtained from the vendor. It is then run on the computer, modifications are entered, and sample test data are run and checked.

Table 13.2 contrasts the batch, interactive, and supplied program modes. The comparisons are based upon general considerations and thus may not be true for all data processing installations.

KEY TERMS

Batch program	Real time
Interactive program	Supplied program
Manufacturer-supplied program	User-supplied program
Proprietary program	

EXERCISES

1. Who develops the logic, flowcharts, and algorithm for the supplied program?
2. Describe several supplied programs and explain how they may be used in a business firm.
3. What are the advantages and disadvantages of the supplied program?
4. What are proprietary suppliers? Give several examples of the type of programs they provide.
5. How does a firm select and implement a supplied program?
6. What is an interactive program? How does it differ from the stand-alone program?

7. Give several examples of available interactive programs.
8. What are the advantages of the interactive program?
9. What are the limitations on interactive programs?
10. What kinds of problems are best suited for online, real-time programming?
11. How does a user implement an interactive program?
12. Contact a time-sharing firm in your area and determine the kinds of interactive programs available from them.

PART FIVE

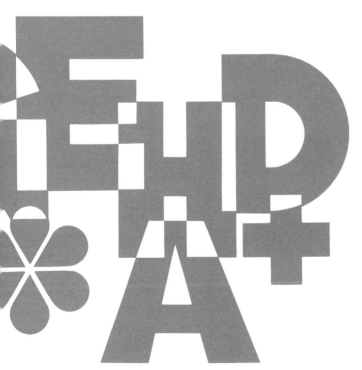

COMPUTER
SOFTWARE

14

OPERATING SYSTEMS

Early in the evolution of computer systems it became obvious that the human operator was a limiting factor in the development of technology. As computer hardware increased in complexity and jobs could be processed more rapidly, human operators could no longer keep up with the system. Minutes, or even hours, were often lost while an operator loaded cards, put paper in the line printer, removed jobs from the machine, logged in runs, and diagnosed errors and problems.

Computer designers realized that the computer could best schedule its own work and diagnose its own troubles. Programs were written to direct the computer through the steps involved in scheduling jobs, accounting for time used, assigning input and output devices and switching them online and offline at the proper times. These programs, called monitor or supervisor programs, were supplied by the computer manufacturer. They enabled the operator to concentrate on physically loading and unloading the jobs from the input and output devices. The computer, controlled by an internal program, processed each job in the most efficient way. Error conditions were immediately brought to the attention of the operator, who, freed of the scheduling responsibility, could apply his or her time to diagnosing and eliminating the error conditions.

As computer hardware developed, more complicated programs, called operating systems, were written to handle even more tasks. Manufacturers call these systems master control programs, executive control systems, or comprehensive operating supervisors. Operating systems differ from source (problem) programs in that they are written by the computer manufacturer. Source (problem) programs are written by the user to solve a direct, local, data-processing problem.

PRINCIPLES OF OPERATING SYSTEMS

An operating system is a complex group of programs and routines that enables a computer to schedule work in the most efficient way. Operating systems supervise the overall operation of the computer, control the flow of jobs in and out of the system, switch input/output machines in and out, and call programs from storage. They include language translators (or compilers), which convert coded programs into machine language. Table 14.1 is a partial list of routines (modules) that make up an operating system. Operating systems are usually written by the computer manufacturer for each series of computers they make.

What An Operating System Does Suppose a source program punched in cards and submitted to the computer for run contains a programming error serious enough to prevent the computer from completing the run. Without an operating system, the job input, processing, error interruption, and output would be handled as follows: The program would be fed to the computer by a human operator who would manually switch in the card reader, place the cards in the hopper, turn on the device, and start the CPU. The operator would also prepare the output device (line printer, for example) and log in the time and job name on the log sheet. Only then could the computer proceed to process the job.

The computer would begin compilation, but the error would prevent it from executing the job. The operator would have to determine the cause of the failure: Is it a machine failure, a programming error, a paper jam, or a mispunched data card?

Suppose the operator were busy loading cards into a card reader. The computer would remain idle until he or she became aware of the stoppage, found and corrected the trouble, and restarted the machine.

When an operating system handles the scheduling, the same situation is handled as follows: The operator loads the cards into the card reader and then starts the processing cycle by pressing a button. The machine switches the card reader online and begins processing the job. When the machine encounters an error in the program, it diagnoses the difficulty as, for example, a programmer error. It immediately prints a message to the operator and runs the cards for that job out of the card reader. Then without delay it begins to input the next run.

Batch and Real-Time Operating Systems One means of categorizing operating systems is based upon their ability to process programs in the batch or real-time operating mode. Batch operating systems are designed to process a job stream consisting of a queue of batch

TABLE 14.1 OPERATING SYSTEM MODULES

PREFIX	IBM-PROGRAM NUMBER	COMPONENT
IHD	360N-CB-452	COBOL Library Subroutines
IJB	360N-CL-453	System Control and Basic IOCS (disk supervisor)
IJC		I/O Card
IJD		I/O Printer
IJE		I/O Paper Tape
IJF		I/O Magnetic Tape
IJG	360N-IO-476	Consecutive Disk IOCS
IJH		Indexed Sequential Direct Access
IJI		Direct Access Method
IJJ		Device Independent Access Method
IJK	360N-PL-464	PL/I Library Subroutines
IJM	360N-IO-478	OCR Devices
IJN	360N-UT-472	Vocabulary File Utility (7772)
IJO	360N-SM-450	Disk Sort/Merge
IJP	360N-SM-400	Tape Sort/Merge
IJQ	360N-AS-465	Assembler
IJR	360N-RG-460	RPG
IJS	360N-CB-452	COBOL Compiler
IJT	360N-FO-451	Basic FORTRAN Compiler
IJU	360N-IO-477	MICR Devices
IJV	360N-PT-459	Autotest
IJX	360N-PL-464	PL/I Compiler
IJY	360N-AS-466	Assembler F
IJZ	360N-DN-481	On-Line Test Executive Program
IKL	360N-CV-489	COBOL LCP

[a]IBM Systems Reference Library, "IBM System/360, DOS: System Generation & Maintenance," C24-5033-8, p. 306.

programs. Each is executed in turn. Real-time operating systems, on the other hand, are designed to respond to events or interruptions and usually to execute several batch or interactive programs simultaneously from online devices. For example, real-time operating systems are required when remote terminals are connected online to the computer. The system must be able to respond promptly to the requests of each terminal user. Real-time operating systems are also used to control processes such as the manufacture of gases, petroleum refining, and food processing.

Some operating systems are designed to handle both batch and real-time tasks at one time. These systems enable the computer to process a stream of batch programs fed into a local card reader or terminal. At the same time, they will respond to a group of real-time terminals, such as teller terminals, located remotely from the processor.

The sets of instructions that make up the operating systems are held in secondary storage on disk, tape, or drum. The unit that holds the operating system is usually referred to as the resident storage device. The particular unit used as resident storage device is reserved exclusively for this purpose.

Manufacturers have given different names to their operating systems according to the media on which they are stored. IBM refers to several operating systems as follows:

TAPE OPERATING SYSTEM (TOS).   This is an operating system that is stored on magnetic tape. When a given routine is needed, it is located on the tape and transferred to primary storage by the system. A number of routines may be called from the tape in the execution of a single program.

DISK OPERATING SYSTEMS (DOS).   Operating systems may also be stored on a disk pack. As various routines are needed, they are called into active storage from the disk.

BASIC OPERATING SYSTEM (BOS).   The Basic Operating System is another method of controlling the computer. The system is stored on disks but differs from the DOS in that the operator communicates with the computer in number codes rather than in English terms. This system is more limited in its functions and is used on smaller computers.

OPERATING SYSTEM (OS).   With the Operating System (OS), used on most large computers, the controlling program is often stored on a random-access magnetic drum. This system allows the computer to process many jobs simultaneously (multiprogramming). Primary storage and input/output devices are assigned with more flexibility than in the previously mentioned systems.

OPERATING SYSTEM/VIRTUAL STORAGE (OS/VS).   This operating system monitors computers that use the virtual storage memory concept. In virtual storage (described in Chapter 8), source programs are stored on a secondary storage device and broken into small segments called "pages." These pages are swapped in and out of primary memory for execution as space becomes available. The OS/VS oversees the "paging" process, keeping track of where all segments are located and what part of the program should be executed next.

Under other systems, large programs are stored as blocks in fixed locations in primary storage. There will often be unused areas between these blocks that are too small to hold another program and are therefore wasted. The OS/VS eliminates this problem, allowing faster and more efficient utilization of the computer's capacities. OS/VS systems are usually

Teaching Computers How to Get Along with People

Machines have a bad reputation when it comes to serving people. They're always giving you the wrong change or the flavor you didn't ask for. Using machines in a business firm that depends on the public's good will can, therefore, be a very dangerous matter.

But automatic teller machines save a lot of money and time for the Wachovia Bank and Trust Company, Winston-Salem, North Carolina, and permit off-hour services to depositors and customers that otherwise would be prohibitively expensive. "People can think of enough reasons for complaining or even moving their accounts without letting a machine hurt their feelings," says a spokesman.

The answer was to teach the computerized terminals to be very polite and understanding when dealing with people. The first thing the bank found out was that people want to tell the machine what to do and not have the machine give them commands. That may be all right in a computer center, but in a bank it can be suicidal. So all machine instructions were very carefully worded.

The bank found customers objected to the typical green cathode ray letters, so printed messages from a revolving film were substituted.

The messages have to be easily understood and not contain a hint of programming jargon. Words with double meanings must be avoided; for example, key in had to be used instead of enter, and money instead of funds. Please and thank you were sprinkled liberally throughout the messages.

Results for the first month of operation have been very good. Each machine averaged 4,300 transactions with no complaints of discourtesy or confusion.

By the way, the most frequent user of the machines during the off hours were young men needing extra cash for the weekend.

SOURCE: "Automatic Tellers Trained in Civility," by Leroy Pope, UPI (dateline Van Nuys, CA).

designed to enable the computer to run both real time and batch programs simultaneously.

System Generation

System generation, sometimes called system initiation, is the procedure of designing, organizing, and setting up an operating system to meet the needs of a specific firm. Programs, utilities, and routines are selected and recorded on the system's resident storage device (tape, drum, or disk). System generation is usually done when a new computer system is installed by a firm. The resources of the operating system are custom tailored to the particular demands of the user.

Functions of the Operating System

Operating systems can be divided into two major types of programs: control programs and service programs. Here are some examples of these two groups.

CONTROL PROGRAMS

1. *Schedule Input and Output Operations.* The CPU can normally process more data per second than a single input and output device can feed in or receive. Thus, many devices must be switched in and out at the proper time.
2. *Communicate with the Operator or Programmer.* The operating system directs the computer to type messages on the console typewriter regarding the status of the computer system, such as I/O devices that need attention, errors in job flow, or abnormal conditions.
3. *Handle Interruptions.* Interruptions caused by errors or input/output problems are processed in an orderly way to reduce time lost from the regular job flow. If an error is detected, the computer does not stop and wait for the operator. It prints a message and goes on to the next job without delay.
4. *Log Jobs.* The program keeps a list of jobs run and clocks them in and out. It records and prints out the elapsed compilation and execution time.
5. *Monitor Status.* The operating program monitors the status of the computer system and performs error and parity checks.
6. *Combine Phases of a Job into a Complete Run.* Parts of a job that is too large to run as a unit can be processed in smaller blocks.
7. *Handle Multiprogramming.* The program will switch between several jobs and allocate time or assign priority. It maintains checkpoints so that jobs can be resumed at the proper place.

SERVICE PROGRAMS

1. *Load Programs and Language Translators (Compilers).* Programs are read from the system's inactive storage areas to active (primary) storage by the operating system.
2. *Maintain the System Library.* Computer systems are capable of storing frequently used routines and programs for use by programmers. These routines are usually held in secondary storage, called the system library. The operating system catalogs and retrieves the routines for the programmer.

EXAMPLE OF AN OPERATING SYSTEM

Although operating systems vary from manufacturer to manufacturer, there are several features common to all. The following describes the organization of an IBM system. (Although the basic concepts are the same, other manufacturers may use different terminology.) The IBM operating system is composed of control programs and processing programs.

Control
Programs

In the IBM system, control programs consist of three types of routines or subprograms:

❶ Supervisor Program

❷ Job Control Program

❸ Input/Output Control Program

SUPERVISOR PROGRAM.   The supervisor program is designed to control the overall scheduling of the computer operations. The supervisor pulls required routines from the resident storage device (disk, tape, or drum) and loads them into primary memory. The supervisor schedules input and output operations and allocates channels to I/O devices. It types messages to the computer operator, indicating error conditions, I/O devices that need attention, etc.

Sidney Harris

"This one writes some fine lyrics, and the other one has done some beautiful music, but they just don't seem to hit it off as collaborators."

JOB CONTROL PROGRAM.   The job control program is designed to facilitate batch processing. In batch processing, the computer operator assembles many individual jobs into a group called a job stream for processing on the computer. (See Figure 14.1.) The job stream is fed to the card reader or other input device, and the machine processes each job in turn, without operator intervention. The computer operator is thus free to perform other tasks.

FIGURE 14.1   JOB STREAM

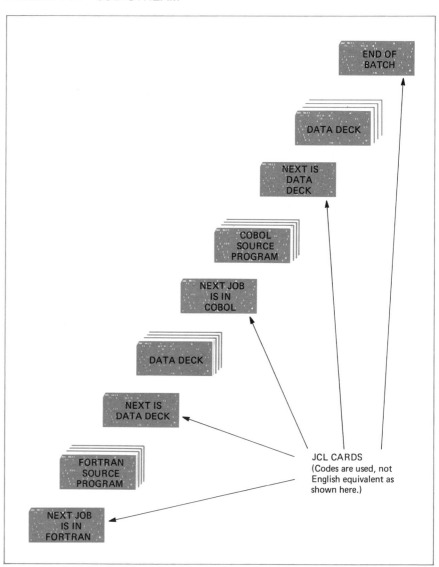

Within the job stream are a number of job control instructions. Some of them indicate the beginning and the end of each job in the group. Others, included in each individual job, give the computer the programmer's instructions for the job. The job control program translates the code on the job control instructions into machine language instructions to the CPU.

INPUT/OUTPUT CONTROL PROGRAM. I/O devices cannot be scheduled for the CPU in an indiscriminate manner. Careful and efficient allocation of card readers, line printers, card punches, tape units, etc. is essential if the CPU is to run at maximum processing speed and without interruption.

In most computers, the Input/Output Control System (IOCS) performs these functions rapidly and efficiently. The IOCS continually monitors the I/O devices. If the line printer is out of paper or the card reader is jammed, it will signal the operator by typing a message on the console typewriter (or displaying it on a video screen). It will substitute other devices if they are available so that processing will not be interrupted.

The IOCS prepares input and output devices for use. For example, it will load reels of magnetic tape, check identification labels, and index the reels to the required point. The IOCS opens the circuitry that permits data to flow between the I/O devices and the CPU. It checks parity of data being transmitted and manages the job of buffering as the data move in and out of the CPU.

Processing Programs
The processing programs work with the control programs to enable the computer to receive a problem written in a programming language, process it, and proceed to the next job in an orderly fashion. IBM classifies their processing programs as

① Language Translators
② Service Programs

LANGUAGE TRANSLATORS. Language translators, often called compilers, were discussed in Chapter 11. Since computers can operate only on instructions coded in machine language, and most programs are written in languages resembling English or mathematical representation, a system of translation is needed. A program called a compiler, or language translator, does the job. (See Figure 14.2) A compiler translates instructions for only one language, or one version of a language, into machine language. The machine language equivalents of the instructions are then fed to the CPU for processing.

Small computers may have only one or two compilers available, for example, for the assembler and FORTRAN languages. Large systems may have compilers for several languages, such as FORTRAN, COBOL, PL/I, RPG, BASIC, ALGOL, and SNOBOL. With the larger system, the programmer

FIGURE 14.2 LANGUAGE TRANSLATOR

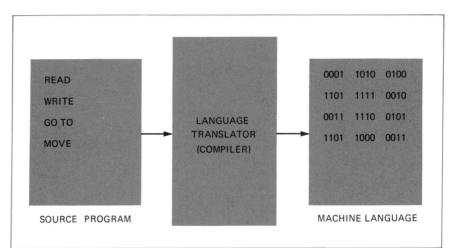

has the option of writing a program in the language best suited to a problem's particular needs. In all cases, the specific compiler is called out by a job control instruction in the job stream.

SERVICE PROGRAMS.   Service programs are subprograms that perform frequently used routines and functions for the programmer. They make a great variety of procedures available to the programmer and thus save much programming time and effort. These programs are called out by job control instructions.

The computer's ability to store and call out these service programs gives it much of its power and capability. Some common service programs are as follows:

1. *Librarian.*   The librarian is a service program that maintains the system library. It allocates a storage area in the computer system for any program, or part of a program, that a programmer wishes to save. It keeps track of where the program has been stored, for future use. This process is called cataloging a program. A system library is usually kept on disk or tape.

   The system library contains programs from many sources. Some are frequently accessed programs or modules cataloged by users. Other programs are cataloged in the system library by the manufacturer. These programs have wide applications in the routine processing performed by many users.

2. *Sort/Merge Programs.*   Much of the data processing task is the preparation and maintenance of files, which must often be merged, updated, or sorted. Routines to perform these common tasks are stored in the operating system and are called out by job control instructions.

Usually sort and merge programs are general in nature and have multiple functions.

3. *Utilities.*   Similar in nature to the sort and merge programs are the utility programs. The utility programs perform such tasks as transferring data from cards to tape or from tape to the line printer, and reblocking data. They are called out by the appropriate job control language.

For example, suppose a programmer has a program that processes data recorded on magnetic tape. But the data are available only on punched cards. The data in the file could be transferred to tape with offline equipment or job control instructions could be used to call out the card-to-tape utility program available in the operating system. The computer would then transfer and process the data during the same run.

PROCESSING THE JOB

When a job stream is fed to the computer for processing, the operating system logs in the name of the job from the first job control instruction and the time on the line printer or the console typewriter. It then reads and follows the instructions on the succeeding job control instruction.

The operating system will load the proper language translator (compiler), read and compile the source program, and prepare an object deck or module. An object module is the machine language translation of the coded programming statements. It is stored as electronic bits in a secondary storage device with other program modules. When ready for execution, the object module and other programs are loaded into primary memory. (See Figure 14.3.) Then the computer executes the program on the data set.

Upon encountering the job control instruction that signals the end of the job, the computer records the elapsed time and logs out the job. Then it moves to the next job in the batch.

Job Control
Instructions

Job control instructions are referred to by various names, depending on the system in which they are used. Burroughs, for example, refers to "program control cards" and "program parameter cards." IBM refers to these instructions as "job control language" (JCL) and the cards on which they are punched as JCL cards. General Electric calls them "control cards."

The job control program recognizes most job control instructions in the job stream by a special symbol, or symbols, appearing in the first one or two columns of a record. Some systems use a "?," others a "$" or the letters "CC." The JCL instructions for the IBM 370 OS/VS system, for example, use a slash in the first column.

When the computer recognizes a job control instruction the Job Control Program translates it and calls the appropriate routine of the operating system into working storage.

FIGURE 14.3   OBJECT MODULE

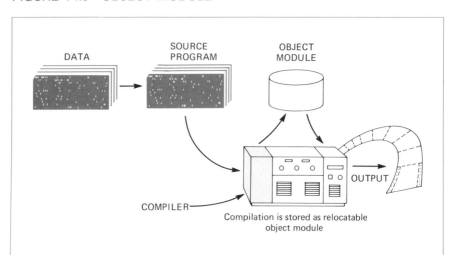

Although variations exist, most systems require similar job control instructions to compile and run a job. The most common ones used in the IBM system are illustrated in Figure 14.4 and include the following.

1. *Job Statement.*   This instruction identifies a new job. Most job statements include an identifying name and the JCL code symbols that identify a new job to the system. The system will log in the name of the job, the time on the console typewriter, and the output medium of the program.
2. *Procedure Statement.*   This instruction directs the computer to call a specific compiler from storage and transfers control of the system to that compiler. Only compilers available to the system can be called. Most machines are equipped with several compilers, so that programs may be written in different languages.
3. *DD Statement.*   This instruction identifies and describes a data set and gives the name of the data set, type of I/O devices that hold the data set, format of records, and the method used to access the data set. In this instance, it describes the source program that is to follow.

   Problem Program.   The source (problem) program is next in line.

4. *Delimiter Statement.*   This instruction marks the end of the source program.
5. *DD Statement.*   This instruction identifies and describes a data set and directs the computer to begin execution. Its purpose is to indicate to the system that it has compiled the programming instructions and execution should begin. (in this instance it describes the data set that is to follow.)

   Data Set.   The data set, if present, follows the DD statement.

6. *Delimiter Statement.* Marks the end of the data set.
7. *End of Job (EOJ).* This instruction tells the computer the end of the job has been reached. It shifts control from the program under execution back to the operating system. Upon encountering the (//) END OF JOB statement, the computer logs out the job on the console typewriter. The system is then ready to begin the next job in the batch.

FIGURE 14.4 COMMON JCL INSTRUCTIONS

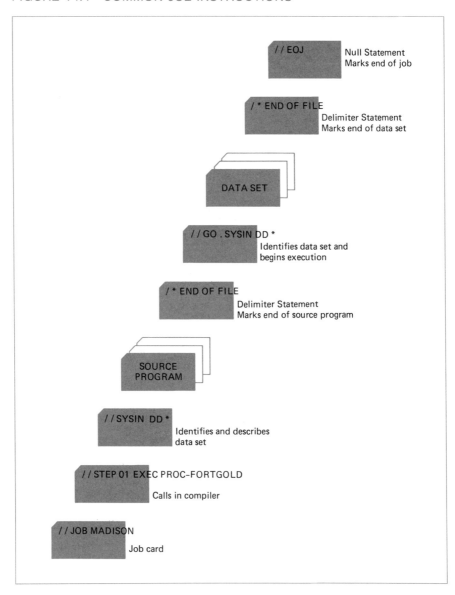

FIGURE 14.5   JOB CONTROL COMBINATIONS

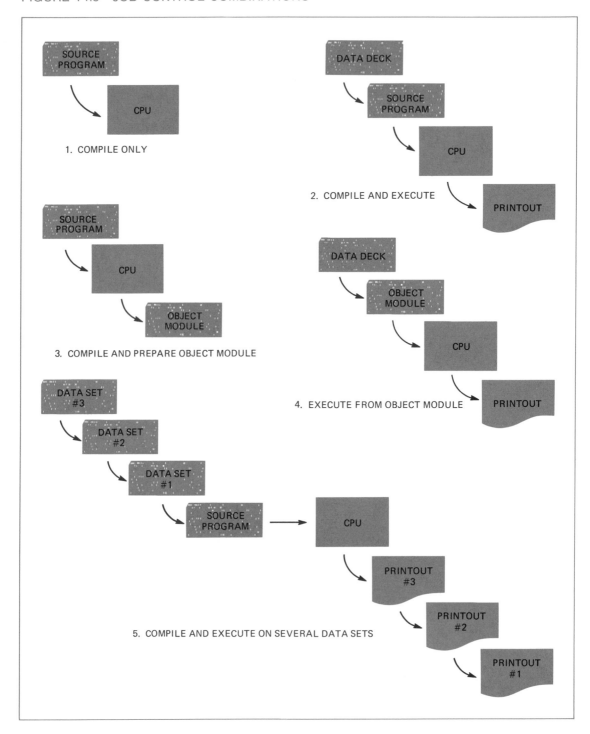

In the example in Figure 14.4, the programmer instructed the computer to compile and execute the job on a data set. This was done with an appropriate set of JCL instructions in the job stream. JCL instructions may also be set up to perform a variety of compile and run combinations.

Options
Figure 14.5 illustrates some of the options available to the programmer using the IBM system. A job can be set up to compile and execute on one data set or on many data sets. At other times during the debugging process, the programmer may only want to see if the program will compile and not include JCL instructions for execution.

The programmer can also use JCL instructions to direct the computer to compile a program and prepare an object module of the machine instructions. (An object module submitted to the computer for execution does not require compilation. This can save considerable CPU time in repetitive runs.)

The options available on a computer system vary. The most common ones on an IBM system are

LIST SOURCE PROGRAM. The computer will list the source program on the output device. Each instruction in the program is listed on the line printer in the order that it is read. This option is important during the debugging phase or when working with a new program.

DUMP MAIN STORAGE. The computer will dump the contents of its main storage in the event of abnormal program termination. A dump is a listing in the hexadecimal code of the contents of each position in storage. It is used in debugging to indicate the point at which a program failed.

LOG. This instruction tells the computer to list the job name and all JCL statements on the console typewriter.

KEY TERMS
Basic Operating System (BOS)
Control program
Disk Operating System (DOS)
Input/output control programs
Job control program
Job stream
Librarian
Object module
Operating System (OS)

OS/VS
Processing programs
Resident storage device
Service program
Supervisor program
System generation
System library
Tape Operating System (TOS)

EXERCISES
1. What are the limitations of using human operators to schedule work for computer systems?
2. Define an operating system.
3. Summarize the functions of the operating system.
4. Compare the major types of operating systems.
5. What is the function of system generation? What are the determining factors in generating a new system?
6. What are the differences in function between control programs and processing programs?
7. Briefly summarize the functions of the major job control instructions.
8. What are some options that may be called out by job control instructions?
9. What are the functions of service programs? How do they save time and programming effort?
10. Obtain a copy of the system log (output from the console typewriter) from the operator in your data center. List the type of information it contains.
11. What language translators or compilers are available on the system in your data center?
12. What service and utility programs are available on your system?
13. What job control instructions are used on your system? If a keypunch is available, punch a set of job control cards to run and execute a simple program.

15

COBOL
PROGRAMMING LANGUAGE

To give directions to the computer, a programmer must be able to communicate with the system. Machine languages can be understood directly by the computer, but they are difficult for people to learn and to use. Therefore, many programming languages have been developed to facilitate people-machine communication. Computer languages, such as COBOL, FORTRAN, and PL/I, are structured to meet the processing needs of the users, not the computer's limitations, and must depend on compilers to translate them into machine language. These languages are called problem-oriented languages, or POLs.

The selection of a specific language for a given programming effort depends upon the needs of the firm, skill of personnel, hardware available, and the nature of the problem to be solved.

In this chapter, we discuss a major POL known as COBOL (COmmon Business Oriented Language), which is used extensively in business and industrial programming.

COBOL is unique because it is supported entirely by its users; that is large firms, governmental agencies, and other users contribute time and money toward the improvement, development, and modification of the language.

Other languages, such as FORTRAN, have no formal sponsor supporting the planning and implementation of improvements. Each computer manufacturer or user is left to his or her own resources to modify the language. Modification is essential if a language is to remain in use and extend its utility.

The initial draft of COBOL was presented in 1960 by the Conference on Data System Languages (CODASYL). This group was formed by many large users, computer manufacturers, and the U.S. Department of Defense to develop a universal language of a business nature. One goal was to develop the language in such a way that COBOL programs could be run on different models and makes of computers. Major interest in the language was generated when the federal government required that all large computers purchased by them be equipped for COBOL. The CODASYL group now meets regularly in committee to evaluate changes, alterations, additions, and improvements to the language.

ADVANTAGES OF COBOL

One of COBOL's major advantages is its close resemblance to English. Since COBOL was intended to reflect common business usage, it incorporates such terms as

ADD   SUBTRACT   MOVE TO   WRITE   PERFORM   PAY-RECORD

Complicated mathematical notation and symbols and binary code have been avoided in favor of common English terms. As a result, programs written in COBOL can be followed by nonprogrammers with little or no training. For example, one does not have to be a computer expert or a mathematician to understand an instruction like

IF PRICE IS GREATER THAN COST, PERFORM LOSS-ROUTINE.

or

ADD STOCK, SHIPMENT, GIVING GOODS.

Because the coding is easy to understand, programs written in COBOL generally require little or no documentation to explain each step in the program. COBOL program documentation does, of course, include flowcharts, descriptive narratives, and input/output specifications.

COBOL has good literal capability. Literal capability is the language's ability to manipulate words, sentences, or paragraphs of textual material. This is an important asset in business data processing, since names, addresses, lists, descriptive material, sentences, etc. are very frequently used.

COBOL is machine independent; that is a program written in the language can run on different makes or models of computers with little or no revision.

Thus, a business firm can change its computer equipment, farm out jobs to other machines, or send programs to other users with considerable assurance that the program will run satisfactorily. (Some programming languages are machine dependent. Programs written in these languages can be run only on a given make or model of computer. To run them on other machines would require that all or part of a program be rewritten.)

COBOL is the major language used in business data processing, and COBOL compilers are available on most large computers used in business.

LIMITATIONS OF COBOL

Although COBOL has many advantages, it does have limitations. Compilers for the full range of statements require a large amount of primary storage. These compilers fill many thousands of bytes of primary storage and therefore cannot be used in small machines. Thus, the utility of COBOL is limited to firms with access to medium or large systems.

COBOL is also verbose. It is not a tightly written language. Programs written in COBOL require dozens of statements, each one like a complete sentence constructed from English language words and names. This structure makes COBOL easy to follow but results in a long, wordy program.

Creative Computing. Nov./Dec. 1976

"Where did you learn to debug a program, Haverstraw?"

For example, a COBOL program to process an employee payroll might require 400 instructions. The same program written in a more terse language, such as FORTRAN, might require only 30 or 40 instructions. However, it should be noted that the more compact the language used and the greater its reliance on symbols and codes, the more difficult it is for the nonprogrammer to follow.

Since COBOL suffers from some mathematical limitations, it is not the preferred language of the scientific or mathematical programmer. It is generally more difficult to perform complex mathematical operations in COBOL than in many other languages.

The COBOL programmer must follow certain rules, conventions, and limitations of form and structure. An error such as a misspelled word or a misplaced period may cause an entire program to fail. However, most POLs have similar limitations.

STRUCTURE OF COBOL

Standard Character Set

All written languages are composed of a group of symbols. These symbols, called letters or characters, are combined into meaningful words to make sentences and phrases.

Programming languages also have standard character sets. Table 15.1 illustrates the set used in COBOL. All programs written in COBOL must be developed from the characters shown here. The program will not compile if any others are used.

Sentence Structure

COBOL, like English, has rules of sentence structure, spelling, and punctuation (called syntax). The basic unit of the COBOL language is the sentence. Sentences are composed of words, which consist of characters from the standard set.

Many COBOL sentences are imperative; that is, they direct the computer to perform a given task. Others are conditional; they direct the computer to follow one of several courses depending upon the value of a quantity in storage or the result of a calculation.

Sentences are grouped to form paragraphs. Each paragraph is assigned a unique name by the programmer. Paragraphs usually contain one or more sentences referring to the same operation. The statements that calculate payroll deductions may make one paragraph; all the instructions needed to print out an overdue notice to a delinquent customer may be another. The programmer can refer to all the steps in a paragraph by the paragraph name.

Paragraphs are further grouped into sections. Sections may be compared to chapters in a book, each concerned with a different aspect of a subject. Finally, all sections are grouped into divisions. Each division performs a different function, but all are interrelated parts of the same program. Figure 15.1 illustrates the structure of COBOL programs.

TABLE 15.1 COBOL STANDARD CHARACTER SET

ALPHABETIC CHARACTERS	NUMERIC CHARACTERS
A	0
B	1
C	2
D	3
E	4
F	5
G	6
H	7
I	8
J	9
K	
L	
M	SPECIAL CHARACTERS
N	
O	(blank) $
P	+
Q	− ;
R	/ >
S	= <
T	.
U	)
V	*
W	'
X	(
Y	' (apostrophe)
Z	

Types of Words   A programmer follows many rules and conventions when composing a sentence in COBOL. The words that make up the sentences are not chosen arbitrarily. Three types of words—reserved words, names, and optional words—are used in COBOL, and each type has its own function.

RESERVED WORDS.   The COBOL language has a group of special reserved words listed in Table 15.2. These words are the commands that direct the computer to perform various tasks. The COBOL compiler will convert them into step-by-step, machine-language instructions, which tell the CPU how to perform a specified activity.

The reserved words have a particular meaning in the language and their use is restricted by several conventions. They may be used only in the way the language allows and spelling must be exact. For example, the reserved word ADD in a COBOL sentence always tells the computer to set up the circuitry to perform addition. A programmer could not use such words as ADDED, PLUS, or AND to perform this calculation.

FIGURE 15.1   COBOL PROGRAM STRUCTURE

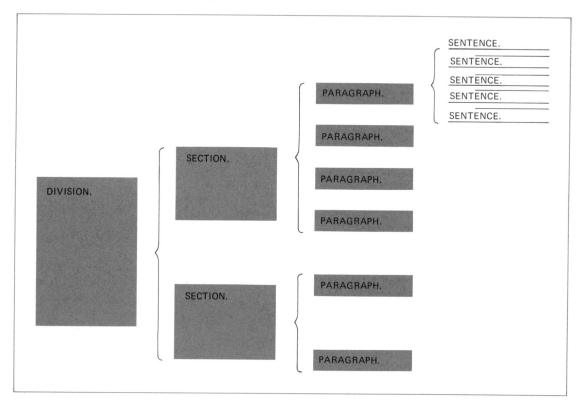

ASSIGNED WORDS.   Assigned words are names selected by the programmer to represent quantities or data calculated or stored in the computer. Names represent the quantities that will be manipulated by the reserved words. In this way, a programmer can refer to and manipulate a quantity even though its value changes during a program.

A programmer assigns names to fields in a data record, to the totals, intermediate totals, paragraphs, and temporary storage areas. Words chosen to be names must conform to certain rules of the language: They may not be more than 30 characters long; they must begin with an alphabetic letter; a reserved word cannot be chosen as a name.

OPTIONAL WORDS.   Finally, optional words are used in composing sentences. These words have no effect on the program flow, but are used in COBOL sentences to improve readability. Some optional words are

IS   THAN   ARE

TABLE 15.2 COBOL RESERVED WORDS

ACCEPT	(DECIMAL POINT)	INPUT-OUTPUT	POSITIVE	STOP
ACCESS	DECLARATIVES	INSTALLATION	(PRINT-SWITCH)	SUBTRACT
ACTUAL	DEPENDING	INTO	PROCEDURE	(SUM)
ADD	(DESCENDING)	INVALID	PROCEED	SYMBOLIC
ADVANCING	(DETAIL)	I-O	(PROCESS)	(SYSIN)
AFTER	DIRECT	I-O-CONTROL	PROCESSING	(SYSOUT)
ALL	DIRECT-ACCESS	IS	PROGRAM-ID	SYSPUNCH
ALPHABETIC	DISPLAY		PROTECTION	
ALTER	DISPLAY-ST	JUSTIFIED		TALLY
ALTERNATE	DIVIDE		QUOTE	TALLYING
AND	DIVISION	KEY	QUOTES	(TERMINATE)
APPLY				THAN
ARE	ELSE	LABEL		THEN
AREA	END	LABELS	RANDOM	THRU
AREAS	ENDING	(LAST)	(RD)	TIMES
(ASCENDING)	ENTER	LEADING	READ	TO
ASSIGN	ENTRY	LEFT	READY	TRACE
AT	ENVIRONMENT	LESS	RECORD	TRACK-AREA
AT END	EQUAL	LIBRARY	RECORDING	TRACKS
AUTHOR	ERROR	(LIMIT)	RECORDS	TRANSFORM
	EVERY	(LIMITS)	REDEFINES	(TRY)
(BEFORE)	EXAMINE	(LINE-COUNTER)	REEL	(TYPE)
BEGINNING	EXHIBIT	(LINE)	(RELATIVE)	
BLANK	EXIT	LINES	(RELEASE)	UNIT
BLOCK		LINKAGE	REMARKS	UNIT-RECORD
BY	FD	LOCK	REPLACING	(UNITS)
	FILE	LOW-VALUE	(REPORT)	UNTIL
CALL	(FILE-LIMIT)	LOW-VALUES	(REPORTING)	UPON
(CF)	FILES		(REPORTS)	USAGE
(CH)	FILE-CONTROL	MODE	RERUN	USE
CHANGED	FILE-ID	MORE-LABELS	RESERVE	USING
CHARACTER	FILLER	MOVE	RESET	UTILITY
CHECKING	(FINAL)	MULTIPLY	RESTRICTED	
(CLOCK-UNITS)	FIRST		RETURN	VALUE
CLOSE	(FOOTING)	NAMED	REVERSED	VARYING
COBOL	FOR	NEGATIVE	REWIND	
(CODE)	FORM-OVERFLOW	NEXT	REWRITE	WHEN
(COLUMN)	FROM	NO	(RF)	WITH
(COMMA)		NOT	(RH)	WITHOUT
COMPUTATIONAL	(GENERATE)	NOTE	RIGHT	WORKING-STORAGE
COMPUTATIONAL-1	GIVING	NUMERIC	ROUNDED	WRITE
COMPUTATIONAL-2	GO		RUN	WRITE-ONLY
COMPUTATIONAL-3	GREATER	OBJECT-COMPUTER		
COMPUTE	(GROUP)	OCCURS	(SA)	ZERO
CONFIGURATION		OF	SAME	ZEROES
CONSOLE	(HEADING)	OMITTED	(SD)	ZEROS
CONTAINS	HIGH-VALUE	ON	SEARCH	
(CONTROL)	HIGH-VALUES	OPEN	SECTION	
(CONTROLS)	(HOLD)	OR	SECURITY	
COPY		ORGANIZATION	SELECT	
(CORRESPONDING)	IBM-360	OTHERWISE	SENTENCE	
COUNT	(ID)	OUTPUT	SEQUENTIAL	
CREATING	IDENTIFICATION	(OVERFLOW)	SIZE	
(CYCLES)	IF		(SORT)	
	IN	(PAGE)	(SOURCE)	
DATA	INCLUDE	(PAGE-COUNTER)	SOURCE-COMPUTER	
DATE-COMPILED	INDEXED	PERFORM	SPACE	
DATE-WRITTEN	(INDICATE)	(PF)	SPACES	
(DE)	(INITIATE)	(PH)	(SPECIAL-NAMES)	
	INPUT	PICTURE	STANDARD	
		(PLUS)		

In COBOL some punctuation marks, such as a comma (,) and semicolon (;), are also optional. Values that will not change may be written directly into the program. For example, if the sales tax, interest rate, or markup is a constant value, the programmer may choose to use it as a number and write it directly into the instructions.

Combinations of these three types of words in sentence form direct the computer to perform various tasks. For example, IF CHARGE-BALANCE IS EQUAL TO 1000, GO TO OVER-LIMIT-NOTICE. In this case, the programmer directs the computer to compare a quantity to 1,000 and branch to a routine if they are equal. The instruction is formed using the reserved words IF, EQUAL TO, and GO TO; assigned names CHARGE-BALANCE and OVER-LIMIT-NOTICE; optional word IS; and constant value 1,000.

Coding Forms and Conventions   A standard coding form, shown in Figure 15.2, is used by COBOL programmers in writing programs. Coded instructions are written longhand on the forms. Then a keyboard operator punches each line on the coding sheet into a separate punched card or keys them onto magnetic tape or disk.

FIGURE 15.2   COBOL CODING SHEET

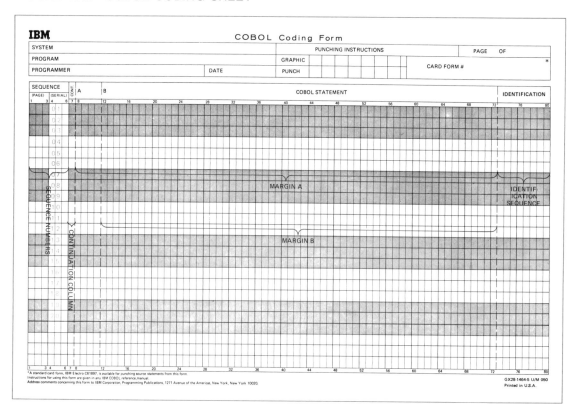

TABLE 15.3   COBOL PROGRAMMING DIVISIONS

DIVISION NAME	FUNCTION
Identification	Identify programmer, program, and company.
Environment	Assign files to input and output devices. Specify computer.
Data	Assign names to quantities and fields, allocate storage spaces, and define format of data records.
Procedure	Define actions and steps computer is to follow in solving problem.

COBOL PROGRAM SHEET LAYOUT.   The standard form contains space at the top of the page for the programmer's name, program name, and other related data. These data are not part of the program deck. The form has 80 columns across the page and 25 lines for instructions.

CONVENTIONS.   The COBOL compiler is designed to expect certain kinds of data in selected columns on the record as shown in Figure 15.2. Columns 1 to 6 are reserved for sequence numbers—numbers assigned to each instruction, in sequence, to help keep instructions in the program in order. These numbers are not used in the actual manipulations within the program.

Column 7 is called the continuation column and is only used to continue a non-numeric literal statement from one line to another. Columns 8 to 72 are reserved for programming statements. Column 8 is called Margin A, and Column 12, Margin B. They are used like headings in an outline to show paragraphs and different levels of statements. Columns 73 to 80 are used to identify each record with a label or program number. They are not read by the COBOL compiler.

COBOL PROGRAM DIVISIONS

A COBOL program has four divisions, each with its own function. These divisions allow "routine housekeeping tasks" to be separated from the steps involved in carrying out the logic of the problem. The programmer can assign input and output devices, set up storage spaces, and assign names without being concerned with the details of the algorithm. Changes in one division can be made without disrupting another division. Table 15.3 lists the four major divisions in the COBOL program and their functions.

Identification
Division

The first division in the COBOL program provides the computer with routine identification data, such as the name of the program, name of the author, the

FIGURE 15.3 IDENTIFICATION DIVISION

```
110 IDENTIFICATION DIVISION.
120 PROGRAM-ID. 'CLIDER'.
130 AUTHOR. JOHN STEIN.
140 INSTALLATION. RETAIL-HOUSE.
150 DATE-WRITTEN. 9-20.
160 REMARKS. THIS PROGRAM READS DATA FROM COL. 1-60 ON CARD.  PRINTS
161     IT OUT RE-FORMATTED.  THIS EXAMPLE IS A NAME AND TELEPHONE
162     DIRECTORY.  THE NAMES ARE PUNCHED IN COL. 1-20, ADDRESSES
163     21-50, PHONE NUMBER, 51-60.  PRINTED SPACED OUT OVER 132
164     CHARACTER LINE .  30 LINES TO A PAGE.
```

installation, and the date written. Figure 15.3 illustrates the Identification Division of a program.

The Identification Division is strictly informational and contains no instructions or procedures. It is not involved with the logic or program algorithm content.

Environment Division

The next division of the program describes the make and model of computer that the program should be run on, and designates the type of input and output media the computer is to use. It specifies whether the input devices are to be card readers, magnetic tape units, etc., and whether the output devices are to be line printers, card punches, or magnetic tape units.

The Environment Division is the only machine-dependent division in a COBOL program. It is tied to the specific installation upon which the job will be run. Since systems have different models of I/O devices available, the programmer must make sure that those designated are available on the system being used. If the job is to be run on another system, the I/O designations in this division must be changed. However, this normally involves only a few cards. Figure 15.4 illustrates the Environment Division of a program.

Data Division

The Data Division tells the computer the kind and format of the data being read in and out and the kinds of temporary storage that will be needed. Figure 15.5 illustrates part of the Data Division. The Data Division is divided into two sections: File and Working-Storage. In the File Section, the programmer details the layout of the data records for each file. Names are assigned to each field, and the kind of data each will hold (such as alphabetic or numeric) is indicated.

In the Working-Storage Section the programmer describes and allocates all temporary and intermediate storage areas needed during processing. He

FIGURE 15.4   ENVIRONMENT DIVISION

```
200 ENVIRONMENT DIVISION.
210 CONFIGURATION SECTION.
220 SOURCE-COMPUTER. IBM-360.
230 OBJECT-COMPUTER. IBM-360.
240 INPUT-OUTPUT SECTION.
250 FILE-CONTROL.
260     SELECT CARD-FILE ASSIGN TO 'SYS001' UNIT-RECORD 2540R.
270     SELECT PRINT-FILE ASSIGN TO 'SYS002' UNIT-RECORD 1403.
```

FIGURE 15.5   DATA DIVISION

```
300 DATA DIVISION.
310 FILE SECTION.
320 FD   CARD-FILE
330      RECORD CONTAINS 80 CHARACTERS
340      BLOCK CONTAINS 1 RECORDS
350      LABEL RECORDS ARE OMITTED
360      RECORDING MODE IS F
370      DATA RECORDS ARE INPUT-CARD.
380 01   INPUT-CARD.
381      03  NAME-1-20X           PICTURE X(20).
382      03  ADDRESS-21-50X       PICTURE X(30).
 .
 .
500 WORKING-STORAGE SECTION.
510 01   SAVE-AREA.
520      03  LINE-COUNT           PICTURE 999.
530 01   DETAIL-LINE.
540      03  CARRIAGE-CONTROL     PICTURE X       VALUE SPACES.
550      03  FILLER               PICTURE X(10) VALUE SPACES.
560      03  NAME                 PICTURE X(20).
570      03  FILLER               PICTURE X(10) VALUE SPACES.
580      03  ADDRESS              PICTURE X(30).
590      03  FILLER               PICTURE X(10) VALUE SPACES.
600      03 TELEPHONE-NUMBER.
610          05  FILLER           PICTURE X       VALUE IS '('.
620          05  AREA-CODE        PICTURE XXX.
```

or she may also include and name values that will be needed for processing but are not read in from a data file.

For example, suppose a programmer is going to compute interest. In the File Section of the Data Division, he or she tells the computer that the data to be read in (principal) will be found in columns 21 to 30 of the card, gives the interest rate in the Working-Storage Section and also sets up and names a temporary storage area for the result. Later in the program, the computer will be directed to print out the results.

Data descriptions should tell the computer how many columns alphabetic and numeric values have, and the position of the decimal point in decimal numbers. Output record descriptions are included, indicating what spacing should be observed if results are to be written on the line printer, or what the record format should be if the output will be on magnetic tape. All this information must be provided before the programmer can give specific instructions on how to calculate the answer.

Procedure Division   In the Procedure Division, the programmer specifies the steps the computer is to follow in executing the program. Figure 15.6 illustrates part of the Procedure Division of a program.

In this section, the powerful COBOL verbs are used to implement the logic and program algorithm chosen to solve the problem. The programmer opens files, moves data, performs mathematical calculations, branches, writes data, closes files, etc. All data are referred to by their assigned names, and instructions are grouped into paragraphs, each with a unique name. The programmer can direct the computer to repeat a group of instructions by referring to its paragraph name.

FIGURE 15.6   PROCEDURE DIVISION

```
1000 PROCEDURE DIVISION.
1010 INITIALIZE.
1020      OPEN INPUT CARD-FILE.
1030      OPEN OUTPUT PRINT-FILE.
1040 WRITE-HEADING.
1050      MOVE HEADING-LINE TO PRINT-LINE.
1060      WRITE PRINT-LINE AFTER ADVANCING 0 LINES.
1070      MOVE SPACES TO PRINT-LINE.
1080      WRITE PRINT-LINE AFTER ADVANCING 1 LINES.
1090      MOVE ZEROES TO LINE-COUNT.
1100 READ-CARD.
1110      READ CARD-FILE AT END GO TO EOJ.
1120      MOVE NAME-1-20X TO NAME.
```

Top Performer at Disney World is a Computer

Visitors to Disney World are filing through the portals of Space Mountain, a brand-new "attraction" in the still-growing fantasy world just outside Orlando, Florida. They are going to take a hair-raising ride "through space," barely missing meteors and other space vehicles.

Controlling the ride and assuring its safety is a computer. The cars race over the tortuous track at up to 28 miles an hour—fast when you're barrelling into a steeply banked horseshoe curve. And although you can't see this, because it's dark, you're shooting up and down space six stories high. For safety, the cars must stay at least 18 seconds apart. If one car begins to gain on the one ahead, the tailgater is braked. And if necessary, the computer can shut down the ride.

The computer keeps tabs on each car's location by a block zone system of magnets using relay logic. When a metal fin extending beneath each car breaks the magnetic field of a magnet alongside the track, the information is fed to the computer. This information is gathered in parallel from the magnetic sensors, from the brakes, from the solenoids that operate the brakes, and from the contactors that are used to confirm that the electrical machinery is running as it's programmed to run. The information is gathered in the relay system and sent to the computer.

The special effects are all operated from a digital animation control center. Computers in the center send instructions to the audio devices in Space Mountain. They release the blast-off roar in the final tunnel of the ride. They control the 40 projectors in Space Mountain that create the Milky Way, meteors, and stars. And they control every movement—even the fluttering of an eyelash—of every animated creature in Disney World.

An elaborate software program has been developed for the entire performance of each animated performer. Stored on magnetic tape, each creature's performance is permanently fixed and coordinated with its fellow performers. The tapes are played over and over again, sending digital instructions by wire to the performer involved.

The actual instructions are received by a proportionate servo-control mechanism in the base of the animated figure. The control converts the digital information into linear motion. Slight movements, such as eyes closing or the movement of a finger, result when the servo-control triggers a magnetic device. The movement of a leg or head, or Lincoln standing up to deliver a speech, is done by a hydraulic double-action piston.

SOURCE: Abstracted from "That Dazzling, Dizzy Disney World Is Run By Computer," John F. Mason, *Electronic Design*, Volume 4, February 15, 1975.

SAMPLE COBOL STATEMENTS

The COBOL language contains many powerful reserved words, which allow the programmer to direct the computer through many sophisticated mathematical and logical operations. The following statements are given as examples of COBOL programming techniques and the use of reserved words and data names. They are only a few of the many statements that could be used.

READ   One of the most fundamental words in COBOL programming is READ. It directs the computer to read data from a file and place it in storage. Once the data are read in, they are available for further processing or output.

EXAMPLE:

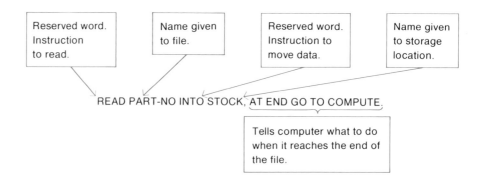

Explanation: In this statement, the programmer instructs the computer to read a record from a file (PART-NO) and place the data in a storage location named STOCK. When it reaches the end of the file, the computer will branch to a portion of the program called COMPUTE. Previous divisions in the program have given all pertinent descriptions. The specific input medium (such as a card reader) was specified in the Environment Division. In the Data Division, the programmer described the data on the input record and set up a storage location named STOCK.

WRITE   The WRITE statement is a basic instruction for outputting data in COBOL programming. It instructs the computer to output data previously read in or calculated during the program.

EXAMPLE:

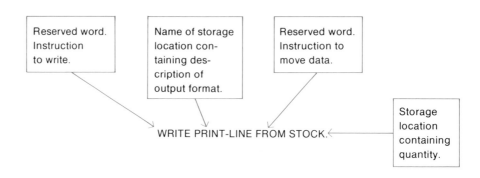

Explanation: In this example, the programmer tells the computer to write a previously read-in or calculated quantity on the line printer. WRITE and FROM are reserved words directing the action. PRINT-LINE is the name for a reformatted location, and STOCK is the assigned name of the storage location containing the required data.

The Data Division gave the computer all instructions for the graphic layout of the output record. The hardware used (line printer in this case) was specified in the Environment Division. The description of the storage location STOCK was given in the Data Division.

Branching   An important ability of the computer is its capacity to test a numeric or non-numeric quantity and make a logical decision to branch to one of several paths. The COBOL language contains several kinds of branch statements. One form uses the reserved word IF in an instruction. In this case, the computer compares two values and branches control of the program to a specified paragraph depending on the results of the comparison.

EXAMPLE:

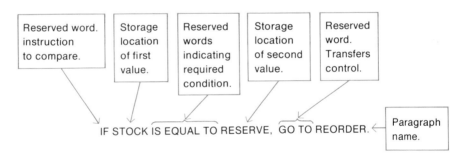

IF STOCK IS EQUAL TO RESERVE, GO TO REORDER.

Explanation: In this instance, the programmer tests and compares the value of STOCK. If the value of STOCK is equal to the value of RESERVE, the computer is to branch to the paragraph labeled REORDER. If the condition for the branch is not met (the value of STOCK is not equal to RESERVE), control will flow to the next statement in the program.

PERFORM   The programmer can instruct the computer to loop through a given sequence of calculations or operations a specific number of times. One way to do this is with a PERFORM instruction. Here the programmer specifies the number of times he or she wants the loop performed. The computer executes the series of steps repeatedly until a counter in the CPU reaches the preset limit. The computer then returns to the statement in the program after the PERFORM instruction.

EXAMPLE:

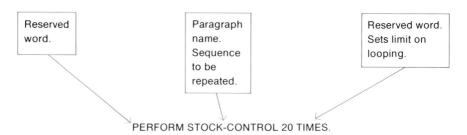

PERFORM STOCK-CONTROL 20 TIMES.

Explanation: Upon encountering the above instruction, the computer will return to the paragraph named STOCK-CONTROL and execute the steps in the sequence 20 times. It will then proceed to the statement following the PERFORM statement and continue processing.

Addition   The computer is capable of performing a variety of mathematical procedures. The COBOL programmer instructs the computer to perform mathematics by including specific reserved words in the instructions. Some reserved mathematical words are ADD, SUBTRACT, and MULTIPLY. The computer will perform the required operation on the data in storage and place the results in the assigned space.

EXAMPLE:

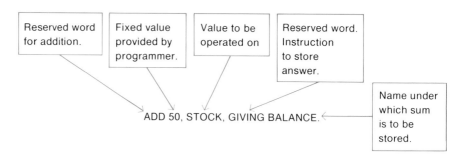

ADD 50, STOCK, GIVING BALANCE.

Explanation: In this case, the programmer wants to add 50 to the value of STOCK. The sum is to be placed in storage under the name BALANCE. Upon encountering the instruction, the computer will perform the required mathematical operation (add 50 to the current value of STOCK) and place the sum in the assigned space, BALANCE. Both STOCK and BALANCE have been described and named in the Data Division.

Arithmetic
Expressions
The computer can be programmed to perform a variety of mathematical steps in a single sentence. This is done by inserting one or more reserved words in the instruction.

EXAMPLE:

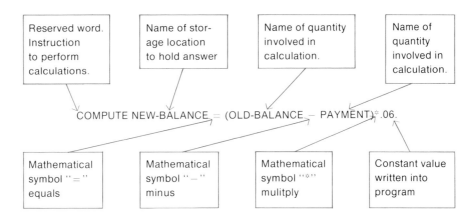

| Reserved word. Instruction to perform calculations. | Name of storage location to hold answer | Name of quantity involved in calculation. | Name of quantity involved in calculation. |

COMPUTE NEW-BALANCE = (OLD-BALANCE – PAYMENT) * .06.

| Mathematical symbol " = " equals | Mathematical symbol " – " minus | Mathematical symbol " * " mulitply | Constant value written into program |

Explanation: This instruction performs several mathematical steps in a single sentence. The programmer directs the computer to calculate a value called NEW-BALANCE. It is found by subtracting PAYMENT from OLD-BALANCE and multiplying the remainder by .06. The parentheses tell the computer to perform the subtraction before the multiplication. The product will be placed in storage under the name NEW-BALANCE. The Data Division contains the descriptions of the quantities and storage areas needed.

SAMPLE PROGRAM

Figure 15.7 is the flowchart for a COBOL program. This program is designed to read in data from one record and manipulate these figures to print out a salary table. The input data are shown in Figure 15.8.

Function of
the Program
The program will read in data from a record called CONTROL-CARD. The data include hourly starting salary, maximum and minimum monthly salaries (named MAX-MON-SAL and MIN-MON-SAL), and an incrementing factor called INCREMENT and DELTA-FACTOR.

The program is shown in Figure 15.9 and the output in Figure 15.10. The steps followed in the algorithm are

❶ The files are opened and title lines written.
❷ The CONTROL-CARD is read and the fields moved into SAVE-AREA.

FIGURE 15.7
FLOWCHART
FOR SALARY
TABLE

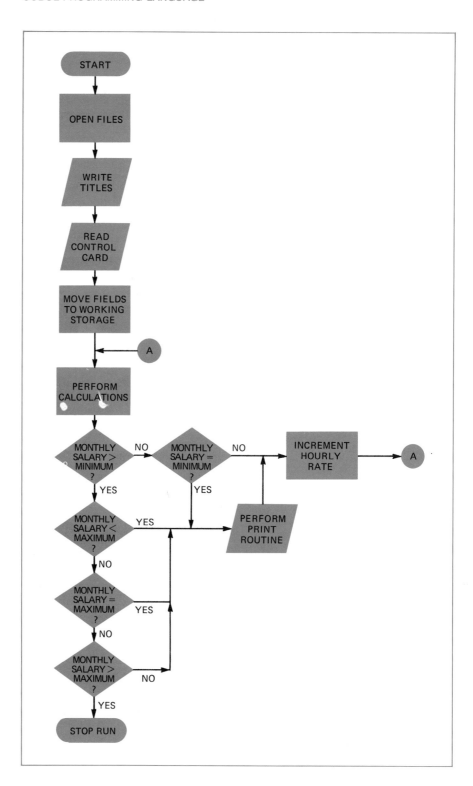

FIGURE 15.8   INPUT DATA LISTING FOR COBOL SALARY TABLE
              PROGRAM

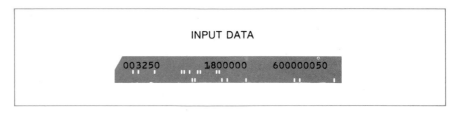

INPUT DATA

003250   1800000   600000050

③ Calculations are performed.

④ Then the computer tests to see that the MONTHLY-SALARY is above
the minimum level required and below the maximum level set by the
programmer.

⑤ All amounts between these limits are printed out.

⑥ Amounts below the minimum cause the computer to branch back to
increment the monthly salary and repeat calculations.

⑦ An amount above the maximum sends the computer to the end of job
routine.

Program   The following discussion traces the program by paragraphs. The numbers
Analysis listed at the left margin are keyed to the line numbers of the program
          illustrated in Figure 15.9.

LINE NUMBER	EXPLANATION
1–18	These are the Identification and Environment Divisions. They identify the program, the computer used, and the input/output devices required.
19–20	Begin Data Division and File Section.
21–33	Describe input CARD-FILE and fields on record. Record is named CONTROL-CARD.
34–40	Describe output PRINT-FILE. Record is named PRINT-LINE.
41	Working-Storage Section.
42–49	Describe, name, and initialize several storage areas used in the program to hold intermediate values. COMPUTATIONAL-3 tells the computer they will be used in mathematical calculations.
50–70	Set up and describe two lines of titles, SALARY-HEADING and TIME-PERIOD-HEADING.
71–82	Set up DATA-LINE, a working area that reformats calculated values and inserts required punctuation where necessary.
83–86	Begin Procedure Division and open files.

FIGURE 15.9   COBOL PROGRAM LISTING—SALARY TABLE

```
1     1010 IDENTIFICATION DIVISION.
2     1020 PROGRAM-ID. 'SALTAB'.
3     1030 AUTHOR. BETTY CHAN.
4     1040 INSTALLATION. STATE JC.
5     1050 DATE-WRITTEN. 3-27.
6     1060 REMARKS.  THIS PROGRAM WRITES A SALARY TABLE. IT CALCULATES DAILY
7     1070      WEEKLY, MONTHLY AND ANNUAL SALARIES, STARTING FROM A GIVEN
8     1080      AMOUNT, ADDING AN INCREMENT EACH CYCLE.  IT LISTS AMOUNT BE-
9     1090      TWEEN THE SPECIFIED MINIMUM AND MAXIMUM MONTHLY SALARY.  IT
10    1095      OPERATES FROM ONE CONTROL CARD.
11    2010 ENVIRONMENT DIVISION.
12    2020 CONFIGURATION SECTION.
13    2030 SOURCE-COMPUTER. IBM-360.
14    2040 OBJECT-COMPUTER. IBM-360.
15    2050 INPUT-OUTPUT SECTION.
16    2060 FILE-CONTROL.
17    2070      SELECT CARD-FILE ASSIGN TO 'SYS001' UNIT-RECORD 2540R.
18    2080      SELECT PRINT-FILE ASSIGN TO 'SYS002' UNIT-RECORD 1403.
19    3010 DATA DIVISION.
20    3020 FILE SECTION.
21    3030 FD  CARD-FILE
22    3040      RECORD CONTAINS 80 CHARACTERS
23    3050      BLOCK CONTAINS 1 RECORDS
24    3060      LABEL RECORDS ARE OMITTED
25    3070      RECORDING MODE IS F
26    3080      DATA RECORDS ARE CONTROL-CARD.
27    3090 01  CONTROL-CARD.
28    3100      03  START-HOURLY-RATE   PICTURE 999V999.
29    3110      03  FILLER              PICTURE X(4).
30    3120      03  MAX-MON-SAL         PICTURE 9(7)V999.
31    3130      03  MIN-MON-SAL         PICTURE 9(7)V999.
32    3140      03  INCREMENT           PICTURE V999.
33    3150      03  FILLER              PICTURE X(47).
34    3200 FD  PRINT-FILE
35    3210      RECORD CONTAINS 133 CHARACTERS
36    3220      BLOCK CONTAINS 1 RECORDS
37    3230      LABEL RECORDS ARE OMITTED
38    3240      RECORDING MODE IS F
39    3250      DATA RECORDS ARE PRINT-LINE.
40    3260 01  PRINT-LINE              PICTURE X(133).
41    4000 WORKING-STORAGE SECTION.
42    4010 01  SAVE-AREA.
43    4020      03  HOURLY-RATE         PICTURE 999V999 COMPUTATIONAL-3.
44    4030      03  DAILY-RATE          PICTURE 9(4)V999 COMPUTATIONAL-3.
45    4040      03  WEEKLY-RATE         PICTURE 9(5)V999 COMPUTATIONAL-3.
46    4050      03  MONTHLY-RATE        PICTURE 9(7)V999 COMPUTATIONAL-3.
47    4060      03  ANNUAL-RATE         PICTURE 9(9)V999 COMPUTATIONAL-3.
48    4070      03  LINE-COUNT          PICTURE 999.
49    4080      03  DELTA-FACTOR        PICTURE V999 COMPUTATIONAL-3.
50    4140 01  SALARY-HEADING.
51    4150      03  CARRIAGE-CONTROL    PICTURE X VALUE IS '1'.
52    4160      03  FILLER              PICTURE X(5) VALUE SPACES.
53    4170      03  AST-1               PICTURE X(37) VALUE  '* * * * * * * *
54    4180-     ' * * * * * * * * * *'.
55    4190      03  AST-2               PICTURE X(13) VALUE ' S A L A R Y '.
56    4200      03  AST-3               PICTURE X(37) VALUE  '* * * * * * * *
57    4210-     ' * * * * * * * * * * *'.
58    4220      03  FILLER              PICTURE X(40) VALUE SPACES.
59    4230 01  TIME-PERIOD-HEADING.
60    4240      03  FILLER              PICTURE X(6) VALUE SPACES.
61    4250      03  HR-6-16X            PICTURE X(11) VALUE 'HOURLY RATE'.
62    4260      03  FILLER              PICTURE X(20) VALUE SPACES.
63    4270      03  DAILY-37-41X        PICTURE X(5) VALUE 'DAILY'.
64    4280      03  FILLER              PICTURE X(10) VALUE SPACES.
```

```
65    4290      03   WEEKLY-52-57X        PICTURE X(6) VALUE 'WEEKLY'.
66    4300      03   FILLER               PICTURE X(10) VALUE SPACES.
67    4310      03   MONTHLY-68-74X       PICTURE X(7) VALUE 'MONTHLY'.
68    4320      C3   FILLER               PICTURE X(10) VALUE SPACES.
69    4330      03   ANNUALLY-85-92X      PICTURE X(8) VALUE 'ANNUALLY'.
7C    4340      03   FILLER               PICTURE X(40) VALUE SPACES.
71    4450 01   DATA-LINE.
72    4460      03   FILLER               PICTURE X(6) VALUE SPACES.
73    4470      C3   HOURLY               PICTURE $$$9.999.
74    4480      03   FILLER               PICTURE X(19) VALUE SPACES.
75    4490      03   DAILY                PICTURE $$,$$9.999.
76    45C0      03   FILLER               PICTURE X(5) VALUE SPACES.
77    4510      03   WEEKLY               PICTURE $$$,$$9.999.
78    4520      03   FILLER               PICTURE X(4) VALUE SPACES.
79    4530      03   MONTHLY              PICTURE $$,$$$,$$9.999.
80    4540      03   FILLER               PICTURE X     VALUE SPACES.
81    4550      03   ANNUALLY             PICTURE $$$$,$$$,$$9.999.
82    4560      03   FILLER               PICTURE X(39) VALUE SPACES.
83    5010 PROCEDURE DIVISION.
84    5020 INITIALIZE.
85    5030      OPEN INPUT CARD-FILE.
86    5C40      OPEN OUTPUT PRINT-FILE.
87    5C50 HEADING-ROUTINE.
88    5060      MOVE SALARY-HEADING TO PRINT-LINE.
89    5C70      WRITE PRINT-LINE AFTER ADVANCING 0 LINES.
9C    5080      MOVE TIME-PERICD-HEADING TO PRINT-LINE.
91    5C90      WRITE PRINT-LINE AFTER ADVANCING 1 LINES.
92    51C0      MOVE SPACES TO PRINT-LINE.
93    5110      WRITE PRINT-LINE AFTER ADVANCING 1 LINES.
94    5120      MOVE ZEROES TO LINE-CCUNT.
95    5130 READ-CONTROL-CARD.
96    5140      READ CARD-FILE AT END GO TO EOJ.
97    5150      MOVE START-HOURLY-RATE TO HCURLY-RATE.
98    5160      MOVE INCREMENT TO DELTA-FACTOR.
99    5170 CALCULATICNS.
10C   5680      MULTIPLY HOURLY-RATE BY 8 GIVING DAILY-RATE, ROUNDED.
101   51SC      MULTIPLY HOURLY-RATE BY 4C GIVING WEEKLY-RATE, ROUNDED.
102   52C0      MULTIPLY WEEKLY-RATE BY 52 GIVING ANNUAL-RATE, ROUNDED.
103   5210      DIVIDE 12 INTO ANNUAL-RATE GIVING MONTHLY-RATE, ROUNDED.
104   5220 CHECK-MONTHLY-RATE.
105   5230      IF MONTHLY-RATE IS LESS THAN MIN-MON-SAL ADD DELTA-FACTOR TO
106   5240         HOURLY-RATE    GO TC CALCULATIONS.
1C7   5250      IF MONTHLY-RATE IS EQUAL TO MIN-MON-SAL GO TO PRINT-DATA.
108   5260      IF MONTHLY-RATE IS LESS THAN MAX-MON-SAL GO TO PRINT-DATA.
1C9   5270      IF MONTHLY-RATE IS EQUAL TO MAX-MON-SAL GO TO PRINT-DATA.
110   5280      IF MONTHLY-RATE IS GREATER THAN MAX-MON-SAL GC TO EOJ.
111   53C0 PRINT-DATA.
112   5310      MCVE MONTHLY-RATE TO MONTHLY.
113   532C      MOVE HOURLY-RATE TO HOURLY.
114   5330      MOVE DAILY-RATE TO DAILY.
115   5340      MOVE WEEKLY-RATE TO WEEKLY.
116   5350      MOVE ANNUAL-RATE TC ANNUALLY.
117   536C      MOVE DATA-LINE TO PRINT-LINE.
118   5370      WRITE PRINT-LINE AFTER ADVANCING 1 LINES.
119   5380      ADD 1 TO LINE-COUNT.
120   5390      IF LINE-CCUNT IS GREATER THAN 29 PERFORM HEADING-ROUTINE.
121   54C0      ACD DELTA-FACTOR TO HCURLY-RATE.
122   5410      GC TC CALCULATIONS.
123   55C0 EOJ.
124   5510      DISPLAY 'NORMAL EOJ' UPCN CCNSCLE.
125   5520 CLOSE-FILES.
126   5530      CLOSE PRINT-FILE.
127   5540      CLOSE CARD-FILE.
128   555C      STOP RUN.
```

FIGURE 15.10   OUTPUT FROM SALARY TABLE PROGRAM

```
* * * * * * * * * * * * * * * * * * * S A L A R Y * * * * * * * * * * * * * * * * * *
HOURLY RATE                    DAILY         WEEKLY         MONTHLY         ANNUALLY
   $3.500                     $28.000       $14C.000       $606.667        $7,280.000
   $3.550                     $28.400       $142.000       $615.333        $7,384.000
   $3.600                     $28.800       $144.000       $624.000        $7,488.000
   $3.650                     $29.200       $146.000       $632.667        $7,592.000
   $3.700                     $29.600       $148.000       $641.333        $7,696.000
   $3.750                     $30.000       $150.000       $650.000        $7,800.000
   $3.800                     $30.400       $152.000       $658.667        $7,904.000
   $3.850                     $3C.800       $154.000       $667.333        $8,008.000
   $3.900                     $31.200       $156.000       $676.000        $8,112.000
   $3.950                     $31.600       $158.000       $684.667        $8,216.000
   $4.000                     $32.000       $16C.000       $693.333        $8,320.000
   $4.050                     $32.400       $162.000       $702.000        $8,424.000
   $4.100                     $32.800       $164.000       $710.667        $8,528.000
   $4.150                     $33.20C       $166.000       $719.333        $8,632.000
   $4.200                     $33.600       $168.000       $728.000        $8,736.000
   $4.250                     $34.000       $170.000       $736.667        $8,840.000
   $4.30C                     $34.400       $172.000       $745.333        $8,944.000
   $4.350                     $34.800       $174.000       $754.000        $9,048.000
   $4.400                     $35.200       $176.000       $762.667        $9,152.000
   $4.450                     $35.600       $178.000       $771.333        $9,256.000
   $4.500                     $36.000       $180.000       $780.000        $9,360.000
   $4.550                     $36.400       $182.000       $788.667        $9,464.000
   $4.600                     $36.800       $184.000       $797.333        $9,568.000
   $4.650                     $37.20C       $186.000       $806.000        $9,672.000
   $4.70C                     $37.600       $188.000       $814.667        $9,776.000
   $4.75C                     $38.00C       $19C.000       $823.333        $9,880.000
   $4.800                     $38.40C       $192.000       $832.000        $9,984.000
   $4.850                     $38.800       $194.000       $840.667       $10,088.000
   $4.900                     $35.20C       $196.000       $849.333       $10,192.000
   $4.950                     $39.600       $198.000       $858.000       $10,296.000
```

87–94	HEADING-ROUTINE paragraph writes titles and initializes LINE-COUNT.
95–98	READ CONTROL-CARD reads in data record, tests for end-of-file and moves data to fields in SAVE-AREA.
99–103	Perform calculations needed for salary table.
104–110	Test for minimum and maximum limits of table.
111–122	Move data from SAVE-AREA to the PRINT-LINE for outputting. Increases and tests LINE-COUNT to see if it is greater than 29. Adds DELTA-FACTOR to HOURLY-RATE and loops back to CALCULATIONS to repeat another cycle.
123–128	End-of-job routine instructs computer to close files and end program.

KEY TERMS

Assigned name
COBOL
Literal capability
Machine dependent
Machine independent
Optional word
Problem-oriented
  language (POL)
Reserved word

Standard Character set
Identification Division
Environment Division
Data Division
File Section
Working-Storage Section
Procedure Division

EXERCISES

1. Give six advantages of COBOL.
2. Give several disadvantages of COBOL.
3. How is a COBOL program structured?
4. What are reserved words? Give three examples.
5. How do assigned names differ from reserved words?
6. Label the reserved columns on a blank COBOL coding sheet.
7. What is the function of the Identification Division?
8. What is the function of the Environment Division? How does running a program on different computers affect this division?
9. What is the function of the Data Division?
10. What is the function of the Procedure Division?
11. What advantage does COBOL offer by separating the Procedure Division from the hardware designation?
12. List the reserved words you would use to write a program that reads a list of numbers, adds them, and writes out the answer.

16

BASIC
PROGRAMMING LANGUAGE

BASIC (Beginner's All-purpose Symbolic Instruction Code) was developed in the early 1960s by John G. Kemeny and Thomas E. Kurtz, two professors at Dartmouth College, working under a grant from the National Science Foundation. BASIC, designed for student use, was planned as an easy-to-learn, interactive language. It resembles the FORTRAN language, but its programming approach is somewhat more simplified.

BASIC has become one of the most widely used languages in schools, colleges, and universities. It is also rapidly becoming the principal language used in commercial time-sharing applications and is widely used for business and scientific programming. BASIC is available on both large and small computer systems.

BASIC is an interactive language. This allows the programmer to interact directly with a program during its execution. The operator uses a terminal, such as the Teletype machine shown in Figure 16.1, to direct the computer, enter programming instructions and data, and receive output.

FIGURE 16.1   BASIC TERMINAL

ADVANTAGES OF BASIC

BASIC is easy to learn and use and does not require a special terminal or keyboard. Programming can be done locally or from a remote terminal connected to the computer via ordinary telephone lines. Since BASIC is real time and interactive, it is a flexible language with a wide range of applications. It has fair mathematical facilities and excellent matrix manipulation capabilities.

LIMITATIONS OF BASIC

Because it is a terminal-oriented language, BASIC is inefficient for handling large quantities of input and output data. It is not suited to processing large files of data. However, large amounts of data may be stored on disk packs at the data center and accessed from the terminal.

Another limitation of BASIC is that at present there is no published language standard. Various manufacturers have extended the language and added features that were not present in the original Dartmouth version. As a result, many versions of BASIC may be found. Programs developed for one system cannot always be easily transferred to other computer systems. The American National Standards Institute (ANSI) is preparing a language standard to be published in the near future. This will expand the use of BASIC and make programs more transferable between systems.

STRUCTURE OF BASIC

Standard Character Set

BASIC has a standard character set consisting of the alphabet, numbers 0–9, and a group of special characters. (See Figure 16.2.) Since the BASIC interpreter reads only these characters, all programming statements must be written from this group.

Statement Structure

BASIC language programs are composed of instructions called statements. Each statement directs the computer to perform one or more operations. BASIC statements consist of words, symbols, and numbers. Each statement is entered as a single line and is assigned a unique, sequential line number.

Types of Words

The BASIC language contains two types of words: reserved and assigned. Both are incorporated with arithmetic and relational operators to form the programming statements.

RESERVED WORDS. The reserved words shown in Table 16.1 have a specific meaning to the computer. They direct it to perform specific actions and can be used only in that way. For example, the word INPUT directs the computer to read in data from the terminal keyboard. The PRINT statement directs it to output data, calculated by the program or stored in the computer, on the terminal print unit.

ASSIGNED WORDS. Assigned words, or names, are assigned by the programmer to represent quantities in storage. They must conform to certain BASIC language rules: They may contain only one or two characters—an alphabetic letter followed by a number or a dollar sign ($). They may not begin with a special character or include embedded spaces. They may not be reserved words.

Names that represent numbers may contain one alphabetic letter, or one alphabetic letter followed by a single digit 0–9. For example, A, B, H, N2, B9, or P7 would be acceptable numeric names. Assigned names for alphabetic quantities consist of an alphabetic letter followed by a dollar sign ($). For example A$, G$ and U$ are acceptable names.

FIGURE 16.2   STANDARD CHARACTER SET

ALPHABETIC CHARACTERS	NUMERIC CHARACTERS
A	0
B	1
C	2
D	3
E	4
F	5
G	6
H	7
I	8
J	9
K	
L	SPECIAL CHARACTERS
M	'
N	-
O	.
P	/
Q	:
R	;
S	<
T	=
U	>
V	?
W	@
X	[
Y	\
Z	]
	↑
	←
	!
	"
	#
	$
	%
	&
	'
	(
	)
	*
	+

TABLE 16.1   RESERVED WORDS

DATA	ABS
DEF	ATN
DIM	COS
END	EXP
FOR/NEXT	INT
GOSUB	LOG
GO TO	RND
IF/THEN	SGN
INPUT	SIN
LET	SQR
MAT	TAN
PRINT	
READ	
REM	
RESTORE	
RETURN	
STOP	

Since each name may have only one or two characters, the number of combinations is limited. This limits the number of variables that may be represented in a single program.

CODING CONVENTIONS

Since BASIC has no reserved columns, formal coding forms are generally not used. Coding is usually done on ordinary ruled paper. Each line of instructions is written on one line on the page, beginning in column 1.

Each BASIC statement must have a line number. Line numbers must be in sequence, with the lowest number assigned to the first statement in the program and the highest assigned to the last statement. The highest statement number that may be assigned in BASIC is 9999.

Programmers generally write BASIC statement numbers in increments of 10, beginning with line number 10. Thus the sequence 10, 20, 30, 40, . . . will be followed. This makes it easier to add lines later if needed.

Most BASIC systems require programs to terminate with a statement consisting of a line number and the word END.

BASIC statements are stored and executed in order by statement number. Statement number 10 will be executed before statement number 20, and so on.

BASIC COMMANDS

Several types of statements are used in BASIC programming. An understanding of all three is needed for successful programming from the BASIC terminal.

Programming commands make up the BASIC program itself. They direct the machine to perform specific activities, such as to read in data or to output information. System commands are used to communicate with the computer's operating system. The operator uses them to sign the computer on and off, open files, begin execution, interrupt execution, etc. Editing commands are used to develop the source program. They enable lines to be added, resequenced, listed, changed, and so on.

System Commands System commands are directions to the computer's operating system on how to handle and process a program. They are the job control language for BASIC. System commands vary from one computer system to another, but all systems have commands that perform the following actions.

LOG ON AND LOG OFF.   These commands direct the computer to begin and end a session with a terminal user. The LOG ON command opens the session, records the user's number and password, and assigns storage space in the computer for the program. The LOG OFF or BYE command terminates the session and disconnects the terminal from the system.

NEW OR NAME.   The system command NEW or NAME directs the computer to assign a name and allot storage space for the program that follows. The computer will then accept programming statements and store them under the assigned name. The program can henceforth be referred to, loaded, and executed by using this name.

RUN.   The command RUN directs the computer to begin executing the program entered into memory by the programmer. Upon completion of execution, the computer will transfer control back to the user at the terminal.

SAVE OR UNSAVE.   The SAVE command directs the computer to save a file of programming statements in its secondary storage system. It copies the program from active storage onto the secondary storage medium specified. The UNSAVE command deletes the file or program from the secondary storage system. These commands are used to maintain a library of programs on the system.

SCRATCH.   This command directs the computer to delete a program from active storage. When SCRATCH is entered, the system will wipe from primary memory any programming statements that are in the presently open file. The

Computer Conserves Energy

The computer may consume a certain amount of energy, but it also can be used to help us conserve and protect our resources. Two innovative means are discussed here:

Five major downtown Los Angeles businesses have formed an energy cooperative with the aid of a $521,000 federal grant as a pilot program in voluntary energy management among heavy consumers of energy.

The program calls for 11 of the city's largest buildings to be hooked to a central computer that will monitor the energy consumption levels of each building. Building operators will be asked to meet reduced consumption goals, and the computer will warn when those goals are threatened. Voluntary use adjustments then would be recommended by the computer.

"If the May Company must use a lot of energy during a period of peak demand, we may have to ask the Occidental Tower to turn off its lights," explained the president of the Central City Association. He said dollar savings to member firms through reduced energy use should be "adequate incentive" to make the program work. The computer will not be capable of shutting down equipment automatically.

Energy officials say similar projects, established in major metropolitan regions alone, could save at least 84 million barrels of oil annually.

The firms involved include United California Bank, the Southern California Gas Company, the Department of Water and Power, the May Company, and Occidental Life Insurance Company of California. The 11 buildings in the project encompass 5 million square feet of commercial floor space (about 10 percent of the downtown total) and house more than 15,000 employees.

Computers can also be used in a more direct manner to save energy: The Data Systems Corporation in Richmond, Virginia, has been designed so that heat generated by the computers will be used to provide heat for the building.

Normally, heat generated by a large bank of computers is carried off by air conditioners and dispersed outside the building. Data Systems is capturing this heat and putting it to work. Based on present electric heating rates, this means a savings of $500 to $600 a month.

SOURCE: "5 Downtown Businesses Form Energy Cooperative," William Rempel, *Los Angeles Times,* November 12, 1975. © 1975, *Los Angeles Times.* Reprinted by permission.

command is used where the programmer desires to delete an old program and enter new statements in their place.

ESC, BREAK, ATTN, CONTROL CHARACTERS. These commands direct the computer to do a variety of actions. As each character is pressed, it sends a signal to the computer to perform a specific action, such as interrupt execution in the middle of a program, delete a partially typed line from memory, or start or stop a paper tape punch. No printed character appears on the Teletype when they are pressed. The actions each performs will vary with the system.

OTHER COMMANDS.   Commands are also available that direct the computer to operate the terminal paper tape unit or magnetic tape units, etc.

Editing Commands

Editing commands also vary with the system. But each system has commands that facilitate development of a BASIC program.

LEFT ARROW (←).   This character causes the computer to delete the previously typed character from memory. Each time the left arrow is struck, the next character to the left is deleted from the line. It is used to correct keyboarding errors when entering programming lines. For example:

$$10 \text{ PRINT ``BEGIN} \leftarrow \leftarrow \leftarrow \leftarrow \leftarrow \text{START''}$$

will cause the computer to delete the five characters BEGIN and replace them with START.

RENUMBER.   The command RENUMBER causes the computer to automatically renumber all statements in a program, usually by 10s, beginning with 10. It allows the programmer to easily reassign uniform line numbers to a program after a number of changes have been made.

EXAMPLE:

```
            2  . .
           10  . .
           15  . .
           23  . .
           30 END

              RENUMBER

           10  . .
           20  . .
           30  . .
           40  . .
           50 END
```

ATTN, # (DELETE).   This command directs the computer to delete a partially typed line from storage. The programmer can then enter the corrected line to replace it.

EXAMPLE:

```
  10 READ          (Incorrect entry; programmer presses)
                   (ATTN or # key to delete line)
  10 INPUT A,B,C    (Programmer enters correct command)
```

LIST. This command directs the computer to list all statements in a program on the print unit of the terminal. LIST provides a convenient means to get a current listing of all statements in their present sequence.

Some systems will list only the entire program, while others will list single lines or sections of a program:

LIST	(Lists entire program)
LIST-10	(Lists only line 10)
LIST-10,50	(Lists lines 10 to 50)

Programming Commands   Programming commands make up the actual BASIC programs. While they vary somewhat from one system to another, all statements will fall into the general categories described here. Explained below are part of the group of core statements found on all systems.

1. ASSIGNMENT STATEMENTS.   The assignment statement assigns numeric or alphanumeric values to the variables used in a program. For example, the statement

$$70 \text{ LET T8} = 100.23$$

assigns the decimal value 100.23 to the name T8, and

$$80 \text{ LET A\$} = \text{''HEAT''}$$

assigns the alphanumeric string HEAT to the assigned name A$. The number of alphanumeric characters that can be assigned to a single name varies with the computer system.

2. ARITHMETIC STATEMENTS.   These statements direct the computer to perform mathematical operations such as addition, subtraction, multiplication, etc. For example,

$$40 \text{ LET A2} = \text{B2*C2}$$

The value of B2 will be multiplied by the value of C2 and the product stored under the assigned name A2. A variety of mathematical operations can be performed on variable and/or constant values with the following arithmetic operators:

FUNCTION	SYMBOL
Addition	+
Subtraction	—
Multiplication	*
Division	/
Exponentiation	** or ↑

3. INPUT/OUTPUT STATEMENTS.   Input/output statements direct the computer to read in data from a program or the keyboard or to output data on the terminal print unit. For example,

60 PRINT S3, B5, M2

directs the computer to print out the values of S3, B5, and M2 on one line across the page. The statement

10 INPUT C

provides a convenient means of inputting data into a program from the keyboard. The computer will print out a question mark (?) and wait for the operator to key in the value of the variable.

4. CONTROL STATEMENTS.   Control statements dictate the sequence or order in which the program instructions will be executed. Normally, flow moves from the first to the last statement in a program. Control statements may be used to branch out of this sequence to other statements in a different part of the program, or to create a loop. For example,

30 GO TO 60
40 . . .
50 . . .
60 . . .

Statement 30 instructs the computer to execute statement number 60 next, rather than 40 and 50. This example illustrates a control statement that creates a branch.

5. RELATIONAL STATEMENTS.   These statements direct the computer to make logical comparisons of data and then branch to a specified statement number if the condition is true. For example,

30 IF A3 > B3 THEN 100
40 . . .

In this example, the computer will compare the value of A3 to B3. If A3 is greater it will branch to statement 100. If the condition is not true, the computer will ignore the branch and execute statement 40 next.
The common relational operators used in BASIC are:

OPERATION	SYMBOL
Greater than	>
Less than	<
Equal to	=
Not equal to	><
Greater than or equal to	>=
Less than or equal to	<=

6. SPECIFICATION STATEMENTS. Specification statements are used to reserve adjacent storage spaces in the computer to hold arrays or groups of related items. For example,

20 DIM A(30)

will reserve 30 spaces in storage to hold the numeric array A. DIM is an abbreviation for dimension.

7. MATRIX STATEMENTS. BASIC has an excellent matrix manipulation capability. The MAT statement directs the computer to perform various manipulations on data stored in an array. For example,

200 MAT C=A+B

directs the computer to add the corresponding elements in array A to array B, forming a new array, C.

8. FUNCTIONS. An important feature of BASIC (also found in FORTRAN) is its built-in functions. A function subroutine is a group of programming statements in the compiler that perform a mathematical routine, such as finding a square root. These functions can be called into the user's program by using their names. Table 16.2 lists some of the built-in functions available in BASIC.

TABLE 16.2 BUILT-IN FUNCTIONS

FUNCTION	PURPOSE
ABS(X)	Absolute value of X
ATN(X)	Angle (in radians) whose tangent is X
COS(X)	Cosine of X radians
EXP(X)	Natural exponential of X (e to the X power)
INT(X)	Integral part of X
LOG(X)	Logarithm of X to the base e (ln x)
RND(X)	A random number between 0 and 1
SGN(X)	Sign of X defined as: If $X < 0$, $SGN(X) = -1$ If $X = 0$, $SGN(X) = 0$ If $X > 0$, $SGN(X) = +1$
SIN(X)	Sine of X radians
SQR(X)	Positive square root of X
TAN(X)	Tangent of X radians

SAMPLE BASIC STATEMENTS

The following statements illustrate some of the operations that can be performed in BASIC.

REM   The REM statement tells the computer to read in a remark and write it out on the terminal as the program is listed. It is used to title a program or a sequence of statements, or to include explanatory information in a program listing.

EXAMPLE:

| Statement number | Indicates this is a remark | | Text or phrase that is to be listed |

10 REM PROGRAM ≠485. WRITTEN BY J. FIELDS

Explanation: The programmer uses a REM statement to include the title, PROGRAM #485, WRITTEN BY J. FIELDS, in the program listing. One or more remarks can be placed at almost any point in the program.

READ/DATA   The READ and DATA statements are used to assign values, listed within a program, to variable names. The READ statement specifies the names under which the data will be stored. The DATA statement includes the values that are to be assigned to the names. The DATA statement is usually placed at the end of the program, before the END statement.

EXAMPLE:

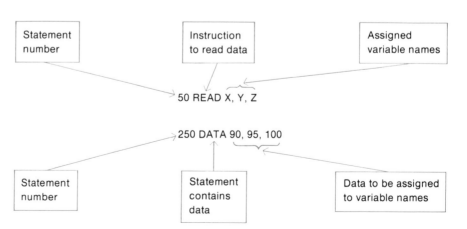

Explanation: Upon encountering the READ statement, the computer will seek out the first DATA statement. It will load the first data item (90) into memory under the name X, the second item (95) under Y, and the third item (100) under the name Z.

Both numeric and alphanumeric data can be assigned with these statements.

PRINT   The PRINT statement directs the computer to output numeric or alphanumeric data on the print unit of the terminal. Upon encountering the PRINT statement, the machine will output the data, stored under the names in the print list, in sequence across the page.

EXAMPLE:

| Statement number | Instruction to output | Names under which data are stored |

200 PRINT X, Y ,Z

Output:

| 90 | 95 | 100 |

Explanation: Upon reaching statement 200, the computer will print out the values of X, Y, and Z. Since a comma is used to separate the names in the PRINT statement, a standard five-column spacing format will be followed. (That is, there will be five columns across the page. Only three are used in this example.)

Had semicolons been used instead of commas, the values would have been output in a more tightly spaced format with only a few spaces between the values.

Assignment   The assignment statement LET assigns a value to the variable name that
Statement   appears to the left of the equals sign. The statement can be used to assign numeric or alphanumeric values.

EXAMPLE:

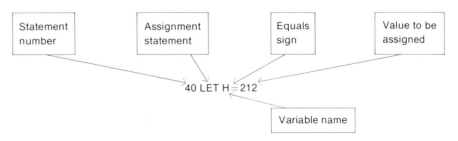

| Statement number | Assignment statement | Equals sign | Value to be assigned |

40 LET H = 212

Variable name

Explanation: This statement will assign the value 212 to the variable name H assigned by the programmer.

50 LET D$= ''TONY''

Explanation: Statement 50 will assign the alphabetic quantity TONY to the name D$.

FOR/NEXT   The two statements FOR and NEXT are used to repeat a sequence of instructions a specified number of times. The FOR statement indicates how many times the sequence will be executed. The NEXT statement marks the end of the sequence. The FOR/NEXT statements are used to create a loop composed of the instructions appearing between them. This loop can read in records in a file, print out lines of data, or perform mathematical calculations many times.

EXAMPLE:

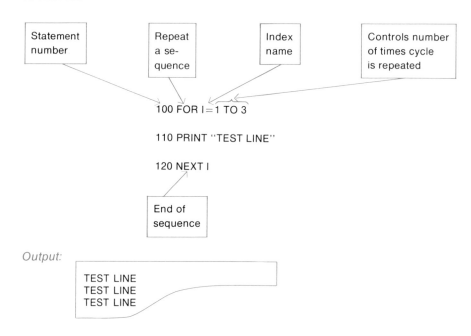

100 FOR I=1 TO 3

110 PRINT ''TEST LINE''

120 NEXT I

End of sequence

Output:

```
TEST LINE
TEST LINE
TEST LINE
```

Explanation: Statement number 100 directs the computer to execute statements 110 and 120 three times. Each time, it will print out the text TEST LINE. After the third execution, the next statement in the program (130) will be executed.

IF/THEN   The IF/THEN statement is used to perform a conditional branch. The computer will test for a specified condition. If the condition is true it will branch to the statement number indicated. The test performed is a relational comparison—the statement tests to see if one value is less than, equal to, not equal to, or greater than another. The value may be a variable (A4), a constant (6.92), or an arithmetic expression (X*3−B). The branch takes place only when the test condition is true. If it is not true, the next statement in the program is executed.

EXAMPLE:

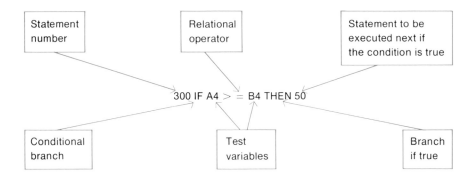

Statement number

Relational operator

Statement to be executed next if the condition is true

300 IF A4 > = B4 THEN 50

Conditional branch

Test variables

Branch if true

"Another advantage is the humming and whirring, which is so much more pleasant than chalk screeching on a blackboard."

Sidney Harris

Explanation: Upon encountering statement 300, the computer will compare the values A4 and B4. If A4 is greater than or equal to B4, the program will execute statement 50 next. If the condition is not true (A4 is less than B4), the branch will be ignored and statement number 310 will be executed next.

SAMPLE PROGRAM

A simple, interactive BASIC language program is illustrated in Figure 16.3. This program calculates the number of student contact hours and assigned hours a professor has per class and the total number for all classes. The variables are input from the terminal during execution.

The flowchart is shown in Figure 16.4. The algorithm is a simple loop that inputs the variables, calculates the contact and assigned hours for a class, prints them out, and then adds them to accumulating totals. The last step in the loop is to ask the user whether the loop should be repeated. The two accumulating totals are initialized before the loop is entered and their values are printed out after the loop is completed.

Program Analysis	STATEMENT NUMBER	EXPLANATION
	10	Program description.
	20	Initializes one accumulating total, G.
	30	Initializes one accumulating total, H.
	40, 50	Asks user to enter A; inputs A.
	60, 70	Asks user to enter B; inputs B.
	80, 90	Asks user to enter C; inputs C.
	100	Calculates student contact hours (D).
	110	Calculates assigned hours (E).
	120–130	Prints out D and E.
	140	Adds D to the accumulating total G.
	150	Printer skips a line.
	160	Adds E to the accumulating total H.
	170	Asks user to enter F (1 if loop is to be repeated, 0 if not.)
	180	Inputs F.
	190	Tests to see if F is 1. If it is, program branches to statement 40.
	200–210	If F is 0, the values of G and H are printed out.
	220	Terminates program.

FIGURE 16.3   BASIC SAMPLE PROGRAM

```
10 REM   CALCULATE STUDENT CONTACT HOURS
20 LET G=0
30 LET H=0
40 PRINT "ENTER NUMBER OF STUDENTS IN CLASS"
50 INPUT A
60 PRINT "ENTER HOURS PER WEEK CLASS MEETS"
70 INPUT B
80 PRINT "ENTER NUMBER OF OFFICE HOURS PER WEEK"
90 INPUT C
100 LET D=A*B
110 LET E=C+B
120 PRINT "YOUR STUDENT CONTACT HOURS ARE ";D
130 PRINT "YOUR ASSIGNED HOURS ARE ";E
140 LET G=G+D
150 PRINT
160 LET H=H+E
170 PRINT "DO YOU WANT TO ENTER ANOTHER WORK LOAD? 0=NO,1=YES"
180 INPUT F
190 IF F=1 THEN 40
200 PRINT "THE FACULTY CONTACT HOURS ARE ";G
210 PRINT "THE FACULTY ASSIGNED HOURS ARE ";H
220 END

RUN
ENTER NUMBER OF STUDENTS IN CLASS
?
50
ENTER HOURS PER WEEK CLASS MEETS
?
3
ENTER NUMBER OF OFFICE HOURS PER WEEK
?
4
YOUR STUDENT CONTACT HOURS ARE   150
YOUR ASSIGNED HOURS ARE   7

DO YOU WANT TO ENTER ANOTHER WORK LOAD? 0=NO,1=YES
?
1
ENTER NUMBER OF STUDENTS IN CLASS
?
45
ENTER HOURS PER WEEK CLASS MEETS
?
3
ENTER NUMBER OF OFFICE HOURS PER WEEK
?
5
YOUR STUDENT CONTACT HOURS ARE   135
YOUR ASSIGNED HOURS ARE   8

DO YOU WANT TO ENTER ANOTHER WORK LOAD? 0=NO,1=YES
?
0
THE FACULTY CONTACT HOURS ARE   285
THE FACULTY ASSIGNED HOURS ARE   15
```

FIGURE 16.4   PROGRAM FLOWCHART

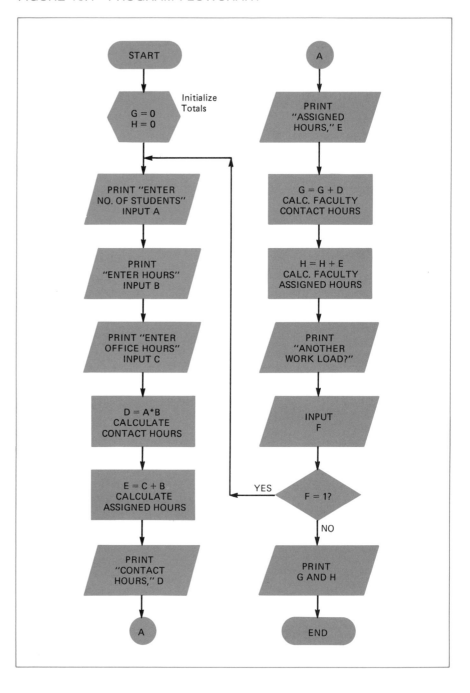

KEY TERMS   Arithmetic operator   Programming command
                            Conditional branch   Relational operator
                            Editing command   System command

EXERCISES

1. What does the name BASIC stand for and how was the language developed?
2. In which areas is BASIC finding wide use?
3. What are three advantages of the BASIC language?
4. What are the advantages of the interactive capability of BASIC?
5. Why does the lack of a language standard pose problems?
6. List three acceptable names for numeric variables and three for alphanumeric variables.
7. What are the rules for the use of line numbers? Why are line numbers important?
8. What are the three types of commands used in BASIC programming?
9. How do system commands differ from editing commands?
10. What is the difference between the UNSAVE and SCRATCH system commands?
11. What three types of statements are used to assign values to variables in a program?
12. What is the purpose of control statements?
13. What are arithmetic operators?

17

FORTRAN PROGRAMMING LANGUAGE

Developed in the late 1950s by a group from IBM, FORTRAN (FORmula TRANslating System) was intended to be a language scientists and mathematicians could use to program their technical problems.

Thousands of hours were invested in writing a compiler that would accept statements in algebraic form and convert them into machine language instructions. During the next two decades, several improved and enlarged versions were written, expanding FORTRAN's utility into many other areas, among them business.

Unlike COBOL, FORTRAN is not supported by a group of users. Instead, manufacturers and users modify, improve, and change the language to suit their own needs.

To eliminate some of the confusion and differences that might arise when a language develops in an unorganized, unplanned way, an effort has been made at standardization. The American National Standards Institute (ANSI) publishes several approved versions of FORTRAN that establish guidelines for computer manufacturers and compiler writers. As new versions and improvements of FORTRAN are written, ANSI studies them for inclusion in their uniform standards. Each manufacturer, however, tends to broaden or expand the available statements in the language for use on its own computers.

The examples and programs in this chapter are illustrative of the ANSI version of FORTRAN IV, X3.9-1966.

ADVANTAGES OF FORTRAN

FORTRAN's primary advantage is its excellent mathematical capability. The language closely resembles algebraic equations, which are familiar to most individuals working in scientific or mathematical areas. In FORTRAN, a programmer can read in and store alphabetic and numeric data, manipulate data, perform complex mathematical and logical operations, and write out the results.

FORTRAN is also a very compact language. Usually only a few statements are necessary to direct the computer to solve a complex problem. COBOL requires many more statements to open files, move, process, and output data.

Because some versions of FORTRAN require a compiler that uses only approximately 4K bytes of storage, FORTRAN compilers are available on small as well as large computers. Most computer manufacturers write FORTRAN compilers for each new machine they put on the market, thus assuring the programmer that a job will run on almost any modern computer.

Improvements in the FORTRAN language have increased its literal capability, and it is no longer limited to mathematical applications. It can manipulate words, sentences, and whole paragraphs of textual material. However, FORTRAN still does not have the ease of literal or alphabetic manipulation that COBOL has.

FORTRAN also eliminates many routine housekeeping details required in COBOL programming. For example, in FORTRAN, storage areas are set up more easily and with less detailed description than is required in the COBOL Data Division. Fields in a data record are more compactly and conveniently described. Open- and close-file routines are handled by the compiler, freeing the programmer from these details.

And finally, FORTRAN was the pattern followed in the development of the BASIC (Beginner's All-Purpose Symbolic Instruction Code) language. A programmer who knows the fundamentals of FORTRAN can write programs in BASIC with little difficulty.

LIMITATIONS OF FORTRAN

FORTRAN bears closer resemblance to mathematical notation than to ordinary business English, because it relies on codes and symbols. It is more difficult for a nonprogrammer to understand or trace program logic in FORTRAN than in COBOL. FORTRAN programs must be fully documented to explain the logic used in the program and the input/output specifications.

As in COBOL, basic rules of punctuation, syntax, spelling, etc. must be followed in FORTRAN programming. The loss of one comma or a misplaced

TABLE 17.1 FORTRAN STANDARD CHARACTER SET

ALPHABETIC CHARACTERS	NUMERIC CHARACTERS
A	0
B	1
C	2
D	3
E	4
F	5
G	6
H	7
I	8
J	9
K	
L	SPECIAL CHARACTERS
M	
N	(blank)
O	+
P	−
Q	/
R	=
S	.
T	)
U	*
V	,
W	(
X	' (apostrophe)
Y	&
Z	$

parenthesis in a FORTRAN program can prevent an otherwise acceptable program from executing.

STRUCTURE OF FORTRAN

Standard Character Set FORTRAN has the standard character set shown in Table 17.1. This set consists of the alphabet, numbers 0–9, and a group of special characters. Since the FORTRAN compiler recognizes only these characters, all programming statements must be written from this group.

Statement Structure In FORTRAN, the basic unit of the language is the statement, not the sentence as in COBOL. The statement is a group of symbols, words, and punctuation formed into an expression. Each expression tells the computer to perform one or more operations.

The statement is composed of names assigned by the programmer, symbols called arithmetic operators ($+$, $-$, $*$, $/$, for example), and reserved words, which direct the computer to perform operations, move data, do calculations, etc.

FORTRAN statements resemble algebraic equations. They do not look like English text matter, do not conclude with periods, and are not formed into paragraphs, as in COBOL.

In Chapter 15 we saw that a COBOL statement took the form of

ADD STOCK, SHIPMENT, GIVING GOODS.

The same instruction in FORTRAN would look like this:

GOODS $=$ STOCK $+$ SHIP

There are several differences between these two examples. The COBOL example is a sentence that ends with a period and uses ordinary English words instead of abbreviations. The instruction to perform a mathematical operation is indicated by the word ADD instead of by an arithmetic operator. In FORTRAN, the statement is written as an equation. STOCK is to be added to SHIP and the sum placed in the location named GOODS. Abbreviations are frequently used in FORTRAN, and more reliance is placed on symbols and codes.

Several other examples will illustrate differences:

COBOL:
MOVE EMPLOYEE-NAME TO PAYCHECK-NAME.

FORTRAN:
PAYNME $=$ EMPNME

COBOL:
IF ITEM IS LESS THAN MINIMUM GO TO ORDER.

FORTRAN:
IF (ITEM $-$ MIN) 50, 100, 100
(50 is the statement number of ORDER)

Types of Words   The FORTRAN language contains two types of words, reserved words and assigned names.

RESERVED WORDS.   The reserved words shown in Table 17.2 have a particular meaning to the computer and can be used only to perform that specific task. They are incorporated into programming statements along with the names of the quantities on which they are to operate.

TABLE 17.2 FORTRAN RESERVED WORDS

BACKSPACE	FIND
CALL EXIT	FORMAT
CALL LINK	FUNCTION
CALL LOAD	GO TO
CALL	IF
CALL PDUMP	INTEGER
CALL SSWTCH	INTEGER FUNCTION
COMMON	PAUSE
CONTINUE	READ
DATA	REAL
DEFINE FILE	REAL FUNCTION
DIMENSION	RETURN
DO	REWIND
END	STOP
END FILE	SUBROUTINE
EQUIVALENCE	WRITE
EXTERNAL	

ASSIGNED NAMES. Assigned names are words chosen by the programmer to represent quantities in storage or data fields on a record. Names must conform to certain FORTRAN rules. They may not be more than six characters long, and in some cases they must begin with certain letters of the alphabet. A reserved word cannot be used as a name.

Optional words, as used in COBOL, are not used in FORTRAN.

Coding Forms and Conventions A standard coding form is used by FORTRAN programmers to write programs. (See Figure 17.1.) After coding, instructions are usually keypunched into cards or keyed onto magnetic tape or disk.

FORTRAN PROGRAM SHEET LAYOUT. At the top of the standard form is a space for entering the programmer's name and other related data. Each page is divided into 80 columns and has approximately 24 lines for writing instructions. Each column corresponds to a column of a record and holds one character.

CONVENTIONS. The FORTRAN compiler is designed to expect certain kinds of data in selected columns. Columns 1 to 5 are reserved for statement numbers. The programmer directs control to different statements during branching and looping by referring to statement numbers.

FIGURE 17.1   FORTRAN CODING FORM

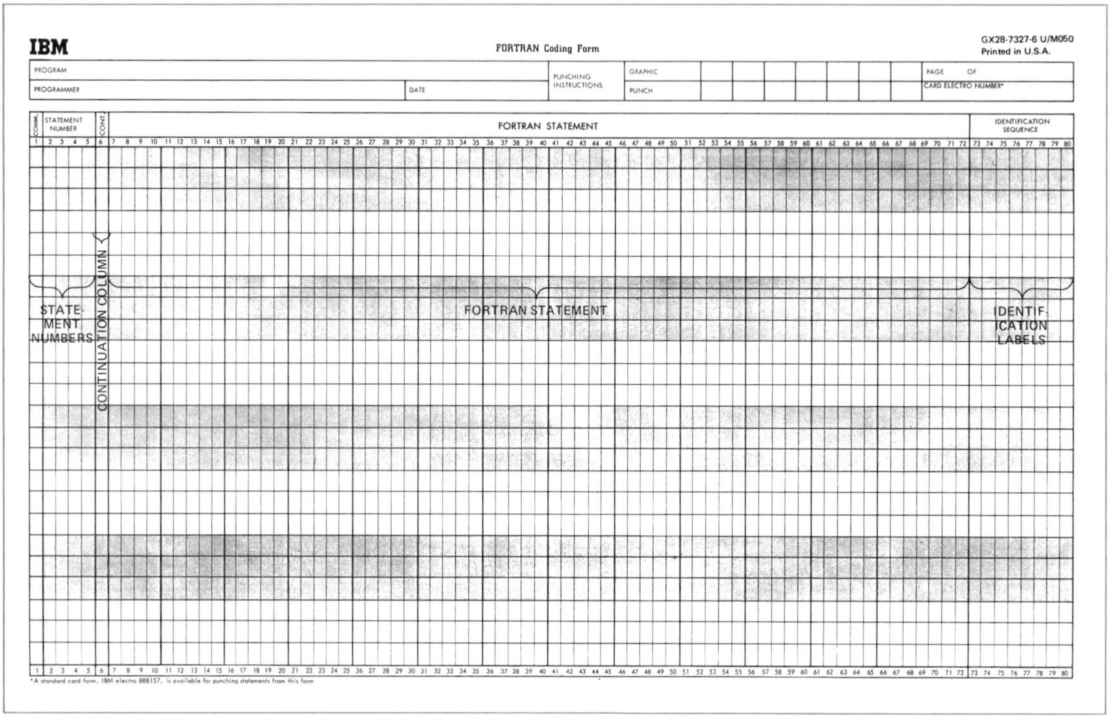

Column 6 is the continuation column. A character is recorded in this column if an instruction is too long to fit on one line. Columns 7 to 72 are reserved for programming statements. The actual coding directions to read data, write data, FORMAT statements, etc. are recorded here. Columns 73–80 are not read by the compiler and are used to record labels, program names, or numbers of identification of each line in the program.

FORTRAN ELEMENTS

A FORTRAN program has no special sections or divisions. FORTRAN statements are placed in the program in the order in which they are to be carried out. The computer executes each instruction, one at a time, branching where directed, until the last statement in the program has been reached.

A programmer constructs FORTRAN statements by combining mathematical operators, reserved words, names, etc. These instructions give certain information to the compiler. They must describe the format of the I/O data. They must indicate whether numbers are whole numbers, decimals, exponentiations, etc.

The FORTRAN language consists of several different types of programming
statements. Four of the most important types are

1. CONTROL STATEMENTS. These statements control the sequence of
operations that the computer is to follow. They instruct the machine to
branch to a given statement, to repeat a sequence a given number of
times, to terminate execution, etc. For example, the statement

    GO TO 50

instructs the computer to execute statement 50 next. It causes the
computer to branch to another statement instead of executing the next
instruction in line.

2. ARITHMETIC STATEMENTS. These statements cause the computer to
perform such mathematical operations as addition, subtraction,
exponentiation, and square root. For example,

    TOTAL = CASH + DEPOS − REFUND

directs an arithmetic procedure. The computer will add the value of CASH
to DEPOS, subtract the value of REFUND, and place the answer in a slot
named TOTAL.

3. INPUT/OUTPUT STATEMENTS. These statements cause the computer to
read in, or write out, data. They call in and out card readers, card
punches, line printers, magnetic tape units, etc. They schedule the flow
of data in and out of the CPU. For example,

    WRITE (6,10) CASH

directs the computer to write the value of CASH on the line printer. The
number 6 within the parentheses is a code indicating the line printer.
The number 10 tells the computer to refer to statement 10 for details
on how the line is to be printed. (See FORMAT statement below.)

4. FORMAT STATEMENTS. These statements give the computer information
on the kind of data to be input and output and the fields where they are
located on a record. FORMAT statements tell the computer whether whole
or decimal numbers are involved, how many digits they have, and how
many places past the decimal point.

    They also give the computer instructions on the graphic layout of the
output. For example, they indicate when lines should be skipped by the
line printer and in what columns data should be printed out.

    A FORMAT statement is associated with one or more input/output
statements. The related I/O statements instruct the computer to read or
write data, the name of the quantities, what I/O units to use, and which
FORMAT statement to refer to for details on how the line is to be printed.

For example,

10 FORMAT (1H1, F5.2)

This FORMAT statement is the one referred to in the previous example. It states that output is to be written at the top of a new page (indicated by the 1H1), that it is a decimal number (indicated by the code F), and that it may fill five columns with two places past the decimal (indicated by 5.2).

FORTRAN Terminology

Several mathematical and general terms are used in specific ways in FORTRAN. Many refer to the data being processed by a program, and others to elements of the program itself. Following are some of the main terms with which a FORTRAN programmer should be familiar:

A constant is a fixed quantity whose value does not change during execution of a program. It may be represented by an assigned name or by the actual value itself. A constant may be a number or an alphanumeric value.

For example, a programmer may want to multiply pay rate by 40 when figuring paychecks. The constant in this program would be 40, since it represents the number of hours each employee works and will be the same for all paychecks prepared.

The programmer may use the number "40" in a programming statement:

PAY = RATE * 40

or assign a name to the constant 40

TIME = 40

and use the name in the statement:

PAY = RATE * TIME

Numeric constants are used in mathematical procedures involving other numbers and constants, but the numeric value they represent does not vary during a program.

Alphanumeric constants can be moved from one location to another within the computer, or input or output. They are not involved in any calculations.

A literal constant is a string of characters the computer considers as a single group. It can be read in, moved in storage, or printed out. It is called "literal" because it may be composed of alphanumeric and special characters, and "constant" because it does not change during the run of a program. Literal constants are often used to label output and to identify data, as in the FORMAT statements below:

80 WRITE (6,90)
90 FORMAT (1H1,14HTAXABLE INCOME)

Not All Computers Are Impersonal

Most of us usually accuse the computer of depersonalizing all of us people. But—believe it or not—the computer is sometimes guilty of humanizing inanimate objects or labels.

For example, invitations to apply for credit cards have been sent out to such unlikely recipients as Mr. Woman's Page on a newspaper (Dear Mr. Page), Mr. Lincoln Tunnel (Dear Mr. Tunnel), Honolulu City County (Dear Mr. County), and a regional electric power authority (Dear Mr. Authority). (The power authority's application was evidently filled out and returned by a human being. Under "annual earnings" was written "$600 million"; under "nature of business" it said "to excrete power.")

How do such letters get into the mail?

For one major credit card company, the first step in mailing personalized letters begins when a direct-mail broker rents 30 to 50 mailing lists from magazines, specialty stores, and so forth. The collected lists are fed into a computer for a merge—purge process. The tapes are first checked out against the names of the 4.5 million people who already have the company's credit card, and any duplications are purged. The next step is to "unduplicate" the outside lists—that is, any name that appears on more than one list is used only once. Another run eliminates (at least theoretically) any nonpersonal "names" like Company or Incorporated. The various purges eliminate nearly a third of the names rented. The system's rate of error is reported to be below one-half of 1 percent. And when an error is found, that name is added to the purge list.

But mistakes still do happen. One application, sent to a resident of Florida, was returned with the following response:

"My thanks and appreciation for your invitation to become a member of your company's customers. But unfortunately, I am not in a position to take advantage of your invitation due to the fact that I am an inmate at Florida State Prison and have been for nine years now."

SOURCE: Adapted from "Beware the Humanity of Computers," by Mike McGrady. © 1975 by *Newsday*. Reprinted by permission.

```
50 WRITE (6,60)
60 FORMAT (1H1,29HCOMMISSION RATE IS 25 PERCENT)
```

In each case above, the literal constant is a string of numbers, letters, or characters that the programmer has written into the program. They will always appear in the printout exactly as in the FORMAT statement. In these examples, the 14H and 29H inform the computer that literal constants of 14 and 29 characters, respectively, follow.

A variable is a quantity whose value will change during a program run. A variable may be alphanumeric characters or a numeric value. It may be read in or out of the computer, or be the result of calculations performed. Since its value changes, the programmer uses an assigned name to refer to it.

In the example above, the programmer uses the name RATE to refer to the hourly wage for each employee. RATE is a variable since its value will not be the same for all employees.

PAY represents a numeric variable that will be calculated by multiplying a constant (TIME) by a variable (RATE).

Numeric variables may be read into a program, printed out, calculated within a program, or used in mathematical procedures to calculate other variables or constants.

Variables can also be alphanumeric characters. For example, in

30 READ (5,40) EMP

Sidney Harris

EMP is an assigned word representing an alphanumeric variable (name) that will be different for each employee. The first paycheck may be prepared for AMOS, the second for DIAZ, etc.

Alphanumeric variables are read into a program from data records and can be listed as part of the output. They usually represent names of parts or people, code identification numbers, labels, etc.

An integer is a whole number. It is a numerical quantity that does not contain a decimal point. Some examples of integers are

1   414   54,675   0002

A real number is a decimal number. It is also called a floating-point number. Some examples of real numbers are

.1   41.4   54,675.00   .0002

Language Features

ARRAYS. FORTRAN is particularly rich in its ability to read in, store, and manipulate large collections of related data. Only a minimum of programming effort is required to direct the computer to set up consecutive storage spaces sufficient to hold several thousand variables and assign a unique name to each location. This storage arrangement is called an array. The process of reading data into an array is called *arraying data*.

The programmer tells the computer the size and name of the array needed. The computer will reserve the storage spaces and assign a name to each location, depending on its position within the array. For example, the first location in an array named MARY might be called MARY(1), the second MARY(2), and the third MARY(3), etc. The number used to indicate the position of a storage location within an array is called a *subscript*. The first subscript may be any number. The computer will automatically assign consecutive numbers as the remaining subscripts.

Subscripts may be used by the programmer for identification. For example,

ARRAY—GROSS NATIONAL PRODUCT

GNP(1970)
GNP(1971)
GNP(1972)
GNP(1973)
GNP(1974)
GNP(1975)

The programmer can have the computer print out the Gross National Product for 1974 by directing it to write the contents stored in GNP(1974). Or GNP(1974) can be added to some other quantity or compared to GNP of another year.

The ability to array and assign subscripts is a powerful tool for the programmer. It enables him or her to read in and store tables of all kinds, lists of numbers, quantities, names, records, etc. Any item in the array can be referred to, processed, or changed by using its subscript.

SUBROUTINES AND FUNCTIONS. Another important aspect of FORTRAN is the availability of built-in functions and subroutines. A function is a mathematical subprogram that can be called into use by a source program to perform a specific mathematical task. A subroutine is a service subprogram that can be called in by a source program to perform a variety of operations.

FORTRAN contains many built-in functions. Some examples are listed in Table 17.3. To illustrate, suppose the FORTRAN programmer wants to find the square root of a number, say 10. He or she can write a program directing the computer to perform each step involved in finding a square root. But it would be much easier to use the square root function (SQRT) available in the compiler, like this

$$ROOT = SQRT(10)$$

When the computer encounters this statement, it will extract the square root of 10 and place the answer in storage under the name ROOT, ready for reading or further processing.

Subroutines may be written by the programmer or the manufacturer and stored in the computer subprogram library. Some subroutines perform housekeeping duties involved in processing a program, such as terminating

TABLE 17.3 FORTRAN LANGUAGE FUNCTIONS

Exponential
Natural logarithm
Common logarithm
Arcsine
Arccosine
Arctangent
Trigonometric cosine
Trigonometric tangent
Trigonometric cotangent
Square root
Error function
Complemented error function
Gamma
Log-gamma
Modular arithmetic
Absolute value
Truncation
Largest value

execution. Others perform alphabetic and numeric sorts, calculate interest payments or payroll deductions, etc. In fact, any frequently used, repetitive procedure can be handled by a subroutine.

To use a subroutine, the programmer inserts a CALL SUBROUTINE statement in the source program at the proper point. The compiler will locate the subroutine named and transfer temporary control to it. When the procedure it performs is completed, the subroutine returns control, and the answer, to the calling program, and processing continues.

SAMPLE FORTRAN STATEMENTS

Many powerful and complex programming statements can be written using the arithmetic operators, reserved words, and assigned names. The following statements illustrate some of the varied operations that can be performed in FORTRAN.

List Comment Statement

This statement tells the computer to read in a comment and write it out as part of the program listing. It is used to identify a part of a program or to include explanatory material in the listing. The statement will be listed but not compiled.

EXAMPLE:

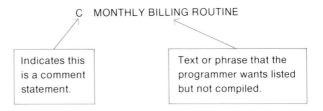

C MONTHLY BILLING ROUTINE

Indicates this is a comment statement.

Text or phrase that the programmer wants listed but not compiled.

Explanation: The programmer wants to include the title MONTHLY BILLING ROUTINE in the program listing. The comment statement is punched in a card and inserted in the program deck. The statement appears at the beginning of the listing, but is not compiled or entered into the working storage of the computer. The "C" in column 1 of the statement tells the computer that this is a comment statement. One or more comment statements can be used at almost any point in the program.

Read a Whole Number

This statement in conjunction with a FORMAT statement tells the computer to read a whole number (integer) and store it in memory ready for further processing.

EXAMPLE:

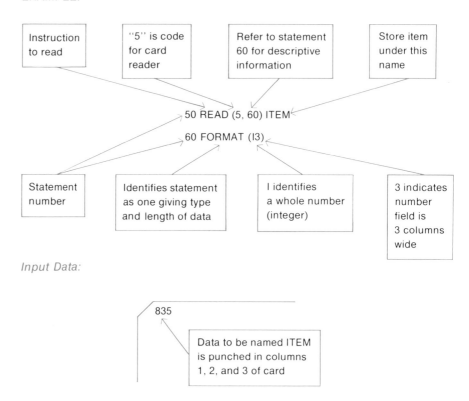

Input Data:

Explanation: The programmer assigns the name of the quantity for later reference. The details of the FORMAT statement are dictated by the number being read in. I must always be used when reading whole numbers.

To read 835, which requires a three-column field, I3 is used in the FORMAT statement. To read the number 3,947, I4 would be used. A six-digit number, such as 845,903, would require the use of I6. In each case, the letter I indicates that the number to be read is an integer. The number following the I indicates how many columns wide the field to be read is. Not all positions in the field need be filled. That is, the width of the field is determined by the maximum number of digits expected in the data appearing in that field.

The 5 in the READ statement is the code number for the card reader. (Code numbers for I/O devices will vary from one installation to another.) The 60 tells the computer that FORMAT statement 60 describes where the number will be found on the card.

Write a
Whole Number

This statement in conjunction with a FORMAT statement tells the computer to write a whole number. The number has been read into storage earlier or calculated by the computer from other data.

EXAMPLE:

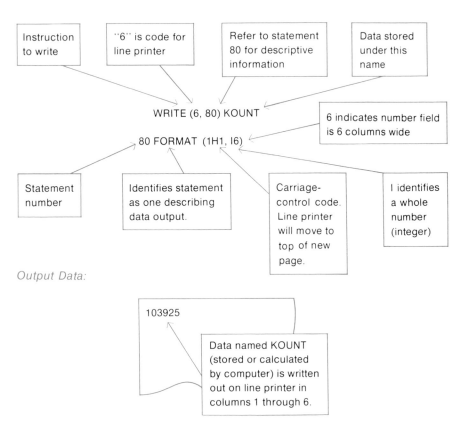

Output Data:

Explanation: The name KOUNT has been assigned earlier by the programmer. The quantity it represents either was read in earlier in the program and given the name KOUNT or is the result of a calculation performed by the computer and named KOUNT.

The details of the FORMAT statement are dictated by the number being output. To write 103,925, a six-column-wide integer, I6 was used.

The 6 in the WRITE statement is the code number for the line printer. The 80 tells the computer that FORMAT statement 80 describes where the data is to be written on the line printer.

Branch—IF   This statement causes the computer to take one of several paths depending on the value of a quantity in storage. Branching is limited to only three paths and is based upon the relationship of the value in storage to zero. This statement enables the programmer to branch back to the beginning, to a point within the program, or to the end of the program.

EXAMPLE:

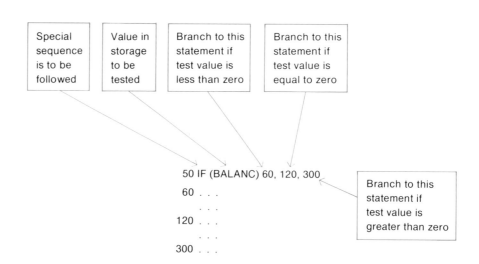

| Special sequence is to be followed | Value in storage to be tested | Branch to this statement if test value is less than zero | Branch to this statement if test value is equal to zero |

50 IF (BALANC) 60, 120, 300

60 . . .

. . .

120 . . .

. . .

300 . . .

Branch to this statement if test value is greater than zero

Explanation: A branch is to be made in the program at statement 50. Control is to branch to statement 60, 120, or 300, depending on the value of BALANC. If the value of BALANC is less than zero, the computer will automatically branch to the statement number in the first position (60). If the value of BALANC is equal to zero, it will branch to the statement number in the second position (120). If the value of BALANC is greater than zero, it will branch to the statement number in the third position (300).

Repeat a Cycle—
DO Loop

Unless otherwise instructed, the computer will execute a statement only once and will follow the instructions in the program consecutively. It is often necessary to repeat a cycle several times. A DO loop statement can be used to instruct the computer to execute a series of statements a predetermined number of times. The maximum times the cycle is executed can be written into the program, or calculated during the time of execution.

EXAMPLE:

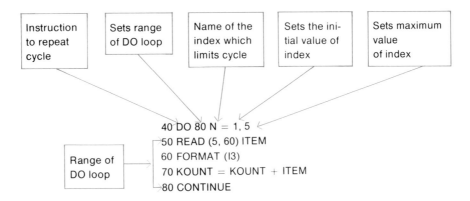

```
40 DO 80 N = 1, 5
50 READ (5, 60) ITEM
60 FORMAT (I3)
70 KOUNT = KOUNT + ITEM
80 CONTINUE
```

Explanation: In this example, a DO loop is used to cause the computer to repeat a READ statement and mathematical calculation five times. The DO instruction consists of the word DO followed by the last statement number in the cycle being repeated, and an index. The index controls the number of times the loop repeats.

The index contains a name (N in this example), followed by its initial value (1) and its limit (5). Each time a loop is performed, the index is incremented by one. When the limit is reached (5), control goes to the next statement following the CONTINUE.

Addition This statement tells the computer to add two or more decimal (real) numbers or two or more whole numbers (integers). (Many compilers cannot add whole and decimal numbers together. Either the whole number must be converted to a decimal and than added, or vice versa.) The computer will perform the indicated calculation and store the answer under an assigned name. This answer may be written out or used for further processing.

EXAMPLE:

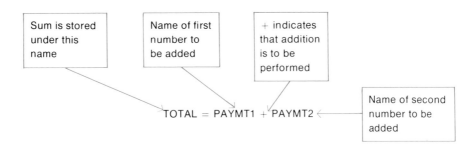

Data in Storage:

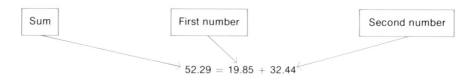

52.29 = 19.85 + 32.44

Explanation: Two numbers are to be added. The first (19.85) has been previously read in or calculated and is stored under the name PAYMT1. The second (32.44) has been assigned the name PAYMT2. The computer will add the numbers on the right-hand side of the expression and place the answer in the location named TOTAL. The values of PAYMT1 and PAYMT2 may change throughout the program. The values that will be summed are always those in storage at the time the computer reaches the instruction.

Compound
Arithmetic
Statements

The computer can be directed to perform more than one arithmetic operation by the same instruction. Calculations using addition, subtraction, multiplication, division, and/or other functions can be indicated in one instruction. The computer will perform all arithmetic procedures indicated and store the answer under the assigned name. This answer may be written out or used for further calculations.

EXAMPLE:

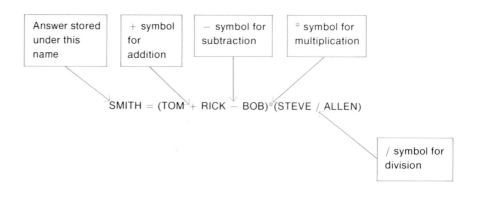

SMITH = (TOM + RICK − BOB)*(STEVE / ALLEN)

Data in Storage:

27.9 = (10.9 + 2.0 − 3.6) * (6.3 / 2.1)

Explanation: The computer performs mathematical calculations according to a definite order or hierarchy

① Exponentiation

② Multiplication and division

③ Subtraction and addition

Unless directed to the contrary, it will move from left to right in performing the hierarchy. Calculations enclosed within parentheses will always be performed before those not enclosed.

The statement in this example includes subtraction, addition, multiplication, and division. The computer will evaluate the terms on the right side of the expression, following the hierarchy, and place the answer on the left under the name SMITH. The parentheses will be cleared first, left to right. The calculation involving addition and subtraction enclosed within parentheses will be performed first. Then the other parentheses, involving division, will be cleared. Finally, the two intermediate results will be multiplied.

SAMPLE PROGRAM

A simple FORTRAN program is given to illustrate how the various statements in the language are assembled.

Function of the Program

The program is designed to calculate and print out the average of a list of wind speeds. The steps in the program are graphically shown in the flowchart in Figure 17.2. The steps the program algorithm follows are:

1. Titles are written and two accumulating totals (CT, TOTAL) are initialized to zero.
2. A simple loop is entered. A record is read and tested for end-of-file. If it is the end, the program branches to the averaging sequence.
3. If the record is not the end-of-file, CT (a counter) is increased by one and the value on the record is added to TOTAL.
4. The data on the record (name of month and wind speed value) are written out on the line printer. The program repeats the loop to read in the next record.
5. When the end-of-file is reached, the average is calculated by dividing TOTAL by CT and is printed out on the line printer. Then program execution terminates.

Program Analysis

The discussion on page 388 traces the program in a step-by-step fashion. The numbers listed at the left margin are the statement numbers shown in Figure 17.3. The input data for this program are shown in Figure 17.4(A); the output is shown in Figure 17.4(B). The input data were punched into cards.

FIGURE 17.2   FORTRAN SAMPLE PROGRAM FLOWCHART

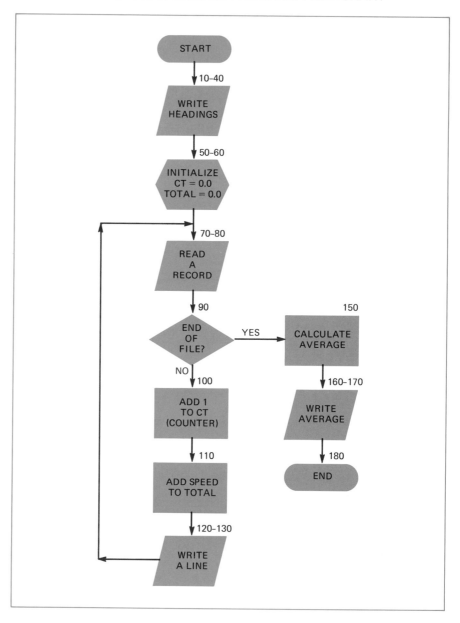

FIGURE 17.3 LISTING OF FORTRAN SAMPLE PROGRAM

```
C        AVERAGE WIND SPEED, OKLAHOMA CITY
C        WRITE HEADINGS
    10 WRITE(6,20)
    20 FORMAT(1H1,21H    AVERAGE WIND SPEED)
    30 WRITE(6,40)
    40 FORMAT(1H0,7H   MONTH,7X,10HWIND SPEED,/)
C        INITIALIZE COUNTER AND TOTAL
    50 CT=0.0
    60 TOTAL=0.0
C        READ IN MONTH AND WIND SPEED
    70 READ(5,80)MTH1,MTH2,MTH3,WIND,LAST
    80 FORMAT(3A4,2X,F4.1,59X,I3)
C        TEST FOR END-OF-FILE
    90 IF(LAST)100,100,150
C        INCREASE COUNTER AND TOTAL
   100 CT=CT+1.0
   110 TOTAL=TOTAL+WIND
C        LIST MONTHS
   120 WRITE(6,130)MTH1,MTH2,MTH3,WIND
   130 FORMAT(1H ,3A4,5X,F4.1)
   140 GO TO 70
C        CALCULATE AND WRITE MEAN
   150 AVRGE=TOTAL/CT
   160 WRITE(6,170)AVRGE
   170 FORMAT(1H0,30HMONTHLY AVERAGE WIND SPEED IS ,F4.1)
   180 STOP
       END
```

FIGURE 17.4 (A) INPUT DATA   (B) OUTPUT

			AVERAGE WIND SPEED	
			MONTH	WIND SPEED
JANUARY	14.6		JANUARY	14.6
FEBRUARY	14.7		FEBRUARY	14.7
MARCH	15.9		MARCH	15.9
APRIL	16.9		APRIL	16.9
MAY	14.4		MAY	14.4
JUNE	13.7		JUNE	13.7
JULY	12.1		JULY	12.1
AUGUST	11.6		AUGUST	11.6
SEPTEMBER	12.4		SEPTEMBER	12.4
OCTOBER	13.0		OCTOBER	13.0
NOVEMBER	13.5		NOVEMBER	13.5
DECEMBER	13.8		DECEMBER	13.8

MONTHLY AVERAGE WIND SPEED IS 13.9

(A)   (B)

STATEMENT NUMBER	EXPLANATION
10-40	Write headings
50, 60	Initialize accumulating totals
70, 80	Read a record
90	Tests for trailer record (end-of-file) and branches to averaging sequence if field contains a value
100	Adds 1 to counter
110	Adds wind speed to accumulating total
120-130	Writes out information that was input
140	Branches to read in the next record
150	Calculates average wind speed
160-170	Writes average wind speed
180	Terminates execution

KEY TERMS

Arithmetic statements
Array
Assigned names
Comment statement
Control statements
DO loop
FORMAT statements
FORTRAN
Function
Index

Input/output statements
Integer
Literal constant
Numeric constant
Real number
Reserved words
Standard character set
Subroutine
Variable

EXERCISES

1. How did the development of FORTRAN differ from that of COBOL?
2. List five advantages and two limitations of FORTRAN.
3. How does the structure of FORTRAN statements differ from that of COBOL?
4. What is the function of control statements?
5. What is the function of input/output statements?
6. What is the function of FORMAT statements?
7. Label the reserved columns on a FORTRAN coding sheet.
8. Define the term *constant* and list three examples.
9. Define the term *variable* and list three examples.
10. How do literal constants differ from other constants?
11. What is an array and what function does it serve in programming?
12. What are functions and subroutines? How are they used in FORTRAN?
13. Write a simple FORTRAN program that includes a DO loop and one or more mathematical calculations.

18

OTHER PROGRAMMING LANGUAGES USED IN BUSINESS

Many other computer programming languages besides BASIC, COBOL, and FORTRAN have been developed and are widely used. Some are interactive, others are batch languages, and a few are both. See Table 18.1 for a partial listing. This chapter will briefly discuss five common languages: PL/I, APL, RPG, assembler language, and ATS.

BATCH PROCESSING LANGUAGES

In this section, we briefly discuss three common batch processing languages, PL/I, RPG, and assembler language.

PL/I
(Programming
Language I)

PL/I was developed by IBM as a multipurpose language. It is a business and scientific language, suitable for batch processing and for use on terminals. Designed to include the best features of FORTRAN and COBOL, PL/I is similar to both, but many new features and capabilities have been

TABLE 18.1   LANGUAGE TYPES

Batch Processing Languages
   COBOL (COmmon Business Oriented Language)
   FORTRAN (FORmula TRANslating System)
   RPG (Report Program Generator)
   Assembler language
   PL/I (Programming Language I)[a]
Interactive Languages (Terminal Languages)
   APL (A Programming Language)
   BASIC (Beginners All-Purpose Symbolic Instruction Code)
   ATS (Administrative Terminal System)

[a]Suitable as a batch processing language and an interactive language.

incorporated. PL/I is used to program a variety of business, educational, social science, scientific, and other problems.

ADVANTAGES. A principal advantage of PL/I is its free style. Unlike other languages, it has no restrictions regarding columns, paragraphs, and statement numbers. PL/I is modular. A novice programmer can use the language after learning only a small part of it. As skills are gained, programming capabilities can be extended by learning additional features. (In many other languages, the programmer needs a fairly thorough understanding of the entire language before using any part of it.)

PL/I has built-in features, called *default options,* that will correct common mistakes made by programmers. Upon detecting a minor programming error or omission, the PL/I compiler will assume it knows what the programmer's intentions were, make a correction, and continue with the program. This makes programming easier and prevents minor errors or bugs from blowing up an otherwise acceptable program.

LIMITATIONS. PL/I compilers require a sizable amount of core storage and cannot be used on small computers. PL/I is a proprietary language: written at the expense of IBM, it is controlled by them. As a result, use of PL/I is limited to IBM computers.

GENERAL CHARACTERISTICS. PL/I is a free-form language, that is, it has few coding conventions. Programming statements are entered as a string of words, numbers, and symbols. Source statements are separated by semicolons. Statements are not confined to individual lines on coding sheets, do not have margin restrictions, and are not blocked into paragraphs.

PL/I has a standard character set, which includes the alphabet, numbers, and a group of special characters. Many of the special characters are code symbols, called operators, that cause the computer to perform various functions.

Special operators have specific meaning for the computer. They include the mathematical symbols $+$, $-$, $*$, and $/$. Additional symbols allow the programmer to call for logical and mathematical comparisons. For example, the computer can be directed to compare two numbers in storage and determine if they are equal, or if one is less than or greater than another. The programmer can connect strings of characters or cause the computer to branch depending on the value of a quantity.

Identifiers are names assigned to quantities in storage or to strings of characters. They can label a single quantity, alphabetic or numeric arrays, entire data files, groups of statements, or even conditions.

Identifiers are combined with operators and reserved PL/I words (called key words) to form statements. With them, the programmer can manipulate data, move quantities, perform calculations, and store or output results. The statements that make up a PL/I program are written on coding sheets as shown in Figure 18.1. These statements may be keypunched and assembled into a source program for batch processing. Or they may be keyboarded and transmitted to the CPU via a remote terminal. Figure 18.2 illustrates a sample program coded in PL/I.

RPG
(Report Program
Generator)

RPG is more a system of preparing reports than a true language. It is widely used on small computers to prepare business reports, accounts receivable, inventory listings, statements, etc.

ADVANTAGES. RPG is one of the easier languages to learn. It has few formal language rules, syntax, or reserved words. It requires a minimum of programming effort and skill to prepare business reports and other documents. The basic pattern of execution is fixed, and the programmer merely determines what will take place within each step. RPG is designed to facilitate the processing, updating, and maintenance of large data files. It requires a smaller compiler than most POLs and is usable on small computers.

LIMITATIONS. RPG is best used for report preparation, since it has restricted mathematical capability. It will perform addition, subtraction,

FIGURE 18.1 PL/I CODING FORM

```
BILLING: PROCEDURE;
    NEXTCARD: READ DATA (MORNO, OBAL, PAYM, RATE);
        CHARGE = OBAL*RATE/12;
        PRINPAID = PAYM - CHARGE;
        BALANCE = OBAL - PRINPAID;
        WRITE DATA (MORNO, OBAL, CHARGE, PRINPAID,
                    BALANCE);
    GO TO NEXTCARD;
END BILLING;
```

FIGURE 18.2   SAMPLE PL/I PROGRAM

```
PRINT: PROC OPTIONS(MAIN);
        DCL IN FILE RECORD SEQUENTIAL INPUT,
                DATA CHAR(100),
                LAB(3) LABEL INIT(A,B,C);
        DO I=1 TO 3;
            ON ENDFILE(IN) GO TO OUT;
            GO TO LAB(I);
            A: OPEN FILE(IN) TITLE('T1');
                GO TO READ;
            B: OPEN FILE(IN) TITLE('T2');
                GO TO READ;
            C: OPEN FILE(IN) TITLE('T3');
            READ: READ FILE(IN)  INTO (DATA);
                    PUT FILE(SYSPRINT) SKIP LIST(DATA);
                    GO TO READ;
            OUT: CLOSE FILE(IN);
                END;
        END PRINT;
```

multiplication, and division, but, compared to FORTRAN or COBOL, its facility for looping, branching, and making decisions is limited.

RPG is not a standardized language. It is machine dependent, and each computer has its own version. A program written in RPG for one computer may need extensive modification before it will run on another.

GENERAL CHARACTERISTICS.   RPG is designed to facilitate file processing. It is concerned with file description, file manipulation, and outputting results.

The language consists of names, codes, numbers, and letters entered in specific columns of coding forms. The specifications sheets used in coding RPG programs, shown in Figure 18.3, are

- file description specifications
- file extension specifications

FIGURE 18.3 RPG CODING FORMS

IBM

International Business Machines Corporation

GX21-9092-2 UM/050*
Printed in U.S.A.

RPG   CONTROL CARD AND FILE DESCRIPTION SPECIFICATIONS

Date _____

Program _____

Programmer _____

Punching Instruction — Graphic / Punch

Page

Program Identification

1 2   75 76 77 78 79 80

Control Card Specifications

Line | Type | Core Size to Compile | Object Output Listing Options | Core Size to Execute | Debug | MFCM Stacking Sequence | Input-Shillings | Input-Pence | Output-Shillings | Output-Pence | Inverted Print | 360/20 2501 Buffer | Number Of Print Positions | Alternate Collating Sequence | Address to Start | Work Tapes | Overlay Open | Overlay Printer | Binary Search | Tape Error | 2152 Checking | Inquiry | Read/Write/Compute | Keyboard Output | Sign Handling | 1P Forms Position | Indicator Setting | File Translation | Punch MFCU Zeros | Nonprint Characters | Table Load Halt | Shared I/O | Field Print | Formatted Core Dump | RPG to RPG II Conversion

Sterling / Model 20 / Model 20

Refer to the specific System Reference Library manual for actual entries.

IBM

International Business Machines Corporation

GX21-9091-1 U/M 050*
Printed in U.S.A.
*No. of forms per pad may vary slightly

RPG   EXTENSION AND LINE COUNTER SPECIFICATIONS

Date _____

Program _____

Programmer _____

Punching Instruction — Graphic / Punch

Page

Program Identification

1 2   75 76 77 78 79 80

Extension Specifications

Line | Form Type | Record Sequence of the Chaining File / Number of the Chaining Field / From Filename | To Filename | Table or Array Name | Number of Entries Per Record | Number of Entries Per Table or Array | Length of Entry | P = Packed/B = Binary / Decimal Positions / Sequence (A/D) | Table or Array Name (Alternating Format) | Length of Entry | P = Packed/B = Binary / Decimal Positions / Sequence (A/D) | Comments

IBM

International Business Machines Corporation

GX21-9094-1 U/M 050*
Printed in U.S.A.

RPG   INPUT SPECIFICATIONS

Date _____

Program _____

Programmer _____

Punching Instruction — Graphic / Punch

Page

Program Identification

1 2   75 76 77 78 79 80

Line | Form Type | Filename | Sequence | Number (1 N) | Option (O) | Record Identifying Indicator or ** | Record Identification Codes 1 2 3 (Position / (N) / Z/D / Character) | Stacker Select | P = Packed/B = Binary | Field Location From To | Decimal Positions | Field Name | Control Level (L1-L9) | Matching Fields or Chaining Fields | Field Record Relation | Field Indicators Plus Minus Zero or Blank | Sterling Sign Position

IBM

International Business Machines Corporation

GX21-9094-1 U/M 050*
Printed in U.S.A.

RPG   CALCULATION SPECIFICATIONS

Date _____

Program _____

Programmer _____

Punching Instruction — Graphic / Punch

Page

Program Identification

1 2   75 76 77 78 79 80

IBM

International Business Machines Corporation

GX21-9090-1 U/M 050*
Printed in U.S.A.

RPG   OUTPUT - FORMAT SPECIFICATIONS

Date _____

Program _____

Programmer _____

Punching Instruction — Graphic / Punch

Page

Program Identification

1 2   75 76 77 78 79 80

Line | Form Type | Filename | Type (H/D/T/E) | AND Select/Fetch Overflow (F) | Space Before After | Skip Before After | Output Indicators And And Not Not Not | Field Name | Edit Codes | Blank After (B) | End Position in Output Record | Packed/B = Binary | Sterling Sign Position

Edit Codes

Commas	Zero Balances to Print	No Sign	CR	-
Yes	Yes	1	A	J
Yes	No	2	B	K
No	Yes	3	C	L
No	No	4	D	M

X = Remove Plus Sign
Y = Date Field Edit
Z = Zero Suppress

· line counter specifications

· input specifications

· calculation specifications

· output format specifications

The specifications forms are used to define files and fields to be read by the computer, the fields to be operated upon, and any mathematical computations to be performed. They also specify how the data are to be output, column heads to be listed, and the graphic layout to be followed.

The information on these sheets is keypunched onto cards to form the source deck. The source deck is combined with control cards and input to the computer for compilation. Then the data set to be processed are entered and the job is run. Figure 18.4 shows a sample RPG program ready for keypunching.

Assembler Language

Assembler language is a machine-dependent, coding language that is more closely related to machine language than the others discussed in these chapters. It is an efficient language from the standpoint of the machine because it can make the most compact use of the computer's primary storage capacity. It is used to program long, repetitive, production-type jobs and system software.

ADVANTAGES. Programs written in assembler language are designed to fully utilize a computer's primary storage and register capacities during all procedures and phases of a program. This can save processing time on a long production run.

Use of assembler language facilitates modular programming. Programs are often written as subroutines or modules. Modules can be combined to solve different problems. Assembler language is available on most computers and requires less primary storage than most POLs.

LIMITATIONS. The efficiency of assembler language on the computer is at the cost of the programmer's time and effort. It is much more difficult to write an assembler language program than a similar program in one of the higher level languages. Each step in processing and manipulation of data must be detailed, byte by byte. Storage areas must be figured and specified.

To use assembler language, the programmer must have a thorough understanding of the computer's architecture, register system, and mnemonic codes. He or she must be familiar with hexadecimal, binary, packed decimal, ASCII, and EBCDIC coding systems and be able to convert from one to the other.

Assembler language is machine dependent. A program written in assembler language for one computer will not necessarily run on a machine of a different model or make.

FIGURE 18.4   RPG SAMPLE PROGRAM

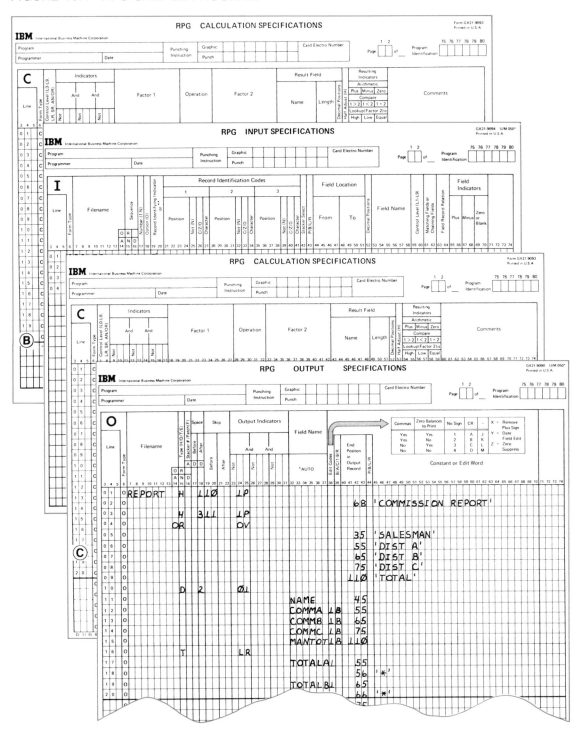

GENERAL CHARACTERISTICS.   Assembler language is a symbolic language based upon mnemonic codes, assigned names, and storage addresses. Each operation, such as add, move data, or compare, is assigned a mnemonic code. Assembler language statements are formed by indicating the mnemonic codes and the assigned names or locations of the operands. This tells the computer what operation is to be performed and the quantities or locations involved. The assembler language programmer uses hexadecimal, binary, packed decimal, ASCII, and EDCDIC codes to increase program efficiency.

"This is truly one of the great poems in the language. Computerese, that is."

Sidney Harris

The basic character set used in assembler language depends upon the particular computer. Generally, it includes the full alphabet, numbers, and a dozen or so special characters.

Each operation or procedure the computer performs, such as add, move data, or multiply, is initiated by a machine language code. The hexadecimal translations of these machine language codes are called operation codes or simply "op codes." Each op code has also been assigned a mnemonic code to identify the operation it performs. The op codes and their mnemonic names used on the IBM System/360 are shown in Table 18.2. For example, addition of values in storage slots is specified by the op code A; addition of values in registers is specified by AR; compare algebraic values is specified by the code C. The assembler translates these codes into the machine language equivalent for execution.

Most assembler language statements are translated line for line into machine language, and each minute step involved in processing and manipulating data must be described to the computer in detail. Only a few of the assembler language statements are designed to generate a group of machine language instructions to direct the computer through a routine. This type of statement is called a *macro instruction.*

The basic assembler language instruction is coded in the following general format:

Name	Operation	Operand A	Operand B	Remarks

The programmer may assign a name to the line of instructions. This name can be referred to later in the program to direct or transfer control during looping and branching. In the operation part of the instruction, the programmer writes the op code mnemonic to indicate the procedure to be performed. Operands are the assigned names or addresses of data that are to be located or moved. Operand A is the address of the first quantity or storage location to be used in the instruction and operand B is the address of the second quantity or storage location involved. (Not all instructions use a second operand.) The programmer may use the rest of the columns for documentation and explanation. Some sample statements are

Name	Operation	Operands A and B	Remarks
ADDSTK	A	3,STOCK	STOCK Add to value in Reg. 3
	MVC	INV(6),SALE	Move value in Loc. SALE to INV
	LA	6,PYROLL	Load address of PYROLL into Reg. 6
OVRAMT	C	10,LIMIT	Compare LIMIT to value in Reg. 10

TABLE 18.2 ASSEMBLER LANGUAGE OP CODES FOR IBM SYSTEM/360[a]

NAME	MNEMONIC	NAME	MNEMONIC
Add	AR	Shift Right Double	
Add	A	Logical	SRDL
AND	N	Store	ST
AND	NI	Store Character	STC
Branch and Link	BALR	Store Halfword	STH
Branch and Link	BAL	Store Multiple	STM
Branch on Condition	BCR	Subtract	SR
Branch on Condition	BC	Subtract	S
Branch on Count	BCTR	Supervisor Call	SVC
Branch on Count	BCT	Test Under Mask	TM
Branch on Index High	BXH	Translate	TR
Branch on Index Low or Equal	BXLE	Translate and Test	TRT
Compare	CR	Unpack	UNPK
Compare	C		
Compare Halfword	CH	**Floating-Point Feature Instructions**	
Compare Logical	CLC	Add Normalized	
Convert to Binary	CVB	(Short)	AE
Convert to Decimal	CVD	Compare (Short)	CE
Divide	DR	Divide (Short)	DER
Divide	D	Halve (Short)	HER
Exclusive OR	X	Load Complement	
Exclusive OR	XI	(Short)	LCER
Execute	EX	Load (Short)	LE
Insert Character	IC	Multiply (Short)	MER
Load	LR	Multiply (Short)	ME
Load	L	Store (Short)	STE
Load Address	LA	Subtract Normalized	
Load and Test	LTR	(Short)	SER
Load Halfword	LH	Subtract Normalized	
Load Multiple	LM	(Short)	SE
Load Positive	LPR		
Load PSW	LPSW	**Decimal Feature Instructions**	
Move	MVI	Add Decimal	AP
Move	MVC	Compare Decimal	CP
Move Numerics	MVN	Divide Decimal	DP
Move with Offset	MVO	Edit	ED
Multiply	M	Edit and Mark	EDMK
OR	OR	Multiple Decimal	MP
OR	OI	Subtract Decimal	SP
Pack	PACK	Zero and Add	ZAP
Set Program Mask	SPM		
Set System Mask	SSM	**Protection Feature Instructions**	
Shift Left Single	SLA	Insert Storage Key	ISK
Shift Right Single	SRA	Set Storage Key	SSK

[a]A Programmer's Introduction to the IBM System/360 Architecture, Instructions and Assembler Language, student text. C20-1646-4, Appendix A, p. 218.

The use of registers is basic to assembler language programming. Registers are temporary storage devices within the CPU that hold data while they are being processed. (Computers may have 16 or more registers for the programmer's use.) Registers serve as counters and indexes; they hold data involved in mathematical calculations or comparisons, etc. Programming instructions direct the computer to move data between general storage and registers, to manipulate quantities stored in registers, to load storage addresses of quantities into a register, etc.

The form shown in Figure 18.5 is used in coding assembler language instructions. The form has provisions for identifying the programmer and other data at the top. Columns 1 to 8 are used for the name of the instructions. Columns 10 to 14 are usually used for the op code; columns 16 to 71 for operands and comments. Column 72 is the continuation column, and columns 73 to 80 are for identification labels. Figure 18.6 is a computer listing of part of a sample program coded in assembler language.

FIGURE 18.5 ASSEMBLER LANGUAGE CODING FORM

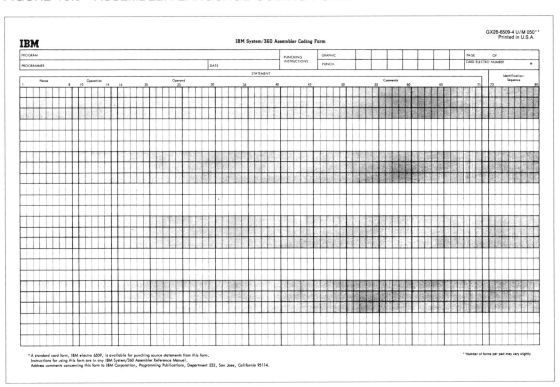

FIGURE 18.6 ASSEMBLER LANGUAGE SAMPLE PROGRAM

```
   LOC  OBJECT CODE    ADDR1 ADDR2  STMT   SOURCE STATEMENT

 000000                             1 SORTPGM  START 0
 000000 05A0                        2          BALR  10,0
 000002                             3          USING *,10
                                    4          OPEN  CDFILE,PTFILE
                                    5** 360N-CL-453 OPEN    CHANGE LEVEL 3-3                            3-3
 000002 0700                        6+         CNOP  0,4
 000004                             7+         DC    0F'0'
 000004 4110 A2D6           002D8   8+         LA    1,=C'$$BOPEN '
 000008 4500 A012           00014   9+TJJ00001 BAL   0,*+4+4*(3-1)
 00000C 00000310                    10+        DC    A(CDFILE)
 000010 00000348                    11+        DC    A(PTFILE)
 000014 0A02                        12+        SVC   2
 000016 5830 A2CE           002D0   13         L     3,TABSTRT          ADD. OF TABLE INTO REG3
 00001A 1822                        14         SR    2,2
 00001C 5A30 A2E6           002E8   15 LOOPA   A     3,=F'80'           ADD 80 TO TABLE LOC FOR NEXT SLOT
 000020 5920 A2EA           002EC   16         C     2,=F'1000'         COMPARE COUNT TO MAXIMUM
 000024 4780 A044           00046   17         BE    SORTA              IF 1000 GOTO SORTA
 000028 5A20 A2EE           002F0   18         A     2,=F'1'            ADD 1 TO COUNT
                                    19         GET   CDFILE,CDWORK
                                    20** 360N-CL-453 GET    CHANGE LEVEL 3-0
 00002C 5810 A2F2           002F4   21+        L     1,=A(CDFILE) GET DTF TABLE ADDRESS
 000030 5800 A2F6           002F8   22+        L     0,=A(CDWORK) GET WORK AREA ADDRESS
 000034 58F1 0010           00010   23+        L     15,16(1) GET LOGIC MODULE ADDRESS
 000038 45EF 0008           00008   24+        BAL   14,8(15) BRANCH TO GET ROUTINE
 00003C D24F 3000 A0EE 00000 000F0  25         MVC   0(80,3),CDWORK     MOVE 80 BYTES TO LOC AT REG3
 000042 47F0 A01A           0001C   26         B     LOOPA              READ ANOTHER CARD
 000046 1852                        27 SORTA   LR    5,2                SAVE COUNT IN REG5
 000048 1842                        28         LR    4,2                SAVE COUNT IN REG4
 00004A 5830 A2CE           002D0   29 SORTB   L     3,TABSTRT          GO AACK TO BEGINNING OF TABLE
 00004E 1824                        30         LR    2,4                RESET COUNTER
 000050 5A30 A2E6           002E8   31 SORTC   A     3,=F'80'           BEGIN COMPARISON, ADD 80 BYTES TAB.
 000054 4620 A07A           0007C   32         BCT   2,SORTD            COUNTS COMPARISONS
 000058 D504 3000 3050 00000 00050  33         CLC   0(5,3),80(3)       COMPARE 5 BYTES OF 2 LINES OF TABLE
 00005E 4720 A064           00066   34         BH    SWITCH
 000062 47F0 A04E           00050   35         B     SORTC              MAKE ANOTHER COMPARISON
 000066 D74F 3000 3050 00000 00050  36 SWITCH  XC    0(80,3),80(3)      TRANSPOSE 80 BYTES
 00006C D74F 3050 3000 00050 00000  37         XC    80(80,3),0(3)
```

INTERACTIVE LANGUAGES

Several interactive languages have been developed to enable the programmer to converse directly with the computer. They are used mainly to solve one-time-only problems where the user needs instantaneous results. They are handled from remote real-time, online terminals and usually involve a limited amount of data input and output.

Interactive languages are translated by a special compiler, sometimes called a processor or interpreter. The processor converts instructions received from a terminal into executable machine instructions. A feature of the interactive language processor is its ability to process many programs simultaneously, enabling several programmers to use the system at the same time. The processor can receive data from each of many terminals, process it, and respond with the answers to the proper terminals. Each user on the system appears to be online with the computer by himself or herself.

Because of the instantaneous response received and the lack of formal coding, the interactive languages are often called conversational languages. Three of the most common are APL, BASIC, and ATS.

APL was developed by IBM specifically as a conversational language. A user with only a minimum amount of programming skill can perform many tasks. For example, he or she can type in two rather large numbers, separated by a plus sign (+) and the computer will sum the two numbers and print out the answer on the next line. Or the user can subtract, multiply, divide, find the square root, or perform many other mathematical calculations by listing only the values and the operator that specifies the procedure.

ADVANTAGES. APL is one of the most powerful interactive languages yet developed. It is modular in structure, offering simple, easy-to-use features for the novice programmer and complex, sophisticated features for the experienced programmer.

APL handles most of the routine housekeeping tasks for the programmer. Data input and output are easily handled with no need for detailed field descriptions, etc. The programmer can assign names to stored values, perform calculations, store arrays of numbers, names, lists, etc., and manipulate data.

APL has a wide variety of sophisticated mathematical and processing tools available for the programmer. These are called out by striking the appropriate symbol on the terminal keyboard.

A feature of APL is its line-by-line execution. Each instruction is executed immediately and the results printed out on the next line. Unacceptable statements are detected immediately. There are no format restrictions on data input and output. The processor accepts decimal numbers, whole numbers, exponent values, and other data as they come in from the terminals. Results are printed out with the required decimal points and exponents supplied by the processor.

A very important advantage of APL is the convenience and efficiency it offers the user. An online, real-time terminal is as easy to use as an adding machine. No formal programming is required on some problems, and no time is lost on visits to the data center.

LIMITATIONS. APL programs can be run only on larger computers, since the processors require a sizable primary storage capacity. APL processors use greater core storage than compilers for FORTRAN. APL programs can be entered only via special terminals.

TERMINALS. An APL terminal and keyboard are shown in Figure 18.7. This terminal is connected to the computer through a unit called a phone coupler. The phone coupler converts the keystrokes to audible sounds, which are transmitted over the telephone line to the APL processor. To use the APL terminal, the user dials the telephone number of the computer and places the phone handset in the coupler. This connects the terminal to the computer and allows the user to enter data, process information, and receive results on the terminal.

FIGURE 18.7   APL KEYBOARD AND TERMINAL

GENERAL CHARACTERISTICS.   APL is a free-form language with very little formal structure. It is composed of symbols called operators, assigned names, and reserved words. Figure 18.8 is a sample APL program showing its general form.

Much of the power of APL is due to its operators. These 50 or more operators are code symbols such as ρ, ι, $\lceil$, ϕ, and Δ. With them the programmer can make many arithmetic or logical comparisons, perform functions, find square roots, determine maximum or minimum values, replace quantities, branch, transfer control, etc.

The APL language can process data in an execution or a definition mode. In the execution mode, the APL language is much like a desk calculator. Data are entered, operations are specified, and results are available instantly.

FIGURE 18.8 SAMPLE APL PROGRAM

```
       ∇ STUCOH
[1]    H←G←0
[2]    D←0
[3]    C←0
[4]    'ENTER NUMBER OF STUDENTS IN CLASS'
[5]    A←□
[6]    'ENTER NUMBER OF HOURS PER WEEK CLASS MEETS'
[7]    B←□
[8]    'ENTER NUMBER OF OFFICE HOURS PER WEEK'
[9]    C←□
[10]   D←A×B
[11]   E←C+B
[12]   'YOUR STUDENT CONTACT HOURS ARE ';D
[13]   G←G+D
[14]   'YOUR ASSIGNED HOURS ARE ';E
[15]   H←H+E
[16]   'DO YOU WANT TO ENTER ANOTHER WORKLOAD? 0=NO, 1 = YES'
[17]   F←□
[18]   →2×ιF=1
[19]   'THE FACULTY CONTACT HOURS ARE ';G
[20]   'THE FACULTY ASSIGNED HOURS ARE ';H
     ∇

     STUCOH
ENTER NUMBER OF STUDENTS IN CLASS
□:
     50
ENTER NUMBER OF HOURS PER WEEK CLASS MEETS
□:
     3
ENTER NUMBER OF OFFICE HOURS PER WEEK
□:
     4
YOUR STUDENT CONTACT HOURS ARE 150
YOUR ASSIGNED HOURS ARE 7
DO YOU WANT TO ENTER ANOTHER WORKLOAD? 0=NO, 1 = YES
□:
     1
ENTER NUMBER OF STUDENTS IN CLASS
□:
     75
ENTER NUMBER OF HOURS PER WEEK CLASS MEETS
□:
     5
ENTER NUMBER OF OFFICE HOURS PER WEEK
□:
     ,5
YOUR STUDENT CONTACT HOURS ARE 375
YOUR ASSIGNED HOURS ARE 10
DO YOU WANT TO ENTER ANOTHER WORKLOAD? 0=NO, 1 = YES
□:
     0
THE FACULTY CONTACT HOURS ARE 525
THE FACULTY ASSIGNED HOURS ARE 17
     ∇STUCOH[□]∇
```

In a definition mode, a list of instructions is entered. Compilation and execution do not occur until after the list is entered and the programmer instructs the computer to begin.

SPECIAL FEATURES. *Editing.* Like most interactive languages, APL has an editing feature to permit corrections and revisions of programming statements and data to be made from the terminal. As the APL programmer enters statements, they are stored in the CPU's memory. They can be changed or replaced by typing in the number of the line and the new information. The computer will automatically make the replacement of the corrected data. This feature permits file updating, selective replacement of values, corrections, etc.

For example, the programmer assigns a value of 50 to the letter A this way:

$$A \leftarrow 50$$

If the programmer types the letter A on the keyboard, the computer will respond with

$$50$$

Later, if $A \leftarrow 100$ is entered, the computer will make the substitution and A will now equal 100 in the computer's memory.

Arrays. An important capability of APL is its ability to handle and process groups of numbers called arrays. For example, a string of numbers can be typed on the terminal and assigned a name.

$$B \leftarrow 2 \ 4 \ 6 \ 8$$

If the programmer later types the letter B, the computer will respond by printing out:

$$2 \ 4 \ 6 \ 8$$

If the programmer types in the statement

$$2 \times B$$

the computer will multiply each item in the array by 2 and print out the results as follows:

$$4 \ 8 \ 12 \ 16$$

ATS (Administrative Terminal System)   ATS is an interactive language designed for preparing reports, bulletins, manuscripts, and other text documents. It is particularly valuable when extensive text editing is required. Text editing, involving revisions, corrections, alterations, and changes in copy, usually requires a great deal of retyping. Each time a revised draft is prepared, most or all of the document must be retyped.

When ATS is used, this procedure is simplified. Revisions, corrections, changes, and alterations can be typed in to replace specified portions of the original copy. Lines, words, phrases, or sentences can be substituted or

The War Between the Computers

Sometimes it seems as though computers resemble their human creators in too many ways . . . two of them at the New York Stock Exchange squabble over which of them is stronger and should be in charge. The resulting brawling has been bloodless so far, but it has left the stock exchange in chaos on several occasions.

The computers are part of a system designed to instantaneously record and report trading transactions as they take place on the New York Exchange and elsewhere. The element that is acting up is the portion that translates the stock market information into a form suitable for the video display screens in use at the exchange.

The kind of data involved and the speed at which the transactions take place demanded a foolproof computer system. Two identical units were programmed so that a sign of weakness or problem in one system would instantly activate the other, bringing it online instead. The problem arises when the systems can't agree on whether or not the online system has a problem. A battle ensues when the offline system decides it's stronger than the online system and tries to take over the other's function. Eventually, if the online system resists, stock exchange personnel have to intervene to straighten out the mess.

Following Exchange rules, if the reports are delayed for longer than five minutes, a trading halt must be called. The resulting confusion takes a half hour or so to straighten out before the computer can resume operation. Meanwhile, floor personnel have to sit around and wait for the all clear. As much as $2\frac{1}{2}$ hours may be consumed after the close of the trading day until the missing 30 or 40 minutes of trading data are reconstructed.

Companies that supply trading data to brokerage houses, wire services and their newspaper clients, and investors who rely on up-to-the-minute reporting will all be grateful when the computers reach agreement.

SOURCE: Adapted from "Computers Battle and Leave NYSE in Dark," by George Wheeler. © 1975 by *Newsday*. Reprinted by permission.

rearranged. The computer inserts all revisions into the stored text, and, at the programmer's request, prints out an updated draft. The programmer can instruct the computer to print out the same copy using a different format, line width, or page depth.

ADVANTAGES. ATS is an efficient method of preparing textual material that must be extensively edited. It saves retyping and allows for reforming. The ATS compiler will center lines, provide automatic page numbering, or insert heads or footings. The ATS system can store data typed in from a remote keyboard in one format and print it out in another. Both line width and page depth can be changed. In addition, lines can be printed out right justified (right margins evenly aligned). ATS requires learning only a few basic instructions and commands.

FIGURE 18.9   MARKED-UP DRAFT OF TEXT STORED IN ATS
PROCESSOR

Simplicity of operation is *the* a keystone of the
ATS/360 System. It does not require the user to
undergo extensive training. ~~Neither does it~~
~~require a special machine operator.~~ After a brief
orientation, anyone who can type can use the system.

One reason for this short learning *period* is that ~~the~~
~~user~~ *you* uses a familiar typewriter keyboard to give
information and instructions to the computer. In
fact, when you are not using the typewriter as a
terminal, you can put it to work to produce fine
quality business correspondence. &Another reason the
system is easy to learn is that ATS/360 operating
procedures are ~~uncomplicated.~~ *straight forward* They were designed
with the secretary in mind, and you will find them
very easy. For example, to correct an error, you
simply backspace and retype.

Everyone in your office ~~can really put the~~
power of the system to work.

Inset: ← THE ATS SYSTEM
makes your job easier!

insert above   *Except for a key which alerts the computer, this keyboard is the same as a SELECTRIC typewriter.*

FIGURE 18.10   FINAL DRAFT PRINTED OUT BY ATS PROCESSOR

```
        Simplicity of operation is the keystone of the
ATS/360 System.  It does not require the user to
undergo extensive training.  After a brief orientation,
anyone who can type can use the system.

        One reason for this short learning period is
that you use a familiar typewriter keyboard to give
information and instructions to the computer.  Except
for a key which alerts the computer, this keyboard
is the same as a SELECTRIC typewriter.  In fact, when
you are not using the typewriter as a terminal, you
can put it to work to produce fine quality business
correspondence.

        Another reason the system is easy to learn is
that ATS/360 operating procedures are straightforward.
They were designed with the secretary in mind, and you
will find them very easy.  For example, to correct
an error, you simply backspace and retype.

        The ATS System makes your job easier!
```

LIMITATIONS.   ATS is a specialized language with a limited application: text editing. The language does not provide branching, looping, or very extensive mathematical manipulation.

GENERAL CHARACTERISTICS.   Information to be processed in the ATS language is typed in from a terminal keyboard without regard to line width or spacing. The text is entered as a stream of characters. Errors are corrected by backspacing and striking over. This corrects the character in the computer's memory. Words, phrases, or sentences may be replaced, rearranged, or deleted. New copy can be added as required.

After all text editing is completed, the user tells the computer the format to use in printing out the draft. The finished draft can contain page headings, footings, page numbers, etc., and can be right justified. It will be evenly spaced and neatly typed.

TABLE 18.3 PROGRAMMING LANGUAGE COMPARISON

	COBOL	BASIC	FORTRAN	RPG	ASSEMBLER	PL/I	APL	ATS
Easy to learn		X		X				X
Programmer oriented	X	X				X	X	
Good math capabilities		X	X		X		X	
Good alphanumeric capabilities	X				X	X	X	X
Resembles English	X					X		X
Self-documenting	X					X		
Available on many machines	X	X	X	X	X			
Standardized	X		X					
Manufacturer controlled					X	X	X	X
Efficient on computers					X			
Large primary storage capacity required	X					X	X	
Interactive capability		X				X	X	X
Default options						X		
Machine dependent				X	X			

Figure 18.9 illustrates a piece of copy that has been keyboarded and stored in the ATS processor. It has been marked with corrections and alterations, which are to be made in the final draft. Figure 18.10 illustrates the reformatted print out as it appears at the ATS terminal, with all changes and alterations made.

Table 18.3 provides a comparison of all the programming languages discussed thus far.

KEY TERMS

APL
Assembler language
ATS
Batch processing languages
Definition mode
Editing
Execution mode
Identifiers

Interactive languages
Mnemonics
Op code
Operand
Operators
PL/I
Processor
RPG

EXERCISES

1. Define batch processing languages and give several examples.
2. Define interactive languages and give several examples.
3. What are the major advantages and limitations of PL/I?
4. How does the PL/I program in Figure 18.2 differ from the FORTRAN program in Figure 17.3?
5. For what kind of job is RPG best suited? What are its limitations?
6. What are the advantages and limitations of assembler language programming? How does the assembler language program in Figure 18.6 differ from the PL/I program in Figure 18.2?
7. What are the major advantages and limitations of APL?
8. What is the difference between the execution mode and the definition mode in APL?
9. What are operators in APL and how are they used?
10. What is meant by text editing? How does ATS facilitate it?
11. If there is a computer terminal at your school, determine what kind it is and what languages can be programmed on it.
12. If an APL terminal is available, enter the program from Figure 18.8 and execute it.

PART SIX

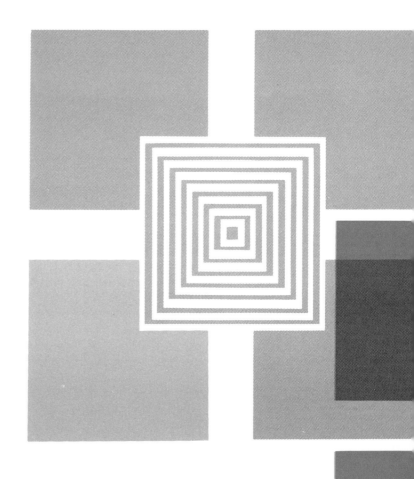

INFORMATION
SYSTEMS

19

INTRODUCTION
TO BUSINESS SYSTEMS

Decision making is a fundamental process and function of a business enterprise. The life and success of the modern firm depend on the right decision quickly arrived at. Vital to the decision-making process is the availability of complete, accurate, relevant data. As our society becomes more complex, so do the factors affecting the decision-making process. The traditional methods of solving problems are often inadequate today. They are being replaced by techniques that rely on information processing, electronic data processing, and the science of business systems analysis.

WHAT ARE BUSINESS SYSTEMS?

Systems are collections of objects, procedures, or techniques that function as an organized whole. They are groups of people, machines, or methods necessary to accomplish specific functions. Business systems are the organizational structures within a firm that enable it to achieve its goals. Business systems include policies, methods, personnel, data processing software and hardware, and communications procedures.

Systems are composed of subsystems. These smaller units have individual functions but act in accord with the goals of the larger system. The advantage of the system is that the total is greater than the sum of the parts. Figure 19.1 shows a simplified business system of a firm. Administration in a business system usually consists of a board of directors and management. An essential function of the board of directors is to select long- and short-range goals or objectives. These goals may be to reach a given dollar volume in sales, realize a given return on investment, earn a specific percentage of profit, or build a new plant.

The establishment of objectives requires a careful analysis of business conditions, the market, customer needs, buying patterns, production capacity, staff, finances, etc. The accurate assessment of each of these elements requires the acquisition, processing, and reporting of data in the form most useful to management.

Once the board of directors has selected certain objectives, it is management's job to direct the subsystems of the firm toward these goals. To effectively measure the amount and direction of progress, even more data are needed. Information such as numbers of hours worked, products shipped, cash flow, receivables due, percentage of plant utilized, and money owed, must be analyzed.

FIGURE 19.1   SIMPLIFIED BUSINESS SYSTEM

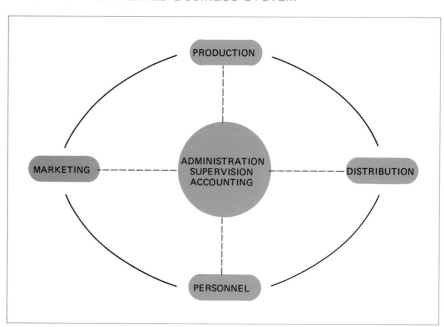

Data in
Business Systems

Since management needs information from all parts of the firm, one of the major assets of a firm can be its facilities for recording, manipulating, and reporting data.

The value of business data varies. Some data are important only at certain times and places in the business cycle. For example, information about an account's purchasing patterns may be needed when a firm is bidding for business. After the contract has been signed or lost, such information may have little value.

To be of greatest value to a firm, data should be

- Available when it is needed
- Available where it is needed
- At the right level of accuracy
- The kind and quality necessary
- Gathered, processed, and reported at a reasonable cost

Need for
Business Systems

Large business firms cannot afford to solve clerical or data flow problems in an unorganized, unsystematic way. Processing costs are high; mistakes are expensive; time is limited.

A planned and organized strategy for processing paperwork and clerical matters is needed by firms to

- Gain maximum cost savings in processing and handling data
- Gain maximum time savings in outputting results
- Establish an orderly procedure for growth
- Develop a uniform method of operation and thus avoid foreseeable problems by establishing policies
- Avoid costly errors
- Improve the quality of business decisions
- Improve organization responsiveness to customers' needs
- Improve allocation of physical resources
- Produce the best product at the lowest cost
- Eliminate duplication of effort

Evolution of
Business Systems

Around 1900, when firms were small and material and labor costs were low, data processing needs were minimal. Few firms used systematic business methods to plan their activities and carry out their goals. When a problem came up, it was solved on the spot, resulting in a patchwork of policies and procedures.

The solution chosen was often the easiest one to implement. Careful analysis of problems and attention to strategy were ignored in favor of finding easy answers quickly. This approach is sometimes called "brush fire" problem solving. Even today some firms use these measures.

As firms grew and the capital investment and costs of labor and materials increased, management turned to more scientific, orderly, and structured means of solving problems. At first, one or two employees were assigned the task of applying scientific methods to solving business problems. They soon became known as business systems engineers or business systems analysts.

Eventually, many firms established a separate unit called the business systems department. This department was responsible for applying scientific methods to clerical and data flow problems in the company.

SCOPE OF MODERN BUSINESS SYSTEMS DEPARTMENTS

Since World War II, the job of the business systems department has grown in importance. The team of business systems engineers, analysts, and data processing specialists has become an indispensable part of many business firms. Figure 19.2 illustrates the organization of an average systems department. The members of the department are brought into many areas and departments of the firm in the performance of their work. They make critical studies and recommendations affecting many operations, procedures, and methods throughout the firm.

Responsibilities
of the
Business Systems
Department

The business systems department is responsible for

- Systems planning and design
- Systems implementation
- Office layout
- Establishment of procedures and policies
- Design of forms
- Work measurement
- Information retrieval and file design
- Selection of personnel
- Software preparation
- Communications
- Hardware selection

SYSTEMS PLANNING AND DESIGN.   A major responsibility of the business systems department is the planning and design of new systems to facilitate the flow of data. The business systems analyst uses scientific methods and techniques to review existing procedures. He or she proposes changes and improvements to overcome weaknesses in existing systems.

FIGURE 19.2   BUSINESS SYSTEMS DEPARTMENT ORGANIZATION
             CHART

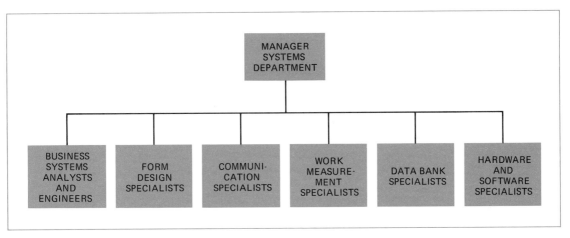

In studying a system, the analyst reviews its forms, procedures, policies, and methods. He or she analyzes the personnel, machines, space requirements, and office layout to determine whether a better system can be developed. The analyst frequently asks six questions in investigating each element in the study:

1. What is done?
2. How is it done?
3. Why is it done?
4. Who does it?
5. When is it done?
6. Where is it done?

The business systems analyst conducts many types of surveys to evaluate the system under consideration. A feasibility study (discussed in Chapter 20), for example, is undertaken to determine whether a new system will be practical from an economic standpoint. Data flow and word processing studies point out bottlenecks, weaknesses, or problem areas. Time and motion studies further define problems and even indicate solutions.

SYSTEM IMPLEMENTATION.   Once a new system has been designed, the business systems department must implement it properly. System implementation requires careful planning to see that the transition is made without waste, errors, or excessive costs. Employee morale must be considered. The business systems analyst must solicit the cooperation of both employees and management. Personnel must be shown the advantages of the new system and how it will affect each individual.

A new system may be implemented in several ways. It can begin "all at once," or "step by step." Sometimes a new system is implemented in a parallel manner. The new system is put into operation alongside the old. When the new system is running smoothly, the old system is dropped. The business systems analyst must observe the new system in operation and see that there is no backsliding into the old, inefficient method.

Implementation sometimes requires designing new forms; writing computer programs; writing procedure, policy, and instruction manuals; acquiring new equipment; rearranging offices; etc.

OFFICE LAYOUT.   A major responsibility of the business systems department is office layout. The analyst must recommend the most efficient office layout to facilitate data flow. (See Figure 19.3.) He or she is concerned with shortening processing time and reducing labor and equipment costs. The analyst may also be responsible for the purchase of any new office equipment required by a system and must then arrange for the efficient use of equipment.

ESTABLISHMENT OF PROCEDURES AND POLICIES.   A new system must be documented to help employees learn how to use it efficiently. The business

FIGURE 19.3   OFFICE LAYOUT

ORIGINAL DESK ARRANGEMENT

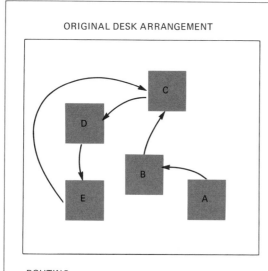

ROUTING
SCHEDULE: A→B→C→D→E→C

CHANGES RECOMMENDED BY ANALYST

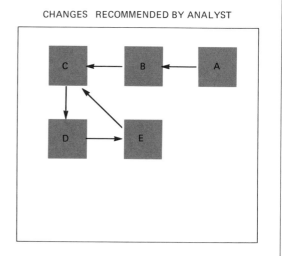

ROUTING
SCHEDULE: A→B→C→D→E→C

systems analyst often uses manuals for this purpose. These manuals are a source of uniform statements on methods and policies. They specify which forms to use, when to use them, how to handle exceptions, and where forms are to be routed.

Well-written policy manuals help both the employee and the organization. They not only provide the employee with a clear statement of company policy and methods but also assure that each branch or division in the company will acquire, report, and process data in the most efficient way.

DESIGN OF FORMS.   Data forms are essential to almost all business systems. In some cases, hundreds of different forms are used within a firm. The success of a new system often depends on whether adequate forms and source documents have been developed.

The business systems analyst must specify contents, layouts, distribution, and routing of the forms. He or she is also responsible for designing source documents and reports.

Forms design includes analysis of the physical characteristics of the form as well as its content. Consideration must be given to size, paper, type size, number of carbons, printing process, and cost. The analyst must also determine the quantity to be ordered, the system of inventory to be used, and the methods of packing and dispensing the forms. Forms must periodically be reviewed to see that they are adequate, necessary, and up to date.

WORK MEASUREMENT.   To test the effectiveness of a new system, or to measure the productivity of an existing system, a method of measuring work must be found. The business systems analyst develops the tools that can assess the output of both personnel and equipment. Some tools used in work measurement are

1. *Time Study.*   The time study consists of observing and timing employees as they perform their duties.

2. *Work Sampling.*   In work sampling, a measure is made of the kinds and types of calculations performed, the number and types of forms handled, and so forth, in order to approximate the content of each job.

Work measurement enables the analyst to compare the output of employees before and after implementing a new system. It allows the quantity as well as the quality of clerical work to be measured.

INFORMATION RETRIEVAL AND FILE DESIGN.   The job of the analyst also includes the design of data files for information storage and retrieval systems. Modern business depends heavily upon data files to store records of transactions in the firm. The analyst should design files that are accurate, complete, compact, and easily corrected and updated.

SELECTION OF PERSONNEL. The business systems analyst may also write job descriptions and orders. Job descriptions outline the duties and functions of each job. Job orders specify the number of employees needed for each job classification. A sample job description and order is shown in Figure 19.4.

In writing a job description, the analyst must indicate the level of skill and training required in performing the job. This information then guides the personnel department in hiring new employees.

The duties of the business systems analyst may include planning programs for job orientation or in-service training. He or she may have to arrange classroom training or instruction from vendors and prepare, revise, and order training manuals, teaching aids, slide films and other media necessary to implement new systems.

SOFTWARE PREPARATION. If a system uses a computer or involves electronic data processing, programs must be written, debugged, tested, and maintained. Often, the analyst must specify the function and purpose of a proposed program, flowchart the preferred algorithm, and indicate the input/output requirements. These specifications are then given to a programmer or other systems analyst who actually writes the program. When the program is running satisfactorily, documentation must be prepared explaining the program logic, how data must be input, program options, etc.

COMMUNICATIONS. The business systems analyst must consider the communications requirements of a new or existing system. If computer

FIGURE 19.4 JOB DESCRIPTION AND ORDER

terminals are needed, he or she determines the type, number, and location and provides instructions so that personnel may use them properly and effectively.

Some firms have access to computers located in different parts of the country and tied into a network by telephone lines (called a tie line service). It is the job of the systems analyst to plan this communications network. He or she must study communications needs, data flow, files, etc., and order the most efficient phone service.

HARDWARE SELECTION. Specifying the type and make of computer and the peripheral equipment needed in the system is also a duty of the business systems analyst, who must review available equipment and judge the cost and capabilities of new equipment.

PROBLEM-SOLVING TECHNIQUES

The business systems department is actively involved in solving company data processing problems. As new tools and techniques have come into use, the methods of solving data flow problems have changed.

Before 1900, techniques such as the guess, the hunch, chance, intuition, habit, routine, or rule of thumb were used to solve clerical and data flow problems. Although some of these methods are still used, they are inaccurate and result in inconsistent or contradictory policies. Modern management personnel should not and cannot rely on these ineffectual methods.

The Scientific Method

About 1900 John Dewey described and documented a series of steps for solving scentific problems. Following these steps greatly increased the chances of a particular solution being precise, accurate, and dependable. This technique, called the scientific method, forms the basis of most logic followed in modern business systems analysis.

The scientific method demands a rigorous, logical approach or strategy. It involves a careful definition of the problem, a thorough analysis of alternatives, an orderly implementation of the best alternative, and, finally, a critical evaluation of outcomes. It is characterized by

- Rigorous attention to detail
- Development and application of precise measuring tools
- Consideration of alternatives
- Use of statistical methods
- Structured methods of implementation
- Use of feedback—that is, use of system output to control system input

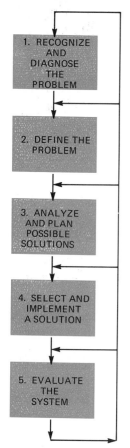

The scientific method leads not to the fastest, easiest solution, but to the most effective solution, indicated by measuring the output.

The five basic steps in the scientific method are illustrated in the marginal figure. They are applied to business systems analysis as follows:

1. RECOGNITION AND DIAGNOSIS OF THE PROBLEM.   Before a problem can be solved it must be recognized. Problems may be brought to the attention of management by employees, customers, or outside consultants, or by systematic observation by management. Then the nature of the problem must be diagnosed. The systems analyst must determine and clearly state the details of the situation. The problem may be, for example, scheduling a new procedure, determining the most efficient way to prepare monthly statements, finding out why a procedure produces inaccurate or inadequate output, or discovering why the cost of a product is higher than projections indicated.

2. DEFINE THE PROBLEM.   The second step in the scientific method is the definition of the problem in measurable terms. In this phase, the business systems engineer states the problem in a quantitative way. If output is low, by how much? If costs are too high, by how much? If data are inadequate, in what way? Reducing the problem to elements that can be measured creates a basis for comparing the output.

3. SYSTEM PLANNING AND ANALYSIS.   The third phase of the activity involves investigating plans to solve the problem. Here the business systems analyst studies different approaches. What will happen if another system is tried? How many dollars will be saved? In what ways will data be more accurate, more prompt, or more economical to prepare? The business systems engineer uses an *if–then* strategy. *If* this method is used, *then* this will result. *If* that strategy is used, *then* that will result. All practical alternatives are considered and analyzed.

4. SELECTION AND IMPLEMENTATION.   In this step, the business systems engineer decides which plan provides the most logical, economical, and sound solution and proposes its implementation to management. Management then decides whether to accept the plan.

In the implementation stage, equipment is studied and purchased, employees are reassigned or new ones hired, policies and practices are defined in detail, manuals are written, forms are designed and printed, and programs are flowcharted and written.

5. EVALUATION.   The final step in the problem-solving process is the measurement of the outcomes of the new system. Were the expected results obtained? Did costs go down? by how much? Are data more

Tell It to the Computer

A team of psychiatrists and psychologists has programmed a CDC 3200 computer to perform the initial data-gathering interview for psychiatric patients at the Utah Veteran's Administration Hospital. The analysis produced by the electronic psychiatrist is less biased and more complete than those produced by humans, according to doctors.

The computer has been programmed to output various psychiatric tests on medical background, personality, and intellect, directly onto a cathode ray tube terminal. The patient answers the computer's questions privately, using a terminal. This encourages the patient to be more frank and uninhibited in his or her answers.

As each test is completed, the computer analyzes the answers and prints out an individualized report. The actual treatment is determined after the staff evaluates these studies. Since reports are generated within a few minutes, data on the patient's treatment and progress can be analyzed daily to provide valuable feedback for the mental health staff. This facilitates adjusting treatment to reflect changes in condition and in designing follow-up procedures.

"The initial data-gathering process, or intake, used to be done by someone who would write down the patient's response on paper," said Dr. Ronald A. Giannetti, a project researcher and instructor in psychiatry.

He said that this procedure often led to personal bias in the written report and in the interpretation. In addition, since many people were involved in preparing the paperwork, each report could take several days to complete.

SOURCE: "Computer Replaces Psychiatric Couch," UPI (dateline Salt Lake City).

accurate? in what way? If the benefits did not materialize, why not? How can the system be improved?

The output of the new procedure is evaluated. The business systems analyst modifies the original solution or selects another alternative for implementation. It is implemented and the output is evaluated again. This procedure is followed until the most efficient arrangement of staff, equipment, office layout, and data processing methods is found.

THE ROLE OF THE COMPUTER

One of the most significant advances in management practices has been the coupling of the scientific method to the power of the computer. The computer's ability to manipulate data at high speed with a high level of accuracy enables the business systems analyst to prepare many of the reports, projections, schedules, and simulations necessary to management decision making.

Simulation and Modeling

An important systems analysis procedure is the modeling and simulation technique made possible by the computer. Simulation is the use of a computer to duplicate a system and then study what would happen if a certain situation occurred. With simulation, different conditions, variations, and alternatives can be tested accurately without the expense and problems that would be encountered in actual marketing or production situations. (See Figure 19.5.)

FIGURE 19.5   SIMULATION

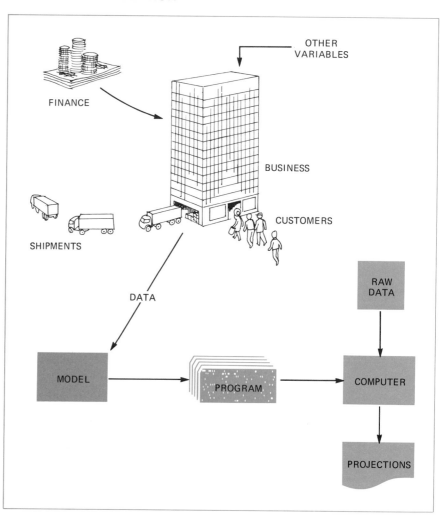

BUILDING THE MODEL.   The first step in simulation is to develop a model. The model is a representation of the situation being tested. Relevant data are gathered, and relationships and cause and effect conditions in the firm are studied by reviewing records and testing. These relationships are restated in quantitative terms to create the model.

For instance, here is the relationship between a retail store's soft drink sales and the temperature.

TEMPERATURE	CASES SOLD
under 60°	1
60°	2
70°	4
80°	8
90°	12
100°	20
over 100°	14

With this information, the store management can make sales predictions and plan advertising and displays, size of orders to suppliers, how much stock to keep on hand, etc.

In effect, we have a mathematical model of a real situation. In this example, however, only two variables are involved. Usually models are complex and include many interdependent relationships and variables. Some even include such random occurrences as water supply or power failures.

Models can be developed of entire firms, such as trucking lines, hospitals, manufacturing companies, retailers, a single department within a company, or even of a product or service. The data that make up the model are programmed and prepared for computer input via punched cards, tape, etc.

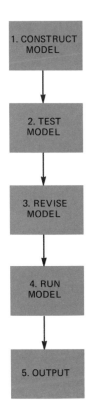

1. CONSTRUCT MODEL

2. TEST MODEL

3. REVISE MODEL

4. RUN MODEL

5. OUTPUT

TESTING THE MODEL.   After the model has been set up, it is tested with known data. The test data are punched into cards, and the program and data are processed. The results of the test simulation are studied to determine the accuracy of the mathematical model. If the model is correctly developed, the predictions generated will represent how costs or conditions actually have behaved. If the model does not deliver predictable results, it is modified or abandoned and a new model begun.

RUNNING THE MODEL.   The accurate model is now ready to simulate what would happen if some variables were changed. What would happen if prices were increased? or another production plant were opened? What would happen if the supply of a certain ingredient were cut off? These data are restated as quantitative values, prepared as input, and fed to the computer with the programmed model. The output should be an accurate prediction of the conditions that will result. The figure on the left summarizes the steps involved in simulation.

ADVANTAGES.   Simulation permits many trial runs to be made with varying conditions. It is less costly to overload a model of a frozen food plant to learn where the system will break down than to actually overload a real plant.

Errors in judgment made with actual customers' goods or services could be disastrous. But errors in judgment in a simulation cause no damage and often point up areas requiring further investigation. However, the results of the model are no better than the quality of the data entered. People tend to assume that the computer output is by its nature always accurate and objective. In reality, output reflects only the nature of the input data and the accuracy of the model.

Linear
Programming

Linear programming (LP) is another quantitative decision-making tool made possible by the computer. Linear programming was developed during World War II to find the fastest, most efficient combination of people and machines to produce war material.

LP produces a mathematical model that will test a combination of elements and determine the most economical or best mix. (See Figure 19.6.) In LP, two statements are entered: one giving the optimum conditions desired and another listing the available resources. The program tests various

Business Automation

"Another way you can save wear and tear on your equipment is to get a more modern entry system."

FIGURE 19.6   LINEAR PROGRAMMING

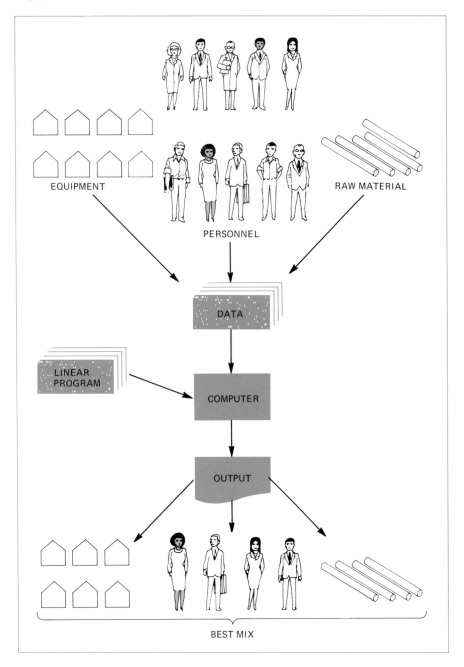

FIGURE 19.7   SCHEDULE FROM A PERT PROGRAM

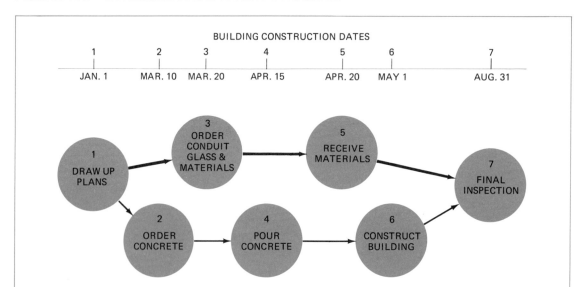

combinations of elements and determines the one that best meets the criteria given.

For example, suppose an airline wishes to find the minimum staff needed to move the maximum number of passengers. The problem is a complex one because of the many employees involved in an airline's operations: pilots, baggage handlers, clerks, ground crews, stewardesses, managers, etc. Will hiring more pilots improve service? Will more clerks at the check-in desk help?

All the salaries and output of employees are stated as quantitative data and fed with a linear program to the computer. The computer will test all possible combinations of employees to determine the one that will allow the airline to handle a given passenger load at minimum salary expense. The results will be printed out as a list of the optimum or best mix of pilots, handlers, clerks, etc.

Performing the same tests in actual situations would be very expensive for the airline. And there would be no guarantee that the optimum arrangement would be discovered.

PERT   PERT (Program Evaluation and Review Technique) is a technique used to find the most efficient scheduling of time and resources for producing a complex product or project.

Firms involved in the manufacture of complicated equipment or the construction of large office buildings constantly face a difficult series of decisions. When should various equipment, supplies, and machines be placed on a job? What steps should be taken first? What elements are critical to the production of the goods and must be kept on schedule to avoid disrupting the other stages? How can the resources of the firm be best used to meet the costs and time deadlines of the project?

A PERT program will output a set of schedules answering these questions as shown in Figure 19.7. With this information, a manufacturer or builder can better control the time, costs, and deployment of resources.

KEY TERMS

Business systems	PERT
Business systems analyst	Scientific method
Job description	Simulation
Linear programming	Tie lines
Modeling	Work measurement

EXERCISES

1. Define business systems.
2. Give four examples of business data with a particular time utility. Name four with a particular place value.
3. Contrast the early methods of solving business problems with those of the computer age.
4. Give several examples in which the guess, hunch, or chance method is used to solve business problems.
5. List the major steps in the scientific method of business systems analysis.
6. Select a simple data flow problem, such as inventory in a small retail store, and trace its solution through the five steps in the analytical approach.
7. What are the major responsibilities of the modern business systems department?
8. Select a data flow problem such as registration and enrollment in your college. Using the six questions often asked by business systems analysts, investigate an improved system.
9. Write a set of policies and procedures for handling returned merchandise in a small retail store.
10. Select a data flow task such as writing up a sales slip in a shoe store. Have several students go through the steps in filling out the forms. Perform a time study and work sampling on the operation.
11. Write a description of a job that involves the handling or processing of data, such as the job of sales clerk or shipping clerk.

20

BUSINESS SYSTEMS
EVALUATION AND PERFORMANCE

In the early days of data processing, the most costly piece of equipment was probably a typewriter, calculator, or desk-top accounting machine. Early systems designers could easily investigate available equipment by calling on a few vendors and checking prices. The decision to buy was often made right on the spot. If a mistake was made, it was easily remedied: The machine was exchanged for another or a new one was purchased. The dollar loss to the firm was nominal.

The decision to implement a modern business system is not a casual one. Alteration of the physical plant, installation of air conditioning equipment, installation of special floors, and the purchase or lease of highly specialized, complex equipment may be involved and costly. The equipment may also require maintenance by trained equipment specialists. Errors in judgment in systems design can cost a firm hundreds of thousands of dollars.

Other factors such as the amount and complexity of data to be processed and the modern business firm's dependence upon it complicate the problem. A new system must be implemented without disrupting the flow of data. Should it be implemented all at once or step by step? Should it operate alongside the old method for a period of time?

These decisions are difficult to make, and once made, often cannot be recalled. If the right decision is made, the firm benefits from an improved data flow. If the wrong decision is made, more money, time, and resources may be needed for correction.

In evaluating and comparing business systems, the business systems analyst weighs many factors. A principal consideration, of course, is cost—any new system must first be justified economically. The analyst must evaluate

- Customer and personnel relations
- Labor cost
- Human factors
- Dependability
- Precision level of results
- Capacity
- Maintenance costs
- Downtime for maintenance and servicing
- Training cost
- Equipment lease or purchase costs
- Profit and return on investment
- Intangible benefits

The feasibility study has become an important technique for evaluating the performance and success potential of a new system. Initially, feasibility studies were used to determine whether a firm should convert from manual or unit record systems to computerized methods. Today, the feasibility study is used to determine whether a computerized system should be updated or replaced. This study does not, however, guarantee results. At times, costly feasibility studies will provide few meaningful results.

WHAT IS A FEASIBILITY STUDY?

A feasibility study is a careful assessment of the benefits expected from a new business system in terms of equipment, personnel, customers, and the physical plant. It aids management in determining whether implementing a new system is practical and economically feasible.

A feasibility study often moves through three phases:

1. Preliminary study
2. Investigative study
3. Final report and recommendations

If the preliminary study does not show promising results, no additional funds or efforts are expended on the next phase, and the approach is abandoned. If the results of the preliminary study are positive, the next phase is begun.

The preliminary and investigative studies build toward the final report and recommendations. Management will decide the fate of a new system on the basis of the recommendations in the final report.

Preliminary Study

The object of the preliminary study is to answer the question, "Does a new system appear to be sufficiently practical and economical to warrant further study and investigation?" The preliminary study looks at the fundamental needs of a business and reviews broad plans for change. It defines the problem, states ultimate objectives, and offers some tentative plans for solution.

During this phase, the business systems analyst discusses data processing needs with various people: employees, managers, division heads, customers, vendors, and others involved in the data cycle.

"I think what we need now is someone called a computer programmer."

Sidney Harris

Computerized Pipe Dream
Plays the Unplayable

For Dr. Prentiss Knowlton, the invention is a pipe dream come true.

The pipes are from a church organ and the invention allows a computer to play it.

Knowlton is a systems analyst with the Jet Propulsion Laboratory in Pasadena. A few years ago, while getting his doctorate in computer science at the University of Utah, he developed and wrote a thesis on a method of permitting musical notes to be flashed on a screen at the same time an organist is playing a piece.

"The value of this is that a composer doesn't have to be distracted while being inspired," explained the scientist. "His ideas are projected and recorded as he gets them."

Seeing that this was possible, Knowlton saw no reason why a computer couldn't be taught to actually play an organ.

And now, from the den of his La Crescenta home, strains from Bach and Mendelssohn flood the air, and the neighborhood thrills to the gifted fingers of a Digital Equipment Corporation PDP-8.

"The concept is along the lines of a player piano, but much more complex," said Knowlton.

The first step is to program the sheet music onto paper tape by punching a Teletype keyboard. This creates perforations on a strip of paper.

For instance, K2# means two sharps. Punching 4-4 tells the machine the number is in 4-4 time. Punching Q=280 says there are 280 quarter notes per minute. And QD3 means a quarter note of D in the third octave.

"It takes about an hour at the Teletype to do a page of music," Knowlton said.

The Teletype is hooked up to the computer, which in turn is hooked up to the organ.

"The possibilities are limitless," Knowlton exulted. "Something like 'The Overture to the Marriage of Figaro' is all but impossible for an organist to play, because of the number of voices or parts. But this way it can be done. The unplayable can be played."

Furthermore, he said, it can be a tool for composers. Once a piano roll is cast, it is virtually unchangeable. But with tape, instructions can be changed at any time.

And Knowlton is even trying to get his baby to do its own composing.

"I instructed it to compose a piece based on the sound of the planets rotating around the sun," he said. "The music wasn't bad."

SOURCE: "Computerized Pipe Dream Plays the Unplayable," David Larsen, *Los Angeles Times*, January 27, 1974. Copyright 1974, *Los Angeles Times*. Reprinted by permission.

SELECTION OF PERSONNEL RESPONSIBLE FOR STUDY.   An important part of the preliminary study is the selection of personnel who will conduct the feasibility study and a definition of their responsibilities. With the task force approach, management forms a committee of knowledgeable employees from various departments. After the committee has completed the study and made recommendations to management, it disbands.

A second approach is to appoint an ongoing committee of individuals from operating units, data processing and business systems departments, and managers. This committee is assigned the task of completing the preliminary study and the investigative phase and making recommendations to management. They have the continuing responsibility of implementing recommendations and monitoring the need for future modifications or changes.

Another approach is to place in charge one individual who is given the title project director and the necessary funds and authority to carry out the feasibility study. He or she may have the additional responsibility of implementing changes and recommendations.

DEFINITION OF GOALS.   One of the first tasks of the preliminary study is to provide a clear definition of the goals of the new system. The outcomes desired from a new system are stated in measurable terms. How many dollars will be saved? What specific problems will be eliminated by the new system? How much faster, more accurate, and precise will the results be? What existing machines can be eliminated?

Often vendors are aware of other studies or have information of value. These companies can provide information that helps the firm set goals and avoid pitfalls experienced by others.

The preliminary phase of the study is essential, since a new system cannot be built until its goals are defined. There would be no way of judging whether it was a success without a measure for comparison.

Investigative Study
The investigative phase of the feasibility study is the most detailed and complex. The elements involved in designing, implementing, and measuring the success of a new system are examined and evaluated.

During this phase, a number of people, from both inside and outside the firm, are called upon for help and cooperation. (See Figure 20.1.) Outside consultants may be hired. Department and branch managers may be interviewed to determine their data needs. Specific pieces of equipment are evaluated in terms of their usefulness in solving the problem under consideration.

A great deal of time is spent working with vendors during the investigative phase. Equipment specifications are studied, machines tested, pilot jobs run on vendors' machines, etc.

As soon as specifications and requirements have been defined, proposals are written and sent to vendors for bids. The vendors review the proposal and prepare price quotations. Sometimes a quotation may outline the methods of solving a problem, suggest specific pieces of equipment, and offer advice for planning and designing a new installation. Many vendors employ a skilled staff of systems engineers, equipment planners, and layout people, whose services are available to clients.

FIGURE 20.1   INTERVIEWS DURING INVESTIGATIVE STUDY

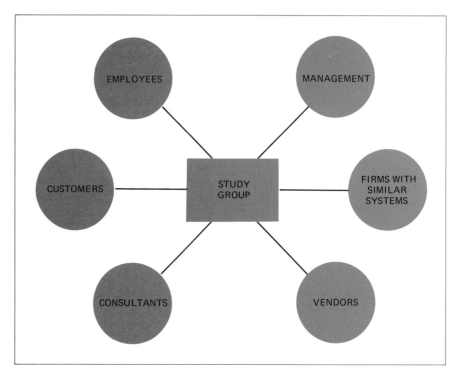

STUDY TECHNIQUES.   A variety of techniques are used in the investigative study. The business systems analyst may observe a machine in operation or personnel at work. He or she may conduct work sampling studies to determine the kind of data being processed or conduct time and motion studies on the methods used to gather data.

Logs, run books, histories, and records may be reviewed for an indication of the quantity of data processed by the firm. Special detailed records may be kept for a short period of time to learn more about the nature of a given data processing problem. For example, all the jobs run on a computer during a period of several months may be logged in a special record and studied in detail. This log will reveal the average length of run, the language compiler most often used, the use of disks, tapes, and primary storage, as well as the demands made on card readers and line printers.

AREAS CONSIDERED.   The investigative phase of the feasibility study deals with several major areas:

❶ Cost
❷ Hardware

❸ Software

❹ Personnel

❺ Time

Cost.   The study team must thoroughly examine all aspects of the new system to determine whether it is worth the expenditure and also to discover the cheapest and most efficient way to implement the system. Some of the questions asked are

- Should new equipment be leased or purchased?
- What will maintenance costs be?
- Which company will provide maintenance service at the lowest cost?
- What one-time costs must be borne?
- What recurrent costs are involved?
- What will be the cost of changing or expanding the new system at a later date?
- What training and implementation costs are involved?
- What will physical plant alterations cost?
- What will air conditioning, power, new floors, exits cost?

Hardware.   Any system that requires the purchase of new equipment will entail some study of the performance, speed, and capacity of key pieces of equipment. The feasibility study asks

- What brand of computer is best?
- What size of CPU and primary storage are best?
- What peripheral equipment should be purchased?
- Should tape drives, disk drives, or drum storage be selected?
- Can selected equipment be expanded to meet growth needs?
- Should equipment be centralized or decentralized?
- Should one large computer or several small ones be purchased?
- Who will be in charge of the new equipment?

Software.   The programming and software costs of a new system must also be studied. The time and effort required to program a given computer, consultation time, and availability of software libraries must all be considered. These questions are asked:

- What new programs will have to be written?
- Should programs be written, or purchased on the outside?
- How long will it take to write, test, and debug new programs?

- What skill will the staff need to write the new software?
- What software is available from vendors at no cost?
- Can existing programs be converted to the new system?
- Can the new programs be run on machines that may be purchased later?

Personnel.   The implementation of a new system affects the people employed by a firm as well as the organization as a whole. The investigative phase studies this area too.

- Will new people be needed?
- How many employees will have to be relocated?
- Will retraining be necessary?
- How will salaries be affected?
- Are there people now employed by the firm with the new skills that will be needed?
- What will the effect be on employee morale?
- How many people will be laid off?

Time Factor.   A new system must be feasible from a time as well as an economic standpoint. The study group asks several important questions:

- What would be the best period in the business cycle to install the new system?
- How long will the installation take?
- Should the old system be operated alongside the new? For how long?
- How long should consultants be employed to monitor the new system?
- Who should supervise the changeover?

Final Report   The last step in the feasibility study is the preparation of the final report and recommendations. This report records the results of the entire study.

A major part of the final report is the economic justification of the new system. The final report includes a statement showing the computed cost savings projected for the new system. It contrasts the new system with the old. It shows benefits expected in hours saved, reduction in personnel needed, and economies that will accrue in equipment lease costs. Figure 20.2 outlines a final report.

BENEFITS OF THE NEW SYSTEM.   A statement lists the benefits of the new system in precise terms. The benefits are expressed in terms of dollars, hours, ratios, etc. Any improvements in error factors, fewer breakdowns, lower maintenance costs, profit, and return on investment are quoted. Often costs go up, but sufficient offsetting benefits may justify a new system.

FIGURE 20.2   FINAL REPORT OF STUDY TEAM

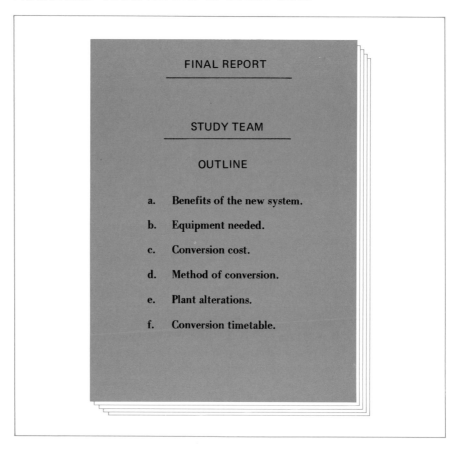

FINAL REPORT
_____

STUDY TEAM
_____

OUTLINE

a.   Benefits of the new system.

b.   Equipment needed.

c.   Conversion cost.

d.   Method of conversion.

e.   Plant alterations.

f.   Conversion timetable.

DETAILED STATEMENT OF EQUIPMENT NEEDED.   A list of the equipment to be purchased or leased is included. This statement gives the vendor name, make, model number, and cost of each piece of equipment. The size of the CPU and model numbers of input and output devices are given.

CONVERSION COSTS.   The procedures needed to convert to the new system are stated. The method of conversion (all at once, step by step, or parallel plan) is outlined. Changes required in the physical plant such as architectural revisions and air conditioning needs are detailed. Often, a timetable is given for implementation for each department.

Sometimes alternate plans are offered and the selection of a specific plan is left up to management. For example, if two methods are feasible, they might be summarized with an assessment of the merits and limitations of each. It is then up to management to select a plan.

Occasionally, the final report contains a quantitative measure of the cost of *not* implementing a new system. The statement may include a detailed estimate of the number of orders lost, cost of errors, and higher operating expenses that will be sustained if the company does not switch to the new system.

BUSINESS SYSTEM SELECTION

One of the major questions treated in the feasibility study is the selection of a business system suitable to the relative size and demands of the task. Complex data processing jobs require extensive processing equipment and a complicated data flow system. Smaller tasks make fewer demands and can often be done on less expensive, less complicated systems.

Criteria
A primary criterion in selecting a system is that it meet the needs of the firm. Needs vary greatly and so do system and hardware capabilities. What may be suitable for one firm may not be adequate for another.

Some companies are file oriented; others are calculation oriented. File-oriented firms require a system to process and perform simple calculations on large files that contain thousands of records. Calculation-oriented firms may have only a few records to be processed, but require computers to perform long and complex arithmetic and CPU-oriented procedures. Some firms are batch-oriented; others require online, real-time capabilities. A mail order house may be able to group its processing in batches. On the other hand, a bank may need real-time processing for its teller terminals.

The firm that must process a large number of card records requires a system that can manipulate large numbers of cards quickly. If many reports or long printouts are generated, the system must have good line printer capacity. If a firm's processing requires a variety of complex sorts and mathematical operations to be performed on a relatively small number of records, a large CPU capacity with limited input/output facilities is adequate. The volume of storage for files affects selection too. For example, the U.S. Internal Revenue Service needs many secondary storage facilities—tape drives, disk drives, etc.—to store millions of tax records.

Comparison of Methods
In selecting a business system, the following must be considered:

- Expansibility
- File type and size
- Kind of problems processed
- Speed

- Online, real-time needs
- Installation and engineering costs
- Programming costs
- Personnel training costs

These characteristics are the criteria used in our comparison of the three types of data processing systems.

MANUAL DATA PROCESSING. Manual data processing methods are relatively low cost for processing a small volume of data. Manual systems are flexible and easily changed, revised, or altered. Installation costs are low, and little specialized equipment is necessary. Operators can be easily trained to perform calculations, file, prepare reports, etc.

Manual data processing is practical for firms with a low volume of data to be processed. It is suitable for one-time problems. Since no programming time or effort is involved, the staff can begin processing the data with little preplanning, testing, or debugging.

UNIT RECORD PROCESSING. Unit record data processing is relatively economical for processing moderate amounts of data. A single unit record machine may lease for $100 to several hundred dollars per month; an entire system for $800 to $1,000 per month, or more. Card-oriented computers, such as the IBM 360/20 or UNIVAC 1004, lease for several thousand dollars per month. Unit record systems are flexible and are easily changed or modified.

Unit record machines, or card-oriented computers, are not, however, suitable for high-volume processing. They would be inefficient for a firm needing a great deal of file storage area and would be unable to meet real-time processing needs.

Unit record equipment is economical to service and does not require an air-conditioned or other specialized environment. It is easier to train operators to run unit record equipment than to train a computer programmer.

ELECTRONIC DATA PROCESSING. Computers range in size from small machines that lease for under $1,000 per month to large systems that lease for several hundred thousand dollars. These systems are expensive and are practical only if fully utilized a large part of each day.

Computer systems are fast, and if a high volume of data is processed, the cost is relatively low. These systems are suitable for firms that have a great number of calculations to perform or need a large storage capacity. They are also suited to real-time processing.

Large systems may be inefficient for one-time data processing problems. In these instances, minicomputers or manual or unit record systems might be more useful.

Computer systems require trained console operators, specialized maintenance staff, and skilled programmers. Some computer systems also require special environmental and plant conditions. Air conditioning, special floors and furniture are a few of the factors involved here.

HARDWARE SELECTION

Another major task of the feasibility study is the selection and specification of hardware for the proposed system. If computers are involved, the job becomes even more complicated and technical. The major elements weighed when selecting a computer are

1. Vendor capability
2. Equipment capability

Vendor Capability Computers are complex machines and need support and maintenance by a team of experts for proper functioning. With this in mind, the systems analyst looks at a vendor's abilities in many areas when selecting a particular brand or make of computer. Several factors are evaluated: the vendor's reputation and past performance, thoroughness and attitude in responding to proposals, capabilities, size of maintenance staff, the number and skill of the systems programmers, and the extent of supporting services. Figure 20.3 is a checklist of important criteria in choosing a vendor.

FIGURE 20.3   CHECKLIST FOR VENDOR CAPABILITIES

✓	REPUTATION
✓	PROPOSAL
✓	EXPERIENCE
	PAST PERFORMANCE
✓	MAINTENANCE STAFF
	SUPPORT SERVICES
✓	SOFTWARE
	TRAINING COURSES
	MANUALS
	LOCAL OFFICES

EXPERIENCE AND STABILITY. A major factor in selection of vendors is their experience in the data processing field and their ability to handle the particular needs of a firm. Some manufacturers have extensive experience in real-time processing, whereas others are batch-processing oriented. Some are specialists in terminal hardware. A number of computer manufacturers have been in business for many years and employ a skilled staff of systems engineers, machinists, technicians, and programmers.

EQUIPMENT SUPPORT. The support services provided by vendors also vary greatly. Some include full maintenance, repair, and installation services in their purchase or lease fee. Some have large branches located in major cities and provide training courses, operating manuals, and extensive help in adapting to a new system.

PROGRAM SUPPORT. To gain the maximum benefits from a computer and other complicated data processing equipment, a firm must have sound programming support from the vendor. Some manufacturers provide complete program packages, including operating systems, compilers, and utility programs. Others offer extensive programming libraries, including scientific and commercial subroutine packages.

An important element in the selection of a computer is the choice of compilers. Some manufacturers have a large number of compilers available for each make or model of machine; others have only one or two compilers available.

Equipment
Capability
Another major criterion in the selection of a computer is the machine's physical capabilities.

Equipment capability is generally related to cost. The higher the cost, the greater the processing speed or storage capacity of the computer. Sometimes there is a trade-off, and a business systems analyst has to choose between high primary storage capacity and high processing speed. For a given dollar amount, it is possible to get one or the other but not both. The analyst must decide which aspect is most important to the system. Figure 20.4 is a checklist of equipment capabilities.

CPU PERFORMANCE. Several measures are used to compare CPU performances. The primary storage capacities, cycle time, and number of instructions processed per second are major factors. Table 20.1 compares different models of one computer brand. A business systems analyst considers the following elements when rating CPU performance:

- Word size
- Instruction cycle time
- Addition time

FIGURE 20.4   CHECKLIST FOR EQUIPMENT CAPABILITIES

✓	CPU PERFORMANCE
✓	I/O PERFORMANCE
	PRIMARY STORAGE
✓	SECONDARY STORAGE
✓	OVERALL EVALUATION
	MAINTENANCE
✓	EXPANSIBILITY
	MULTIPROCESSING

- Number of programmable registers
- Number of input/output channels
- Primary storage capacity
- Arithmetic capability
- Physical size and characteristics

I/O PERFORMANCE.   The capabilities of the I/O devices are deciding factors in selecting peripheral equipment. Slow or insufficient card readers or line printers can cause a computer to become I/O bound. Under such conditions the amount of work processed during a shift would be far less than the maximum expected. Some of the measures compared are

- Number of cards read per minute
- Number of cards punched per minute
- Number of lines printed per minute
- Size and number of characters displayed on a video screen
- Speed at which data can be transmitted between CPU and I/O devices
- Number of terminals that can be operated at one time

SECONDARY STORAGE PERFORMANCE.   The capacity of secondary storage devices is an important factor, particularly in a system that depends on data accessed from storage. If a large number of files must be kept online for access by the CPU, adequate secondary storage facilities must be provided. The elements studied in comparing secondary storage devices are

- Number of disk drives on the system
- Number of tape drives on the system

TABLE 20.1 CPU COMPARISONS

IBM MODEL	NUMBER OF INDEX REGISTERS	CPU CYCLE TIME[a]	MAIN STORAGE READ/WRITE	MAXIMUM STORAGE CAPACITY	CPU CHANNELS AVAILABLE
125	—	0.98 μs	—	131 kilobytes	16
135	16	0.75 μs	0.77 μs	245 kilobytes	3
145	16	0.2 μs	0.54 μs	524 kilobytes	4
155	6	2.1 ms	2.1 ms	2 megabytes	—
165	12	2 ms	2 ms	3 megabytes	—

[a]μs (microsecond) = 0.000001 second
ms (millisecond) = 0.001 second
Source: *Infosystems,* May 1974, p. 52.

· Data cell and data drum storage capacity

· Density of media (bytes per inch on tape)

· Capacity in bytes per device

OVERALL SYSTEM PERFORMANCE. Several additional elements must be evaluated in a comparison of computer systems. Business systems analysts must know what provisions have been made for peripheral devices. Can the computer support a plotter or graphic display devices? Can it handle paper tape? Can the system remote process? Can it multiprogram (run several jobs at one time)?

Other important questions concern a computer's primary storage capacity and utilization. The storage areas of some computers are divided into fixed sections called partitions. These partitions cannot be adjusted or changed, even if one is overloaded and another is not. Some computers are designed for dynamic allocation of storage. The CPU can assign storage modules to different functions as needed by the problem program.

Sometimes a test or "benchmark" program is used to compare machines. The same program will be tested on several different computers to determine the different time and cost benefits.

KEY TERMS

Feasibility study
Final report
Investigative study
Ongoing committee

Preliminary study
Project director
Task force committee

EXERCISES

1. Why is it important to measure business system performance?
2. List and discuss six important elements measured in evaluating system performance.

3. What are the three main phases of the feasibility study? What is the purpose of each?
4. Discuss three approaches for selecting personnel to implement a feasibility study.
5. What questions does the investigative study analyze? Give several examples.
6. What support can a vendor provide when a firm plans a new business system?
7. Describe the kinds of findings presented in the final report and how they are used by management.
8. How do the needs of file-oriented firms differ from calculation-oriented firms? Give three examples of each.
9. When selecting a system, what characteristics are considered? How are they important?
10. Contrast the suitability of manual, unit record, and computer data processing methods for a medium-sized firm.
11. Summarize the major points a firm must evaluate when selecting hardware.
12. List and discuss six items that must be evaluated when judging computer capabilities.
13. What elements are evaluated when comparing input/output equipment capabilities?
14. Use your phone directory to determine what computer equipment vendors serve your local community.
15. As an individual assignment, make an appointment with a computer equipment vendor. Discuss the services, support, and help the firm provides clients.

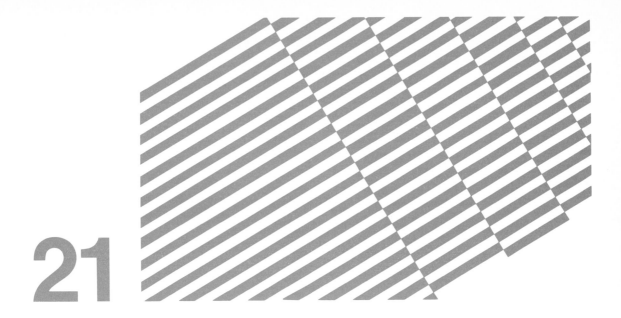

21

INTRODUCTION
TO TELEPROCESSING

Teleprocessing is a method of processing data in which the input and output devices are in a different location from the computer. Teleprocessing is the result of the synthesis of the techniques and principles of both electronic data processing and telecommunications. Telecommunications is the science of moving data through wires, radio waves, or microwave transmission circuits. In teleprocessing, these methods are used to transmit data between the input/output devices and the CPU.

Teleprocessing involves a network of one or more computers and one or more terminals. A teleprocessing system may be as simple as one terminal connected to a computer by telephone lines, or as complex as a network of computers tied to hundreds of terminals throughout the country.

Figure 21.1 illustrates a simple teleprocessing system, with capabilities for input, output, processing, and storage. The input/output devices and the CPU are connected by a communications link.

A communications link is the physical means of connecting locations for the purpose of transmitting and receiving information. It is the circuitry that ties two devices together and permits data to flow between them.

FIGURE 21.1   TELEPROCESSING SYSTEM

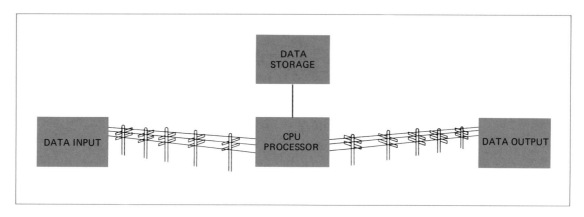

HISTORY OF TELEPROCESSING

Early telegraph systems often used paper tape to store and transmit information. This laid the groundwork for teleprocessing. Before World War II, teleprocessing was limited to transmitting data punched in paper tape to calculators several hundred miles away for processing. The results were punched into paper tape and transmitted back to the receiving station.

One of the first significant applications of teleprocessing, developed by the military after World War II, was the teleprocessing system called SAGE (Semi-Automatic Ground Environment) in which telephone lines tied several remote terminals to a CPU. The availability of real-time data increased the military's ability to make rapid, accurate judgments for air defense strategies.

The practicality of the military teleprocessing system was evident. Business firms began to use teleprocessing as a tool for solving business data processing problems. One early successful system was SABRE (Semi-Automatic Business Research Environment), which processed airline reservations. A listing of available seats was stored in a central computer. Terminals were placed in airline ticket offices. Ticket agents could query the system to learn the number of unsold seats on any given flight. This reliable and highly successful method of handling seat reservations pointed the way toward other teleprocessing applications.

Today, teleprocessing is invaluable to businesses with large inventories or costly remote data flow problems and is used for such tasks as credit checking, hotel and motel reservations, inventory control, auto license verification, controlling shipments in transit, sales reports, order entry, and ticket sales.

Point-of-
Sale (POS)
Terminals

The most recent growth in teleprocessing has been in the area of point-of-sale (POS) terminals. (See Figure 21.2.) These terminals are special cash registers that are connected to a central computer via a communications link. They allow the clerk to perform sales and order processing and gather marketing data at the point of sale.

POS terminals are now located in a variety of retailing and wholesale establishments, including department stores, variety stores, supermarkets, discount stores, and clothing, dress, and shoe shops.

FIGURE 21.2 POINT-OF-SALE TERMINAL

No More Paychecks for the Air Force

The Air Force is doing away with paychecks.

Early in 1975 it began paying its personnel in western states through an electronic funds transfer system.

Devised in cooperation with the Treasury Department and the Federal Reserve, the system works like this: Payroll data are entered onto magnetic tapes and sent to a regional office for initial processing. From there the tapes are forwarded to the appropriate Federal Reserve Bank. The Fed sorts the data electronically and transfers funds to financial institutions handling the payees' acounts.

Not only is the federal government saving thousands of dollars in processing expenses, but everyone gets paid on time. And there's no chance of a check getting lost in the mail.

Officials estimate that by 1980 about 16 million recurring federal payments will be transferred directly to recipients' accounts through the Fed's EFTS network.

SOURCE: Adapted from "60,000 Airmen Will Get Paid Electronically—No Checks" (UPI), Van Nuys News and Green Sheet, February 2, 1975.

In operation, the clerk enters sales data such as the amount of purchase, stock number, and units purchased. This information is relayed to a central computer, where the charges are computed and posted to the proper account. A customer receipt is prepared at the terminal.

Some POS terminals provide a variety of management reports including cash disbursements, receipts, charge, check, credit card, return, and refund reports. POS applications will continue to increase as more retail establishments install these terminals.

ADVANTAGES AND LIMITATIONS OF TELEPROCESSING

Teleprocessing is a flexible and fast means of accessing files. It eliminates the necessity of physically carrying data to the computer center, and its remote entry capabilities make real-time applications from the field possible. Teleprocessing enables many users to share the same system at the same time, thus reducing cost. Each user is given greater computer capability than could be afforded otherwise.

Teleprocessing permits more efficient use of computers, since users can take advantage of the time difference between the East and West Coasts. For example, users in the East can process jobs on computers in California before the working day begins in the West. And conversely, western users can use New York computers after the working day in the East has ended.

Teleprocessing has its limitations. Since all parts of the system are bound by a communications link, expensive tie lines, interconnecting lines, telephone lines, etc. must be installed. Additional equipment and complex programming are also involved.

Cost accounting procedures must be designed to handle a large volume of users. Records must be kept so that each user can be charged for CPU time and storage used. Job control procedures must be set up to handle jobs coming in from all users. Security measures must be available to prevent unauthorized users from querying or accessing files.

Finally, teleprocessing is subject to communications failures. A downed line, or interruption in the transmission between the CPU and terminal causing loss of data, is an ever-present problem.

Sidney Harris

"What I had in mind was topographical elevations and circuit schematics."

EXAMPLES OF TELEPROCESSING SYSTEMS

Teleprocessing systems are flexible arrangements of machines, programs, and communications equipment. A system may have one or many terminals. A single CPU may serve all needs of the system, or several CPUs may be linked together. Users may be located within the same building, or separated by thousands of miles.

Simple
System

Figure 21.3 illustrates the simplest teleprocessing system. One CPU with batch processing capability serves one remote terminal. Jobs can be entered and output on the batch I/O device at the CPU site. At the same time, the system can handle queries and input from the remote terminal. In this example, the terminal in the sales department is tied to the CPU by hard wires (that is, the terminal is wired directly to the CPU).

FIGURE 21.3 SIMPLE TELEPROCESSING SYSTEM

COMPUTER CENTER

CPU

INPUT/
OUTPUT
DEVICE

TRANSMISSION
LINE

SALES DEPARTMENT

TERMINAL

OFFICE BUILDING

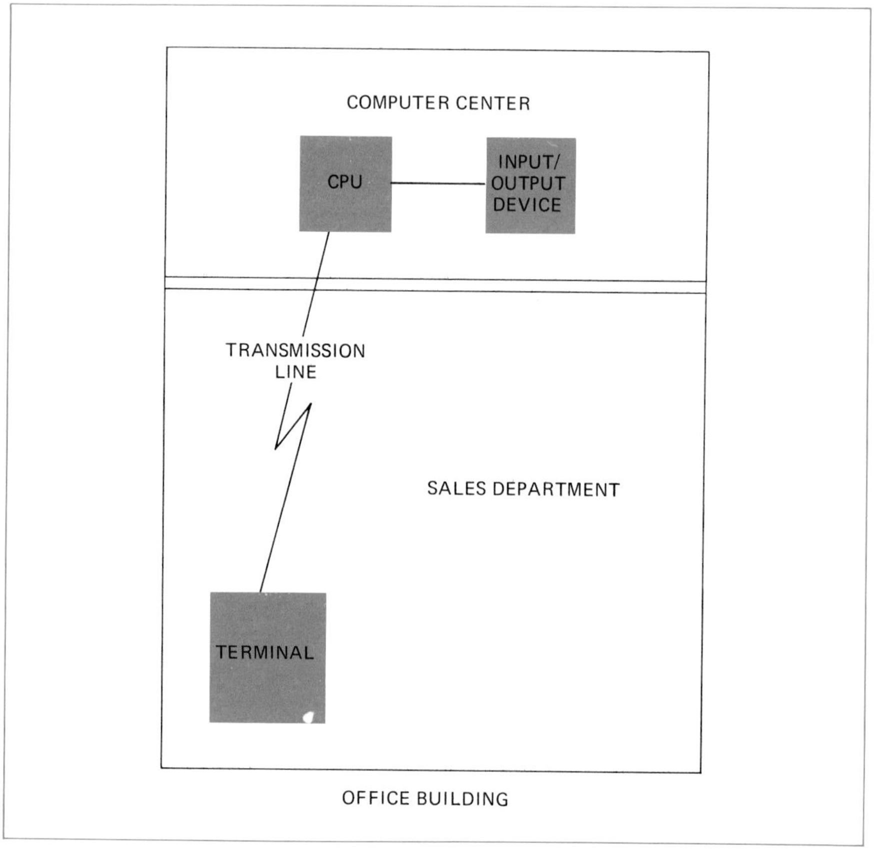

FIGURE 21.4 MORE COMPLEX TELEPROCESSING SYSTEM

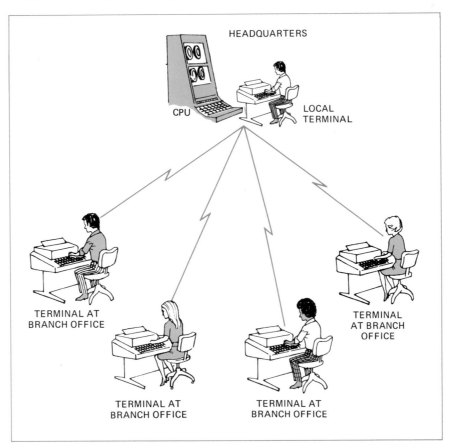

In a variation of this arrangement the computer could be located in the accounting department with additional terminals in other parts of the building.

More Complex System

A more complex teleprocessing system is shown in Figure 21.4. Here, the computer is located in the firm's main office. Each branch in the same city has a terminal. The remote terminals are tied to the computer through telephone lines. Data can be entered or output at the computer site or at any of the remote terminals on the line. With this system, each branch office has computer capacity available, without requiring the actual installation of a machine.

Complex Network

The firm in Figure 21.5 has one large computer in its home office. Each branch, located in a major city, has several terminals connected to it from outlying areas. This enables each local branch to serve several terminals on one transmission line.

FIGURE 21.5   NATIONAL TELEPROCESSING SYSTEM

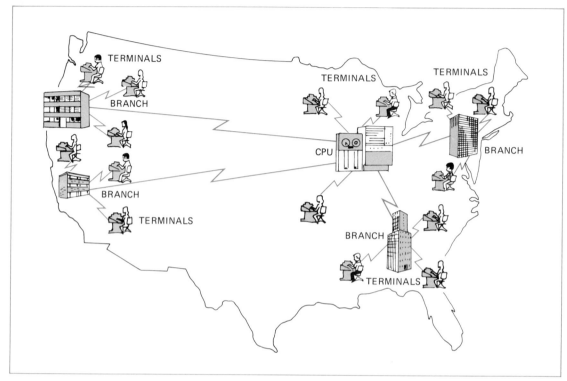

Figure 21.6 illustrates a similar arrangement, except that two computers are on the system. Since the computers are tied online, it is possible to use either or both to process data from any remote terminal. This arrangement is called multiprocessing. It allows the computer network to handle overloads and breakdowns more efficiently. Either computer serves as a backup in the event of a CPU failure. In the system in Figure 21.5 a failure of the central CPU would cause the entire system to go down.

CYBERNET.   Cybernet, the computer utility service of Control Data Corporation, is a good example of a complex teleprocessing system. The Cybernet system consists of more than 60 data centers in the United States and over 40 international centers. More than 70,000 miles of communications lines link the system together (as shown in Figure 21.7).

Cybernet has a network of 28 large-scale computer systems located in major cities of the country. A communications network, composed of voice grade and wide band lines, links the CPUs in this system.

Customers gain access to the computing system via a terminal installed in their office as shown in Figure 21.8. Telephone lines are used to tie remote terminals to the data centers. Several types of terminal systems with differing

FIGURE 21.6   NATIONAL TELEPROCESSING NETWORK WITH TWO CPUs

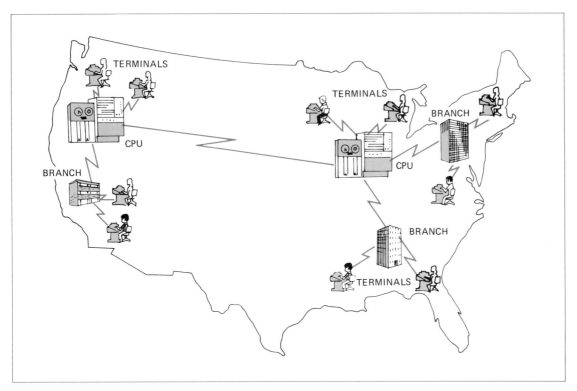

capacities are available. Card readers, video display terminals, plotters, magnetic tape and paper tape drives, line printers, etc. can be connected to the system. A small 12K computer can be installed in the user's office to further expand the system's applications.

A large staff of programmers, systems engineers, computer operators, librarians, communications specialists, managers, and marketing people are employed. Both batch processing services and real-time, conversational programming are available to remote users.

Cybernet has many languages available on its system, including BASIC, COBOL, and FORTRAN. Many applications programs are online, providing data analysis, linear programming, structural analysis, mathematical and electronic-circuitry programming, and simulations and modeling.

THE BASIC TELEPROCESSING SYSTEM

Elements in the
Teleprocessing
System

The basic teleprocessing system has several elements or components:

❶ Data entry

FIGURE 21.7 CYBERNET NETWORK

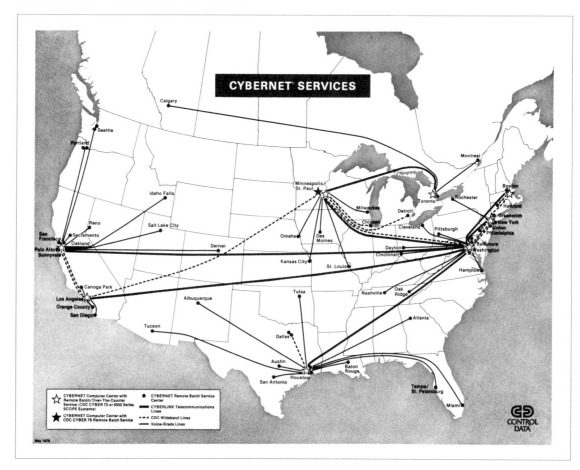

② Data transmission
③ Data processing
④ Data storage
⑤ Data inquiry

Data entry is the operation of inputting data to the system through a network of remote terminals. Data are sent to the CPU through the data transmission system. Data processing is performed in the CPU. Files and programs are kept in data storage accessible to the CPU. Data inquiry is made from remote terminals to the master file.

Data Entry   The method of data entry depends on the type of teleprocessing system, the needs of the firm, and the time element.

FIGURE 21.8   CYBERNET REMOTE ACCESS TERMINAL

Some teleprocessing systems, as shown in Figure 21.9, are essentially nothing more than data input systems. All data come in to a central computer through a system of remote input terminals. Data processing and output take place at the central computer location. No output goes to the remote terminals. These systems do not bring the resources of the computers or results of the output to the terminals, but use each remote terminal as a data entry point.

Systems such as these are useful when a home office wants to collect data from local units and do all processing and outputting in the central office. An example would be a centralized billing system. All sales from branches would be entered on terminals and the data transmitted to the main office. There, bills, invoices, and other accounting data would be prepared, and statements would be mailed out to customers.

MODES OF DATA ENTRY.   There are four major modes of data entry.
1. *Offline Data Preparation—Online Data Entry.*   In this mode, data are collected offline and sent to the CPU in a batch for processing. For example, data may be collected throughout the day and recorded on punched cards, magnetic tape, or paper tape. When data are ready for entry, or at the close of the working day, an operator would place the tape or cards on a terminal, signal the computer to prepare for data input, and

FIGURE 21.9   SIMPLE DATA ENTRY SYSTEM

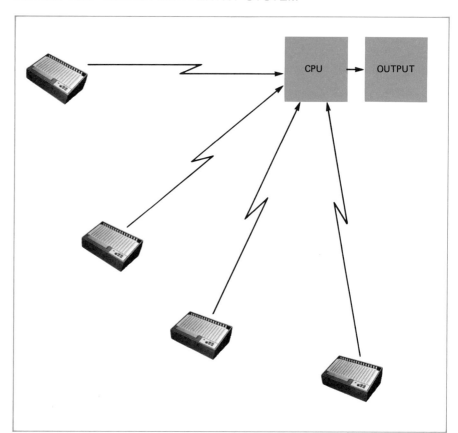

begin transmission. Offline data entry might be used to run a payroll or a statistical procedure.

2. *Online Data Preparation—Online Data Entry.*   In this mode, data are keyboarded and transmitted to the central computer at the time the transaction occurs. A signal from the remote terminal initiates the transmission. No intermediate storage device, such as paper or magnetic tape, is used. However, a buffer is sometimes placed in the system to see that characters are fed to the CPU with the proper timing.

Bank teller terminals use this mode. The data are sent to the CPU at the instant the teller enters the details of the transaction on the terminal.

3. *Computer-Accessed Data Entry.*   In this mode, the computer is programmed to call the terminal when the CPU is ready to receive the data. This mode differs from those above in that the computer rather than the terminal operator initiates the transmission. Data are gathered, entered, and stored in the terminal over a period of time. When the CPU is ready to

receive and process the data, it signals the terminal to begin transmission. The terminal then sends the CPU all the data it is holding in storage.

Applications of this mode include billing, payroll, and inventory systems. Data are collected and entered in the terminal during the working day. The CPU receives and processes the data at the end of the working day, when its workload is smaller, or at periods when the transmission lines are not in heavy use.

4. *Shared Data Input.* In this mode, several remote terminals are connected to the CPU through one transmission line. The arrangement is similar to a telephone party line. A terminal can go online and send data *only* when the line is not being used by another terminal.

Data
Transmission

One of the essential elements in a teleprocessing system is the transmission of data between terminals and CPU or between several CPUs. The data are usually transmitted over telephone, telegraph, or leased lines, or through microwave or radio wave circuits. The selection of the transmission mode for a teleprocessing system depends on the needs of the firm and the available computer hardware and related equipment.

DATA TRANSMISSION LINES. Communication lines for teleprocessing systems are priced according to their ability to transmit data, which is determined by type of circuit and grade of line or volume of data that can be fed from point to point.

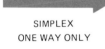

SIMPLEX
ONE WAY ONLY

Circuits Used. Three types of circuits are in common use, as shown in the margin. They are

❶ Simplex circuits

❷ Half-duplex circuits

❸ Full-duplex circuits

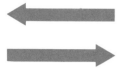

HALF DUPLEX
SEND OR RECEIVE
ALTERNATELY

In the simplex circuit, data can flow in only one direction. A line either receives data or transmits data. It cannot do both, and is therefore a limited means of data transmission. A terminal coupled to a simplex line that only transmits data is called a send-only terminal. A terminal coupled to a simplex line that only receives data is called a receive-only terminal.

A half-duplex line, on the other hand, can receive and transmit data, but can do only one at a time. The half-duplex line can be shifted from one direction of data flow to the other by the CPU or the terminal, but its utility is still limited. If a terminal is transmitting data over a half-duplex line, the computer cannot interrupt the input flow to send back an important message. It must wait until the terminal shifts the line to the receive mode before delivering the information. The half-duplex line is the most widely used because it handles most communication needs at a reasonable cost.

FULL DUPLEX
SEND AND RECEIVE
SIMULTANEOUSLY

A full-duplex circuit is obviously the most efficient because it allows a two-way transmission of data to occur simultaneously. Suppose an operator is entering data through a terminal to the computer and is unaware that the system's storage capacity has reached its limit. With a full-duplex circuit, the computer can signal the terminal to stop inputting data before the system becomes overloaded.

Speed of Data Transmission. Communication lines are also classified by the volume of data they can transmit. The greater the number of characters transmitted per second, the higher the grade of line. The lower the volume, the lower the grade.

The standard measure of data transmission speed is *bits per second* (*bps*). (The term baud is sometimes inaccurately applied here. Baud refers to a measure in the teletypewriter industry.) The higher the bps or line capacity, the more data it can move per given interval of time.

Three grades of lines are used for data transmission:

1. Narrow band line
2. Voice grade line
3. Wide band line

The narrow band line usually has a maximum transmission speed of 300 bps. These lines are less than voice grade in quality and are not widely used. They are, however, more economical to lease than other grades.

Voice grade, or voice band, lines can transmit more than 300 bps. They are called voice grade because they are commonly used for ordinary telephone conversations.

Wide band lines are capable of transmitting data at 18,000 bps or higher. Of the three lines available from the telephone company, these lines have the greatest capacity for moving data and are the most expensive to lease.

Thus, we see that the most versatile and expensive line would be a full-duplex, wide band line. A simplex, narrow band line would be less expensive but more limited in use.

CHANNELS. A channel is the path between each terminal and its CPU. A CPU that services 30 terminals simultaneously would require 30 channels. With appropriate equipment it is possible to transmit up to 45 channels of information over one communication line. Specialized data transmission equipment must be installed to make multiple channels available on a single line. But regardless of the number of channels on the same circuit, the user pays only the basic charge for a single line.

MULTIPLEXERS. Multiplexers are designed to provide up to 45 or more channels of communications over a single voice grade line. Figure 21.10 illustrates a system with two multiplexers, one at each end of the communications line. The multiplexer on one end sets up channels over which to transmit the data coming in from the terminals. The multiplexer at the other end of the line separates the data and sends them to the CPU.

FIGURE 21.10   DATA TRANSMISSION SYSTEM WITH
                          MULTIPLEXERS

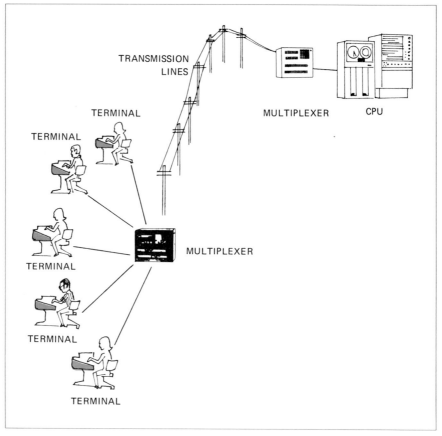

This arrangement provides an efficient low-cost means of coupling up to
45 terminals online to a computer using only a single voice grade line.

COUPLERS.   A coupler is a device used to connect a terminal or a
CPU to a telephone line. These devices are also called modems
(MOdulator-DEModulators) or interface facilities.
   As keys are depressed on the terminal keyboard, the coupler converts the
characters into pulses suitable for transmission over the telephone line. At
the computer, another coupler converts the pulses back to a form suitable
for processing in the CPU.
   Couplers may be either hard wired or acoustic. A hard-wired coupler is
permanently connected to the telephone line and the data transmission
device. It forms a direct physical and electronic path between the elements
on the circuit. Couplers at the CPU end of a system are usually hard wired.
   Acoustic couplers are not permanently connected to either the CPU, the
terminal, or the telephone line. This has the advantage of allowing a terminal

FIGURE 21.11　ACOUSTIC COUPLED TERMINAL

to be connected to any telephone line in the field. Acoustic couplers convert signals from the terminal into an audible tone for transmission over ordinary telephone lines. See Figure 21.11.

Data Processing　The full potential of teleprocessing was not realized until two major developments in technology occurred: the designing of computers capable of multiprogramming and real-time processing.

MULTIPROGRAMMING.　A multiprogramming system consists of a computer capable of executing several jobs at one time. At any given moment, the computer may be compiling several jobs, executing several others, and handling the inquiries and transactions of others.

　　A major capability of a multiprogramming computer is its ability to interrupt the processing of one or more jobs and to execute higher priority work first. When a multiprogramming computer receives an interrupt message from a high-priority job, it will temporarily store all data being processed at that moment. It will execute and output the job with the higher priority and then return to the original jobs at the point where it left off.

REAL-TIME PROCESSING.   In real-time processing, transactions are processed by a computer as they occur, and results are available to the user immediately. Data are input and output via online devices.

Figure 21.12 illustrates a real-time terminal system. Today, many computer manufacturers market real-time computer systems capable of multiprogramming. They can service many remote terminals on a real-time basis and at the same time handle batch processing jobs fed from on-site devices.

REMOTE JOB ENTRY.   Teleprocessing brings the power of the computer to users in remote locations. (See Figure 21.13.) Via remote job entry, they can process data in much the same way as in batch job processing. The difference is that the I/O devices are located away from the CPU. Data in the remote job entry (RJE) system are input to a computer and output from it via an elaborate terminal system consisting of card readers, card punches, line printers, typewriters, keyboards, etc.

The terminal transmits data from cards, tape, or keyboard to the CPU. Programs including job control cards and data decks are input in this way. The data are processed by the CPU and the results sent back to the remote terminal for output. With remote job entry, a user thousands of miles away from a computer can maintain large files, or prepare the monthly billing or the firm's payroll, as if he or she were at the CPU site.

Data Storage   Data storage is an essential part of teleprocessing, since each user stores master files, programs, etc. at the CPU site. The computer must be able to access files quickly in order to properly service a group of remote terminals. Large secondary storage systems of magnetic tape, disk, and drum must be maintained for all computers used for time-sharing applications.

Data Inquiry   Some teleprocessing systems designed only to output data are called inquiry systems. (See Figure 21.14.) Remote users can only request the computer to output information from a file accessible to the CPU. (See Figure 21.15.) They cannot update or add data to a file. File maintenance and data input are done at the site of the CPU.

Examples of data inquiry systems include stock market quotation and inventory inquiry systems. In these systems, the user queries the computer about the status of a given file. Usually he or she cannot change or update the information in the file.

If the system is modified to permit file maintenance and data input from the terminals, it is called a remote processing system.

Files can be queried by

❶ Telephone inquiry with audio response

❷ Keyboard inquiry and response

❸ Keyboard inquiry with video display

FIGURE 21.12 REAL-TIME TERMINAL

FIGURE 21.13 REMOTE
JOB ENTRY TERMINAL

FIGURE 21.14   DATA OUTPUT (INQUIRY) SYSTEM

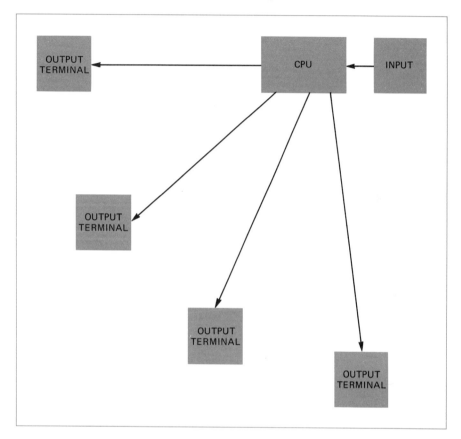

TELEPHONE INQUIRY WITH AUDIO RESPONSE.   Audio response terminals are sometimes used to output data from a teleprocessing system. The user calls the system and inputs a key number, such as part number or item number. The computer then accesses the master file and locates the requested record. It assembles a verbal message, which is fed back over the telephone line to the terminal. The user receives a spoken reply to the query over the telephone.

KEYBOARD INQUIRY AND RESPONSE.   In this mode, the operator keyboards a part number, name, or other descriptive information. The computer processes the inquiry and transmits the results to the remote terminal for output.

KEYBOARD INQUIRY WITH VIDEO DISPLAY.   In this mode, the user keyboards in the descriptive data and the computer processes the request.

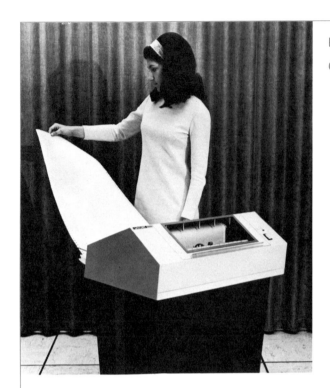

FIGURE 21.15
OUTPUT STATION

FIGURE 21.16
REAL-TIME DISPLAY

The results of the processing are sent back to the terminal and displayed on a video screen.

Figure 21.16 illustrates the output from a real-time application, displayed on a video display system.

KEY TERMS

Acoustic coupler
Channel
Communications link
Full-duplex circuits
Half-duplex circuits
Hard-wired coupler
Modem
Multiplexer
Multiprocessing

Multiprogramming
Point-of-sale terminal
Real-time processing
Receive-only terminal
Remote job entry
Send-only terminal
Simplex circuits
Telecommunications
Teleprocessing

EXERCISES

1. Define teleprocessing and explain how it differs from conventional or local processing.
2. Summarize the five major elements in the basic teleprocessing system.
3. How does online data entry differ from offline? Give several examples of data entry applications suitable to each.
4. List the three kinds of transmission circuits used in teleprocessing and explain how they differ.
5. How do narrow band, voice grade, and wide band lines differ?
6. What are the advantages of an acoustic coupler? Suggest several applications for portable terminals with acoustic couplers.
7. Define multiprogramming and explain how it is important to teleprocessing.
8. How does remote job entry processing differ from real-time processing? Give examples of processing jobs suitable to each.
9. Summarize the major advantages and disadvantages of teleprocessing.
10. Visit a stockbroker's office, business firm, or small engineering company that uses teleprocessing. Determine what kinds of equipment are online, their applications, and the advantages of the system.

22

INFORMATION SYSTEMS

One of the major results of the computer's ability to process large volumes of data quickly, accurately, and economically is the development of information systems. Information systems are collections of people, machines, computers, and communications equipment designed to capture, transmit, store, process, retrieve, or display information.

Information systems are now used in government, business, education, banking, finance, and other fields to perform a variety of activities. They are used to process orders, check credit, process job applications, facilitate the flow of funds, prepare management reports, or even replace money.

This chapter discusses information systems, their construction, and some typical applications. It describes data banks, retrieval systems, and electronic funds transfer systems (EFTS). It concludes with a discussion of the problems related to information systems and data center operations, including security, protection of vital data, and unauthorized access to files.

IMPORTANCE OF INFORMATION SYSTEMS

Information systems improve management's ability to make effective decisions in several ways. Elements used in the decision-making process must be reduced to quantitative terms. This decreases the time required to make a decision and increases its accuracy. Information systems affect a firm's financial capability. They provide current data on changing business cycles and conditions that give management better control over the flow of funds. They can produce information on various activities early enough in the business cycle to enable management to take effective corrective action before problems arise.

Information systems improve the marketing and distribution capacity of an organization. They facilitate the process of bringing the right kind of product to market at the right time, at the right price, and in the right quantity to make a profit.

Information systems foster better control of production processes and procedures. The computer can be used to control the flow of goods into the manufacturing cycle, to schedule work output, personnel workloads, shipments, deliveries, and the ordering of raw materials.

With labor an increasingly costly item in the manufacture of goods, one of the most important benefits is the improved deployment of human resources within an organization. Information systems can be designed to maintain a complete and current description of employees, their training, skills, assignments, and special capabilities.

MAJOR ELEMENTS OF AN INFORMATION SYSTEM

Basically, an information system consists of a data bank containing pertinent files and information and the computer's ability to input, retrieve, and output information. (See Figure 22.1.).

What Is a Data Bank?

The American National Standards Institute (ANSI) defines a data bank as "a comprehensive collection of libraries of data used by an organization." It contains all the information related to the information system.

A data bank for a credit processing system may include information on a customer's purchasing patterns, payment history, inventory, and personal or financial status. A system may include data on employees, their families, medical history, bank savings, means of transportation, etc. In government, a data bank may contain information on citizens' physical and mental health, legal difficulties, arrest records, employment histories, travel, income, and military experience.

A data bank may be maintained either at the user's site or at a timeshare firm. The data may be stored as paper documents, microfilm or microfiche records, photographs, audio or video tape recordings, on punched cards, or on computerized media such as magnetic tape, disk, or drum storage systems.

FIGURE 22.1   INFORMATION SYSTEM

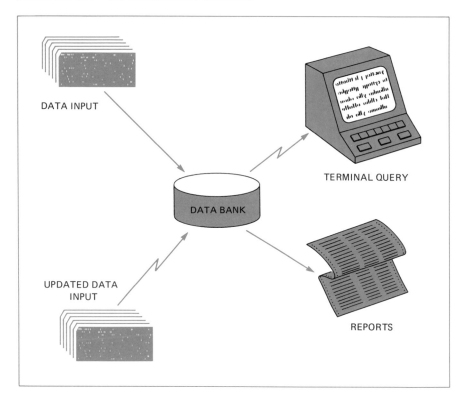

Data banks are used in several ways. The computer can be instructed to access specific information in the bank and prepare various reports from it. Or users at local or remote terminals can send queries to the computer asking it to locate specific pieces of information and display or output them on the terminal. For example, a savings and loan association that queries a data bank hundreds of times in a working day may have terminals at each teller's window, at loan desks, and in executive offices. Output may be hard-copy reports printed on a line printer, a display on a video terminal, or a message given on an audio response unit.

Structuring a Data Bank

The steps involved in developing and implementing a data bank include

1 Definition of data in the bank

2 Structuring of files and input media

3 Structuring of query procedures and output media

4 Inputting of raw data to build bank

⑤ Opening of system to users

⑥ Continual updating of data by inputting new information

Information drawn from many sources within the company may be placed in a data bank. Some common items included are

- Sales information
- Order backlog
- Customer buying patterns
- Current selling prices
- Shipping information and costs
- Supply of raw materials
- Cost of materials
- Equipment and plant capacity
- Financial data
- Personnel data

These items are supplied by departments as raw data input, and new data are continually input to keep the file current.

How are Data Banks Accessed? Figure 22.2 illustrates a video terminal (CRT), which is one method of accessing a data bank. The operator keys in an identifier such as a name, social security number, or driver's license number. The computer locates the specified file and displays all or part of it on the screen. Some terminals print out a permanent hard copy of the information at the same time.

Since file security is an important concern, some systems require elaborate access codes and passwords before certain kinds of information can be displayed. Others do not include file security systems and allow the entire contents to be displayed to anyone possessing the name or other file identifier.

EXAMPLES OF INFORMATION SYSTEMS

The following examples are indicative of major types of information systems:

① Management Information Systems (MIS)

② Information Retrieval Systems

③ Electronic Funds Transfer Systems (EFTS)

Management Information Systems A management information system (MIS) provides information to management for effective decision making. These systems vary in their scope, size, and

FIGURE 22.2 ACCESSING DATA BANK

capacity. Figure 22.3 illustrates the MIS used by B. F. Goodrich.* It is a comprehensive financial management system, using a computer data bank and online terminals.

The data bank contains information on the firm's budgets, sales, engineering, billing, assets, payroll, transportation, and accounts receivable and payable. It is composed of several subsystems that handle order

*Datamation, September 1974, page 53.

FIGURE 22.3   MANAGEMENT INFORMATION SYSTEM

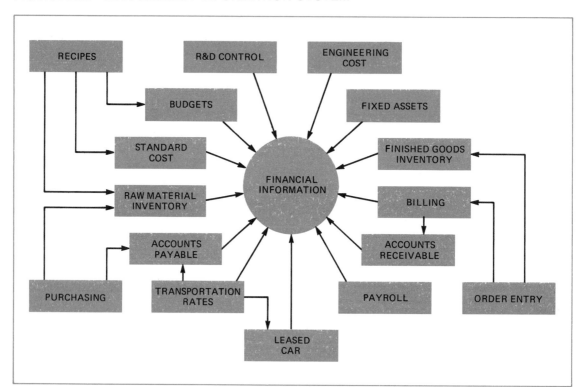

processing, inventory, payroll, and accounting functions. The order processing portion captures data on customer orders and includes data on routing, shipment, contract price, base price, credit, and raw materials and finished goods inventories.

The entire system is maintained on a large computer system that includes magnetic tape drives and several disk drive storage devices. The system can perform both batch and interactive (real-time) processing. It is equipped with line printers for preparing reports and CRT display units for updating and inquiry.

Management information systems may be structured to provide critical data on financial management, cost accounting, cost control, personnel management, etc. For example, reports can be generated for such matters as cash flow, trends in accounts payable and receivable, earnings ratios, and turnover ratios.

The MIS can give management data concerning distribution functions. These reports can provide information on finished goods in stock or in transit, goods in production, or backlogged orders. They can prepare shipping schedules, routing data, and shipping cost tables. This type of information decreases late deliveries, misrouted goods, and over- or underproduction of goods.

Investment planning and management of capital assets can be included in an MIS. For example, managers can receive reports on capital outlays, returns on investment, cost centers, depreciation schedules, and equipment maintenance and installation costs. This facilitates planning the acquisition of new capital goods or the sale of outdated or unproductive equipment.

Cost accounting information can be processed by an MIS. An MIS can be programmed to give reports on the cost of goods in manufacture. It can print out breakeven points, points of diminishing returns, fixed and variable expense reports, and costs by product line, model, or individual unit produced.

Information Retrieval Systems

An information retrieval system is a large data bank maintained in a central location and accessed by users in many remote locations. Maintenance is usually performed at the central location. Access is usually via remote terminals or telephone.

The Medical Information Bureau (MIB)* is a good illustration of a large national data bank owned and operated outside of government. It was established in 1902 by the Association of Life Insurance Medical Directors to prevent insurance fraud and to disseminate information on applications to member companies. Today, more than 700 life insurance firms use this massive information system headquartered in an Information Center in Greenwich, Connecticut. Reports received from the MIB are attached to policy applications and are used in determining whether to underwrite a given insurance risk.

Each member company of the MIB pays between $2,000 and $30,000 per year for access to the master file via online computer terminals located in their own home offices. Within 30 minutes, the master file can be queried for a prospective client's name. Member companies are charged between 21¢ and 50¢ per name searched, depending upon the type of report generated and its urgency. Each "hit" or report provides the insurance company with important decision-making data. It eliminates the possibility of an applicant who was denied insurance by one company from making false statements to another in order to qualify for insurance.

The MIB master file contains extensive information on more than 12 million people, including their names, addresses, and occupations. Extensive medical histories and documentation regarding complications are coded into the file. Hundreds of medical conditions are reported and indexed by a coding system. When a "hit" is returned from MIB, the report specifies what medical conditions were diagnosed and what parts of the body were involved.

*Prism, June, 1974, page 31.

Mind-Reading Computers

Shades of science fiction . . . now they're trying to teach the computer to read minds!

Scientists working under contracts from Advanced Research Projects Agency at the University of Illinois, UCLA, Stanford, Massachusetts Institute of Technology, the University of Rochester, and in laboratories at other facilities have been studying ways to plug a computer into a person's brain waves—electroencephalograph (EEG) signals.

They expect to be able to use these EEG signals in a myriad ways. So far, researchers have been able to determine not only an individual's alertness, but how he or she learns and perceives colors and shapes. They can tell whether a subject is fatigued, puzzled, or daydreaming. Now, they are attempting to use the brainwaves to control machines.

A pilot's brainwaves could be read by electrodes placed in his radio earphones. A small special-purpose computer could scan the peaks and valleys of the EEG to determine what the pilot is concentrating on and what he is ignoring. If he should intentionally put his plane into a dive, the computer would let it pass. But if he took a potentially hazardous action through inattention, the computer would alert him.

In the classroom, the EEG–computer system could discover how students learn and when they are most likely to learn. It could also advise teachers about the most effective way to teach. In a test, it could tell the difference between a right answer based on knowledge and one that was merely a lucky guess.

At UCLA, scientists are using EEG signals to control machines, bypassing the body's motor and muscle system. Brainwaves are linked directly to a machine that has been programmed to perform various operations depending on the particular brainwave pattern being received.

In one experiment, a student whose EEG signals were being fed to such a machine sat in front of a television screen. Using only her brainwaves, she was able to move a symbolic mouse through a maze on the screen. Examples of potential applications are wheelchairs that quadriplegics could command without manipulating levers, and cockpit controls that could be operated by brainwaves if the pilot's arms and legs were immobilized.

Other studies are seeking ways to use the EEG to improve computer-based teaching programs by showing which lessons are effective and which are not, to determine the part of the brain that is in use when people are in the process of remembering pictures or graphs, and to aid in air-traffic control by selecting the controller whose brain is most ready to handle work at any particular time.

Is it only a matter of time before the computer will be able to read a person's brainwaves to determine just what he or she is thinking?

SOURCE: Abstracted from "Mind-Reading Machine Tells Secrets of the Brain," Norman Kempster, *Los Angeles Times*, March 20, 1976, and "Machines Controlled by Brainwaves?" Harry Nelson, *Los Angeles Times*, May 21, 1976. © 1976, *Los Angeles Times*. Reprinted by permission.

Adverse information is also given, such as number of heart attacks, high blood pressure, etc.

Several sensitive categories of information were previously maintained in the MIB files such as information on an individual's nervous conditions, sexual problems and deviations, alcoholism, drug abuse, social maladjustment, prostitution, reckless driving, and participation in hazardous sports.

Because of the threats to personal privacy, much of the MIB information system is being reviewed by both the insurance industry itself and outside sources. Some sensitive categories of information are being deleted. There has been pressure on MIB to eliminate data on an individual's financial and nonmedical conditions.

Electronic Funds Transfer Systems

Figure 22.4 illustrates an electronic funds transfer system (EFTS). Systems such as these are being developed in the United States through the mutual efforts of banks, merchants, employers, credit unions, and savings institutions.

In this system, one or more large computers are used to control and process the transfer of all funds throughout the system. EFTS may contain several segments including a retail point-of-sale (POS), customer's bank, remote bank (money machine), direct payroll, and electronic bill-payment segments. The system can be arranged in different ways to meet the needs of customers, banks, retailers, and employers.

All elements in the system operate as a totally integrated network, providing for the payment of goods and services, transfer and deposit of funds, payroll, and credit authorization. Some segments of the EFTS are described below.

CENTRAL COMPUTER. In EFTS a large central computer system coordinates and controls all parts of the system. It serves the teller terminals located in banks, point-of-sale terminals at retail establishments, terminals located at business firms, and "money machines."

The central computer system maintains files on all accounts including retailers, customers, employers, etc. All debits and credits to these accounts are posted by the central computer to the proper account. Some electronic funds transfer systems under design will be very extensive and incorporate segments into a statewide or nationwide network of terminals located in banks, shopping centers, supermarkets, and elsewhere.

RETAIL POINT-OF-SALE (POS) SEGMENT. Many retailers now have POS terminals installed in showrooms, sales offices, and retail counters. Figure 22.5 illustrates point-of-sale terminals located in a retail establishment. Each terminal is connected via telephone lines to the central computer. The POS terminal receives data either input from a keyboard located on the terminal or from a credit card placed in a slot located on the terminal. The credit cards used in the system have a magnetic stripe across the back on which

FIGURE 22.4   ELECTRONIC FUNDS TRANSFER SYSTEM (EFTS)

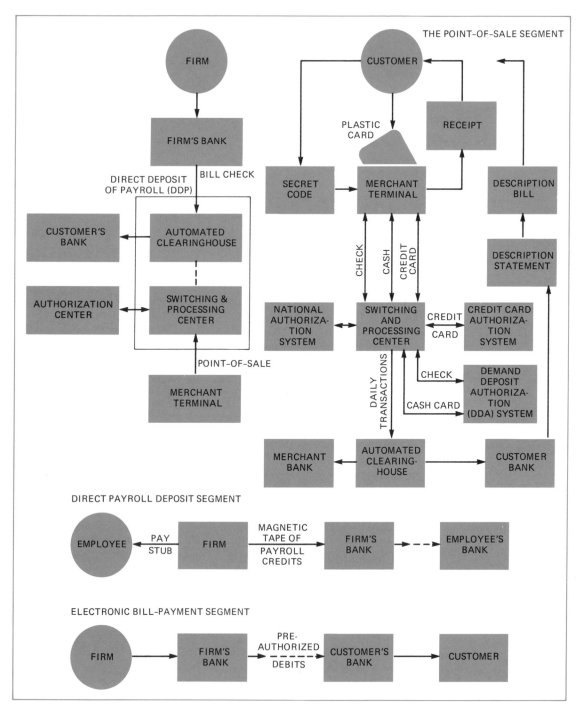

FIGURE 22.5   RETAIL POINT-OF-SALE TERMINALS

is encoded the name of the customer, account number, and other pertinent information.

When a retail purchase is made, the clerk keys in such data as the amount of the purchase, the stock or part number, and quantity ordered. Then the credit card is inserted into the terminal and customer data are read from it. All of this information is relayed by telephone lines to the central computer. The computer first processes the credit authorization, checking the customer's credit limit and status. If the account is in good order, the terminal posts the debit to the customer's account and credits the retailer's account. The terminal then prints out a hard copy receipt of the transaction for the customer.

BANK TELLER SEGMENT.   Principal banks tied to the system are equipped with a number of teller terminals. (See Figure 22.6.) These terminals are located at the bank teller windows and are used to process normal banking transactions for the system. Merchants and customers may make deposits or withdrawals from them. The teller enters the desired amount of deposit

FIGURE 22.6

TELLER TERMINAL

FIGURE 22.6

TELLER TERMINAL

FIGURE 22.7

REMOTE BANKING

TERMINAL

or withdrawal by keying in the account number and data. The terminal posts the transfer accordingly.

REMOTE BANK OR "MONEY MACHINE" SEGMENT.   A group of specially equipped money-changing terminals, connected to the system, are located in shopping centers, supermarkets, and other public places. (See Figure 22.7.) They provide users with a 24-hour banking service.

A customer inserts his or her credit-money card into the terminal, keys in a code number, and enters the transaction request—deposit, withdrawal, or transfer of funds between accounts. Even direct cash withdrawals are acceptable. The terminal checks the account status, proceeds with an authorization, and services the request. No live teller is involved in the transaction. Virtually all bank services, except for large loans, may be processed by the "money machine" terminal.

DIRECT PAYROLL SEGMENT.   Paycheck distribution may be processed by the system in different ways. Some employers will simply mail their employees paychecks that are then endorsed and deposited in the bank. Sometimes deposits will be made through the mail.

PROBLEMS RELATED TO INFORMATION SYSTEMS

One of the limitations of the information system is the potential for misuse of stored data. Many problems exist when the system holds vital data on a firm's customers, personnel, goods, inventory, services, and so on. In the following pages we consider the accessibility of computers and data to users and the protection of important files. Protection can often involve costly and time-consuming procedures to prevent unauthorized access, resulting in theft and misuse of data. Finally, the question of centralization versus decentralization of the information system must be considered.

ACCESSIBILITY

The modern data center is often considered a support unit whose services extend across many organization and division lines. This concept raises several questions regarding management and control of the data processing center and access to files. Where does the data center fit into the organization chart? Who is to have control? What security measures should be instituted? What jobs are suitable and acceptable for run? What jobs are to be given highest priority? Who should schedule jobs? What kinds of data should be gathered? Who shall have terminals and passwords?

Computer installations must be fully utilized if they are to be run economically. This is particularly important in large data centers with expensive, high-capacity hardware and a highly skilled supporting staff. Close attention to scheduling and priorities is important. For this reason, few large data centers permit hands-on operation of large computers. They prefer to control access, use, and scheduling of the machine for maximum efficiency.

Originally, the same individual programmed, operated, and, in fact, sometimes built a computer. During the late 1940s and early 1950s, a computer operator had to be a "jack of all trades." Only those who understood the internal mechanisms of the computer could write programs. Today, such knowledge is no longer necessary to use the computer effectively in business.

Sidney Harris

"The databank is slightly mistaken. I'm not an alcoholic. I never attempted to assassinate the governor. I haven't been married 17 times. I don't owe $86,000 in gambling debts . . ."

OPEN SHOP.   Early computer installations were operated by an open shop or "hands-on" arrangement. In "hands-on," programmers operate the computer as well as write the program. Today only a few computer installations allow hands-on use, and usually only on the smaller machines. Although it is convenient for many programmers, the hands-on arrangement tends to be inefficient because work cannot be grouped or scheduled to increase productivity.

A problem with hands-on use is the difficulty in maintaining security in the computer area. Important business records, documents, files, and confidential data are often accessible in the room. This exposes confidential records and vital information to anyone in the center.

CLOSED SHOP.   Most computer installations now maintain a closed shop or "hands-off" arrangement. Programmers must submit their programs to a control clerk who in turn gives it to a trained, supervised operator. The advantages of this arrangement are that only qualified operators have access to the machine and tight security can be maintained in the computer area. In addition, since similar work can be grouped and run in batches, output is increased and rush work can receive preference.

TELEPROCESSING.   A third method of gaining access to a computer is by a remote terminal. Remote terminals have become an important means of accessing computers and data banks. In one sense, each user has "open shop" access from his or her desk or office, and a staff of professional operators is available to process jobs. The next decade should see great expansion in the use of remote terminals and teleprocessing.

SECURITY

In many firms, the data center has become the central depository for the firm's most important records, statistics, data, and files. The loss of these records and data could threaten the very existence of the firm.

The data center is subject to both internal and external hazards. Earthquakes, fires, and other natural disasters are external threats. Theft, vandalism, fraud, and unauthorized use of data constitute internal dangers that threaten security.

It is essential to protect the privacy of important records and data. Much of the information stored in a data center is irreplaceable. Money from insurance policies may replace equipment, but this money may not be able to undo the damage if records are lost or tampered with.

Several measures can be taken to reduce these security and disaster threats. They include screening personnel, physical plant security, backup copies of files, and provisions for substitute computers in emergencies.

Screening Personnel Extensive security and personnel investigations are made on employees who will work in the data center or have access to files. Security bonds are sometimes required.

Physical Plant Protection In an effort to provide maximum security for the computer installation, data centers use several techniques to deter unauthorized entry. These include burglar alarms, keycard door locks, and security police. Other measures include the installation of closed-circuit television, antisabotage devices, and ultrasonic and audio detection systems. Figure 22.8 illustrates a double-door entry control system.

Backup Files Since it is virtually impossible to protect against all natural and physical calamities, backup files and computers are often used. Backup files are duplicate files maintained in another building or at a remote location. The files may be transmitted or updated by telephone communications links. Some duplicate files are shipped to storage facilities.

FIGURE 22.8 DOUBLE-DOOR ENTRY CONTROL SYSTEM

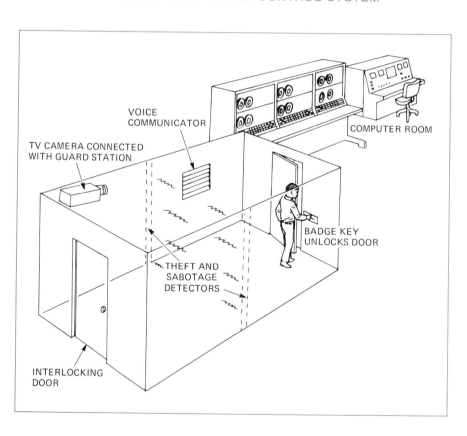

Backup computers are used to reduce the problem of disruption in service. Important programs and operating routines are written to run on several different computers. Arrangements are made with other companies, service bureaus, or other branches of the firm to run the jobs on their computers in the event of trouble.

Unauthorized Use of Files Special labels and passwords are used to limit access to certain files. Elaborate software and hardware systems have been developed to prevent unauthorized users from gaining access to data files.

CENTRALIZED VERSUS DECENTRALIZED DATA PROCESSING

A major question facing a firm's top-level management is whether data processing facilities should be centralized or decentralized. Figure 22.9 shows these two systems.

Should one large computer be purchased to serve the needs of the entire firm? Or would several smaller computers located in different branches or cities be more useful? The answer depends on the firm's needs—its volume of data processing and other factors. Generally, a high volume of centralized data processing operations justifies a large computer installation. In this way a firm has the advantage of operating one large computer, with its greater power, speed, and storage capacity. Security problems are minimized at the same time.

With decentralized data processing, on the other hand, decisions can be made closer to the source. Since they will usually be concerned with a smaller part of the total enterprise, they are less subject to gross error. But decentralizing can often mean difficulties in standardizing procedures and coordinating data processing functions.

Distributive Data Processing During the past decade, the cost of computer systems, including memory, has declined considerably. On the other hand, the costs of communications lines and data transmission have increased. These factors have led to a reduction in the economies gained from large-scale centralized computer systems. Furthermore, the introduction of intelligent terminals—computer terminals with integrated microprocessors built into them—provides computer capability at a reasonable cost. (See Figure 22.10.)

Many firms have therefore moved to decentralized data processing systems, called distributive systems. These systems, which use low-cost, smaller equipment, allow data to be processed locally. They also provide greater reliability since the entire firm is not dependent upon a single computer to do all of its work or to maintain its data bank and files. Such systems are often integrated into *networks* or groups of related, small computers.

FIGURE 22.9   CENTRALIZED AND DISTRIBUTIVE DATA
PROCESSING SYSTEMS

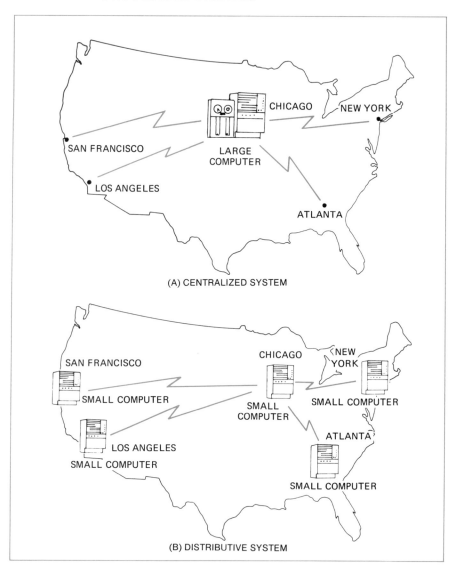

(A) CENTRALIZED SYSTEM

(B) DISTRIBUTIVE SYSTEM

KEY TERMS

Closed shop	Information system
Data bank	MIB
Distributive data processing	MIS
EFTS	Open shop
Information retrieval system	

FIGURE 22.10   INTELLIGENT TERMINAL

EXERCISES
1. What are information systems?
2. List three advantages of information systems.
3. What are the elements of an information system?
4. What is a data bank, and what kinds of information might be in it?
5. What are the steps involved in structuring a data bank?
6. What are management information systems, and what type of information can they produce?
7. What is an information retrieval system, and how is it accessed?
8. What is an electronic funds transfer system?
9. What are some of the questions that must be answered when considering management and control of the data processing center?
10. What is the difference between open and closed shop operations?
11. What measures are taken to reduce security and disaster threats to data centers?
12. What is centralized data processing, and when is its use indicated?
13. What is decentralized data processing, and what are its advantages?

PART SEVEN

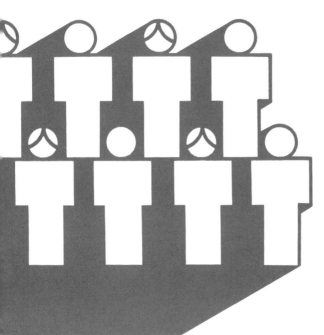

THE
COMPUTER
IN
SOCIETY

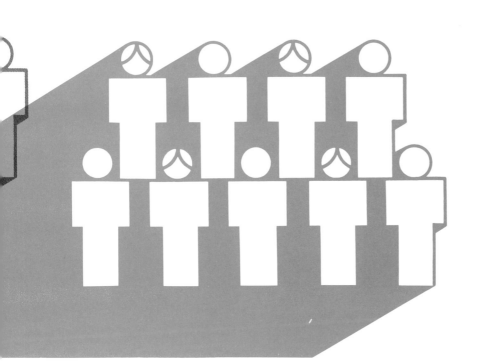

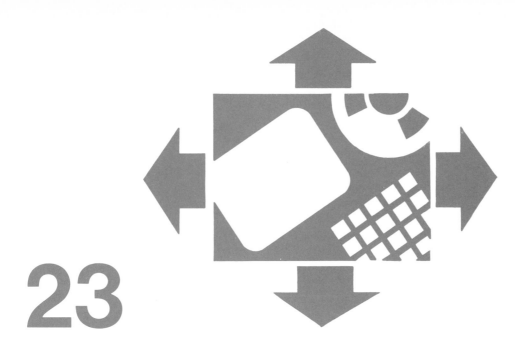

23

IMPACT ON SOCIETY

The computer, like all other great inventions, has permanently altered our way of life. Our society will never be the same again. There is no way of stopping progress or declaring a moratorium on change. Whether for good or for bad, the computer influences how we think, how we live, our way of conducting business, our interaction with each other, and even how we perceive ourselves.

This chapter examines the impact the computer has had on the social, legal, educational, and political structures in our society.

HOW PEOPLE SEE THE COMPUTER

People vary greatly in their attitudes toward the computer . . . often in relation to the age group to which they belong.

Adults educated before the computer age may fear and resent its intrusion. They remember a different way of life—slower, less demanding, more predictable. Some members of this generation consider the computer a villain that has forced change and automation upon them too fast. Many see it as the cause of unemployment, relocation, and social unrest. They worry about the long-term effects of the computer and automation. At the same time, this generation has seen technology help bring about a higher standard of living, improved health care, faster communications, and more efficient business operations.

Those educated during the 1950s and early 1960s—the years that gave birth to the computer—react somewhat differently. Major events and changes have always been occurring in their lives . . . each one hailed as the panacea for the world's problems. And each one, in turn, failing to keep all the promises, indeed often creating different problems for society to solve.

Most people in this age group have very mixed feelings about the computer. They find themselves interacting with it more and more—in their jobs, in all aspects of personal finances—and yet many still feel a strong sense of mysticism and amazement toward this "giant electronic brain which can out-think a thousand scientists."

Young people educated since the advent of the computer have a very different reaction. To them, along with TV, jet airplanes, and the atom bomb, it's part of their lives. It's always been there. It's just a tool like the typewriter, telephone, or pocket calculator, to be mastered and used.

EMPLOYMENT

One of the most important and direct ways in which the computer has affected people is in the area of employment. The computer has brought a great deal of automation to business and industry. It has sometimes resulted in unemployment, relocation of families, job transfers, and extensive retraining of personnel. Alienation, distrust, and fear often result from such forced changes. On the other hand, the computer has created many new jobs, unheard of only a decade or two ago. (See Figure 23.1.)

For some, the computer has meant new goals and aspirations, higher incomes, better working conditions, and more free time. For others, it has meant layoffs, periods of unemployment, and uncertainty about the future.

LEISURE TIME AND RECREATION

Computer technology influences the amount of time we spend on the job and how we use our time when we are off the job. In many instances, the computer has increased industrial productivity, allowing factories and shops to produce more goods and services with less input of human time, energy, and effort. This gives us more time to read, play, travel, relax, think, or just daydream.

One interesting development is the growth of the computer hobbyist. The computer has become a hobby or avocational interest for thousands of men, women, and children across the country. (See Figure 23.2.) They are building computers from parts or kits, writing programs, playing computer

FIGURE 23.1 COMPUTER LIBRARY AND LIBRARIANS

FIGURE 23.2

THE COMPUTER PLAYS CHESS

games, or designing and studying computers and information systems. This fast-growing activity has led to the emergence of hundreds of clubs that meet regularly to exchange programs, software, and hardware, share ideas, buy equipment as group purchases, etc.

PRESSURE TOWARD UNIFORMITY AND STANDARDIZATION

Of particular significance is the pressure the computer exerts on society toward uniformity and standardization. All names must fit within the number of spaces allocated for the field; responses to questions must conform to one of those in the list so that the proper code number can be checked; items produced by a manufacturing process controlled by computer will be held to a high quality control standard, but be all alike. (See Figure 23.3.)

How will this tendency toward uniformity be developed by society? Will it be used to create a dull, lifeless, and rigid society? Or will it be used to stimulate diversity and individuality? To free people from structure, or to force them into rigid molds?

IMPACT UPON THE GROUP

The computer has an effect on how people respond and interact in groups. It is influencing our working structures, play, travel, and family groups; it has affected our communication, educational, and transportation systems. (See Figure 23.4.)

The computer is changing some aspects of our social status system. An individual's status in our society is often measured by his or her job, amount of money in the bank, or kind of auto or home. Another important criterion of social status is the individual's proximity to control centers in an organization or system. In some areas of society, those closest to the computer and the associated data banks enjoy higher status and influence than others.

Huge empires of people, machines, money, and resources have been built around the computer. One need only look at the giant data processing and paperwork mills found in various governmental agencies, schools, and large corporations to see part of the impact of the computer.

Consider the social implications of the Consumer Price Index (CPI), which is published regularly by the U.S. Department of Labor. This index is used as a cost of living index and is the basis for granting salary and wage adjustments to millions of Americans. Yet the preparation, gathering, and processing of information is in the hands of a few data processing professionals.

FIGURE 23.3   UNIFORMITY AND STANDARDIZATION IN INDUSTRY

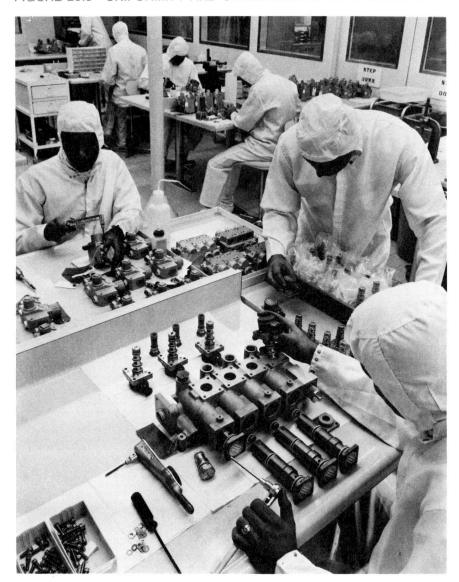

INDUSTRIAL COMPUTER MONOPOLIES

The rich railroad, steel, and oil barons of the past century have been replaced by a new type of industrial giant, the multinational industrial conglomerate. Control of these monopolies is one of society's major problems. In the

FIGURE 23.4   COMPUTER-BASED CAR POOL SYSTEM, DETROIT AREA

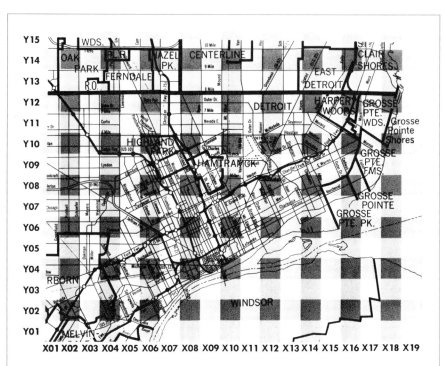

computer industry, for example, IBM Corporation controls approximately 70 percent of the large-scale computer market. It also is a major force in computer and business machine sales and leases, software development, programming, and business systems. In 1974 IBM ranked number two in net income and ninth in net sales of all industrial firms in the United States.

The last decade has seen the demise of many competitors, including the computer divisions of RCA, General Electric, Xerox, and Singer.

Such concentration of industrial power has many critics. Suits by the Department of Justice and attempts by Congress to form an Industrial Reorganization Commission are efforts at reducing the power, scope, and size of such giant conglomerates.

DEPENDENCE UPON COMPUTERS

There is little doubt that society, business, and government are largely dependent upon computers. Without them we simply could not process the

FIGURE 23.5 COMPUTER-DESIGNED FEED RECIPES INCREASE EGG PRODUCTION

vast amount of data our society consumes . . . quickly, accurately, and inexpensively. (See Figure 23.5.)

Is it sound or safe for a society to become so totally dependent upon any industrial machine or process for its existence? (See Figure 23.6.) What would happen, if for whatever reason, suddenly all the giant computers in the country failed? What would happen to the millions of paychecks, social security checks, internal revenue documents, and other matters processed by computer? Could business and government survive? Should a small army of people be maintained as a backup in the event such a failure should occur?

There are no simple answers. Clearly, we depend upon these machines; but that's also true of the electric light, the automobile, telephone, and TV. Some people predict that because of computers and calculators we will lose our ability to reason and think. In another generation, we will have forgotten how to perform mathematics and solve problems.

Others find this view simplistic. They believe the computer increases our abilities. It forces us to be more logical in our reasoning, to analyze problems more critically, to state problems in quantitative terms. They point out that computers, after all, only follow directions. Someone has to prepare those

FIGURE 23.6   SCIENTIST GUIDING LUNAR MODULE IN MOON
                      FLIGHT SIMULATION

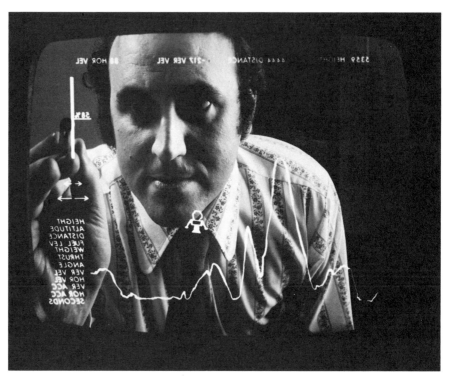

directions. What the computer will do, it is to be hoped, is free us from the
drudgery of dull, repetitious details and allow us to spend our time developing
creative, innovative solutions to age-old problems.

LEGAL CONSIDERATIONS

Questions have been raised about the legal implications of computerized
information systems. Computer errors have denied individuals credit, loans,
or the right to purchase a home or automobile. They have caused people to
lose their jobs or have their lives or homes placed in jeopardy. Such
occurrences are forcing society to take another look at our laws regarding
fault and liability.

   Who is at fault when the computer makes a mistake and lives are
disrupted or millions of dollars lost? People have been erroneously picked
up by police and put in jail because of computer errors. (See Figure 23.7.)

FIGURE 23.7   POLICEMEN CHECKING COMPUTER CRIME FILE

In one instance, a driver was pulled over to the curb and shot and killed while being arrested. Later, police discovered that a computer error had been made in processing his driver's license number. Who is responsible for this death? The clerk who entered the data into the computer, the computer programmer, the systems engineer, the computer manufacturer, or the policemen? Or is our entire society at fault for allowing the situation to develop?

Other legal issues concern property rights. Should computer programs and programming logic be patented? Some computer programs may cost millions of dollars to write, debug, test, and document. Questions concerning protection against theft and unauthorized use must be considered and answered.

THE NEW CRIMES

The computer has forced society to take a new look at crime and even to redefine criminal behavior as it relates to business practices. The old crimes of fraud, burglary, theft, robbery, breaking and entering, and embezzlement are, of course, still with us. But a host of new crimes, executed on or assisted by a computer, are occurring with increasing frequency. These crimes are often very subtle in nature and extremely difficult to detect. Electronic breaking and entering of a computer file is quick and quiet, and leaves no trace such as a jimmied lock or fingerprints.

The new criminal is not the unsophisticated clerk who sees the opportunity to pocket a few dollars from the till. This criminal is a sophisticated person with skills in computer technology, programming, communication science, and cryptology. He or she can steal millions of dollars and cover up virtually every trace, using the computer to hide any clues.

Some of the new crimes consist of entering fraudulent data into a computer, changing a program to print out unauthorized checks or release funds, and altering records to conceal cash thefts. Some crimes consist of merely stealing data or information. Others involve stealing computer processing time.

The New "Cops" As a result of the new crimes, a group of computer "cops" have evolved. These individuals, trained in the computer sciences, accounting, programming, and auditing fields, use specialized computer programs to detect fraud and embezzlement. For example, one system, "Culprit," sold by Cullinane Corporation, is an electronic data processing auditing program. It consists of a group of routines that leave an audit trail and provide an elaborate series of controls. A set of monitor programs control access to the auditing system. Culprit also trains auditors to use the system to detect criminals attempting computer fraud.

The Los Angeles Sheriff's Department has implemented a special training program for deputies who handle computer crime investigations. The program, which requires six months to complete, brings an investigator to the point where he or she can understand the way computer thieves operate and how to apprehend them.

A number of special techniques have been developed by firms to provide a high level of computer security. These include passwords and identification

"Do you realize that without computers it would be impossible to assess the impact of computers on our society?"

codes, locks and keycards, TV cameras and alarm systems. No one can enter the secured computer room until he or she presents a badge keycard, which contains a numeric or alphabetic code. If anyone attempts to gain access to the computer room with an illegal key or number, the system sounds an alarm, and closed circuit TV records the image of the intruder.

IMPACT ON EDUCATION

Educational institutions across the country are experiencing a certain amount of change and stress as a result of the computer. All levels of education —elementary, secondary, college, and university—as well as all instructional, curricular, and administrative processes are being affected.

The computer has proven to be a useful, sometimes revolutionary, tool in the presentation of instruction to students, as well as assisting teachers in managing instruction. It is used for a variety of administrative tasks, such as processing student records, counseling and advisement, and grade reporting. It is appearing in classrooms, laboratories, lecture halls, admissions offices, libraries, study halls, and dormitories around the country.

Role of the Computer

In computer-assisted instruction (CAI), the student interacts directly with the computer via a terminal during the learning process. The computer may either supplement or replace the teacher. The student is given instructions, is asked questions, and receives responses from the computer. CAI can provide drill work, exercises, and remedial or enrichment material, prepare tests, or simply carry on a dialogue with the student. Figure 23.8 shows some students involved in CAI.

In the computer-managed instruction mode (CMI), the computer is used to assist the teacher in keeping track of student progress. The instructor or teacher, rather than the student, interacts with the computer. The computer is used to grade or prepare tests, maintain roll records, prepare rosters, do statistical evaluations on classes, or prepare enrichment or remedial programs for individual students or entire classes.

Both CAI and computer-managed instruction can be used to provide a degree of individualization that a teacher alone cannot do. Each student can progress at his or her own rate and can study different materials that are relevant to his or her particular interests or aptitudes.

Other attributes of the computer are also advantageous to the learning process. A computer never loses patience or interest or becomes tired. Studies have shown that many students learn better and faster at a lower cost and have greater retention with computer-managed or computer-assisted instruction.

The individualization made possible by computers can change the whole approach to education. Large, central schools can be replaced by a

FIGURE 23.8   STUDENTS USING INTERACTIVE TERMINALS

decentralized system with terminals in the students' homes. Education can
be delivered to each student at the most convenient time and place.

This raises many questions. What will be the teacher's role if the work
load is taken over by the computer? Will he or she become a manager of
instruction, or merely a programmer? Will the human aspect of the
instructional process be affected if people are replaced, even in part, by
machines? What will the next generation be like if they have been trained,
educated, influenced, nurtured, and stimulated by a computer? What will
be their attitudes toward "teachers" and society?

Curriculum   Other questions raised by the computer concern the curriculum and content
of course work in the future. What kind of knowledge will students need
to survive in our future society? Learning about the computer itself may
be the most important. The educated student will need to know how
computers work and are programmed, their potential, problems, and liabilities,
and how to use them as a general purpose problem-solving tool.

One of the big challenges of education today is to teach students to cope
with a rapid rate of change. Alvin Toffler points out that it is not change
itself, but the rate of change, that creates chaos in society. Computers have

Minicomputers Used on Cars to Improve Fuel Economy

Minicomputers are likely to be part of all new cars by 1980–81 to help meet stricter pollution limits and demands for better fuel economy, according to a top executive of American Motors Corporation.

George E. Brown, AMC's executive director of vehicle emissions and safety, said that, in order to meet the double goals of economy and pollution control, cars of the 1980s will have to make progress in three areas: (1) more control of exhaust gas as it leaves the engine, (2) more precise ignition control, and (3) better control of the fuel and air mixture being burned.

Brown said minicomputers are one of the few currently known ways to meet both standards—"unless we have some oddball breakthrough."

General Motors Corporation announced that it would make the first use of a microprocessor aboard a production automobile on some 1977 Oldsmobile Toronados. The small computer device will be used continuously to adjust the car's timing for better fuel economy and pollution control, GM said.

Other automobile makers are developing other ways to utilize the computer to improve car performance. Ford Motor Company, for example, is using a computerized mechanism to bring to fruition a 60-year-old dream: turning off half the cylinders in an engine when full power is no longer needed.

A tiny computer is connected to sensors that continually monitor engine speed, throttle setting, and several other factors. When the sensors indicate that full power is no longer needed, the valves on three cylinders close. This usually occurs at about 45 miles per hour. The cylinders will remain off until the car accelerates rapidly or slows down to 25 miles per hour, at which point they will refire.

Ford engineers still have some problems to solve: reducing vibration enough to allow operation on three cylinders when the car is idling, controlling the increased emissions of nitrogen oxide vapors, and smoothing out the rough feeling when the engine shifts from six to three cylinders.

The major advantage of the on-again, off-again engine is that it is expected to boost fuel mileage an average of at least 10 percent. It is an option on some 1977 trucks and is expected to be used more widely on 1979 models.

SOURCES: "Autos: On Again, Off Again," *Newsweek*, October 4, 1976. "Minicomputers Likely on All New Models in 1980," Harry Anderson, Times Staff Writer, *Los Angeles Times*, September 13, 1976. © 1976, *Los Angeles Times*. Reprinted by permission.

been accused of placing the fast pulley on the social machine and cranking up the speed control. And computer technology itself changes so fast that textbooks are often obsolete by the time they are printed. Should we stop teaching about computers? Should we place a moratorium on the introduction of new technology into society? Should we concentrate on teaching students the meaning and implications of established technology before introducing them to the new?

THE CASHLESS SOCIETY

The Electronic Funds Transfer System (EFTS) was discussed in Chapter 22. Now we consider the social implications of the largely cashless society that may result from the widespread application of EFTS.

The EFTS enables goods to be purchased, merchandise sold, employees paid, and funds deposited or withdrawn from banks without cash actually changing hands. The point-of-sale (POS) terminal, computer systems, money machines, and bank teller terminals make possible an electronic flow of funds between employer, employee, customer, and merchant without the use of checks or the mails.

The EFTS will change the time frame in which sales, purchases, and payments are made. Transactions will be posted immediately rather than waiting for bills and payments to move through the mails. For example, employees could be paid hourly, and their wages credited throughout the business day to their accounts. Purchases could be billed to customers' accounts at the time of purchase instead of waiting for the usual billing and collection cycle.

The cashless society will reduce the need for physically mailing checks between banks, customers, and employees. The government has already tested a system that sends reels of magnetic tape to banks to deposit funds into social security accounts. This system will reduce delays in payments to recipients, reduce lost or stolen checks, and provide a more complete and accurate record of transactions.

The social implications of this system are manifold. We will ultimately be able to buy everything from a postage stamp to a new home or automobile using a "cash card." On the one hand this will stimulate purchasing because of the "credit card psychology"—"buy now, pay later." This may encourage people to overspend and go into considerable debt. On the other hand, the instantaneous processing of these transactions may prevent people from spending money they do not have and reduce business losses due to bad credit risks.

IMPACT OF DATA BANKS

It has been reported that there are five files on every living American, containing information from the moment of birth to some time after death.* The last decade has seen a huge growth and proliferation of data banks in government and private industry. These banks collect information on an

*Prism, June 1974.

FIGURE 23.9   COMPUTER KEEPS TRACK OF PAPAGO INDIANS'
HEALTH RECORDS

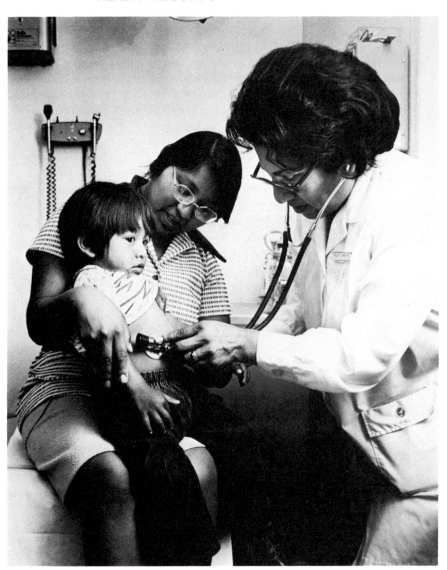

individual's health, employment, family life, medical records, and social
habits. (See Figure 23.9.)

The Department of Defense maintains a data bank on 1.6 million persons.
The FBI files cover 450,000 people. The National Driver Registration files
cover over 3,300,000 people. The Small Business Administration files
encompass over 500,000 citizens, and the IRS intelligence file over 220,000,

not to mention the IRS data base on each taxpayer. Add to this more than 204 million records maintained by the U.S. Department of Census and another 212 million files on Social Security participants.

The social impact of this massive data gathering and collection system must be considered carefully. The dissemination of information into the wrong hands creates many problems and invades one's right to privacy. Data on citizens can be used to hurt their employment situations, their ability to obtain credit or financing, or their entrance into schools and universities.

On the positive side, data banks provide business and government with a valuable resource of information on which to make sound and rational decisions. They produce factual, quantitative data that can be used to improve service, facilities, and efficiency and to reduce waste.

STANDARD UNIVERSAL IDENTIFIER

It has been proposed that the government issue a standard universal identifying number (SUI) to every citizen that would remain with the individual from birth until death. It would be used as the basis for maintaining and preparing files, posting to accounts, and keying all information regarding that person.

Some have argued that the issuance of an SUI to all citizens would create more problems than it would solve. On the one hand, it would eliminate or reduce errors in identifying files. Built-in error-check digits would prevent transposing of digits or dropping digits when communicating the number.

On the other hand, the SUI could provide government or business firms with a "key" to a citizen's total file. This would allow them to gain access to a variety of information that would not be available otherwise. In the wrong hands, the SUI could be used to spy and maintain surveillance files and dossiers on innocent citizens.

SOCIAL SECURITY NUMBER

It has been proposed that the social security number (SSN) now in use be used as an SUI. There are inherent problems in this idea. In some instances, dozens of citizens are using the same SSN to identify their accounts. The SSN does not have a built-in checking feature or check digit. Since Congress authorized the SSN number to be used principally within the social security system, there is some question about the legality of using it for private commercial use. Regardless of whether the SSN should be used as an SUI, it has become a *de facto* SUI. Each year, more and more business firms and governmental agencies use the SSN as their principal file identifier.

LEGISLATION TO CONTROL THE USE OF DATA BANKS

Several pieces of legislation have been passed at the state and national levels to control the abuses and misuse of credit information and data banks.

Fair Credit Reporting Act

The Fair Credit Reporting Act was passed by Congress in an attempt to regulate abuses found in the consumer credit reporting industry. The act requires agencies to follow reasonable procedures to safeguard credit information and gives the responsibility of enforcement to the Federal Trade Commission. It requires that a subject be informed when a credit investigation is being conducted.

Freedom of Information Act

Passed in 1970, this act gives citizens and other agencies the right to have access to many kinds of government data. It was an attempt by Congress to provide for the open flow of data in government and to protect the public's right to know about government activities. A safeguard was built in to protect the rights of individuals. It provided that government agencies could withhold data of a personal nature from the public. With this major exception, the Freedom of Information Act established a formal declaration of availability of records and information of all government agencies.

Federal Reports Act

This piece of legislation was designed to minimize the burden of furnishing information to the government and regulate its collection. It forbids a federal agency from conducting or sponsoring the collection of identical items of data on ten or more persons, other than federal employees, without approval from the Office of Management and Budget.

Privacy Act of 1974

This act requires that each federal agency identify each system of records that it maintains and regularly review the contents of its files to assure that information is necessary and relevant. It specifies that files may not contain data on citizens' religious or political affiliations or activities.

The Privacy Act requires each federal agency to publish a list of the systems of records it maintains. This list must include the name and location of the data system and the category of individual on which records are maintained.

Information must be made accessible and available to citizens. Each federal agency may establish a fee to copy a record, but it cannot charge for locating or searching for it. Agencies are required to acknowledge a receipt of a request for information within ten days. In cases where an individual disputes the accuracy of an agency's records, the agency is required to note this in the file. Finally, a citizen may ask for an accounting from the agency of all disclosures made from his or her file.

MAJOR SOCIAL ISSUES TO BE CONSIDERED

Limitations on space preclude an extensive discussion of the social issues raised by the computer. The list below summarizes some of the principal concerns that must be resolved:

1. How can society preserve individuality while fully implementing the computer? Ways will have to be found to utilize the computer's capabilities to benefit creativity and individuality rather than to foster stifling standardization.
2. How can privacy and individual freedom be preserved in the face of expanding data banks? Social controls will have to be developed and implemented to control abuses and misuse of data while enabling us to exploit the advantages of data banks.
3. How can society prevent the loss of humanism in the computer age? Ways will have to be found to allow people to grow and live in a mechanized, automated world without experiencing the negative aspects of a machine-manipulated society.
4. How can society preserve its independence? Ways will have to be found for society to continue to utilize the computer but not become so dependent upon it that people lose control or cannot survive without it.
5. How can employment and jobs be preserved in the face of continuing automation? As machines take over more activities, ways must be found to direct people's intellectual potential into areas that are beneficial to the development of society.
6. How will legal issues regarding failures and mistakes made by the computer be resolved? Who will be responsible and to what extent when errors are made by a computer? Will computer malpractice insurance have to be written for computer programmers and operators?
7. How can feelings and attitudes of alienation and resentment be handled in the face of widespread introduction of computers into the educational, social, and political structures?
8. How can we moderate the introduction of new technology (such as new computers and languages) into society at a rate that allows humans to respond without frustration and "future shock"?

SOME PRINCIPAL NEEDS OF THE FUTURE

There are several important aspects of the future for which society must prepare in order to ease the widening proliferation of computers.

1. COMPUTER LITERACY.   There is a growing need for people of all ages to learn more about the computer—its potential and its limitations and shortcomings.
2. REGULATION AND CONTROL OF COMPUTER USE.   The introduction of computers into society must be guided and controlled to minimize stresses and disruptions.
3. INDUSTRY STANDARDS.   The growth of computer languages, data banks, and communications indicates the need for a system of standards. New machines and systems will have to be able to interface and communicate with one another with a minimum of adjustment. Without standards, society may find itself helplessly adrift in a world of machines, languages, and systems that cannot work together.
4. CONTROL OF COMPUTER MONOPOLIES.   There will be an increased need to control monopolies in the computer industry. Regulations will be needed to place limits on firms that seek to control entire markets, languages, or software to the detriment of society.
5. RESPONSIVE EDUCATION.   The computer and other new technology places heavy demands on schools and colleges to expose the student to a much wider body of knowledge, much of it more technical. But there must still be a balance preserved with general education and the humanities.
6. COMPUTER-INDUCED ALIENATION.   Ways must be found to deal with the distrust and fear of computerized activites.
7. THE COMPUTER'S ROLE IN SOCIETY.   Society will have to define what tasks are best suited for machines and which are best suited for people. Individuals displaced from traditional roles must be helped to learn new ones. For while the computer takes over people's roles in some areas, it creates new jobs that require trained personnel.

KEY TERMS   CAI   SSN
               Cashless society   SUI
               CMI

EXERCISES   1. List five areas in which the computer has had significant social impact.
               2. What efforts are being made to control large computer monopolies?
               3. List three major legal concerns regarding the use of computers in society.
               4. What techniques are used to combat the new crimes?
               5. Contrast the differences between CAI and CMI.
               6. What major changes may result from the cashless society?
               7. What are the benefits and dangers of data banks?

8. How does the SUI differ from the SSN?
9. Why is the SSN unsuitable for use as an SUI?
10. List and briefly describe three major pieces of legislation that control data banks.
11. Obtain a list of all major files maintained by your school. Describe the kinds of records kept in each file.
12. Check the credit cards in your possession. Determine which cards use the SSN as the file identifier. Is there a check digit in the number?

APPENDIXES

A

EMPLOYMENT
IN DATA PROCESSING

Electronic data processing offers interesting, satisfying career opportunities for men and women who have the necessary skills, training, and experience. The growth rate of data processing exceeds that of most other American industries and is expected to continue to increase very rapidly.

Types of Jobs Data processing is a diverse field employing individuals in business establishments, government, schools and universities, and private institutions. Most individuals in data processing are employed in the business area in the following categories: manufacturing, public utilities (transportation, electric power, communications), wholesale trade, retail trade, finance (real estate, insurance), and services.

Job opportunities exist in relatively small as well as large firms, in different geographic areas, and in communities of all sizes.

As more firms acquire EDP systems, more jobs will be created for those with the necessary skills, knowledge, and abilities. Other jobs related to manual accounting, such as hand-posting in ledgers, filing, and operating a comptometer, are being absorbed in EDP.

515

Job environments differ widely. Some individuals work in relative isolation in a private office. Other travel thousands of miles each year and meet hundreds of people. Some jobs require a high degree of manual dexterity; others, virtually none. Some require years of study in mathematics or electronics; for others, a practical knowledge of selling and marketing principles is basic.

SALARIES.   Salaries vary according to job classification, years of experience, and training. They vary also with the geographic area, need for individuals with a given specialty, and current business and economic conditions. As a rule, salaries paid in data processing are above the national average and reflect the degree of training and experience. As in any business, however, a surplus of applicants in a particular job category will affect salaries.

WORKING CONDITIONS AND BENEFITS.   Generally, employment in the data processing industry requires little physical effort. Since most firms house their data processing equipment in modern, air-conditioned quarters, EDP employees, as a rule, work in newer, better equipped, and more comfortable quarters than other clerical and office workers.

Some firms offer fringe benefits such as educational allowances. Company health plans, profit sharing, bonus programs, and liberal vacation benefits are common in this industry.

SKILLS AND APTITUDES.   Generally, the specific job determines the skills and aptitudes required. The student should talk to a school counselor or guidance officer and review aptitude test scores and interest measures to evaluate his or her capabilities.

EDUCATION AND TRAINING

Schools and Colleges

Schools, colleges, and universities offer a variety of courses in data processing.

INDIVIDUAL COURSES.   Short courses may last from six or ten weeks to one year. They usually cover a specific, but limited skill. A course in COBOL or FORTRAN programming is an example. Another course may train the student to be a computer console operator for a particular brand and size of computer or to operate a single machine such as the keypunch or verifier.

These short courses permit the student to enter the industry with a minimum of time and money devoted to training and preparation. However, for advancement and greater opportunity, additional academic coursework, training, and supervised on-the-job instruction are usually required.

COMPREHENSIVE PROGRAMS—COMMUNITY COLLEGES.   Many community colleges offer two-year programs that grant the student either an A.A. degree or a certificate of proficiency in data processing. Either of these is valuable on entry into the job market.

The emphasis in coursework varies. Some community colleges stress data processing for business and industry with the curriculum designed to suit students for employment in insurance, banking, manufacturing companies, and government. Other schools stress equipment and hardware and provide coursework in practical operations and maintenance. The student may, for example, be taught how to service card punches and tape readers, and be given instruction in electronics and electromechanical theory and practice, computer logic, arithmetic and mechanics, including trouble-shooting, testing, and repairing computer systems.

Still other colleges offer strong mathematically oriented computer courses, which stress numerical methods and the mathematical elements of computer programming.

Graduates of a two-year course may qualify as beginning programmers, salespersons, or for jobs in computer maintenance or installation. Or the student may transfer to a university and pursue a B.S. or B.A. degree.

COLLEGES AND UNIVERSITIES.   As in the two-year programs, EDP curriculums vary greatly in the four-year schools and universities. Most programs have been developed to meet special needs or the employment demands of firms in a given community.

Most four-year schools offer courses in programming languages and an introduction to data processing. Business schools offer undergraduate and graduate work in business management and business systems analysis. Other programs develop information systems technology, systems analysis, or computer technology.

Many universities offer graduate work—leading to M.B.A. degrees—in electronic data processing, computer science, and business administration. Colleges of Education frequently offer undergraduate and graduate concentrations in data processing for teachers through the Business Education program.

Home Study Courses

Several equipment manufacturers and private schools offer comprehensive home study courses in basic computer systems, programming, and systems engineering. These programs utilize programmed instruction, film strips, audio and video tapes, self-testing, and supervised reading.

Firms such as IBM maintain customer education centers offering coursework in basic systems, programming languages, and applications. They provide packaged home study courses, examinations, and advisory services, and give certificates of completion.

Manufacturers'
Training Programs

Some firms provide customers with training programs designed primarily for in-service training of employees, or for orientation to their services.

Manufacturers' courses cover engineering, manufacturing, project management, and systems programming. Courses offered by time-sharing firms teach users how to operate remote terminals and cover programming languages.

Certificate in
Data Processing

A Certificate of Proficiency is awarded by the Data Processing Management Association (DPMA) to individuals who pass a written examination. The examination is offered annually at over 100 schools and colleges throughout the country and is open to those who have five years experience in data processing.

The certificate is an asset when seeking employment in the data processing field. It certifies that the holder has a broad educational background and practical knowledge of data processing. The student interested in more details should contact the association at 505 Busse Highway, Park Ridge, Illinois 60068.

The educational background recommended by the DPMA provides a balanced coverage of essentials. The following abstract of their study outline lists the main topics of study. It should be noted that the list is extensive and covers advanced mathematical and systems theory. All jobs in data processing do not require such extensive preparation, however.

1. Data processing equipment. The student should understand the basic principles of data processing equipment and its evolution.
2. Computer programming and software. An understanding of computer programming, compilers, methods of addressing, loops, subroutines, sorts, and memory systems is necessary.
3. Principles of management. The student should understand the fundamentals of general management and organization principles, management techniques, corporate organization structure, and data processing management practice.
4. Quantitative methods. A foundation in quantitative methods is essential for the specialist. These include the basic principles of accounting, cost accounting, internal control and auditing, operations research and statistics.
5. Systems analysis and design. The student should understand the principles of systems analysis, hardware evaluation techniques, systems design, and implementation.

JOB DESCRIPTIONS

Jobs in data processing may be classified in many ways: for example, by necessary skills, salary, or industry group.

The Dictionary of Occupational Titles (D.O.T.), available in most school and public libraries, gives a thorough description of the various job categories. These volumes outline in detail the duties, skills, and aptitudes necessary for performance of each job.

Occupational guides published by state employment offices are another useful source of job descriptions. These guides usually outline job duties, working conditions, employment, pay and hours, promotion, and training, and provide information about where to find additional data.

Many large-scale employers, such as state and local government, school districts, and private firms, publish job availability and employment bulletins, which discuss job descriptions, requirements, salary, and how to apply for the job.

Major Data
Processing
Opportunities

The following list of jobs and their descriptions is an overview of the diverse nature of the industry.

KEYPUNCH OPERATOR.   The keypunch operator uses key-driven machines to record data as punched holes in cards. Keypunch operators usually work in large rooms, with many other employees. Operating noise is thus a factor and should be considered by anyone sensitive to sound.

Speed, accuracy, and concentration are essential. Operators must be able to accept instruction and cooperate with fellow workers. This job is primarily sedentary; hours are good; and work may be available around the clock. Innovations in data input methods and equipment may affect job availability and some of the skills required of keypunch operators.

TABULATING MACHINE OPERATOR.   The "tab" operator works with unit record equipment such as sorting machines, collators, reproducing punches, interpreters, and tabulators.

With the growth of EDP, the reliance upon unit record equipment has diminished to some extent. Unit record installations are primarily found in the small to medium-sized firm, or in firms that operate unit record equipment as well as electronic computers.

The "tab" operator should enjoy working with machines, have good eyesight, and be able to lift from 20 to 60 pounds of punched cards. The employment outlook for this group is less optimistic because of the trend toward EDP.

PROGRAMMERS.   A programmer's responsibilities range from planning and flowcharting a problem to coding (writing the instructions for the computer) and debugging it (locating errors in programs). Generally, he or she plans the solution of a stated clerical, administrative, or statistical problem.

The programmer must determine what information should be entered in the program and in what form, the mathematical and logical operations the computer must perform, and the type of output desired. Sometimes the work is divided into several groups: one person does the research and early planning of the program; another, the actual coding of the instructions.

Working conditions are good, and jobs are available in a variety of establishments. The long-range employment outlook is optimistic and will parallel the growth for skilled office employees. As new programming languages enter the industry, some new skills and retraining may be necessary.

SYSTEMS ANALYST.   The systems analyst studies business problems and formulates procedures for solving them, using EDP equipment. He or she then develops a set of guidelines that the programmer converts into computer instructions. The work involves analyzing subject matter and identifying conditions and criteria required to automate a procedure. The analyst specifies the number and type of records, files, and documents to be used; outlines actions to be taken by personnel and computers in sufficient detail for programming; presents recommendations and proposed procedures to management; recommends equipment configurations; coordinates the development of test problems; and participates in trial runs of new and revised systems.

The employment outlook for this group is good. As more firms begin to utilize data processing, there will be an increased need for individuals who can diagnose business data problems and propose solutions.

DIGITAL COMPUTER OPERATOR (Console Operator).   The console operator monitors and operates the control console of the computer and determines the procedures to be followed from the programmer's instruction sheet for the run. An operator readies the equipment, loads the computer with tape, reels, disks, or cards, and starts the run. If the computer stops, or signals an error, he or she must try to locate the source of the trouble. The operator communicates with the computer by typing instructions on a console typewriter. Messages may be received on the typewriter or on a video screen.

Console operators may operate a variety of auxiliary equipment. These machines may transfer data from one medium to another.

The console operator may work alone on a single computer or with several others in a computer installation. Many firms operate their computers around the clock, using second and third shifts. The need for console operators is basic to the industry and should grow in the next decade.

Improvements in computers and programming languages have simplified, rather than complicated, machine operations. Because of these changes, machines are often less complex to operate than a decade or two ago. As a result, those studying for careers in computer console operations and even programming will discover that it is now easier to qualify for these openings.

LIBRARIAN, DOCUMENTATION SPECIALIST.   This occupational category supports the activities of the programmers and systems engineers. Librarians catalog and file data, reports, programs, and documentation on programs. Documentation specialists write up the details and specifications on running programs. They prepare notes, drawings, and textual statements regarding the program flow, format of input and output records, etc. Tape librarians file and catalog magnetic tape, disks, and even tab cards in large computer installations.

DATA PROCESSING MANAGER, DIRECTOR.   This individual is responsible for the overall output and operations of the data processing department. The Director coordinates the activities of the computer installation with those of other departments and organizations and must provide uninterrupted service to the firm. As an administrator, he or she supervises the other employees in the data processing department and plans workloads, staffing, selection and training, and promotion. A manager must remain aware of new equipment and systems and be able to communicate well, both verbally and in writing.

The employment outlook for managers is good and will increase as more firms adopt EDP methods.

SALES AND MARKETING.   A wide variety of positions are open in the sales and marketing of computers, terminals, time-sharing services, and related hardware. Those engaged in this job classification demonstrate equipment, analyze needs, and make recommendations concerning new devices and services.

The sales staff for time-sharing companies calls upon both large and small businesses to explain and demonstrate computer terminals and software services. The hours and working conditions vary greatly with the kind of equipment or service sold and the employer. Some travel may be involved.

The successful salesperson must have a good grasp of data processing fundamentals, enjoy being with people, and like selling.

CUSTOMER ENGINEERING AND MAINTENANCE.   Customer engineers are employed by computer manufacturers to call upon firms that use their systems. They help the customer make the most efficient use of the available equipment.

The installer often travels to new installations and remains with the account until the system is in operation and performing properly.

Maintenance people visit computer installations at regular intervals to perform preventive maintenance procedures or to service the equipment. They clean, lubricate, and adjust machines, and perform routine diagnostic tests on computers, line printers, card punches, and other equipment.

The employment outlook for this group is good and will grow as more machines go into service. Technical skills and a knowledge of electronics and hardware are required. Many smaller firms that make computer components and supporting equipment also hire technicians, installers, maintenance people, and engineers.

STRUCTURE OF DATA PROCESSING DEPARTMENT

The size and complexity of data processing departments vary with the kind and size of the business they serve. For a small firm, a few data processing employees operating a small computer or a limited amount of EAM equipment may be sufficient. Medium-sized organizations may employ from 5 to 20 individuals and operate both unit record equipment and a computer. Large firms, on the other hand, may employ many thousands of people in data processing and operate a computer network that ties together several large computers in various parts of the country.

Small Data Processing Department

The smallest and simplest organization is one in which one or two employees are responsible for data processing operations. In a small firm, these individuals serve as combination programmers, computer operators, keypunch operators, systems analysts, and managers.

But data processing is a complex field and different skills are required of the programmer and the systems analyst. The skills that make a good computer operator differ from those required of EAM operators. Because of this, there is a need for specialization within the data processing department. Figure A.1 shows a typical organization chart for a small data processing department, with four specialized employees: a programmer, an input/output operator (who may be a keypunch operator), a computer operator, and a manager.

The relatively low volume of work processed by a small business usually limits the need for programming languages to only a few, easily handled by

FIGURE A.1   ORGANIZATION CHART OF SMALL DATA PROCESSING DEPARTMENT

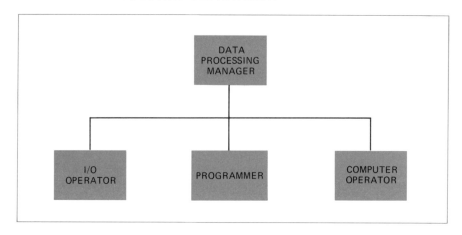

FIGURE A.2   ORGANIZATION CHART OF MEDIUM-SIZED DATA
                    PROCESSING DEPARTMENT

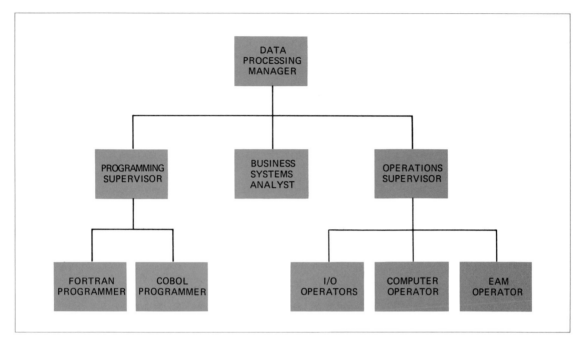

one or two programmers. Little or no systems programming, such as
modifying the operating system of a computer or altering compilers, is done.

Medium-Sized   More and more medium-sized firms are using computerized data processing
Data Processing   systems. Insurance companies, manufacturers, sales agents and brokers,
Department   advertising agencies, and other moderately sized companies employ from 5 to
                  20 employees in their data processing departments.
                      The increase in size permits more specialization within the department.
                  Figure A.2 is an organization chart of a medium-sized company. The
                  department is headed by a data processing manager who supervises
                  employees and guides the operation of the department. The manager has
                  a staff of programmers, business systems analysts, and EAM and computer
                  operators. If the workload merits 24-hour operation, an operation supervisor
                  may be in charge of three shift supervisors.
                      If the firm needs to program in more than one language, it may employ
                  several programmers, each proficient in a different language, and assigned
                  to different types of problems. One or more keypunch operators may be
                  assigned to each programmer. The punched programs are turned over to a
                  computer operator for running.

A data center in a large firm may employ from a dozen to several hundred workers and occupy an entire floor of a large office building. Figure A.3 is an organization chart of a data processing department in a large business firm.

There may be dozens of keypunch operators, supervisors, systems analysts, systems engineers, programmers, business systems analysts, operators, clerks, librarians, and documentation specialists. The larger the company, the greater the specialization that can take place in the data processing department. With specialization comes greater efficiency and output. Since large firms process a high volume of work, the department can also be put on a 24-hour operating schedule, which further maximizes equipment utilization.

SYSTEMS GROUP.   The systems group is responsible for planning and expanding the operating system and computer control programs and for altering compilers. They are also responsible for the maintenance and development of all systems software. The systems group employs systems analysts, systems programmers, and librarians.

PROGRAMMING GROUP.   Some companies need to process a wide variety of problems in business, engineering, mathematics, graphics, and research. They employ programmers with specialized abilities in such languages as COBOL, FORTRAN, RPG, and assembler language.

With more personnel available, the functions usually performed by the programmer can be further specialized and assigned to different individuals. Documentation and keypunching can be assigned to specialists. Even the job of programming instructions can be reduced to different levels. A senior programmer may lay out the overall program and assign separate sections of the program to other programmers for coding. Finally, the parts are assembled into a running program and it is documented by another specialist.

OPERATIONS GROUP.   The operation function is also divided into specialized activities. Large computer centers often operate EAM facilities alongside of computers. Some have several sizes and types of computers available in one installation.

These firms employ several supervisors to coordinate the operations group. Their staff may be assigned to operate a particular computer or I/O device, the computer console, tape and disk drives, or some other component of the system.

SUPPORT GROUP.   Large firms employ a large support staff for the data processing department. The greater volume of programming increases the need for tape and program librarians, mathematicians, statisticians, technicians, clerk typists, supervisors, and so on.

FIGURE A.3 ORGANIZATION CHART OF LARGE DATA PROCESSING DEPARTMENT

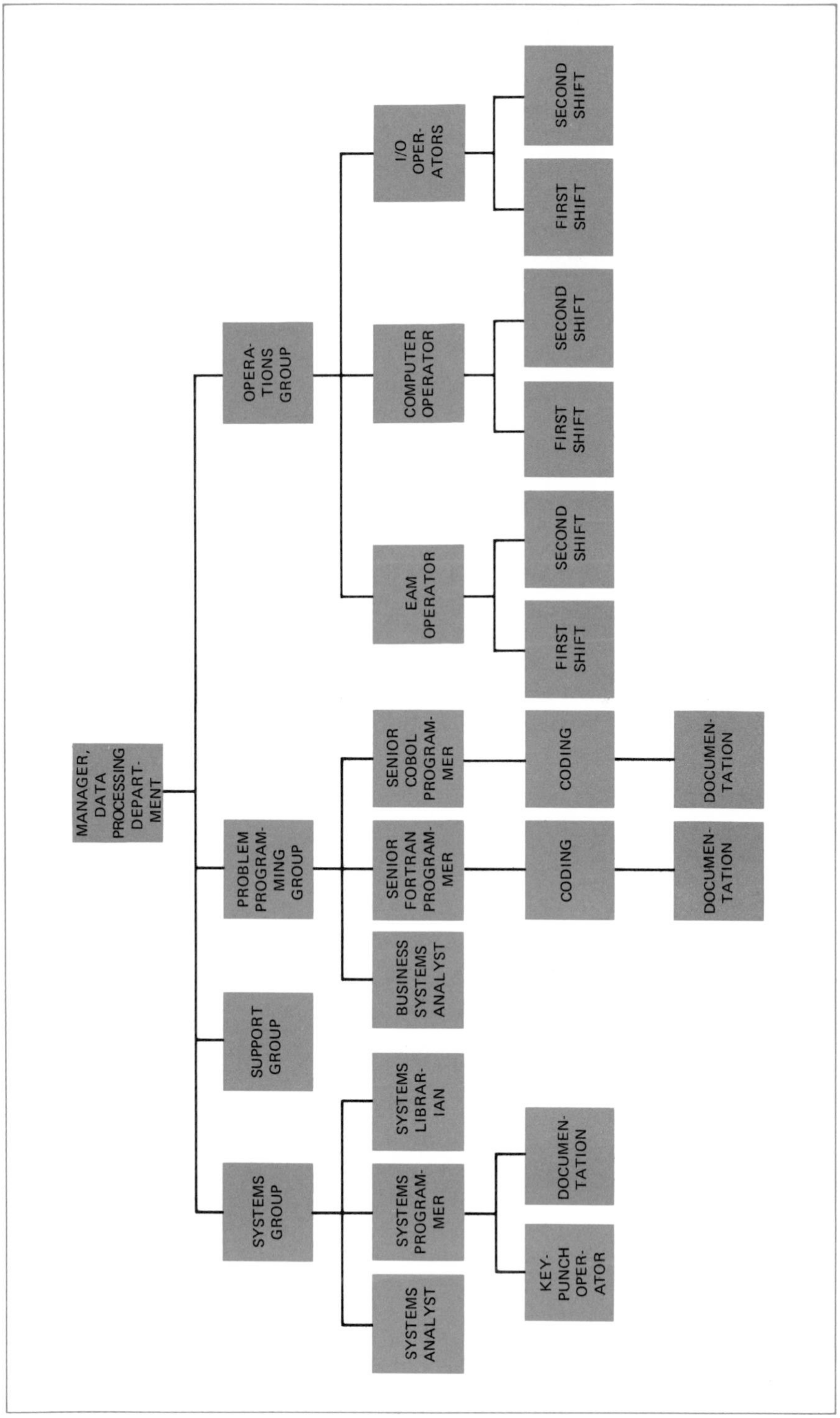

Personnel needs are usually dictated by the volume and type of programming done by a firm, as well as its kind, size, and degree of sophistication. The personnel department and the data processing manager use job description outlines as a guide when considering applications for employment.

The number of positions needed in each department is obtained from a review of reports and records. Obviously, a firm requiring a great deal of keypunching or data input will employ more keypunch operators and supervisors than firms that do more systems design and programming. The latter will need coders, programmers, and systems analysts.

To staff the positions in the department, the personnel department and data processing manager usually follow several routine procedures. Applicants are first interviewed and screened by the personnel department. They fill out applications for employment, giving pertinent data such as previous employment, experience, and education. The personnel department may also test the applicant to evaluate his or her mental capacity and performance. Then the applicant is interviewed by the data processing manager or supervisor. The results are evaluated and a selection made.

The data processing manager or supervisor introduces the new employee to the job. Usually the employee takes a training or indoctrination course or is placed under close supervision for a period of time. Some firms use periodic employee evaluation procedures to advance employees in status, pay, and responsibility.

In-service training is another responsibility of data processing management. As new equipment is acquired or new procedures installed, retraining programs, seminars, and courses may be offered to employees to enable them to adjust to the new operations with a minimum of delay and inconvenience.

CONVERSION TABLE:
DECIMAL, BINARY, HEXADECIMAL

DECIMAL	HEXA-DECIMAL	BINARY	DECIMAL	HEXA-DECIMAL	BINARY	DECIMAL	HEXA-DECIMAL	BINARY
0	00	0000 0000	21	15	0001 0101	42	2A	0010 1010
1	01	0000 0001	22	16	0001 0110	43	2B	0010 1011
2	02	0000 0010	23	17	0001 0111	44	2C	0010 1100
3	03	0000 0011	24	18	0001 1000	45	2D	0010 1101
4	04	0000 0100	25	19	0001 1001	46	2E	0010 1110
5	05	0000 0101	26	1A	0001 1010	47	2F	0010 1111
6	06	0000 0110	27	1B	0001 1011	48	30	0011 0000
7	07	0000 0111	28	1C	0001 1100	49	31	0011 0001
8	08	0000 1000	29	1D	0001 1101	50	32	0011 0010
9	09	0000 1001	30	1E	0001 1110	51	33	0011 0011
10	0A	0000 1010	31	1F	0001 1111	52	34	0011 0100
11	0B	0000 1011	32	20	0010 0000	53	35	0011 0101
12	0C	0000 1100	33	21	0010 0001	54	36	0011 0110
13	0D	0000 1101	34	22	0010 0010	55	37	0011 0111
14	0E	0000 1110	35	23	0010 0011	56	38	0011 1000
15	0F	0000 1111	36	24	0010 0100	57	39	0011 1001
16	10	0001 0000	37	25	0010 0101	58	3A	0011 1010
17	11	0001 0001	38	26	0010 0110	59	3B	0011 1011
18	12	0001 0010	39	27	0010 0111	60	3C	0011 1100
19	13	0001 0011	40	28	0010 1000	61	3D	0011 1101
20	14	0001 0100	41	29	0010 1001	62	3E	0011 1110

DECIMAL	HEXA-DECIMAL	BINARY	DECIMAL	HEXA-DECIMAL	BINARY	DECIMAL	HEXA-DECIMAL	BINARY
63	3F	0011 1111	109	6D	0110 1101	155	9B	1001 1011
64	40	0100 0000	110	6E	0110 1110	156	9C	1001 1100
65	41	0100 0001	111	6F	0110 1111	157	9D	1001 1101
66	42	0100 0010	112	70	0111 0000	158	9E	1001 1110
67	43	0100 0011	113	71	0111 0001	159	9F	1001 1111
68	44	0100 0100	114	72	0111 0010	160	A0	1010 0000
69	45	0100 0101	115	73	0111 0011	161	A1	1010 0001
70	46	0100 0110	116	74	0111 0100	162	A2	1010 0010
71	47	0100 0111	117	75	0111 0101	163	A3	1010 0011
72	48	0100 1000	118	76	0111 0110	164	A4	1010 0100
73	49	0100 1001	119	77	0111 0111	165	A5	1010 0101
74	4A	0100 1010	120	78	0111 1000	166	A6	1010 0110
75	4B	0100 1011	121	79	0111 1001	167	A7	1010 0111
76	4C	0100 1100	122	7A	0111 1010	168	A8	1010 1000
77	4D	0100 1101	123	7B	0111 1011	169	A9	1010 1001
78	4E	0100 1110	124	7C	0111 1100	170	AA	1010 1010
79	4F	0100 1111	125	7D	0111 1101	171	AB	1010 1011
80	50	0101 0000	126	7E	0111 1110	172	AC	1010 1100
81	51	0101 0001	127	7F	0111 1111	173	AD	1010 1101
82	52	0101 0010	128	80	1000 0000	174	AE	1010 1110
83	53	0101 0011	129	81	1000 0001	175	AF	1010 1111
84	54	0101 0100	130	82	1000 0010	176	B0	1011 0000
85	55	0101 0101	131	83	1000 0011	177	B1	1011 0001
86	56	0101 0110	132	84	1000 0100	178	B2	1011 0010
87	57	0101 0111	133	85	1000 0101	179	B3	1011 0011
88	58	0101 1000	134	86	1000 0110	180	B4	1011 0100
89	59	0101 1001	135	87	1000 0111	181	B5	1011 0101
90	5A	0101 1010	136	88	1000 1000	182	B6	1011 0110
91	5B	0101 1011	137	89	1000 1001	183	B7	1011 0111
92	5C	0101 1100	138	8A	1000 1010	184	B8	1011 1000
93	5D	0101 1101	139	8B	1000 1011	185	B9	1011 1001
94	5E	0101 1110	140	8C	1000 1100	186	BA	1011 1010
95	5F	0101 1111	141	8D	1000 1101	187	BB	1011 1011
96	60	0110 0000	142	8E	1000 1110	188	BC	1011 1100
97	61	0110 0001	143	8F	1000 1111	189	BD	1011 1101
98	62	0110 0010	144	90	1001 0000	190	BE	1011 1110
99	63	0110 0011	145	91	1001 0001	191	BF	1011 1111
100	64	0110 0100	146	92	1001 0010	192	C0	1100 0000
101	65	0110 0101	147	93	1001 0011	193	C1	1100 0001
102	66	0110 0110	148	94	1001 0100	194	C2	1100 0010
103	67	0110 0111	149	95	1001 0101	195	C3	1100 0011
104	68	0110 1000	150	96	1001 0110	196	C4	1100 0100
105	69	0110 1001	151	97	1001 0111	197	C5	1100 0101
106	6A	0110 1010	152	98	1001 1000	198	C6	1100 0110
107	6B	0110 1011	153	99	1001 1001	199	C7	1100 0111
108	6C	0110 1100	154	9A	1001 1010	200	C8	1100 1000

DECIMAL	HEXA-DECIMAL	BINARY	DECIMAL	HEXA-DECIMAL	BINARY	DECIMAL	HEXA-DECIMAL	BINARY
201	C9	1100 1001	220	DC	1101 1100	239	EF	1110 1111
202	CA	1100 1010	221	DD	1101 1101	240	F0	1111 0000
203	CB	1100 1011	222	DE	1101 1110	241	F1	1111 0001
204	CC	1100 1100	223	DF	1101 1111	242	F2	1111 0010
205	CD	1100 1101	224	E0	1110 0000	243	F3	1111 0011
206	CE	1100 1110	225	E1	1110 0001	244	F4	1111 0100
207	CF	1100 1111	226	E2	1110 0010	245	F5	1111 0101
208	D0	1101 0000	227	E3	1110 0011	246	F6	1111 0110
209	D1	1101 0001	228	E4	1110 0100	247	F7	1111 0111
210	D2	1101 0010	229	E5	1110 0101	248	F8	1111 1000
211	D3	1101 0011	230	E6	1110 0110	249	F9	1111 1001
212	D4	1101 0100	231	E7	1110 0111	250	FA	1111 1010
213	D5	1101 0101	232	E8	1110 1000	251	FB	1111 1011
214	D6	1101 0110	233	E9	1110 1001	252	FC	1111 1100
215	D7	1101 0111	234	EA	1110 1010	253	FD	1111 1101
216	D8	1101 1000	235	EB	1110 1011	254	FE	1111 1110
217	D9	1101 1001	236	EC	1110 1100	255	FF	1111 1111
218	DA	1101 1010	237	ED	1110 1101			
219	DB	1101 1011	238	EE	1110 1110			

C

KEYPUNCHING

Keypunching is done on a machine resembling a typewriter that has provisions for handling cards. When a key is pressed, the machine simultaneously punches a machine-readable code into the card and prints the corresponding character at the top of the column. Most keypunch machines punch letters, numbers, and special characters; some have only numeric keyboards.

THE STANDARD CARD

The most common input medium for the computer is the 80-column card shown in Figure C.1. Available in a variety of colors and printed forms, it is $3\frac{1}{4}''$ by $7\frac{3}{8}''$, with a corner cut or a colored stripe for identification. The most important terms related to the card are:

BIT   A bit is one punch position in a card; it is treated as a binary digit by the computer.

BYTE   A byte is one vertical column of bits, forming one character.*

---

*Each column of holes represents one alphabetic character or one number. A different code system is used within the computer's storage to represent numbers and characters, but since the computer automatically translates the holes in the card into the proper storage code, the beginning student need not be concerned with this difference.

FIGURE C.1   THE STANDARD PUNCHED CARD

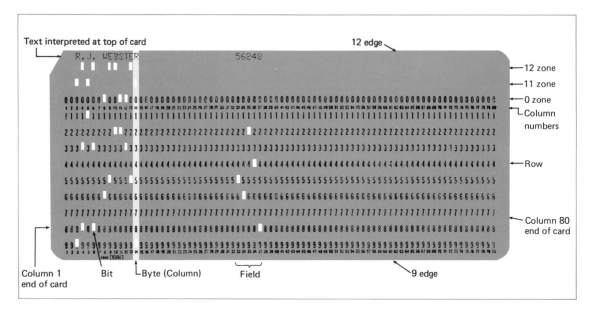

ROW   A row is a horizontal group of 80 bits across the card. There are 12 rows on a card. The top two, called the 12 and 11 rows, are not labeled; the other rows are labeled 0–9.

ZONE   A zone is one of the three top rows of the card. The row nearest the top of the card is the 12 zone, the one below it is the 11 zone, and below that is the 0 zone. Zones are usually not labeled. The 11 zone is sometimes called the X punch.

COLUMN   The face of each card has 80 vertical columns. Each column contains a 12 zone, an 11 zone, and 10 bits labeled from 0 to 9. Each vertical column can record one alphabetic, numeric, or special character.

FIELD   A field is a group of columns containing related information. Fields can range from 1 to 80 columns in width. For example, a 5-digit identification number punched in columns 10–14 of a card is a field of 5 columns, and 20 columns punched with a name is a 20-column field.

12 EDGE   The 12 edge is the top edge of the card, the one nearest the 12 zone.

9 EDGE   The 9 edge is the bottom edge of the card, the one nearest the 9 row.

COLUMN 1 END   The column 1 end is the left edge of the card, nearest column 1.

COLUMN 80 END   The column 80 end is the right edge of the card, nearest column 80.

INTERPRETING   Interpreting is the conversion of the punched code into a form readable by humans, namely the characters typed at the top of the card over each column. Interpreting is done automatically when the print switch is on and the card is punched. Each character appears directly over the column in which it is punched. If desired, cards can be keypunched without interpreting by turning off the print switch.

PUNCHED CARD CODES

A code based on the one developed by Herman Hollerith is used for punching alphabetic and numeric data into cards. The code uses a unique set of holes or bits for each letter, character, and number. The code for the numbers uses only one bit punched in rows 0–9. Letters require one punch in zone 12, 11, or 0 and one in rows 1–9. Special characters require from one to three holes. This code is illustrated in Figure C.2.

The IBM 029 card punch is one of the most common keypunch machines in use today. This machine, designed around 1965 for use with the IBM 360 computer, is a refinement of the earlier 026 card punch. Many 026 machines are still in use today. The major differences between the two machines are the 029's larger character set and improved styling and operating features.

FIGURE C.2   PUNCHED CARD CODE

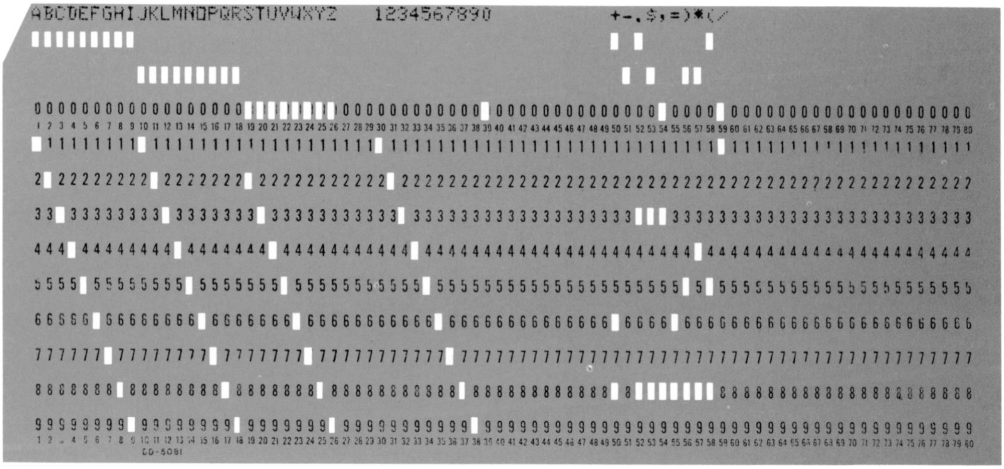

FIGURE C.3   IBM 029 CARD PUNCH

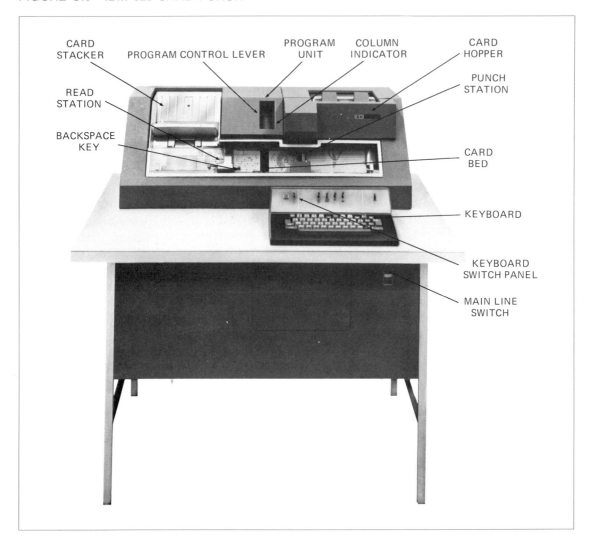

The larger character set may be punched on the 026 by using the MULT PCH key (described later).

The plus sign ($+$), equals sign ($=$), and left and right parentheses are standard on the IBM 029. They are also present on the keyboard of some models of the IBM 026, but they punch a different combination of holes, which will be interpreted incorrectly by the computer and can cause program failure. If in doubt, check Table C.1 for the combinations required by the computer.

Figure C.3 shows the major parts of the 029 card punch. This machine will feed cards from the card hopper to a punch station. There data are punched into the card from a typewriterlike keyboard. After being punched, the card moves to a read station and then to the card stacker. These movements are controlled from the keyboard, without the operator actually handling each card.

Figure C.4 shows this path. Cards to be punched are loaded into the card hopper, which holds 500 cards and is located in the upper right part of the machine. Cards should be placed in the hopper face forward, with the 12 edge up. A pressure plate holds the cards firmly from behind, and cards leave the hopper one at a time.

At the punch station, the card moves under a set of punch dies. As a key is pressed, the dies punch the appropriate holes in the column and the character is printed at the top. As the punching proceeds, the card moves from right to left, under the punch station.

Next, the card moves to the read station, which is used for duplicating cards. A series of contacts sense the holes punched in the card and transmit this information to the punch station. A duplicate card can thus be punched without rekeying.

From the read station, the card moves to the card stacker. The stacker, located in the upper left portion of the machine, is capable of holding 500

FIGURE C.4   CARD PATH

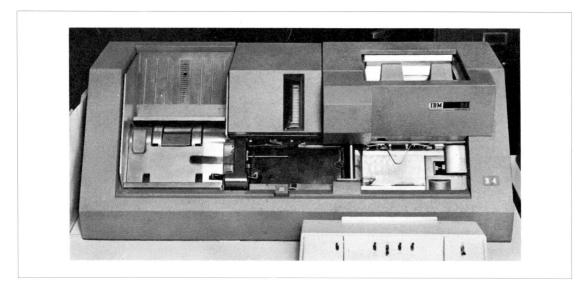

cards. When the stacker is full, the keyboard locks and no more cards can be punched until it is emptied.

KEYBOARD SWITCH PANEL

The keyboard switch panel, located just above the keyboard (Figure C.5(A)) has six toggle switches mounted on it. These switches are set by the operator to make the machine perform tasks such as automatically feeding cards, printing left zeros in the number field, and automatically skipping columns.

Figure C.5(B) shows the switch panel in detail. The extreme left switch is the AUTO SKIP/DUP switch. It is used in conjunction with the program control unit. This unit is useful when punching large numbers of data cards. It will automatically shift and tab to specified columns. For most routine keypunching, the switch may be left in the OFF position.

Four switches are located in the center of the panel. The PROG SEL switch is used in conjunction with the program control unit and may also be disregarded on simple jobs. The AUTO FEED key is used to feed cards automatically. When it is in the ON position, a new card will be fed from the

FIGURE C.5

(A) COMBINATION KEYBOARD

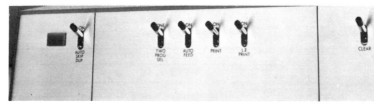

(B) KEYBOARD SWITCH PANEL

TABLE C.1   IBM 029 CARD PUNCH CODE

KEY	ALPHABETIC		NUMERIC	
NUMBER	CARD CODE	GRAPHIC	CARD CODE	GRAPHIC
1	11-8	Q	12-8-6	+
2	0-6	W	0-8-5	−
3	12-5	E	11-8-5	)
4	11-9	R	12-8-2	¢
5	0-3	T	0-8-2	0-8-2
6	0-8	Y	12-8-7	I
7	12-1	A	none	none
8	0-2	S	0-8-6	>
9	12-4	D	8-2	:
10	12-6	F	11-8-6	;
11	12-7	G	11-8-7	¬
12	12-8	H	8-5	'
13	0-9	Z	None	None
14	0-7	X	0-8-7	?
15	12-3	C	8-7	''
16	0-5	V	8-6	=
17	12-2	B	11-8-2	!
18	11-5	N	12-8-5	(
19	11-7	P	12	&
20	0-1	/	0	0
21	0-4	U	1	1
22	12-9	I	2	2
23	11-6	O	3	3
24	11-1	J	4	4
25	11-2	K	5	5
26	11-3	L	6	6
27	11-4	M	7	7
28	0-8-3	,	8	8
29	12-8-3	.	9	9
33	11	-	11	-
40	8-4	@	8-3	#
41	0-8-4	%	0-8-3	,
42	11-8-4	*	11-8-3	$
43	12-8-4	<	12-8-3	.

card hopper as soon as a data item is punched in column 80 of the preceding card. With the switch in the OFF position, cards are fed by pressing the FEED key on the keyboard.

When the PRINT switch is in the ON position, it causes each letter to be printed at the top of the column as it is punched. When PRINT is in the OFF position, cards can be punched but not printed. The LZ PRINT switch automatically fills in zeros to the left of a numeric field. For most jobs, this switch will be in the OFF position.

On the extreme right of the panel is the CLEAR switch. This switch moves all cards from the punch and read stations to the card stacker. It is spring loaded and when held up will cause the machine to cycle cards out of the punch and read stations and into the stacker.

Several different keyboards are available on the 029 card punch. The most common layout is shown in Figure C.6. This is the standard 64-character keyboard. It has a space bar that is used in the same manner as the one on a typewriter.

The keyboard has several rows of characters similar to those on a typewriter. Most of the keys have two characters marked on them. Two shift keys, labeled NUMERIC and ALPHA, determine which half of the key will punch. The letter on the lower half of each key will be punched unless the NUMERIC shift key is pressed. To punch the top character, the NUMERIC key is held down while the character key is struck.

The ALPHA shift key, on the right, is pressed when the program control unit is being used and the operator desires to override it. It allows the lower half of the key to punch, even though the control card is set to punch the upper half. For most jobs, the operator can ignore this key.

Other important control keys include:

DUP   This key is used to duplicate a card. When the DUP key is held down, the read station will send the signals to the punch station. As the card advances from right to left, data will be transferred, column for column.

FIGURE C.6   COMBINATION KEYBOARD

REL   This key advances a card to the next station. When pressed, the REL key will move a card from the punch station to the read station, or from the read station to the card stacker.

FEED   This key controls the card feed mechanism. It feeds a card from the card hopper to the punch station. A card cannot be punched, however, until it is properly registered by pressing the REG key.

REG   This key properly positions the card in the punch and read stations. The REG key must be pressed before a card can be read or punched.

ERROR RESET   This key resets the keyboard when it is locked. The keyboard will lock for several reasons, such as the main-line switch turned off while a card is in the punch station or a card not registered at the punch station.

MULT PCH   This key prevents a card from moving after it has been punched and thus allows another character to be punched in the same column. In this way, any combination of holes can be punched in a card, regardless of the letters appearing on the keyboard.

OTHER CONTROLS AND ADJUSTMENTS

BACKSPACE   The backspace button is located at the center of the machine, below the card bed. When this key is pressed, it will backspace cards in the punch and read stations.

MAIN-LINE SWITCH   The power switch is located below the desk top, on the lower right portion of the machine. The machine should be turned off when not in use.

READING DESK AND ADJUSTABLE KEYBOARD   A workspace is provided to the left of the keyboard for holding coding sheets or other documents while keypunching. The keyboard is adjustable and can be set at a convenient angle for the operator.

COLUMN INDICATOR   A column indicator, or pointer, is located in the window of the program control-card unit, just above the read station. It shows which column of the card is in position for reading and punching.

The programmer will rarely need to use the other control keys on the punch. These include the program control unit, the AUX DUP, SKIP, PROG ONE, and PROG TWO keys.

HOW TO USE THE KEYPUNCH

A variety of jobs can be done on the keypunch, including punching single cards, duplicating, correcting, and interpreting. A few of the major operations the beginning programmer will need to know are discussed below. The reader should refer to the IBM 029 Card Punch Reference Manual, GA24-3332, for a more detailed and thorough discussion on keyboard functions and operating instructions.

First, the operator should load the card hopper. Do not use folded, bent, or used cards. Discard mispunched cards promptly.

Cards should be carefully jogged to see that all edges are neatly aligned. Place the cards in the card hopper face forward, with the 12 edge up.

TO PUNCH ONE CARD

1. Turn on the main-line switch (located under the desk on the right side of the machine). Hold the CLEAR switch up to remove any cards from the card bed.
2. Set the AUTO FEED switch to OFF, PRINT to ON, and the LZ to OFF. The AUTO SKIP/DUP and PROG SEL switches are not used, and the program control lever should be set to disengage the program control unit.
3. Press the FEED key once to feed a fresh card from the hopper to the punch station.
4. Press the REG key to properly register the card in the punch station.
5. All characters on the bottom half of the key are punched if the program control unit is disengaged, and the ALPHA and NUMERIC shift keys are not held down. To punch a letter on the top half of the key, hold down the NUMERIC key. Continue punching data until the line is finished or until column 80 has been reached.
6. Remove the card from the card bed by holding up the CLEAR switch until the machine cycles the card out to the stacker.

If two or three cards are to be punched in succession, the REL key may be pressed after each card has been punched. This will move it out of the punch station and to the read station. The FEED key is then depressed and a new card fed to the punch station while the first card remains in the read station. Press the REG key to register the card and begin punching. Several cards can be punched in this manner by pressing the FEED, REG, and REL keys, in that order.

If many cards are to be punched, the AUTO FEED switch can be put in the ON position. This will automatically feed a card each time the REL key is pressed. Most beginning operators, however, will find it easier to feed cards with the FEED key. If the operator is not careful when the AUTO FEED key is ON, the machine will feed several cards to the punch station and jam.

TO INSERT A CARD INTO THE CARD BED MANUALLY

1. Set up the machine as described in steps 1 and 2 above.
2. Insert the card manually in the card bed, behind the punch station. Carefully slide it into position to the right of the punch unit. Cards may also be manually inserted behind the read station.
3. Press REG to position the card properly for punching.
4. Data can be punched in any column of the card. Manual insertion is useful when the operator desires to insert a character or word on a previously punched card.

TO DUPLICATE ONE CARD

1. Turn on the machine and arrange the switches as described previously.
2. Manually insert the card to be duplicated at the read station. From the right side, carefully position it behind the read unit.
3. Press the FEED key to feed a new card from the hopper to the punch station.
4. Press the REG key. This aligns the cards under their respective stations, ready for duplicating.
5. Hold down the DUP key until all columns of the card have been duplicated.

TO DUPLICATE SEVERAL CARDS

1. Turn on the machine and arrange the switches as described before.
2. Interlace the deck of cards to be duplicated with blank cards. (See Figure C.7.) The first card in the deck should be the first card to be duplicated, followed by a blank, and so on.
3. Place the interspersed deck into the card hopper.
4. Press the FEED key to feed the first card to the punch station.
5. Press the REL key to move the first card to the read station.
6. Press the FEED key again, to feed the blank to the punch station.
7. Press the REG key to register the cards properly for duplicating.
8. Hold down the DUP key until all characters have been duplicated.
9. Press the REL key to move the first card to the card stacker and the second card down to the read station.
10. Continue the cycle REL, FEED, REL, FEED, REG, DUP, until all cards have been duplicated.

FIGURE C.7   DECK INTERLACED TO DUPLICATE CARDS

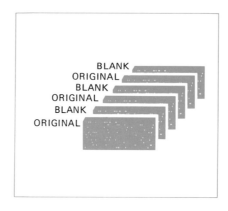

TO INTERPRET A CARD

1. Turn on the machine and arrange the switches as described previously.
2. Follow the procedure for duplicating one card. Insert the uninterpreted card under the read station and a blank card under the punch station.
3. Be sure the PRINT switch is ON.
4. Depress the DUP key until the card has been duplicated and interpreted.

TO CORRECT AN ERROR

1. Turn on the machine and arrange the switches as described before.
2. Follow the procedure for duplicating one card. Hold the DUP key down until the point of error has been reached. Errors can be easily corrected by duping all columns except those that need corrections.
3. Punch in the correct data. In this way it is possible to change one or two characters and duplicate the rest of the line from the original card. Or the card may be only partially duplicated and completed by keyboarding entirely new data on the rest of the line.

TO INSERT A CHARACTER IN THE LINE

1. Set up the keypunch and arrange the switches as described previously.
2. Follow the procedure for duplicating one card. Hold the DUP key down until the point where the character to be inserted has been reached.

3. Place your left hand on the card under the read station. Firmly hold the card in position and press the space bar once. This will advance the card under the punch station one space, but will retard the movement of the card under the read station.
4. Press the BACKSPACE button once. This will back up both the original card and duplicated card.
5. Punch in the character to be inserted.
6. Hold down the DUP key until the remainder of the card has been duplicated.

TO MULTIPLE PUNCH A CARD

1. Hold down the MULT PCH key. This will prevent the advance of the card and enable you to punch several keys in one column.
2. Strike two or more keys, one at a time.

TO CLEAR A CARD JAM AT FEED OR PUNCH STATION

1. Hold down the pressure roll release lever with the left hand. The lever is located at the right of the base of the program drum and is accessible by lifting the cover of the program unit.
2. Carefully pull the card with the right hand. Do not tear the card. (If the card is torn, pieces can be removed from either station by using another card to push them out while depressing the pressure roll release lever.) Be very careful not to damage the punch dies.

CHECKING ACCURACY OF CARDS

Lay a duplicated card over the original and hold it up to a window or lamp. The holes should agree.

Fan out the deck of cards and align them on a table top to check column alignment. The entire group of cards can then be easily scanned to see that all statement numbers, continuation cards, and statements are punched in the right columns.

Use a card-verifying machine to verify punching and keying accuracy. It resembles a keypunch and is used for checking the accuracy of a set of data cards against the original data. The cards to be verified are placed in the machine and the data rekeyed. If they agree, a notch is punched on the side of the card.

Batch and hash totals can also be used to detect errors. The totals from the source documents can be run on an adding machine, and the tape can be compared with totals run from the cards.

EXERCISES

1. Explain the function of keypunching. In what form are data given to the keypunch operator, and how are data returned?
2. Obtain a standard 80-column card. Using differently colored pencils, draw lines marking one of the nine rows, one of the zones, and several vertical columns. Label the 12 edge, the 9 edge, and the column 1 and column 80 ends.
3. Lay a standard card on top of a blank coding sheet. How are the two similar? How do they differ?
4. Define the following terms:

   row   byte
   field   9 edge
   bit   12 edge

5. The punch code is shown in Figure C.2. Print your name and age on a sheet of paper. Identify the bit combinations associated with each letter.
6. On a piece of paper, draw a diagram of the card path through the keypunch. Label the keyboard and switch panel, card hopper, punch station, read station, and stacker. Using a line of arrows, trace the path of the card from hopper to stacker.
7. Briefly describe the function of the following keys:

   DUP   REG
   MULT PCH   FEED
   REL   ERROR RESET

8. Using the keypunch, punch your name on a card. Summarize the steps involved in this operation.
9. Prepare a duplicate card of your name using the DUP key. Summarize the steps involved in the operation.
10. Describe several ways in which errors can be corrected using the keypunch. Must all data be rekeyboarded if an additional character is to be inserted in the line?
11. Keypunch a data set consisting of 10 cards, following this arrangement:

   Name   Columns 1–20
   Address   Columns 31–60
   Phone   Columns 71–80

D

CASE PROBLEMS

This chapter relates the theories and principles discussed in previous chapters to real-life, day-to-day situations. The examples are drawn from actual case histories of firms that developed electronic data processing systems to solve problems or improve services.

Each case is presented from the user's viewpoint. It is assumed that a business systems analyst has studied the situation, planned a solution, and directed its implementation.

Each example states the background of the firm and gives size, location, markets, product, and other pertinent data. Then it either outlines the old data flow system and its weaknesses, or describes existing conditions and explains why they are unsatisfactory.

The solution to the problem is given next in a description of the new business system. Procedural changes are explained, new software and hardware are discussed. Finally, the benefits gained from the implementation of the new system are summarized.

In reviewing the cases in this chapter, you should keep two points in mind. First, the benefits of a new system are usually measured in terms of profits, income, or return on investment of the entire company. Implementing a new system may double or triple EDP costs, but increase profit.

The benefits realized may also be nonmonetary, such as improved customer relations, a better corporate image, or higher employee morale. These benefits may be at the cost of higher data processing expenditures.

Second, this chapter discusses successful case histories. It is quite possible that other firms, with different management, product lines, personnel, etc. may not experience similar results.

INVENTORY–WAREHOUSE PROBLEM

Alchemy Chemical Corporation

Alchemy Chemical is a large supplier of industrial chemicals and equipment. It markets thousands of chemicals and reagents, glassware, microscopes, laboratory apparatus, and testing instruments.

Alchemy has its headquarters in a large urban city. Twenty smaller branches, located in eight other cities, serve various geographic areas. (See Figure D.1.) A team of salespersons call upon customers to inform them of new products, solicit business, and take orders.

Orders are either phoned into the branch or carried by hand to the sales desk. Under the old system, written orders were prepared at the sales desk and given to the shipping department, where goods were picked, wrapped,

FIGURE D.1   ALCHEMY CHEMICAL CORPORATION

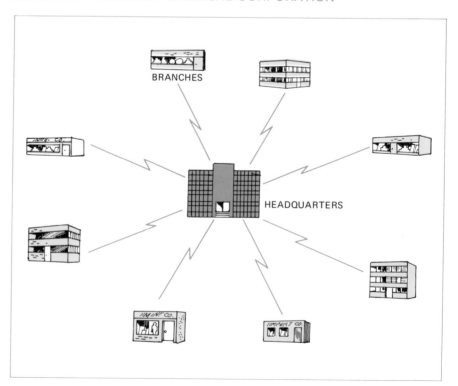

and shipped. If an item was not in stock, it was ordered from another branch and shipped directly to the customer.

Each branch warehouse stocked about 75,000 different items. When an order was received, the item was checked against inventory by manually pulling the proper card from a file that contained the names of all goods and their current inventory.

THE PROBLEM The inventory system was costly and inefficient. Many clerks were required to maintain the 75,000 inventory cards. Items were often out of stock because the order clerk did not complete the inventory card in time. Cards were sometimes misfiled, or errors were made as the records were updated. When cards were misfiled or lost, several hours were wasted in taking a physical inventory. Often salespersons had to keep customers waiting on the phone while a clerk checked stock.

Since the data on the inventory cards were hard to summarize, management did not have sufficient or current information. Turnover on each item in stock was hard to determine.

THE SOLUTION A computer system was installed in the Alchemy headquarters. Two video display terminals were installed in each branch, one at the order desk and another in the sales department. Telephone lines linked the computer at the head office with the terminals at the branches.

A data base, consisting of inventory information from all branches, was gathered and recorded on magnetic disks. This file included part number, current inventory, price information, and the name of the supply source for each item in stock. This file could be updated by any of the sales desks or warehouses. In addition, the file was structured to display a warning when items were low in stock and should be reordered.

Under this new system, the salesperson calls the branch office to place an order. An order clerk, seated before the video terminal in the sales department, queries the data bank by keying in the part number and quantity ordered. The terminal immediately responds with a display showing the quantity in stock, cost, and other data. As items are sold or removed from stock, the inventory is updated from the sales desk and warehouse. The stock available in each branch warehouse can be queried from any terminal. Figure D.2 contrasts the old inventory system with the new computerized method.

The computer is programmed to print out management reports at weekly intervals. These reports give the current inventory of all items in stock and turnover factor. Reports summarize sales by product line, branch, and supplier.

BENEFITS With the new system, Alchemy's customers benefit from faster information. As a result, service and sales have increased and the company has realized greater profits.

FIGURE D.2   ALCHEMY FLOWCHART

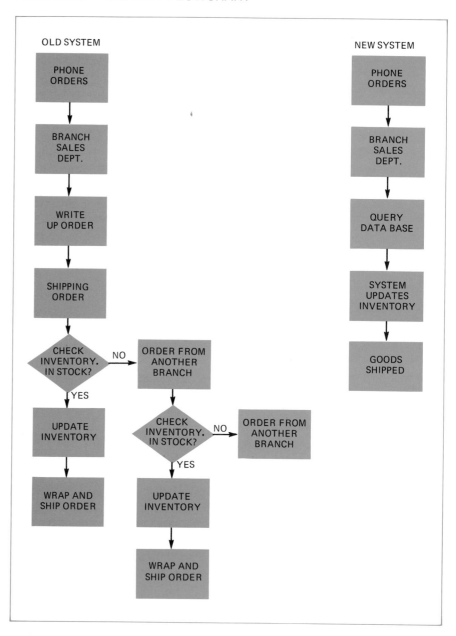

Management has more complete information and control of inventory. The turnover rate of each item in stock is known. Fewer runouts occur, since the system prepares a report listing the low items, supplier, and time required for order to be received.

SALES MANAGEMENT INFORMATION PROBLEM

Babbage Office Machines and Supplies

Babbage sells adding machines, desk calculators, and office photocopy equipment. The product line also includes desks, chairs, filing cabinets, and other office equipment.

A general sales manager, who coordinates the sales efforts of the entire firm, is employed at the home office. (See Figure D.3.) Several branch sales offices are located in other cities. Each branch is headed by a sales manager who oversees its activities. Each branch hires its own salespersons. The general sales manager frequently visits the individual units to conduct sales meetings, review reports, and guide and coordinate the sales activities.

Under the old system, branch salespersons called on customers and phoned in orders. Orders were also received directly from the customers by phone or mail. Each salesperson completed a weekly sales report giving his or her total calls for the week and the amount and type of goods sold.

FIGURE D.3   BABBAGE OFFICE MACHINES AND SUPPLIES

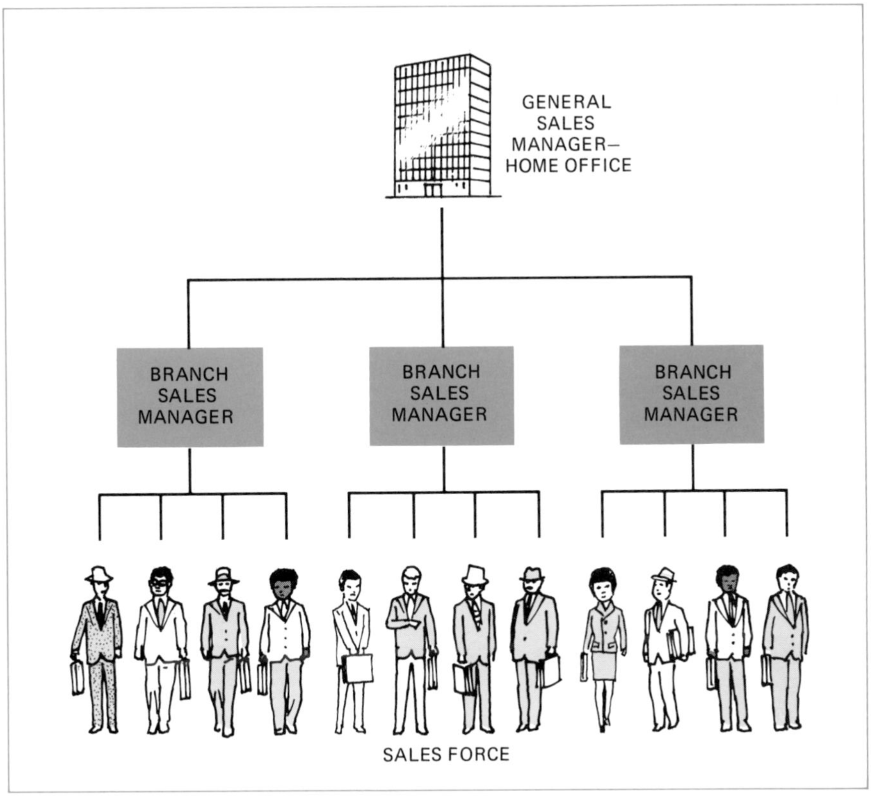

THE PROBLEM   The problem was a lack of current information and incomplete sales and marketing information. The salespersons often neglected to turn in their weekly reports on time and to complete them accurately. Much time was lost locating and organizing records. The general sales manager had little time to plan sales and marketing strategies.

Because of inadequate data and incomplete reports, it was hard to distinguish the best-selling products from those that were not moving. It was difficult to identify the salespersons who were doing a successful job and those who needed help. Often sales information would not be ready until after the close of the period, thus delaying reports to the home office. With inadequate or nonexistent information, management could not make intelligent decisions or even determine where changes or improvements were required.

THE SOLUTION   A computerized system was installed in the home office and an offline terminal in each branch. The typewriter-like terminal is coupled to the computer by calling the home office on the telephone. The phone handset is placed on the coupler connecting the terminal to the computer. Data, keyboarded on the terminal, are fed to the computer.

As orders are written up at the branch, items are removed from stock and shipped. At the end of each day, the sales data are transmitted to the bank at the home office. The salesperson prepares a weekly log of sales calls, and it is regularly transmitted to the data bank. Figure D.4 contrasts the old and new systems.

The system is programmed to print out sales reports. The Branch Sales Profile, printed each day for the branch sales manager, lists sales by amount, salesperson, and product. Slow-moving items and large single sales are extracted and reported separately.

A report is also printed at the home office for the general sales manager. He can also query the system about any branch and thus review the current status of a branch before a visit.

BENEFITS   With the new system, the branch sales manager has sales figures and related information available promptly. He knows which products are selling and which salespersons are effective.

The reports prepared at the home office enable the general sales manager to spot overall problems faster and give him a better picture of the entire operation. His visits to the branches are more effective, since both he and the branch sales managers have common statistics for decision making. Time can be spent planning and developing new marketing strategies instead of reviewing incomplete reports.

FIGURE D.4 BABBAGE FLOWCHART

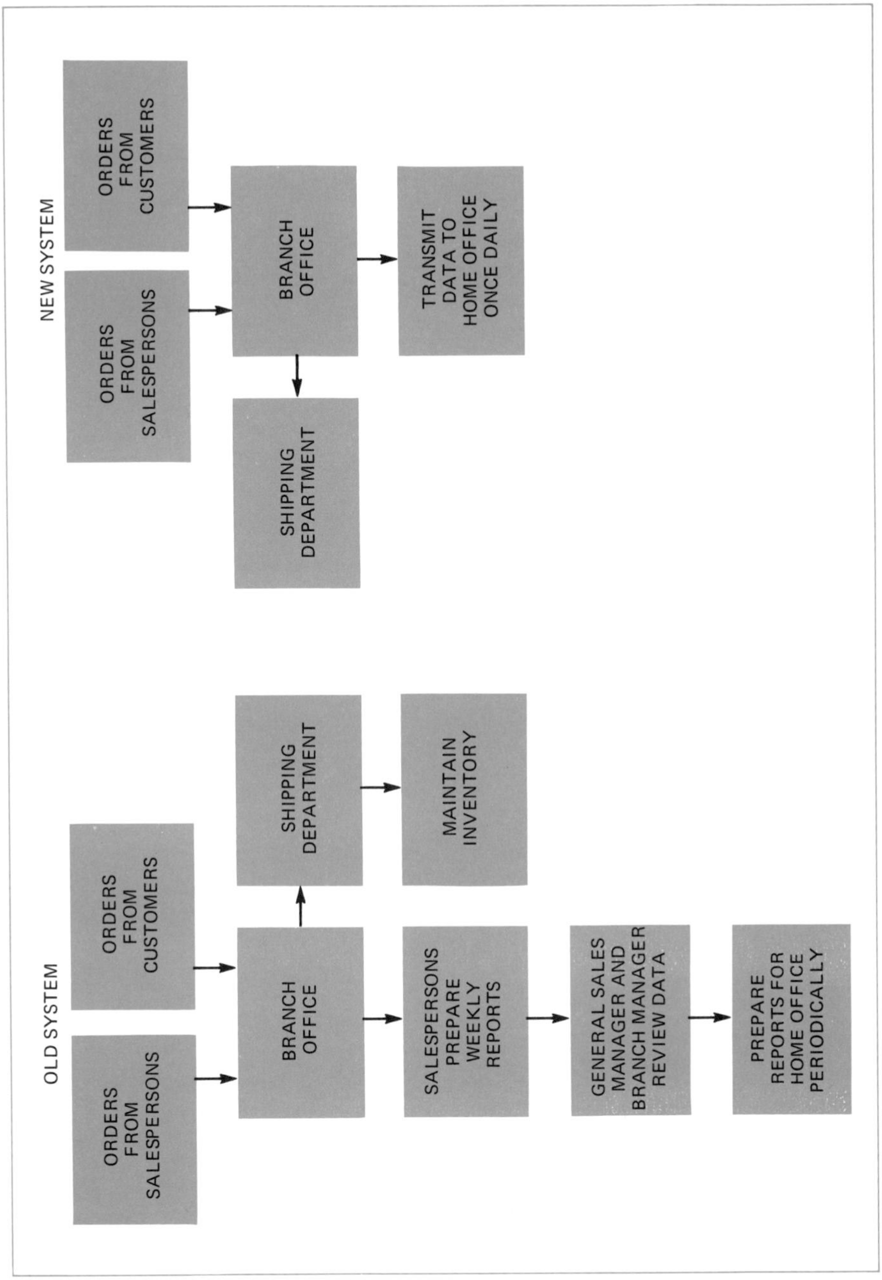

DISTRIBUTION PROBLEM

Volta Parts Company

Volta Parts Company is located in the suburb of a large city. It manufactures electronic parts, components, testing equipment, and instruments, which are sold to customers throughout the country. Customers are concentrated in several large cities. (See Figure D.5.)

Customers require very fast service on replacement parts. All orders arrive at the main plant by airmail or long distance telephone. Orders are filled promptly and wrapped or crated for shipment. Each evening, Volta ships about 300 packages (total weight about 10,000 lbs) by truck lines or rail.

THE PROBLEM   The use of ground carriers is both slow and expensive. The preferred mode would be air freight. But the great number of small packages make the cost prohibitive.

THE SOLUTION   The solution to Volta's problem was the installation of a computer programmed to output information on the best way to consolidate and direct

FIGURE D.5   VOLTA PARTS COMPANY

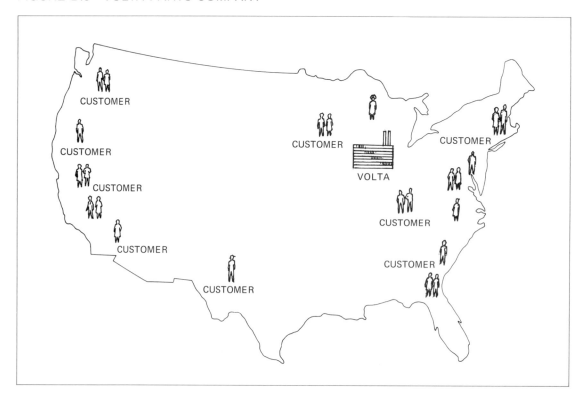

shipments. With the new system, shipping information, data on customers, shipper tariffs and schedules, etc. are stored in the computer. Data regarding goods ready for shipment are entered during the day. At the end of each day, the computer prints out a schedule indicating the most efficient way to group packages for shipping.

All packages going to each of five major cities are put in one large crate and sent air freight. Upon arrival at their destination, the large crates are opened and individual packages are delivered to the customer via local carriers. (This is done by the local carrier at no charge.) Shipments to smaller communities are sent by the most efficient ground transportation. Figure D.6 contrasts the old and new systems.

BENEFITS   Using the computer to help consolidate and plan shipments, Volta can take advantage of reduced air freight rates.

FIGURE D.6   VOLTA FLOWCHART

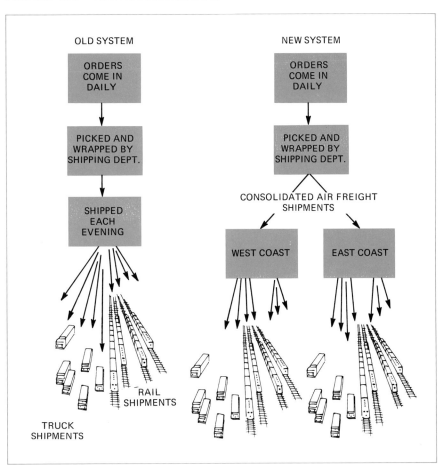

The computer provides management with several reports. It prints out cost reports and a comparison of shipping rates using different media. Customers get faster service at the same rate because, with air freight, shipping time has been reduced from an average of 15 days to 4 days.

PERSONNEL INFORMATION PROBLEM

Bleriot Airparts Company

Bleriot's twelve plants produce airframe parts and guidance and radar equipment. (See Figure D.7.) Each plant has its own personnel department responsible for hiring and selecting employees, including engineers, scientists, designers, technicians, clerks, and typists. The plants range in size from about 75 employees to more than 1,500.

Each employee's personnel record includes such data as age, military service, health history, previous employer, special training courses taken, education, special abilities and skills, language skills, and marital status.

FIGURE D.7   BLERIOT AIRPARTS COMPANY

LOCATION OF PLANTS

THE PROBLEM Bleriot has a labor pool of about 10,000 people, who range from those with limited skills such as file clerks or typists to those with highly specialized knowledge such as aerospace engineers.

Bleriot is expanding into a more diverse line of equipment and products. These new lines are developed by ''project groups,'' a staff of technicians, engineers, typists, etc. assigned to a particular problem. Bleriot must find the best staff for these new project groups.

The personnel department in the plant planning a project had to review 10,000 personnel files to identify employees with requisite skills who could be transferred to the new group. This method was slow, and employees who could do the job best were often overlooked. As a result, Bleriot would hire new personnel for a group, and then later discover an employee with the required skills.

THE SOLUTION A computer was already available in the data processing department. A master file, including all of the pertinent information for each employee, was developed. A computer program was designed and written to process personnel records in the file. Under the new system, the personnel department,

FIGURE D.8 BLERIOT FLOWCHART

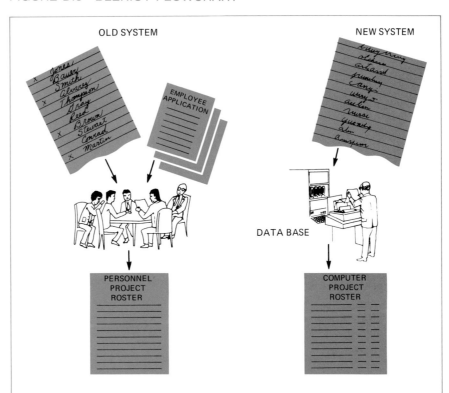

or a project director, can query the files with the list of requirements and the computer will output a list of employees who can fill the position. Queries are fed to the computer via a terminal or other input device. Figure D.8 contrasts the old method with the new system.

BENEFITS   Not only is the new system economical, but it has boosted employee morale because it enables employees to increase their job mobility. Since fewer new employees are being hired, the costs for training and indoctrination programs are reduced.

Management can get a closer look at employees. They are aware of the mix of personnel with specialized skills, language skills, security clearance, and special training. The system gives valuable information regarding medical-safety hazards and is useful in planning security, recruiting, and training programs.

CONSUMER CREDIT PROBLEM

Central City Merchants Association

The Central City Merchants Association is composed of a group of retail merchants located in a large midwestern city. Members include department stores, appliance dealers, garages, clothing stores, and furniture stores. (See Figure D.9.)

Each merchant extends credit to customers. Before reform, credit standing was learned by checking records kept by each merchant and calling the Association headquarters for a review of its files. (The Association's files include information on delinquent accounts, pending lawsuits, bad check passers, and so forth.) While the merchant waited on the phone, an Association clerk would search through several lists and file folders for the customer's name. If no negative credit information was found, the clerk reported that the customer had a good credit rating.

THE PROBLEM   The major limitations of the credit system were its high cost of maintenance and the delays in reporting important credit information. All credit data were recorded manually in files and searched by hand. It sometimes required several hours or more to check a name and clear credit if a suit were pending or if special instructions were noted in the file. The merchant either had to wait for clearance from the Association or extend credit without it and run the risk of a loss.

In some instances, customers would run up large bills at several stores at one time, or issue bad checks in payment for merchandise. It often took several weeks before this information filtered back to the Association's credit office and was recorded in the file. In the meantime, the merchant might extend even more credit or accept bad checks as payment.

FIGURE D.9   CENTRAL CITY MERCHANTS ASSOCIATION

THE SOLUTION   The Association solved its problem by implementing a computerized consumer credit system. A computer was installed in the Association office. A master file containing all credit information was recorded on magnetic disk. Included were the names of accounts, delinquencies, bad check passers, etc. Several clerks were assigned the task of maintaining the master file and entering new credit data. The master file was updated promptly to guarantee accurate credit ratings.

   With the new system, several clerks are assigned to handle phone queries from the merchants. A clerk keyboards credit request information on a video display terminal connected to the computer. The computer searches the master file and displays any data pertaining to that customer on the video terminal. The clerk then relays this credit information to the merchant. It now takes only a few minutes to process a query. Figure D.10 contrasts the old and new systems.

FIGURE D.10   CENTRAL CITY FLOWCHART

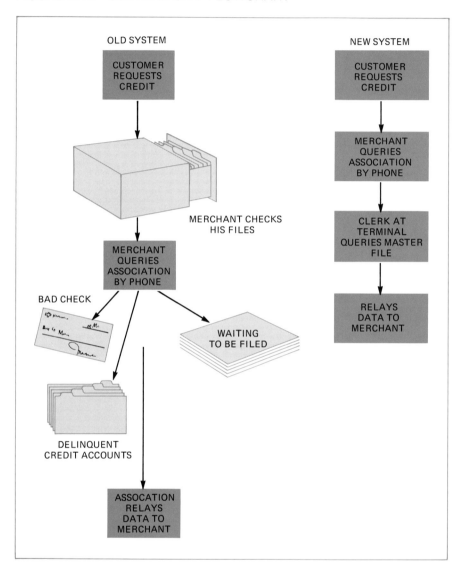

BENEFITS   The immediate benefits of the new system were the reduction in credit losses suffered by the merchants, improved customer relations, and, in some cases, an increase in sales. With credit information relayed immediately, delays in accepting checks and processing new orders are avoided. The incidences of accepting bad checks are substantially reduced.

Other benefits appeared later. As the bulk of credit data went online, costs for maintaining the credit check system were reduced and fewer clerks were required.

BANK TELLER PROBLEM

Trustworthy Bank

Trustworthy Bank is a medium-sized banking firm located in a northern state. It provides full banking facilities for its users, including loans, escrow accounts, and note collection service. There are 15 branches with a total of 150 teller windows in operation on an average business day. (See Figure D.11.) Each branch employs from 4 to 12 tellers.

At the end of the day, deposits, debits, and credits were processed in a batch system on the firm's computer. To process a deposit, for example, a teller stamped the customer's deposit slip and entered the amount in a deposit book. Each day, tellers checked the contents of their drawers

FIGURE D.11   TRUSTWORTHY BANK

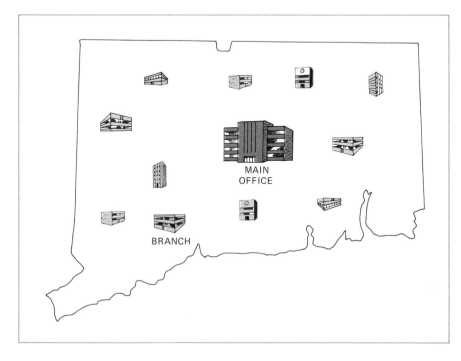

against the paperwork for that day. Later the deposits were sent to the main branch for posting to accounts. Reports and audits were handled at the main branch after all data were in. Withdrawals in excess of a minimum amount routinely required verifying the customer's balance.

FIGURE D.12   TRUSTWORTHY FLOWCHART

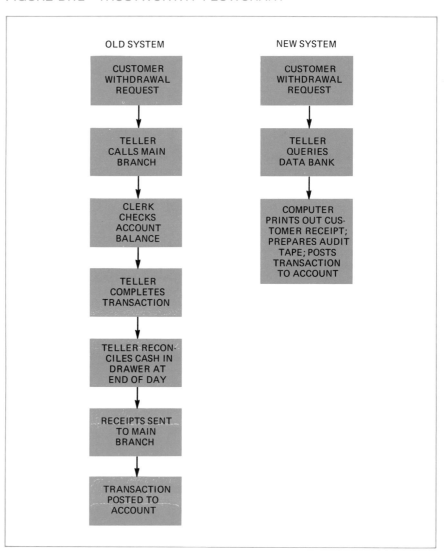

THE PROBLEM   This system had several inadequacies. Since data were not processed until the end of the day, phone queries to check balances and authorize customer withdrawals had to be made frequently. If clerks at the data center were busy, the customer had to wait at the window until the withdrawal was cleared.

Each teller spent a good deal of time at the end of each day reconciling the day's cash flow. Without an hourly record of transactions, auditing of teller windows was difficult and reports for management could not be prepared until all posting was completed.

THE SOLUTION   Trustworthy Bank installed a group of real-time teller terminals, coupled online to its computer in the main branch. A teller can query a data bank at any time during the day. All deposits and withdrawals are posted immediately from the terminal as they occur.

For example, when a customer makes a withdrawal, the teller keys in the account number and the amount of the transaction. The computer accesses the customer's account in the data bank and determines whether there are sufficient funds to cover the withdrawal. A receipt for the customer, showing the teller number, amount of withdrawal, and other data is printed out by the terminal. As the withdrawal is entered in the data bank, an audit tape is prepared, giving a complete record of the transaction. Figure D.12 contrasts the old and new systems used at Trustworthy Bank.

BENEFITS   The new system has benefited both Trustworthy and its customers. Since all transactions are handled online, tellers can query the account balance immediately to update passbooks and customers can make large withdrawals or cash checks without delay. Transactions now take less time and tellers can serve more customers per hour. As a result, some of the tellers have been reassigned to other duties, thus reducing labor costs.

The audit tapes generated by each teller terminal facilitate the general audit. In addition, the computer prints out management reports that list the number of checks cashed and deposits received by each branch, total the cash in and out, and give the net cash.

TAX SERVICE PROBLEM

Loophole Tax Service

Loophole Tax Service operates a group of 42 income tax offices. During peak periods, Loophole employs extra tax consultants to staff additional temporary offices. (See Figure D.13.) Each year the firm processes thousands of federal and state tax returns for clients.

The consultants interviewed clients to gather data on their tax liability.

FIGURE D.13   LOOPHOLE TAX SERVICE

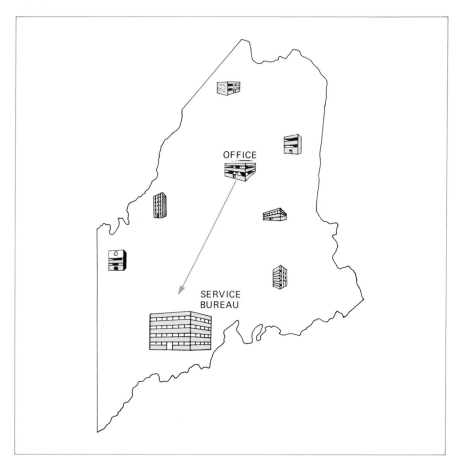

After the client left, the consultant reviewed the figures and calculated the tax liability, payments, etc. with an adding machine.

The figures were then given to a typist, who completed the tax forms. The forms were reviewed by the consultant and then given to the client.

THE PROBLEM   This system was slow and inefficient. Consultants wasted time on routine calculations, such as adding up itemized deductions. Many typists were required to prepare the forms. This work was slow since figures had to be carefully positioned on the forms. Sometimes important items were overlooked or errors crept into calculations.

One of the greatest difficulties was the rush during the tax season,

FIGURE D.14   LOOPHOLE FLOWCHART

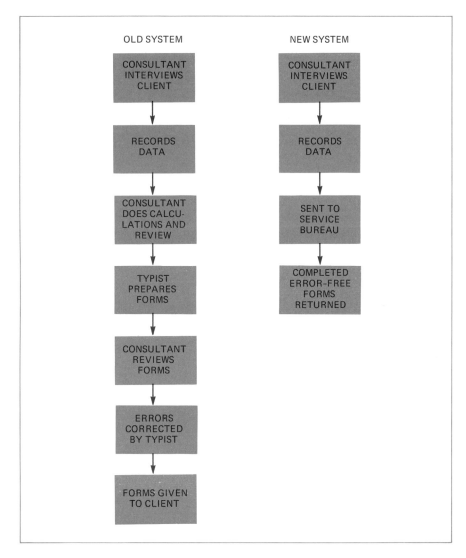

especially just before the tax forms were due. Typists and consultants were at their busiest, increasing overtime costs and chances of errors. Unfortunately, many last-minute clients had to be turned away.

THE SOLUTION   The solution to Loophole's problem was to buy computer time and software from a service bureau. On a piecework price arrangement, the service bureau does all keypunching, processing, and preparing of finished tax returns.

With the new system, a standard data sheet is used by all consultants to record data obtained during the client interview. The consultant pencils in such things as tax liability, deductions, and exemptions in the spaces provided. The forms are then given to the service bureau and the data are keypunched into cards. These cards are fed to the computer with the service bureau's tax preparation program. The line printer is loaded with a multipart, three-carbon form, imprinted with the standard tax form. The computer performs all calculations and prints out the results in the proper areas on the tax forms. The forms are returned to Loophole. One copy is for the client; one for the government; and the third is for Loophole's records. Figure D.14 contrasts the old and new systems.

BENEFITS   With the new system, Loophole Tax Service has been able to reduce costs and errors and handle more clients during the busy tax season. Since the computer performs all routine calculations, fewer clerical and mathematical errors occur. Important items are less likely to be overlooked, since the computer flags omissions and any items that appear to be excessive or in error.

The system has substantially reduced the amount of time a consultant spends on each return. Each consultant can now serve many more clients. Labor costs have fallen since far fewer typists are employed. Loophole's customers benefit because computer-printed tax forms are much neater than manually typed forms.

FIGURE D.15   ADAM SMITH MANUFACTURING COMPANY

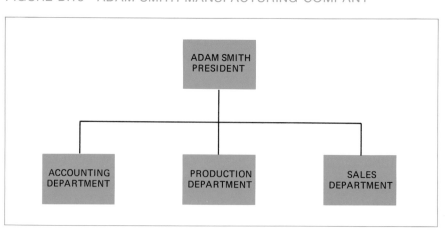

SMALL BUSINESS FIRM PROBLEM

Adam Smith Manufacturing Company

Adam Smith is the president of a small company that has been in business for 16 years. Thirty-three people are employed by the company, which manufactures small precision parts. (See Figure D.15.)

Six clerical employees are needed to handle data processing and paperwork. They process the weekly payroll, mail out over 300 checks per month to suppliers and vendors, prepare 2,000 invoices per month, and prepare statements for their several hundred accounts. In addition, Smith must keep many records, including ledgers, accounts payable, and accounts receivable. He must send out collection letters to overdue accounts. Current operating figures, such as sales analysis, projections, and inventory records, are needed for management decision making.

THE PROBLEM The six employees handling the paperwork faced many problems. When the workload was very heavy, they often mailed out invoices and statements late and made errors. Records were not maintained, and data flow and reports were inadequate.

Smith felt that inefficiencies in paperwork and data processing prevented his company from expanding and increasing earnings.

FIGURE D.16 ADAM SMITH FLOWCHART

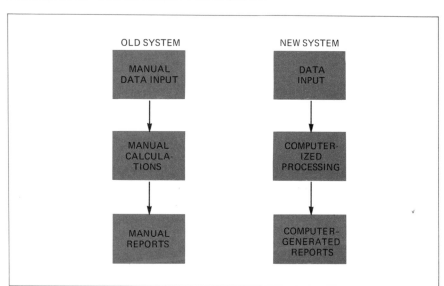

FIGURE D.17   MAKEMONEY CONSULTANTS

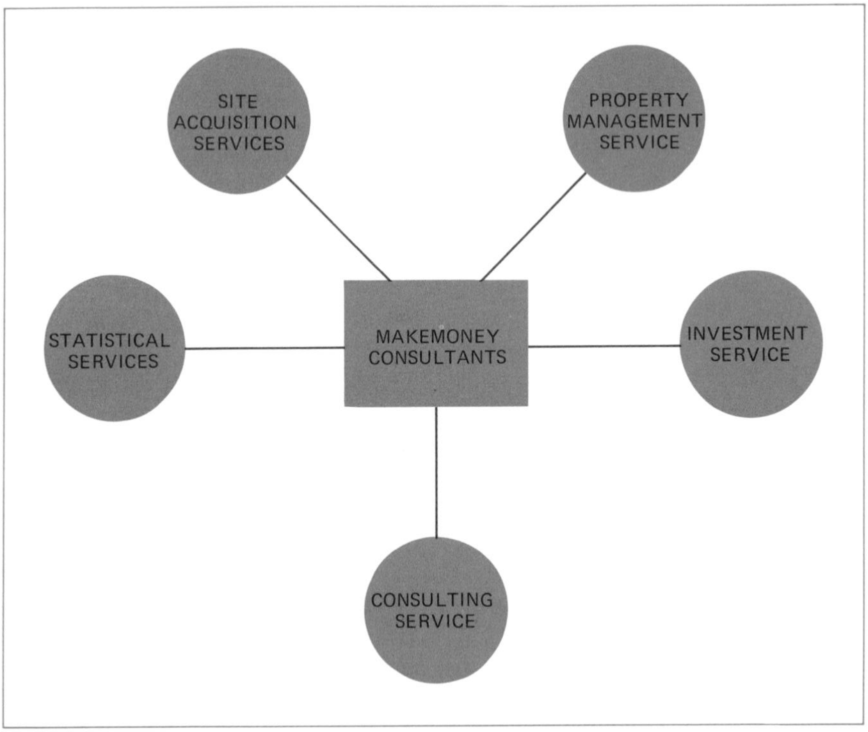

Smith presented his problem to several computer companies. They suggested a systems approach to his business. Smith leased a computer for $1,500 per month and, with the help of the manufacturer's systems engineers, shifted the bulk of his data processing to the new system.

Some ready-made programs were available from the computer systems library to process the payroll, invoicing, inventory, etc. These programs were implemented by the systems engineers with only a few minor changes and program modifications. Figure D.16 contrasts the old system with the new one.

Smith had hoped the new system would reduce his payroll costs. But this did not materialize. Instead, he hired a computer programmer/operator and transferred four of his employees from the accounting department to the sales and production departments.

Smith has been able to increase his sales 20%, while costs are up only 5%. As a result, capacity and profit have increased substantially. The computer system handles the general ledger, accounts receivable, and accounts payable. It handles the entire payroll and issues the company checks. It prepares earnings reports and government forms.

Invoicing procedures have improved. Smith has a better picture of his cash flow and more adequate information on inventory. Collections have improved, since bills are mailed out promptly and delinquent accounts are called to his attention sooner. The computer prepares the collection letters, which used to be typed by a secretary.

Smith has discovered added benefits. His production foreman found that several other computer programs available from the manufacturer were of value in the development and production of new products. These programs save the foreman and his staff about 50 hours each month. They are run during off hours, when the computer is not busy on other work. Smith feels this totally unexpected benefit has an economic value of several hundred dollars per month.

REAL ESTATE MANAGEMENT PROBLEM

Makemoney Consultants

Makemoney is a real estate and investment management consulting service. It offers investment, brokerage, site acquisition, and property management services to investors and landowners. Clients rely on Makemoney to analyze investment transactions and offer advice concerning land and building purchases. A staff of sales consultants deals directly with the clients. Analysts, statisticians, and forecasters work in the office preparing reports and data. (See Figure D.17.)

THE PROBLEM   The previous data processing system at Makemoney involved the preparation of estimates and typewritten reports.These required many hours of laborious manual calculations and a considerable amount of repetitive figuring. A full-time staff of ten employees was needed to figure rates of return, profit on real estate transactions, investment projections, and routine statistical work. During peak periods, errors occurred more frequently, and the analysts and statisticians sometimes fell behind in their work.

Because it is a small company, Makemoney could not afford to purchase or lease a computer large enough to handle its work, but it had a clear need for computerized data processing.

THE SOLUTION   Makemoney arranged to purchase computing time and software from a local time-sharing company. Two typewriter terminals connected by existing telephone lines to the time-sharing computer were installed. The terminals lease for about $100 per month each, and the charges for computing time from the company average $600 per month.

FIGURE D.18   MAKEMONEY FLOWCHART

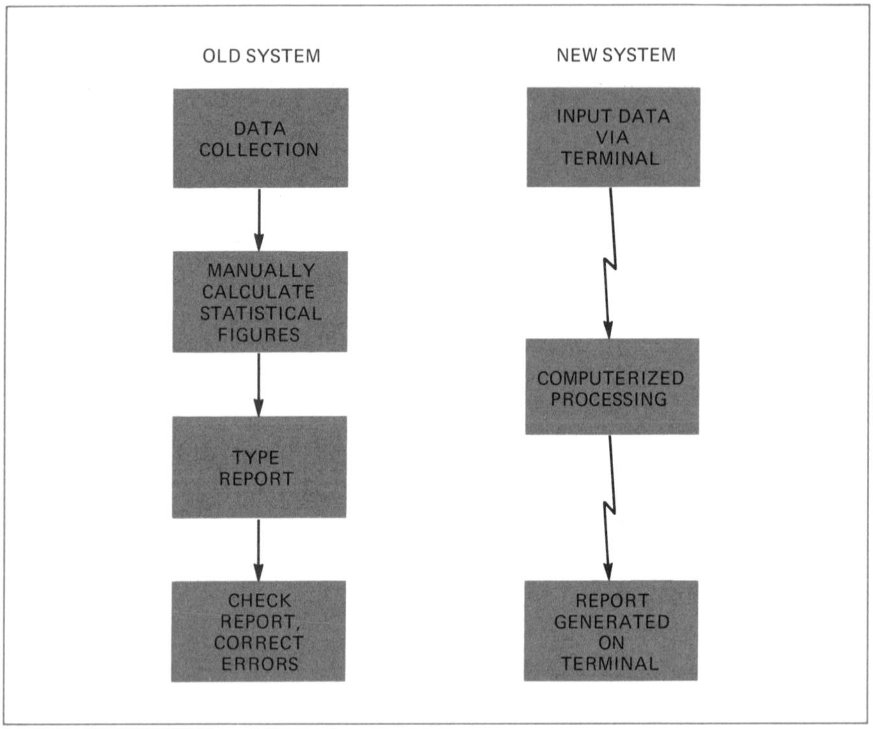

The time-sharing company has a variety of programs available for its customers. Makemoney uses a group of financial, real estate, money handling, interest, and statistical programs to service its needs. It also uses software to process cash flow, trend analysis, profit and loss statements, etc. These programs are on-line, ready for use, and Makemoney is able to use them with little or no changes.

Several employees are assigned the task of inputting and processing data on the terminals. The results are given to the sales consultants, who in turn review the information with their clients. Figure D.18 contrasts the old and new systems.

BENEFITS   With its new computer system, Makemoney is able to give its clients more accurate, complete, and prompt consulting services. The sales consultants can quickly advise clients concerning land transactions, enabling the clients to act faster and take advantage of lower market prices.

With the computer processing all calculations, projections, and estimates, statisticians and analysts no longer fall behind during peak periods. The reports printed out by the terminals in Makemoney's office are neat and accurate. Makemoney can give them directly to their clients without any retyping or correction.

Makemoney was able to promote several of its analysts and statisticians to sales consultants. The new business they bring in far exceeds the cost of the time-sharing service. As a result, Makemoney is doing about a 20% greater volume of business, with little increase in operating costs. As Makemoney continues to expand, the installation of extra Teletype terminals will handle the increased volume of work.

EXERCISES   Answer the questions below for each of the nine cases presented in this chapter.

1. Prepare a list of hardware the firm might use in implementing the new system.
2. What computer language would be most valuable to the firm?
3. What proprietary programs, if any, might be used?
4. What further changes or improvements would you suggest?

GLOSSARY[1]

*ABSOLUTE ADDRESS   An address that is permanently assigned by the machine designer to a storage location. A pattern of characters that identifies a unique storage location without further modification. Synonymous with machine address, specific address.

*ACCESS TIME   The time interval between the instant at which data are called for from a storage device and the instant delivery begins. The time interval between the instant at which data are requested to be stored and the instant at which storage is started.

ACTIVITY   A term to indicate that a record in a master file is used, altered, or referred to.

*ADDRESS   An identification as represented by a name, label, or number for a register, location in storage, or any other source or destination, such as the location of a station in a communication network.

*ALGOL   *Algo*rithmic *L*anguage. A language primarily used to express computer programs by algorithms.

*ALGORITHM   A prescribed set of well-defined rules or processes for the solution of a problem in a finite number of steps.

*ALPHAMERIC   See Alphanumeric.

*ALPHANUMERIC   Pertaining to a character set that contains letters, digits, and usually other characters such as punctuation marks. Synonymous with alphameric.

*ANALOG COMPUTER   A computer in which analog representation of data is mainly used. A computer that operates on analog data by performing physical processes on these data. Contrast with *digital computer.*

ANALOG DATA   Data represented in a continuous form, as contrasted with digital data represented in a discrete (discontinuous) form. Analog data are usually represented by means of physical variables, such as voltage, resistance, and rotation.

ANSI   American National Standards Institute. Formerly ASA and USASI.

[1]All entries marked with an asterisk are reproduced with permission from the *American National Standard Vocabulary for Information Processing,* © 1970 by American National Standards Institute, copies of which may be purchased from the American National Standards Institute at 1430 Broadway, New York, New York 10018.

APL *A Programming Language.* A mathematically oriented language.

*ARITHMETIC UNIT The unit of a computing system that contains the circuits that perform arithmetic operations.

*ARRAY An arrangement of elements in one or more dimensions.

*ASCII American Standard Code for Information Interchange. The standard code, using a coded character set consisting of seven-bit coded characters (eight bits including parity check), used for information interchange among data processing systems, communication systems, and associated equipment. The ASCII set consists of control characters and graphic characters. Synonymous with USASCII.

*ASSEMBLE To prepare a machine language program from a symbolic language program by substituting absolute operation codes for symbolic operation codes and absolute or relocatable addresses for symbolic addresses.

ASSEMBLER LANGUAGE A symbolic programming language that uses symbolic operation codes and addresses. The translation of these codes into machine language is called an assembly.

ATS *Administrative Terminal System.* A text processing language.

AUDIO RESPONSE UNIT A device that outputs information, recorded on a magnetic storage medium, using the spoken word.

*AUXILIARY STORAGE A storage that supplements another storage. In flowcharting, an offline operation performed by equipment not under control of the central processing unit.

*BACKGROUND PROCESSING The automatic execution of lower priority computer programs when higher priority programs are not using the system resources. Contrast with *foreground processing.*

BACKUP SYSTEM Standby facilities such as a computer or files, for use in case of damage, loss, or overloading.

BASE The number of characters used in a digital numbering system.

BASIC *Beginners All-Purpose Symbolic Instruction Code.* A programming language used in time sharing.

*BATCH PROCESSING Pertaining to the technique of executing a set of programs such that each is completed before the next program of the set is started. Loosely, the execution of programs serially. Pertaining to the sequential input of computer programs or data.

BAUDOT CODE A code for the transmission of data in which five equal-length bits represent one character.

*BCD (BINARY CODED DECIMAL NOTATION) Positional notation in which the individual decimal digits expressing a number in decimal notation are each represented by a binary numeral.

BCDIC (BINARY CODED DECIMAL INTERCHANGE CODE) An extension of the BCD numeric code, consisting of six intelligence channels and one parity check-bit channel. Up to 64 different characters can be transmitted.

BINARY NOTATION A fixed-base notation where the base is two.

BINARY SEARCH A search procedure that locates the object of search by successively dividing a file, or part of a file, in half and searching for the object at the midpoint.

BIT Contraction of "binary digit," the smallest unit of information in a binary system. A bit may be either one or zero.

BLANK-COLUMN DETECTION A unit record procedure that detects unpunched or uncoded columns.

*BLOCK A set of things, such as words, characters, or digits, handled as a unit. A collection of contiguous records recorded as a unit. Blocks are separated by block gaps and each block may contain one or more records.

BLOCKING Combining two or more records into one block.

BPS (BITS PER SECOND) In serial transmission, the instantaneous bit speed within one character, as transmitted by a machine or a channel.

*BRANCH A set of instructions that are executed between two successive decision instructions. To select a branch as above. Loosely, a conditional jump.

*BUFFER A routine or storage used to compensate for a difference in rate of flow of data, or time of occurrence of events, when transmitting data from one device to another.

*BUG A mistake or malfunction.

*BYTE A sequence of adjacent binary digits operated upon as a unit and usually shorter than a computer word.

CARD PUNCH A device to record information in cards by punching holes in the cards to represent letters, digits, and special characters.

CARD READER A device that senses and translates into internal form the holes in punched cards.

CATHODE RAY TUBE (CRT) DISPLAY A device that presents data in visual form by means of controlled electron beams. The data display produced by such a device.

CENTRALIZED DATA PROCESSING A computer system in which the processor facilities are located at a single geographic site.

*CENTRAL PROCESSING UNIT (CPU) A unit of a computer that includes circuits controlling the interpretation and execution of instructions. Synonymous with *main frame*.

*CHAIN PRINTER A printer in which type slugs are carried by the links of a revolving chain.

*CHANNEL A path along which signals can be sent—for example, data channel, output channel. The portion of a storage medium that is accessible to a given reading or writing station—for example, track, band. In communication, a means of one-way transmission.

CHANNEL ADDRESS The code that refers to a particular circuit that connects the CPU to an I/O device.

CHANNEL SCHEDULER In the Disk and Tape Operating Systems (DOS and TOS), that part of the supervisor that controls all input/output operations.

*CHARACTER A letter, digit, or other symbol that is used as part of the organization, control, or representation of data.

*CHARACTER SET A set of unique representations called characters—for example, 26 letters of the English alphabet, 0 and 1 of the Boolean alphabet, the set of signals in the Morse code alphabet, the 128 characters of the ASCII alphabet.

*CHECK BIT A binary check digit—for example, a parity bit.

CLASSIFY To arrange into classes of information according to a system or method.

*CLOCK A device that generates periodic signals used for synchronization. A device that measures and indicates time. A register whose content changes at regular intervals in such a way as to measure time.

*CLOSED SHOP Pertaining to the operation of a computer facility in which most productive problem programming is performed by a group of programming specialists rather than by the problem originators. The use of the computer itself may also be described as closed shop if full-time trained operators, rather than user/programmers serve as the operators. Contrast with *open shop.*

*COBOL   *Common Business-Oriented Language.* A business data processing language.

CODASYL   *Conference of Data Systems Languages.* The group of users and manufacturers of data processing systems that developed and maintain the COBOL language.

CODING   The operation of converting instructions into language commands that can be processed by a computer.

*COLLATE   To combine items from two or more ordered sets into one set having a specified order not necessarily the same as any of the original sets. Contrast with *merge.*

*COLUMN   A vertical arrangement of characters or other expressions. Loosely, a digit place.

*COMMUNICATION LINK   The physical means of connecting one location to another for the purpose of transmitting and receiving data.

*COMPILE   To prepare a machine language program from a computer program written in another programming language by making use of the overall logic structure of the program, or generating more than one machine instruction for each symbolic statement, or both, as well as performing the function of an assembler.

*COMPILER   A program that compiles.

*COMPUTER   A data processor that can perform substantial computation, including numerous arithmetic or logic operations, without intervention by a human operator during the run.

COMPUTER UTILITY   An organization that provides data processing consultation, services, and time-share support to another firm, usually via remote processing facilities.

*CONSOLE   That part of a computer used for communication between the operator or maintenance engineer and the computer.

CONSTANT   A fixed or invariable value or data item.

CONTROL PROGRAM   See Operating System.

CONTROL UNIT   In a digital computer, those parts that effect the retrieval of instructions in proper sequence, the interpretation of each instruction, and the application of the proper signals to the arithmetic unit and other parts in accordance with this interpretation.

CORE STORAGE   A form of high-speed storage, using magnetic cores.

COUNT DATA FORMAT   A system of organizing records in a disk file containing one home address area, with count and data areas for each record.

*COUNTER   A device such as a register or storage location used to represent the number of occurrences of an event.

COUNT KEY DATA FORMAT   A system of organizing records in a disk file containing one home address area, with count, key, and data areas for each record.

COUPLER   See Modem.

CYLINDER   The group of data tracks accessed simultaneously by a set of read and write heads on a disk storage device.

*DATA   A representation of facts, concepts, or instructions in a formalized manner suitable for communication, interpretation, or processing by human or automatic means. Any representation, such as characters or analog quantities, to which meaning is, or might be, assigned.

*DATA BANK   A comprehensive collection of libraries of data. For example, one line of an invoice may form an item, a complete invoice may form a record, a complete set of such records may form a file, the collection of inventory control files may form a library, and the libraries used by an organization are known as its data bank.

DATA BASE   See Data Bank.

DATA CELL DRIVE   A random-access storage device that holds millions of characters on strips of magnetic material. The strips are filed in groups called cells.

DATA COLLECTION   The act of bringing data from one or more points to a central point.

DATA CYCLE   The fundamental data processing sequence of operations, composed of input, processing, and output.

DATA DECK   That portion of a job that contains the data or information to be processed by the program.

DATA FLOW   The data path through a problem solution.

DATA INQUIRY   One element of a teleprocessing system in which remote files can be accessed by a request for information.

DATA MANAGEMENT   A general term that collectively describes those functions of the control program that provide access to data sets, enforce data storage conventions, and regulate the use of input/output devices.

DATA MANIPULATION   See Data Processing.

*DATA PROCESSING   The execution of a systematic sequence of operations performed upon data. Synonymous with *information processing.*

DATA TRANSMISSION   The sending of data from one part of a system to another.

*DEBUG   To detect, locate, and remove mistakes from a routine or malfunctions from a computer. Synonymous with *troubleshoot.*

DECENTRALIZED DATA PROCESSING   A computer system in which the processor facilities are located at a variety of geographic sites rather than at a single site.

DECIMAL NOTATION   A fixed-base notation, where the base is ten.

*DECISION   A determination of future action.

DECISION TABLE   A tabular form showing the alternative conditions and actions that may take place in a program.

*DECODER   A device that decodes. A matrix of logic elements that selects one or more output channels according to the combination of input signals present.

*DETAIL FILE   See Transaction File.

DETAIL PROGRAM FLOWCHART   A flowchart that shows a step-by-step diagram of each detail involved in the solution of a problem. Synonymous with *micro* or *detail flowchart.*

DIAGNOSTIC MESSAGE   Messages printed out by the computer during compilation or execution of a program, pertaining to the diagnosis or isolation of errors in the program.

DIGIT ROW   One of the horizontal rows of bits on a punched card, generally referring to rows 1 to 9.

*DIGITAL COMPUTER   A computer in which discrete representation of data is mainly used. A computer that operates on discrete data by performing arithmetic and logic processes on these data. Contrast with Analog Computer.

DIGITAL DATA   Data represented in discrete, discontinuous form, as contrasted with analog data represented in continuous form. Digital data are usually represented by means of coded characters, such as numbers, letters, and symbols.

DIRECT ACCESS   See Random Access.

DISK   See Magnetic Disk.

DISK PACK   A direct access storage device containing magnetic disks on which data are stored. Disk packs are mounted on a disk storage drive.

DISPLAY   A visual presentation of data.

DISTRIBUTIVE DATA PROCESSING   See Decentralized Data Processing.

DOCUMENT   A medium and the data recorded on it for human use—for example, a report sheet, a book. By extension, any record that has permanence and that can be read by person or machine.

*DOCUMENTATION   The creating, collecting, organizing, storing, citing, and disseminating of documents or the information recorded in documents. A collection of documents or information on a given subject.

DOS   Disk Operating System.

*DUMP   To copy the contents of all or part of a storage, usually from an internal storage into an external storage.

EAM   Electrical Accounting Machine. Pertaining to data processing equipment that is predominantly electromechanical, such as card punch, mechanical sorter, collator, and tabulator.

EBCDIC   Extended Binary Coded Decimal Interchange Code. A coding system widely used in modern computers, which can represent up to 256 characters. Consists of eight-bit coded characters and a ninth parity bit.

*EDIT   To modify the form or format of data—for example, to insert or delete characters such as page numbers or decimal points.

EFTS   Electronic Funds Transfer System.

*ELECTRONIC DATA PROCESSING (EDP)   Data processing largely performed by electronic devices. Pertaining to data processing equipment that is predominantly electronic, such as an electronic digital computer.

END-OF-FILE MARK   A code that signals that the last record of a file has been read.

*END-OF-TAPE MARKER   A marker on a magnetic tape used to indicate the end of the permissible recording area—for example, a photoreflective strip, a transparent section of tape, or a particular bit pattern.

END PRINTING   A form of interpreting in which large numbers, approximately $\frac{1}{4}$ inch high, are printed on the end of a punched card, at right angles to the zone and digit rows.

*ERROR   Any discrepancy between a computed, observed, or measured quantity and the true, specified, or theoretically correct value or condition.

EVEN PARITY   A checking system in which a binary digit is added to an array of bits to make the sum of the bits even.

EXECUTE   To carry out an instruction or perform a routine.

EXECUTION CYCLE   The phase in the CPU operating cycle during which an instruction is performed or carried out.

FEASIBILITY STUDY   A planning study, made to evaluate the aspects of implementing a new system or modifying an existing one. The study involves consideration of such elements as cost, time, labor.

*FIELD   In a record, a specified area used for a particular category of data, for example, a group of card columns used to represent a wage rate or a set of bit locations in a computer word used to express the address of the operand.

*FILE   A collection of related records treated as a unit. For example, one line of an invoice may form an item, a complete invoice may form a record, the complete set of such records may form a file, the collection of inventory control files may form a library, and the libraries used by an organization are known as its data bank.

FILE LABEL   A unique name assigned to a file to identify its contents.

*FILE MAINTENANCE   The activity of keeping a file up to date by adding, changing, or deleting data.

FILE PROTECTION RING   A plastic ring placed around the hub of a reel of magnetic tape to allow data to be written on the tape. It is a means of error prevention.

FIXED-LENGTH RECORD   Pertaining to a file in which all records are constrained to be of equal, predetermined length.

*FIXED-POINT REPRESENTATION   A positional representation in which each number is represented by a single set of digits, the position of the radix point being fixed with respect to one end of the set, according to some convention.

FLEXIBLE DISK   A secondary storage device composed of a thin flexible storage medium coated with ferromagnetic compound.

*FLIP FLOP   A circuit or device containing active elements, capable of assuming either one or two stable states at a given time.

*FLOATING-POINT REPRESENTATION   A number representation system in which each number, as represented by a pair of numerals, equals one of those numerals times a power of an implicit fixed positive integer base where the power is equal to the implicit base raised to the exponent represented by the other numeral.

*FLOWCHART   A graphical representation for the definition, analysis, or solution of a problem in which symbols are used to represent operations, data, flow, equipment, etc.

*FOREGROUND PROCESSING   The automatic execution of the programs that have been designed to preempt the use of the computing facilities. Usually a real-time program.

*FORMAT   The arrangement of data.

*FORTRAN   *For*mula *Tran*slating system. A language primarily used to express computer programs by arithmetic formulas.

*FULL DUPLEX   In communications, pertaining to a simultaneous two-way independent transmission in both directions. Synonymous with duplex.

*FUNCTION   A specific purpose of an entity or its characteristic action. In communications, a machine action such as a carriage return or line feed.

GANG PUNCH   To punch all or part of the information from one punched card into succeeding cards.

*GATE   A device having one output channel and one or more input channels, such that the output channel state is completely determined by the input channel states, except during switching transients. A combinational logic element having at least one input channel.

*GENERAL-PURPOSE COMPUTER   A computer designed to handle a wide variety of problems.

*GENERATOR   A controlling routine that performs a generate function, for example, report generator, I/O generator.

GRAPHIC OUTPUT   Symbols output from a system. Includes plots, drawings, curves, and lines.

GROUPING   Combining records into a unit to conserve storage space or reduce access time.

*HALF DUPLEX   In communications, pertaining to an alternate, one way at a time, independent transmission.

HARD COPY   See Document.

*HARDWARE   Physical equipment, as opposed to the program or method of use—for example, mechanical, magnetic, electrical, or electronic devices. Contrast with *software.*

*HEADER CARD   A card that contains information related to the data in cards that follow.

HEXADECIMAL NOTATION   A numeration system with a base of sixteen.

*HOLLERITH Pertaining to a particular type of code or punched card utilizing 12 rows per column and usually 80 columns per card.

HOLLERITH CARD See Punched Card.

HOUSEKEEPING Operations or routines that do not contribute directly to solution of the problem but do contribute directly to the operation of the computer.

*INDEX An ordered reference list of the contents of a file or document together with keys or reference notations for identification or location of those contents. To prepare a list as in the above. A symbol or numeral used to identify a particular quantity in an array of similar quantities. To move a machine part to a predetermined position, or by a predetermined amount, on a quantized scale.

INFORMATION See Data.

*INFORMATION PROCESSING See Data Processing.

*INFORMATION RETRIEVAL The methods and procedures for recovering specific information from stored data.

INFORMATION RETRIEVAL SYSTEM A computer system that provides for data storage and rapid retrieval and display of the stored information.

*INITIALIZE To set counters, switches, and addresses to zero or other starting values at the beginning of, or at prescribed points in, a computer routine.

*INPUT Pertaining to a device, process, or channel involved in the insertion of data or states, or to the data or states involved.

INPUT/OUTPUT Commonly called I/O. A general term for the equipment used to communicate with a computer. The data involved in such communication. The media carrying the data for input/output.

INPUT/OUTPUT CONTROL SYSTEM (IOCS) A control program designed to schedule the flow of data into and out of the computer system.

*INSTRUCTION A statement that specifies an operation and the values or locations of its operands.

INSTRUCTION CYCLE The phase in the CPU operating cycle during which an instruction is called from storage and the required circuitry to perform that instruction is set up.

INTEGER A positive or negative whole number or zero.

INTELLIGENCE CHANNEL In communications, a pathway for meaningful or useful information (as contrasted with the check-bit channel, which transmits parity information).

INTEGRATED CIRCUIT A combination of interconnected circuit elements inseparably associated on, or within, a continuous substrate.

INTERACTIVE LANGUAGE A language designed to allow the programmer to communicate with the computer during the execution of the program.

INTERACTIVE PROGRAM A computer program that permits data to be entered, or the course of programming flow to be changed, during its execution.

*INTERPRETER A computer program that translates and executes each source language statement before translating and executing the next one. The device that prints on a punched card the data already punched in the card.

*INTER-RECORD GAP (IRG) An area on a data medium used to indicate the end of a block or record.

*INTERRUPT To stop a process in such a way that it can be resumed.

*JOB A specified group of tasks prescribed as a unit of work for a computer. By extension, a job usually includes all necessary computer programs, linkages, files, and instructions to the operating systems.

JOB CONTROL LANGUAGE   A language for communicating with the computer to identify a job or describe its requirements to the operating system.

JOB STREAM   The flow of cards, or records input to a computer system, containing the job control statements, source program, and data deck.

*K   An abbreviation for the prefix kilo, that is, 1000, in decimal notation. Loosely, when referring to storage capacity, two to the tenth power, 1024 in decimal notation.

*KEY   One or more characters within an item of data that are used to identify it or control its use.

*KEYPUNCH   A keyboard-actuated device that punches holes in a card to represent data.

*LABEL   One or more characters used to identify a statement or an item of data in a computer program.

*LANGUAGE   A set of representations, conventions, and rules used to convey information.

*LIBRARY   A collection of organized information used for study and reference. A collection of related files.

*LIBRARY ROUTINE   A proven routine that is maintained in a program library.

*LINE PRINTER   A device that prints all characters of a line as a unit.

*LINEAR PROGRAMMING   In operations research, a procedure for locating the maximum or minimum of a linear function of variables that are subject to linear constraints.

LISTING   To print every item of input data. Loosely, a printout of all cards or records in a program or file.

LOAD-POINT MARK   A marker on a magnetic tape used to indicate the beginning of the permissible recording areas. For example, a photoreflective strip, a transparent section of tape, or a particular bit pattern.

*LOGICAL RECORD   A collection of items independent of their physical environment. Portions of the same logical record may be located in different physical records.

LONGITUDINAL PARITY CHECK   In magnetic tape, on a tape in which each lateral row of bits represents a character, the last character placed in a block and which is used for checking parity of each track in the block in the longitudinal direction.

*LOOP   A sequence of instructions that is executed repeatedly until a terminal condition prevails.

*MACHINE LANGUAGE   A language that is used directly by a machine.

MAGNETIC CORE   A configuration of magnetic material that is used to concentrate an induced magnetic field to retain a magnetic polarization for the purpose of storing data, or for its nonlinear properties as in a logic element. It may be made of such material as iron, iron oxide, or ferrite and in such shapes as wires, tapes, toroids, rods, or thin film.

*MAGNETIC DISK   A flat, circular plate with a magnetic surface on which data can be stored by selective magnetization of portions of the flat surface.

*MAGNETIC DRUM   A right circular cylinder with a magnetic surface on which data can be stored by selective magnetization of portions of the curved surface.

*MAGNETIC INK CHARACTER RECOGNITION   The machine recognition of characters printed with magnetic ink. Abbreviated MICR.

*MAGNETIC TAPE   A tape with a magnetic surface on which data can be stored by selective polarization of portions of the surface. A tape of magnetic material used as the constituent in some forms of magnetic cores.

*MAIN FRAME   Same as *central processing unit*.

*MANAGEMENT INFORMATION SYSTEM Management performed with the aid of automatic data processing. An information system designed to aid in the performance of management functions. Abbreviated MIS.

MANUAL DATA PROCESSING Data processing procedures using pencil, paper, adding machine, calculator, etc.

MARK SENSE To mark a position on a punched card with an electrically conductive pencil, for later conversion to machine punching.

*MASTER FILE A file that is either relatively permanent or that is treated as an authority in a particular job.

*MATCH To check for identity between two or more items of data.

*MATHEMATICAL MODEL A mathematical representation of a process, device, or concept.

*MATRIX In mathematics, a two-dimensional rectangular array of quantities. Matrices are manipulated in accordance with the rules of matrix algebra. In computers, a logic network in the form of an array of input leads and output leads with logic elements connected at some of their intersections. By extension, an array of any number of dimensions.

*MEMORY See Storage.

*MERGE To combine items from two or more similarly ordered sets into one set that is arranged in the same order. Contrast with *collate*.

MICRO FLOWCHART See Detail Program Flowchart.

MICROPROCESSOR A miniature computer manufactured on a small chip, using solid state integrated circuitry, that possesses characteristics of larger systems.

MICROSECOND One-millionth of a second.

MILLISECOND One-thousandth of a second.

MINICOMPUTER A small, desk-top, digital computer, with a CPU, at least one I/O device, and primary storage capacity of 4K bytes.

MIS Management information system.

*MNEMONIC SYMBOL A symbol chosen to assist the human memory—for example, an abbreviation such as "mpy" for "multiply."

*MODEM *Mo*dulator-*Dem*odulator. A device that modulates and demodulates signals transmitted over communications facilities.

MONITOR PROGRAM See Operating System.

*MULTIPLEX To interleave or simultaneously transmit two or more messages on a single channel.

MULTIPLEXER CHANNEL Feeds data between a group of slow speed input/output devices and the CPU.

*MULTIPROCESSING Pertaining to the simultaneous execution of two or more computer programs or sequences of instructions by a computer or computer network. Loosely, parallel processing.

*MULTIPROGRAMMING Pertaining to the concurrent execution of two or more programs by a computer.

NANOSECOND One billionth of a second (10^{-9} sec).

*OBJECT PROGRAM A fully compiled or assembled program that is ready to be loaded into the computer.

OCTAL REPRESENTATION Pertaining to the numeration system with a base of eight.

ODD PARITY A checking system in which a binary digit is added to an array of bits to make the sum of the bits odd.

*OFFLINE Pertaining to equipment or devices not under control of the central processing unit.

OFFLINE SYSTEM   In teleprocessing, that kind of system in which human operations are required between the original recording function and the ultimate data processing function. This includes conversion operations as well as the necessary loading and unloading operations incident to the use of point-to-point or data gathering system.

*ONLINE   Pertaining to equipment or devices under control of the central processing unit. Pertaining to a user's ability to interact with a computer.

ONLINE SYSTEM   In teleprocessing, a system in which the input data enter the computer directly from the point of origin and/or in which output data are transmitted directly to where they are used.

OP CODE   See Operation Code.

*OPEN SHOP   Pertaining to the operation of a computer facility in which most productive problem programming is performed by the problem originator rather than by a group of programming specialists. The use of the computer itself may also be described as open shop if the user/programmer also serves as the operator, rather than a full-time trained operator. Contrast with *closed shop.*

*OPERAND   That which is operated upon. An operand is usually identified by an address part of an instruction.

*OPERATING SYSTEM   Software that controls the execution of computer programs and that may provide scheduling, debugging, input/output control, accounting, compilation, storage assignment, data management, and related services.

*OPERATION CODE   A code that represents specific operations.

*OPTICAL CHARACTER RECOGNITION   Machine identification of printed characters through use of light-sensitive devices. Abbreviated OCR.

OUTPUT   Data that have been processed. The state or sequence of states occurring on a specified output channel. The device or collective set of devices for taking data out of a device. A channel for expressing a state of a device or logic element. The process of transferring data from an internal storage to an external storage.

OVERLAP   To do something at the same time that something else is being done; for example, to perform input/output operations while instructions are being executed by the central processing unit.

PAGING   A procedure for maximizing the memory capacity of a computer by swapping data between primary memory and a secondary storage device. See also Virtual Storage.

*PARALLEL   Pertaining to the concurrent or simultaneous occurrence of two or more related activities in multiple devices or channels.

*PARITY CHECK   A check that tests whether the number of ones (or zeros) in an array of binary digits is odd or even.

*PERIPHERAL EQUIPMENT   In a data processing system, any unit of equipment, distinct from the central processing unit, that may provide the system with outside communication.

PERT   *Program Evaluation and Review Technique.* A systems analysis technique used to find the most efficient scheduling of time and resources when producing a complex project or product.

PHOTOTYPESETTER   An output device that prints out characters using a photographic imaging system.

PHYSICAL RECORD   A record from the standpoint of the manner or form in which it is stored, retrieved, and moved—that is, one that is defined in terms of physical qualities.

PICOSECOND   One-thousandth of a nanosecond.

PL/I   *Programming Language I,* a high-level programming language.

PLOT   To map or diagram. To connect the point-by-point coordinate values.

PORTABLE PUNCH   A hand-held device that allows the operator to manually punch out precut holes. Used to encode data in machine-readable form while in the field.

POL·   See Problem-Oriented Language.

PRIMARY STORAGE   The main internal storage.

*PROBLEM-ORIENTED LANGUAGE   A programming language designed for the convenient expression of a given class of problems.

PROBLEM PROGRAM   See Source Program.

*PROCESSOR   In hardware, a data processor. In software, a computer program that includes the compiling, assembling, translating, and related functions for a specific programming language, COBOL processor, FORTRAN processor.

PRODUCTION RUN   A computer run, involving actual data, as contrasted with a test run, using data for checking purposes.

*PROGRAM   A series of actions proposed in order to achieve a certain result. Loosely, a routine. To design, wire, and test a program.

PROGRAM FLOWCHART   A step-by-step diagram, showing each discrete procedure and element in the solution of the problem.

PULSE TRAIN   The resulting electronic impulses that transmit encoded information.

*PUNCHED CARD   A card punched with a pattern of holes to represent data. A card as above, before being punched.

*PUNCHED TAPE   A tape on which a pattern of holes or cuts is used to represent data.

QUEUE   A waiting line formed by items in a system waiting for service—for example, customer at a bank teller window or messages to be transmitted in a message switching system. To arrange in, or form, a queue.

*RANDOM ACCESS   Pertaining to the process of obtaining data from, or placing data into, storage where the time required for such access is independent of the location of the data most recently obtained or placed in storage. Pertaining to a storage device in which the access time is effectively independent of the location of the data.

READ/WRITE HEAD   That part of a magnetic tape drive that records electronic pulses on magnetic tape, or reads data from tape.

*REAL TIME   Pertaining to the actual time during which a physical process transpires. Pertaining to the performance of a computation during the actual time that the related physical process transpires in order that results of the computation can be used in guiding the physical process.

*RECORD   A collection of related items of data, treated as a unit. For example, one line of an invoice may form a record; a complete set of such records may form a file.

*RECORD LENGTH   A measure of the size of a record, usually specified in units such as words or characters.

*REGISTER   A device capable of storing a specified amount of data, such as one word.

*REMOTE ACCESS   Pertaining to communication with a data processing facility by one or more stations that are distant from that facility.

REMOTE JOB ENTRY (RJE)   A system of hardware and software that enables jobs to be input, processed, and output via remote terminals.

REPORTING   Data outputted in a form usable to people, for example, information transferred from magnetic tape to printed payroll checks.

REPORT PROGRAM GENERATOR (RPG)   A computer language used for processing large data files.

REPRODUCE   To prepare a duplicate of stored information, especially for punched cards, punched paper tape, or magnetic tape.

*ROUTINE   An ordered set of instructions that may have some general or frequent use.

*ROW   A horizontal arrangement of characters or other expressions.

*RUN   A single, continuous performance of a computer program or routine.

*SEARCH   To examine a set of items for one or more having a desired property.

SECONDARY STORAGE   Auxiliary storage.

SECTOR   A pie-shaped portion or area on the surface of a magnetic disk storage device.

SELECTOR CHANNEL   Feeds data between a single high-speed input/output device and the CPU.

SEMICONDUCTOR   A solid-state electronic switching device that performs functions similar to an electronic tube.

SEQUENCE CHECKING (CHECKING SEQUENCE)   A unit record procedure that determines whether all records in a file are ordered in a series, or according to rank or time.

SEQUENTIAL ACCESS   Pertaining to the sequential or consecutive transmission of data to or from storage. Pertaining to the process of obtaining data from or placing data into storage where the time required for such access is dependent upon the location of the data most recently obtained or placed in storage. Synonymous with serial access.

SEQUENTIAL SEARCH   A search procedure in which the object of the search is located by systematically evaluating each record in the file in sequence.

*SERIAL   Pertaining to the sequential or consecutive occurrence of two or more related activities in a single device or channel. Pertaining to the sequencing of two or more processes. Pertaining to the sequential processing of the individual parts of a whole, such as the bits of a character or the characters of a word, using the same facilities for successive parts.

*SIMULATION   To represent certain features of the behavior of a physical or abstract system by the behavior of another system.

*SOFTWARE   A set of computer programs, procedures, and possibly associated documentation concerned with the operation of a data processing system, for example, compilers, library routines, manuals, circuit diagrams. Contrast with *hardware*.

*SORT   To segregate items into groups according to some definite rules. Same as order.

SOURCE DOCUMENT   A record prepared at the time, or place, a transaction takes place. These documents serve as the source for data to be input to the computer system.

*SOURCE PROGRAM   A computer program written in a source language.

*SPECIAL-PURPOSE COMPUTER   A computer that is designed to handle a restricted class of problems.

SPOOLING   A process of writing output data on a temporary storage device (usually a magnetic drum) until an output unit is available.

STANDARD CHARACTER SET   The limited collection of letters, numbers, and characters used to encode a program in a given language.

*STATEMENT   In computer programming, a meaningful expression or generalized instruction in a source language.

STATISTICAL SEARCH   A search procedure that relies upon statistics and the laws of probability to locate the object of search in a file.

*STORAGE   Pertaining to a device into which data can be entered, in which they can be held, and from which they can be retrieved at a later time. Loosely, any device that can store data. Synonymous with *memory*.

*STORAGE PROTECTION   An arrangement for preventing access to storage for either reading or writing, or both.

*STORED PROGRAM COMPUTER   A computer controlled by internally stored instructions that can synthesize, store, and in some cases, alter instructions as though they were data, and that can subsequently execute these instructions.

*SUBROUTINE   A routine that can be part of another routine.

SUBSYSTEM   A part of a larger system, which in itself forms an organized whole.

SUMMARY PUNCH   A card-punching machine that can be connected to an accounting machine to punch totals or balance cards. To punch summary information in cards.

SUPERVISOR   A routine or routines executed in response to a requirement for altering or interrupting the flow of operation through the central processing unit, or for performance of input/output operations, and, therefore, the medium through which the use of resources is coordinated and the flow of operations through the central processing unit is maintained. Hence, a control routine that is executed in supervisor state.

*SYMBOLIC ADDRESS   An address expressed in symbols convenient to the computer programmer.

*SYSTEM   An assembly of methods, procedures, or techniques united by regulated interaction to form an organized whole. An organized collection of men, machines, and methods required to accomplish a set of specific functions.

SYSTEM ANALYSIS   The analysis of an activity to determine precisely what must be accomplished and how to accomplish it.

SYSTEM FLOWCHART   A diagram that shows the data flow in an entire organization or system. It specifies the work stations, operations to be performed, communications links, etc.

SYSTEM GENERATION   The procedure of designing, organizing, and setting up an operating system to meet the needs of a specific organization.

SYSTEM LIBRARY   The collection of all cataloged data sets at an installation.

*TELECOMMUNICATIONS   Pertaining to the transmission of signals over long distances, such as by telegraph, radio, or television.

TELEPROCESSING   A form of information handling in which a data processing system utilizes communication facilities.

*TERMINAL   A point in a system or communications network at which data can either enter or leave.

THROUGHPUT   A measure of system efficiency; the rate at which work can be handled by a system.

*TIME SHARING   Pertaining to the interleaved use of the time of a device.

TOS   Tape Operating System.

*TRACK   The portion of a moving storage medium, such as a drum, tape, or disc, that is accessible to a given reading head position.

TRAILER RECORD   A record that follows one or more records and contains data related to those records.

*TRANSACTION FILE   A file containing relatively transient data to be processed in combination with a master file. For example, in a payroll application, a transaction file indicating hours worked might be processed with a master file containing employee name and rate of pay.

TRANSISTOR   A small solid-state, semiconducting device, ordinarily using germanium, that performs nearly all the functions of an electronic tube, especially amplification.

*TROUBLESHOOT   See Debug.

TURNAROUND TIME   The elapsed time between submission of a job to a computing center and the return of results.

TYPE BAR   A linear type element containing all printable symbols.

UNIT RECORD   Historically, a card containing one complete record. Currently, the punched card.

UPDATE   To modify a master file with current information according to a specified procedure.

USASCII   *U*nited *S*tates of *A*merica *S*tandard *C*ode for *I*nformation *I*nterchange. Code consisting of seven intelligence channels and an eighth check-bit channel.

*VARIABLE   A quantity that can assume any of a given set of values.

*VARIABLE-LENGTH RECORD   Pertaining to a file in which the records are not uniform in length.

*VERIFY   To determine whether a transcription of data or other operation has been accomplished accurately. To check the results of keypunching.

VIRTUAL STORAGE   A computer memory system that expands the primary memory beyond its physical limitations by means of additional secondary storage capacity and the use of paging.

VOLUME   That portion of a single unit of storage media that is accessible to a single read-write mechanism.

WIRING CONTROL PANEL   Device used to program unit record equipment. Consists of a frame with rows of hubs. The hubs are connected in various patterns using jumper wires.

*WORD   A character string or a bit string considered as an entity.

*WORD LENGTH   A measure of the size of a word, usually specified in units such as characters or binary digits.

*WRITE   To record data in a storage device or a data medium. The recording need not be permanent, such as the writing on a cathode ray tube display device.

*X PUNCH   A punch in the second row from the top on a Hollerith punched card. Synonymous with eleven-punch.

Y PUNCH   A punch in the top row of a Hollerith punched card. Synonymous with twelve-punch.

ZONE PUNCH   A punch in the eleven, twelve, or zero row of a Hollerith punched card.

CREDITS

CHAPTER 1

1.1 Reprinted from the May 1975 issue of MODERN OFFICE PROCEDURES and copyright 1975 by Penton/IPC, subsidiary of Pittway Corporation. **1.2** From *Electronic News*, May 19, 1975. **1.4** Courtesy of IBM Corp. **1.5** Courtesy of Control Data Corp. **1.6** Sperry Univac Division, Sperry Rand Corp. **1.7** Courtesy of Honeywell Inc. **1.8** Courtesy of Burroughs Corporation. **1.9** Courtesy of Digital Equipment Corp. **1.10** Courtesy of Texas Instruments, Inc. **1.11** Courtesy of *Computer Decisions* © 1970, Hayden Publishing Co.

CHAPTER 2

2.2 Courtesy of Planning Research Corporation. **2.3** Courtesy of Planning Research Corporation. **2.4** Courtesy of Planning Research Corporation. **2.5** Courtesy of Planning Research Corporation. **2.6** Courtesy of Planning Research Corporation. **2.7** Courtesy of The Bettmann Archive, Inc. **2.8** Courtesy of Planning Research Corporation. **2.9** Courtesy of Planning Research Corporation. **2.10** Courtesy of Planning Research Corporation. **2.11** Courtesy of Planning Research Corporation. **2.12** Courtesy of Henry Tropp. **2.13** Courtesy of Henry Tropp. **2.14** Courtesy of Amcomp, Inc. **2.15** Courtesy of BASF Systems. **2.16** Courtesy of Burroughs Corporation. **2.17** From AMERICAN BUSINESS, 3 ed., by Mauser and Schwartz, Copyright © 1974, by Harcourt Brace Jovanovich, Inc. and reproduced with their permission. **2.18** Courtesy of Teletype Corporation. **2.19** Courtesy of Tektronix, Inc. **2.20** Courtesy of Intel Corporation. **2.21** From *Electronic News*, August 4, 1975. **2.22** Reprinted by permission from *Reference Manual, IBM 519 Document-Originating Machine,* © 1961 by IBM Corp.

CHAPTER 3

3.1 Courtesy of U.S. Census Bureau. **3.3** From SIMPLIFIED ANSI FORTRAN IV PROGRAMMING, 2nd ed., by Gerald A. Silver and Joan B. Silver, copyright © 1971, 1976, by Harcourt Brace Jovanovich, Inc. and reproduced with their permission. **3.5** Reprinted by permission from *IBM Data Recorder Operator's Guide,* © 1971 by IBM Corporation. **3.9** Courtesy of IBM Corp. **3.10** Courtesy of Sperry Univac Division, Sperry Rand Corp. **3.11** Courtesy of IBM Corp. **3.12** Courtesy of Computer Elections Systems, Inc.

CHAPTER 4

4.10 Reprinted by permission from *Reference Manual, IBM 519 Document-Originating Machine,* © 1961 by IBM Corp. **4.15** Top left and right, Center left and right courtesy of IBM Corp.; Bottom courtesy of Sperry Univac Division, Sperry Rand Corp. **4.16** Courtesy of Sperry Univac Division, Sperry Rand Corp.

CHAPTER 5

5.3 Courtesy of IBM Corp. **5.4** Courtesy of IBM Corp. **5.5** Courtesy of Burroughs Corporation. **5.6** Courtesy of NCR Corporation. **5.9** Courtesy of Digital Equipment Corp. **5.10** Courtesy of NCR Corporation. **5.11** Courtesy of Hewlett-Packard Company. **5.12** Courtesy of IBM Corp. **5.13** Courtesy of Honeywell Inc. **5.14** Courtesy of Burroughs Corporation. **5.15** Courtesy of Sperry Univac Division, Sperry Rand Corp.

CHAPTER 6

6.4 Courtesy of IBM Corp. **6.6** Courtesy of Tally Corporation. **6.7** Courtesy of IBM Corp. **6.9** Courtesy of Thom McAn Shoe Company. **6.10** Courtesy of Scan-Data Corp. **6.11** Courtesy of IBM Corp. **6.14** Courtesy of IBM Corp. **6.15** Courtesy of NCR Corporation. **6.16** Courtesy of Singer, Business Machines Division. **6.17** Courtesy of Data Action Co. **6.18.** Courtesy of Data Action Co. **6.19** Courtesy of Inforex Corporation.

CHAPTER 7

7.6 Reprinted by permission from *Introduction to IBM Data Processing Systems* © 1970 by IBM Corp. **7.7** Reprinted by permission from *Introduction to IBM Data Processing Systems* © 1970 by IBM Corp. **7.8** Reprinted by permission from *Introduction to IBM Data Processing Systems* © 1970 by IBM Corp. **7.9** From *ABC'S of Teletype Equipment,* Teletype Corp. **7.10** Reprinted by permission from *IBM Systems 1360 Component Description, 2400 Series Magnetic Tape* © 1970 by IBM Corp.

CHAPTER 8

8.1 Reprinted with special permission from *Infosystems Magazine,* October, 1972 issue, Hitchcock Publishing Co., Wheaton, Ill. 60187. All rights reserved.   **8.2** Courtesy of Datapac Inc.   **8.3** Courtesy of Intel Corp.   **8.4** Reprinted by permission from *Introduction to IBM Data Processing Systems* © 1970 by IBM Corp.   **8.5** Reprinted by permission from *Introduction to IBM Data Processing Systems*   **8.5a** © 1970 by IBM Corp.   **8.6** Courtesy of IBM Corp.

CHAPTER 9

9.1 Harbrace Photo.   **9.2** Reprinted by permission from *IBM 729, 7330, and 727 Magnetic Tape Units, Principles of Operation* by IBM Corp.   **9.3** Reprinted by permission from *Introduction to IBM Data Processing Systems* © 1970 by IBM Corp.   **9.4** Reprinted by permission from *Introduction to IBM Data Processing Systems* © 1970 by IBM Corp.   **9.6** Reprinted by permission from *IBM System 1360 Disk Operating System, System Control and System Service Program* © 1971 by IBM Corp.   **9.7** Courtesy of IBM Corp.   **9.9** Harbrace Photo   **9.11** Courtesy of Sperry Univac Division, Sperry Rand Corp.   **9.12** Courtesy of IBM Corp.   **9.16** Courtesy of California Computer Products (Calcomp Corp), Anaheim, Cal.   **9.17** Courtesy of IBM Corp.   **9.18** Reprinted by permission from *Introduction to IBM Data Processing System* © 1970 by IBM Corp.

CHAPTER 10

10.1 Harbrace Photo.   **10.2** Courtesy of Trendata, Inc.   **10.3** Reprinted by permission of Centronics Data Computer Corp. © 1976.   **10.4** Reprinted by permission from *Introduction to IBM Data Processing System* © 1970 IBM Corp.   **10.5** Reprinted by permission from *IBM 1403, Printer Component Description,* IBM.   **10.6** Courtesy of IBM Corp.   **10.7** From "Typesetting" by Gerald O. Walter © May, 1969, *Scientific American.*   **10.8** Courtesy of Singer Friden Division.   **10.10** Courtesy of NCR Corporation.   **10.11** Courtesy of IBM Corp.   **10.12** Courtesy of Hewlett-Packard Company.   **10.13** Courtesy of California Computer Products Inc. (Calcomp Corp.), Anaheim, Ca.   **10.14** Courtesy of Datapoint Corp.   **10.15** Courtesy of IBM Corp.

CHAPTER 11

11.1 From SIMPLIFIED ANSI FORTRAN IV PROGRAMMING, 2nd ed., by Gerald A. Silver and Joan B. Silver, copyright © 1971, 1976 by Harcourt Brace Jovanovich, Inc. and reproduced with their permission.   **11.2** Reprinted by permission from *IBM Data Processing Techniques,* © 1962 by IBM Corp.   **11.3** Reprinted by permission from *IBM Data Processing Techniques,* © 1962 by IBM Corp.   **11.6** From SIMPLIFIED ANSI FORTRAN IV PROGRAMMING, 2nd ed., by Gerald A. Silver and Joan B. Silver, copyright © 1971, 1976 by Harcourt Brace Jovanovich, Inc. and reproduced with their permission.   **11.7** From SIMPLIFIED ANSI FORTRAN IV PROGRAMMING, 2nd ed., by Gerald A. Silver and Joan B. Silver, copyright © 1971, 1976, by Harcourt Brace Jovanovich, Inc. and reproduced with their permission.

CHAPTER 12

12.2 From Gerald A. Silver, Joan B. Silver, INTRODUCTION TO SYSTEMS ANALYSIS, © 1976, p. 250. Reprinted by permission of Prentice-Hall, Inc., Englewood Cliffs, New Jersey.   **12.3** From SIMPLIFIED ANSI FORTRAN IV PROGRAMMING, 2nd ed., by Gerald A. Silver and Joan B. Silver, copyright © 1971, 1976, by Harcourt Brace Jovanovich, Inc. and reproduced with their permission.   **12.5** Courtesy of Rapidesign, Inc.

CHAPTER 13

13.5 Courtesy of Applied Digital Data Sytems Inc.

CHAPTER 16

16.1 Courtesy of Teletype Corporation.

CHAPTER 17

17.2 From SIMPLIFIED ANSI FORTRAN IV PROGRAMMING, 2nd ed., by Gerald A. Silver and Joan B. Silver, copyright © 1971, 1976, by Harcourt Brace Jovanovich, Inc. and reprinted with their permission.   **17.3** From SIMPLIFIED ANSI FORTRAN IV PROGRAMMING, 2nd ed., by Gerald A. Silver and Joan B. Silver, copyright © 1971, 1976, by Harcourt Brace Jovanovich, Inc. and reprinted with their permission.   **17.4** From SIMPLIFIED ANSI FORTRAN IV PROGRAMMING, 2nd ed., by Gerald A. Silver and Joan B. Silver, copyright © 1971, 1976, by Harcourt Brace Jovanovich, Inc. and reprinted with their permission.

CHAPTER 18

18.1 Reprinted by permission from *An Introduction to PL/I: Student Text,* by IBM Corp.   **18.2** Reprinted by permission from *PL/I (F) Programmer's Guide, IBM System 360,* © 1972 by IBM Corp.   **18.4** Courtesy of IBM Corp.   **18.7A** Reprinted by permission from *IBM APL/360 Primer,* © 1969 by IBM Corp.   **18.7B** Courtesy of University Computing Co.   **18.9** Courtesy of Proprietary Computer Systems Inc.   **18.10** Courtesy of Proprietary Computer Systems Inc.

CHAPTER 21

21.2 Courtesy of NCR Corp.   **21.7** Courtesy of Control Data Corp.   **21.8** Courtesy of Control Data Corp.   **21.9** Courtesy of IBM Corp.   **21.10** Courtesy of American Data Systems.   **21.11** Courtesy of Digi-Log Systems, Inc.   **21.12** Courtesy of NCR Corporation.   **21.13** Courtesy of Burroughs Corporation.   **21.15** Courtesy of Sperry Univac Division, Sperry Rand Corp.   **21.16** Courtesy of Control Data Corp

CHAPTER 22

22.2 Courtesy of NCR Corp.   **22.3** Reprinted with permission of Datamation®, Copyright 1974 by Technical Publishing Company, Greenwich, Connecticut 06830.   **22.4** Reprinted from *Computer Decisions,* Nov., 1972, © 1972 by Hayden Publishing Co.   **22.5** Courtesy of NCR Corp.   **22.6** Courtesy of Burroughs Corp.   **22.7** Courtesy of NCR Corp.   **22.8** Reprinted with special permission, INFOSYSTEMS magazine, Hitchcock Publishing Co., Wheaton, Ill. 60187, all rights reserved.   **22.10** Courtesy of Burroughs Corporation.

CHAPTER 23

23.1 Courtesy of Sperry Univac Division, Sperry Rand Corp.   **23.2** Courtesy of Burroughs Corp.   **23.3** Courtesy of IBM Corp.   **23.4** Courtesy of Burroughs Corp.   **23.5** Courtesy of IBM Corp.   **23.6** Courtesy of Digital Equipment Corp.   **23.7** Courtesy of Sperry Univac Division, Sperry Rand Corp.   **23.8** Courtesy of IBM Corp.   **23.9** Courtesy of IBM Corp.

Appendix C

C.1 From SIMPLIFIED ANSI FORTRAN IV PROGRAMMING, 2nd ed., by Gerald A. Silver and Joan B. Silver, copyright © 1971, 1976, by Harcourt Brace Jovanovich, Inc. and reprinted with their permission.   **C.3** Courtesy of IBM Corp.   **C.4** From SIMPLIFIED ANSI FORTRAN IV PROGRAMMING, 2nd ed., by Gerald A. Silver and Joan B. Silver, copyright © 1971, 1976, by Harcourt Brace Jovanovich, Inc. and reprinted with their permission.   **C.5** From SIMPLIFIED ANSI FORTRAN IV PROGRAMMING, 2nd ed., by Gerald A. Silver and Joan B. Silver, copyright © 1971, 1976, by Harcourt Brace Jovanovich, Inc. and reprinted with their permission.   **C.6** From SIMPLIFIED ANSI FORTRAN IV PROGRAMMING, 2nd ed., by Gerald A. Silver and Joan B. Silver, copyright © 1971, 1976, by Harcourt Brace Jovanovich, Inc. and reprinted with their permission.   **C.7** From SIMPLIFIED ANSI FORTRAN IV PROGRAMMING, 2nd ed., by Gerald A. Silver and Joan B. Silver, copyright © 1971, 1976, by Harcourt Brace Jovanovich, Inc. and reprinted with their permission.

Cartoons

Chapter 1 Reprinted with permission of Datamation®, copyright 1972 by Technical Publishing Company, Greenwich, Conn. 06830.   **Chapter 2** Reprinted with special permission, INFOSYSTEMS magazine, Hitchcock Publishing Co., Wheaton, Ill. 60187, all rights reserved.   **Chapter 3** Reprinted with permission of Datamation®, copyright 1975 by Technical Publishing Company, Greenwich, Conn. 06830.   **Chapter 4** Cartoon by Saxon reprinted with permission by Oxford Pendaflex Corporation.   **Chapter 5** Sidney Harris.   **Chapter 6** *Dunagin's People* by Ralph Dunagin courtesy of Field Newspaper Syndicate.   **Chapter 7** Reprinted with permission of EDN Magazine, Cahners Publishing Co., Inc.   **Chapter 8** Sidney Harris.   **Chapter 9** Sidney Harris.   **Chapter 10** Sidney Harris.   **Chapter 11** Reprinted with permission of EDN/EEE Magazine, Cahners Publishing Co., Inc.   **Chapter 12** *Grin and Bear It* by George Lichty, Courtesy of Field Newspaper Syndicate.   **Chapter 13** Sidney Harris.   **Chapter 14** Sidney Harris.   **Chapter 15** Reprinted with permission of *Creative Computing.*   **Chapter 16** Sidney Harris.   **Chapter 17** Sidney Harris.   **Chapter 18** Sidney Harris.   **Chapter 19** Reprinted with special permission, INFOSYSTEMS magazine, Hitchcock Publishing Co., Wheaton, Ill. 60187, all rights reserved.   **Chapter 20** Sidney Harris.   **Chapter 21** Sidney Harris.   **Chapter 22** Sidney Harris.   **Chapter 23** Reprinted with permission of Datamation®, copyright 1975 by Technical Publishing Company, Greenwich, Conn. 06830.

INDEX